the rebel café

the rebel café

*Sex, Race, and Politics in Cold War America's
Nightclub Underground*

Stephen R. Duncan

Johns Hopkins University Press   Baltimore

Johns Hopkins University Press
2715 North Charles Street
Baltimore, Maryland 21218-4363
www.press.jhu.edu

Library of Congress Cataloging-in-Publication Data

Names: Duncan, Stephen R., 1970– author.
Title: The Rebel Café : sex, race, and politics in Cold War America's
    nightclub underground / Stephen R. Duncan.
Description: Baltimore : Johns Hopkins University Press, 2018. |
    Includes bibliographical references and index.
Identifiers: LCCN 2017058442 | ISBN 9781421426334 (hardcover : alk. paper) |
    ISBN 1421426331 (hardcover : alk. paper) | ISBN 9781421426341 (electronic) |
    ISBN 142142634X (electronic)
Subjects: LCSH: Nightlife—United States—History—20th century. |
    Nightclubs—United States—History—20th century. | Popular
    culture—Political aspects—United States. | Bohemianism—United States. |
    United States—Social life and customs—1945–1970.
Classification: LCC GT3408 .D86 2018 | DDC 306.4/0904—dc23
LC record available at https://lccn.loc.gov/2017058442

A catalog record for this book is available from the British Library.

Maps by Meredith Duncan

Special discounts are available for bulk purchases of this book.
For more information, please contact Special Sales at 410-516-6936
or specialsales@press.jhu.edu.

For Meri
And in memory of John David Duncan

I have always been struck, in America, by an emotional poverty so bottomless, and a terror of human life, of human touch, so deep that virtually no American appears able to achieve any viable, organic connection between his public stance and his private life.
James Baldwin, 1957

The *return of the repressed* makes up the tabooed and subterranean history of civilization.
Herbert Marcuse, *Eros and Civilization*, 1955

For the most wild yet most homely narrative which I am about to pen, I neither expect nor solicit belief. . . . Yet, mad am I not—and very surely do I not dream.
Edgar Allan Poe, "The Black Cat," 1843

contents

acknowledgments

It is nearly ubiquitous for academics to point out that writing is no solitary endeavor and that it takes the generous input of multiple colleagues and friends to finish a project like this one. Yet it bears repeating, because it's true. I owe thanks to more individuals than I can name here, but I at least want to express my gratitude to those who contributed most directly to the ideas and content of this book.

First, I will always be indebted to the scholars who supported my early work at the University of Maryland with their mentorship and their service on my dissertation committee: David Sicilia, Robyn Muncy, David Freund, and Zita Nunes. Throughout my time there, Saverio Giovacchini and, especially, my graduate advisor, James Gilbert, guided my training as a cultural historian with patience, generosity, and acumen that were seemingly limitless. Stephanie Hinnershitz also gave me useful feedback on early chapters, as did Thomas Bender. And a very special thanks to Jon Shelton, without whom this book would not exist. My conversations with Jon over the years (and, often, over a beer or two . . . or three) were foundational, and his insights were always sharp (even considering his baffling dismissal of Billy Joel's songwriting genius: "You may be right, I may be crazy . . .").

Many thanks to the archivists at Columbia University's Butler Library, the San Francisco History Center, Stanford University's Green Library, the University of California at Los Angeles' Charles E. Young Research Library, the New York Performing Arts Library, New York University's Tamiment Library, and the Wisconsin History Center in Madison. Thanks to Shan Sutton and the University of the Pacific for a summer research grant that allowed me to exhaustively explore the Dave Brubeck Collection. I am especially grateful to Trish Richards, Keith Hatcheck, and Michael Wurtz for their knowledgeable guidance through that collection. I am equally indebted to the staff of the Bancroft Library at the University of California, Berkeley, in particular to Susan Snyder for assistance with the Henri Lenoir Collection, and to Heather Smedberg and the entire staff of the Mandeville Special Collections at the University of California, San Diego, for their assistance with the Joanne Kyger Papers.

Several people were kind enough to sit down and talk with me about their experiences in the postwar nightlife scenes in New York City and San Francisco. Their perspectives were important, even when they were not included formally in the finished product. Lorraine Gordon of the Village Vanguard graciously shared her memories. Charles and Marlene Inman generously talked at length about the San Francisco jazz scene, as did Herbie Wong. Ragland Tolk Watkins offered his time and a collection of crucial materials, as well as the most valuable gift of all: his friendship. Gerald Nachman's background as a journalist and humor scholar informed my examination of Mort Sahl, in particular. Also, sincere thanks to Clinton Starr for sharing a rare recording of "Blabbermouth Night" at The Place. In addition, several people were also helpful in providing access to photographs: C. R. Snyder, the staff at Found SF, Yvette Torres, and Genie Stressing. And special thanks to Kush at the Cloud House in San Francisco. Kush's insights and encyclopedic knowledge of the North Beach and Greenwich Village poetry scenes were fundamental to the framing of this book and made possible whatever richness I was able to bring to the subject.

In the final stages of completing the manuscript, I received support from multiple quarters. Johns Hopkins University Press's editorial and faculty boards strengthened the book with their comments and suggestions, as did my editors, Elizabeth Demers and Lauren Straley. Kathleen Capels's meticulous copyediting immensely sharpened its prose. Sincerest thanks also to my colleagues in the Department of History at Bronx Community College (BCC), who have welcomed me so warmly as one of their own: Simon Davis, William deJong-Lambert, Jordi Getman-Eraso, David Gordon, Chris Grenda, Liz Hardman, Prithi Kanakamedala, Mara Lazda, Sibongile Mhlaba, Seth Offenbach, Ahmed Reid, Vava Roczniak, and Tamar Rothenberg. In particular, Kate Culkin offered important feedback at a crucial moment. Thanks also to Paulette Randall, who keeps our department functioning and (mostly) sane. A special thank-you to the students at BCC, who remind me daily why I love being a teacher. And while my own work as an undergraduate is not reflected directly in this book's topic, I will always be grateful to Stephanie Cole at the University of Texas at Arlington for providing a methodological bedrock and for reigniting my passion for history.

Last, but certainly not least, I would like to thank my family for their continual encouragement: Patti and Mike Pinkston, Matt and Ana Duncan, Daniel and Kristine Duncan, and Leah Miller. And to my other "brother," Digant Kasundra, who put me up (and put up with me) so many times I've lost count, many thanks. Most of all, my life-partner, Meredith Knoll-Duncan, has shown the patience of a saint when so much of my attention was absorbed by research, travel, and writing. Her critiques, suggestions, and assistance have been invaluable, from the beginning of the project through the very moment of finishing it. Every day she shows me how to approach the world with thoughtfulness and empathy. And every day that I get to spend with her makes me feel like the luckiest person on Earth. This book is dedicated to her.

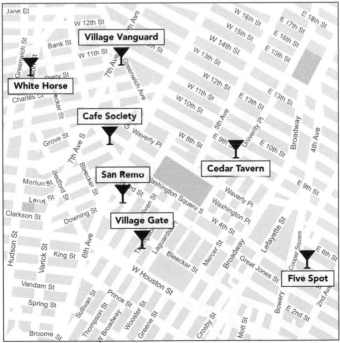

Lower Manhattan, New York City, and detail map of Greenwich Village

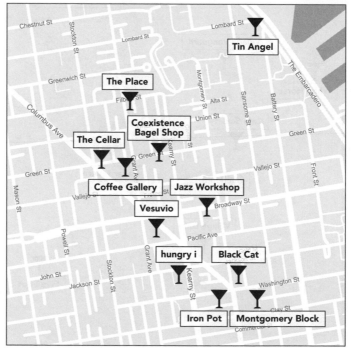

San Francisco and detail map of North Beach

the rebel café

the metal cafe

introduction

can you show me the way to the rebel café?

> They were planning a revolution / to end want & hunger / They were
> plotting a new form of thinking / They were arguing in blue smoke /
> a direction for art . . . / in the rebel cafe . . . The Philadelphia taverns /
> of 1776 / were rebel cafes . . . / Thomas Paine / in a three-cornered
> blue / lifting pewter tankards in the Indian Queen / the night a pam-
> phlet called *Common Sense* / came off the press / They were drawing
> a nation with ink / inside the rebel cafe . . . —da da da da— / in the
> Cabaret Voltaire . . . Jean-Paul Sartre / sitting with Simone de Beau-
> voir / in the Cafe Flore / waiting for Hitler to fall / . . . Janis Joplin /
> leans against the bar / with a guy from Detroit, a / guy from Texas /
> and a guy from / Salem, Missouri / to sing Amazing Grace / in the
> rebel cafe
> **Edward Sanders, "Hymn to the Rebel Cafe," 1993**

On June 6, 1945, as Nazi Germany smoldered in the wake of firebombs and defeat and the United States persevered in the Pacific conflict, delegates from fifty nations gathered in San Francisco's Civic Center to establish the framework for the United Nations. Meanwhile, as conference chairman (and soon-to-be-convicted Soviet spy) Alger Hiss presided over debates and draft revisions, a less conspicuous group of young idealists gathered at a café called the Iron Pot, in the nearby neighborhood of North Beach, to hash out the future of "world security." This small, scruffy clique had no delusions of grandeur, well aware that their plans in no way rivaled the world-historical diplomacy occurring twenty blocks south. Yet, in their own raffish way, they were charting a new path for America in the coming postwar era. "It is our intent," they cried amid the smoke and the smell of beer, fists pounding the table in enthusiasm, "to have a club where no one shall be denied membership because of race, creed or color; to have a club whose atmosphere shall be, if you will, Bohemian, and whose purpose shall be the serious furtherance of good living . . . through the media of such diverse means as art, writing, music, drama, chess, cards, food and drink, discussion groups and organized pressure groups." Housing discrimination, asserted one African American member, should be their first target. Yes, agreed a writer from a "local left-wing paper," adding that they should not only fight racism but also advocate on behalf of all workers. Concerned that their new endeavor signaled a lack of gratitude toward their meeting's host, they concluded, "We want it clearly and absolutely understood that the club in no way, shape or form, has any unfriendly intent toward . . . 'The Iron Pot.'"[1]

This scene was not, by itself, an earth-shattering historical moment; the little gang of Iron Pot radicals did not bloom into a renowned civil rights organization, a new political party, or even a social movement, as commonly conceived. It did represent, however whimsically, the kind of conversation that was happening all over the United States, in cafés and bars and coffeehouses and nightclubs, as the Second World War drew to a close. Just as this idealistic band sat among the revelry of the Iron Pot, nightspot patrons in American cities downed drinks and *talked*—of politics, art, sex, society, and self-expression. Such intimate gatherings in no way rivaled the immensity of the wave of labor strikes that erupted at the war's end and the civil rights organizing that grew from black America's Double-V campaign for victory over fascism both at home and abroad. But the sum of these small café conversations perhaps held as much significance. Like the tiny intracellular mutations that drive evolution, invisible until we recognize a new species in retrospect, these nocturnal discussions incrementally changed the shape of America's body politic.

Despite the affluence that defined much of the postwar era, the specters of atomic apocalypse, the Cold War, racial oppression, the triumph of corporate liberalism, and concomitant conformity led some Americans to wonder whether the promise of plenty was worth less than the sum of its parts. This discontent spawned a national community of bohemians and cultural dissidents in the two decades following World War II. Connected by complex social networks and aesthetics—and often by left-wing political views—this community constituted an important Cold War counterculture. Music, literature, visual arts, journalism, and standup comedy were all transformed as cultural producers emphasized "authenticity," claiming honesty and even purity in their work and espousing immediacy in language, experience, and ideology. As a result, a diverse coalition of devotees, including artists, performers, and audiences, united in an informal project to redefine the meaning of America, placing an experimental pluralism alongside demands for personal liberty.

Many historians have discussed urban bohemia as a background for radical politics from the 1910s to the 1960s. But while offhandedly mentioning bars, coffeehouses, and nightclubs as bohemian locales, they seldom examine these nightspots as social and cultural institutions, nocturnal nodal points that connected social networks into a national circuit. These urban underground nightspots—what the radical poet Ed Sanders has called, collectively, the Rebel Café—provided spaces for interaction, public discussion, and identification for patrons, while also shaping the form and content of cultural productions. In "Hymn to the Rebel Cafe," Sanders situates his own activism in a lineage of rebellion spanning back to the American Revolution, following a path that meandered through nineteenth-century working-class saloons, the cabarets of Berlin, and Parisian cafés to the nightspots of New York and San Francisco, which are the subjects of this book.[2]

This Rebel Café image and history encapsulates a cultural scene (including visual arts, literature, and music) that developed in the United States from the 1930s through the early years of the Cold War. In the 1930s, the political Left established ties with cultural producers and intellectuals through a range of institutions, from the Communist Party's literary John Reed Clubs to the New Deal's arts programs. Amid the upheavals of World War II and the resultant Red Scare, many who deplored the inequalities of capitalism and embraced social democracy had to go underground. Leftists in the culture industry faced direct or indirect oppression for their views, seen most dramatically in the prosecution of the Hollywood Ten and the anticommunist blacklist. As a result, oppositional performers, writers, poets, and painters made a place for themselves in a world of coldwater flats, jazz clubs, and literary cafés. Tucked away in the underground, politically conscious cultural producers carried forward a species of left-wing activism that repopulated American politics in the 1960s.

My own interest in the subject of nightclub culture started with a casual conversation with a colleague about how to theorize "the public." Probably because I had spent so much time in nightclubs during the years when I worked as a rock musician, I was struck by the thought that standup comedy found a new kind of public audience with Lenny Bruce's nightclub act in the 1950s. I quickly realized, however, that a more compelling question was how nightclubs themselves played a role. So I followed the threads of connection from clubs where Bruce performed, such as New York City's Village Vanguard or San Francisco's hungry i, and what I found intrigued me. These clubs were part of a much deeper milieu, as well as a long, socially conscious, even radical intellectual and cultural genealogy. This line stretched from the first-known cabaret, Le Chat Noir in Paris, through politically tinged Depression-era performances in the United States, the jazz clubs of the 1940s and 1950s, and into the Beat generation's literary movement. At the end of this timeline, the Rebel Café expanded and was absorbed into the broader culture through the sociopolitical shifts that were visible by the end of 1963, including a folk music revival and other expressions of freedom that found a more direct political form in the civil rights movement and the New Left. Over the next six years, its ethos of rebellion became intertwined with the explosion of the counterculture and liberation movements—the gay rights uprising at New York City's Stonewall Inn being the most dramatic moment when this underground culture erupted into the mainstream. Moreover, while my focus on New York and San Francisco was originally guided by nightclub comedy, as I traced the outlines of the Rebel Café I discovered a bicoastal bohemia whose social networks functioned by using those cities as twin poles. In important ways, I had stumbled on the cultural roots of what journalist Bill Bishop termed "the big sort," which has made California and New York the coastal bastions of blue-state liberalism in an America that is otherwise bathed in red.

This volume therefore offers four ways to take a fresh look at midcentury America. First, it shows that nightspots were social, cultural, and, ultimately, political institutions for radicals and left-wing bohemians and artists, which changes our picture of the 1950s by showing what was underground, despite the disruption of the formal Left. Rebel Cafés were an integral part of a postwar counterpublic that, as it grew in scope and prominence, helped to shape the contours of left-leaning liberalism. And here is where I found the most surprising links, as this milieu influenced and connected public figures like Paul Goodman and Susan Sontag with performers such as Charles Mingus and Nina Simone. Second, it uncovers the function of nightspots within marginal groups, bohemia, and dissidents, connecting social networks. This tied New York City and San Francisco socioculturally, but it also shows the Rebel Café's sheltering role for leftists, which allowed a continuity with the 1930s, challenging the notion that the Red Scare marked a complete disruption. Third, media publicity has long been part of the story of New York intellectuals and leftists, but this study offers a window onto San Francisco as a national touchstone in the twentieth century, indicating that it was fundamental in changing musical and literary styles (and even aspects of film and television), as well as the scene's most lasting contribution—socially satirical "brick wall" comedy. Fourth, the book offers a synthesis of histories previously separated by the scholarship growing from identity politics. I am able to demonstrate that in the 1950s, the civil rights movement, left-wing bohemianism, gay rights activism, and feminism were more intertwined than previously recognized.

This synthesis also gives insight into the origins of identity politics, helping to reveal the motivations of those seeking liberation from the social hierarchies that persisted even within the Rebel Café milieu. In the postwar context of the Red Scare, rising wages and unionism, the expansion of higher education, and a widespread acceptance of psychoanalysis's inward reflection, identity politics moved alongside left-leaning liberals' reduced focus on workers, as class became increasingly associated with lifestyle, professionalism, and education, rather than on the relationship between labor and capital. From the 1940s to the 1960s, sophisticated consciousness and cultural knowledge—rather than income alone—gradually became key measures of middle-class status. For many, Rebel Café nightspots were places to put this status on display.

Norman Mailer once said of the Vietnam War, "It is self-evident that the *Readers Digest* and Lawrence Welk and Hilton Hotels are organically connected with the Special Forces napalming villages." I would like to demonstrate a related proposition, linking early twentieth-century Parisian cabarets and the birth of Dadaism in the Cabaret Voltaire with San Francisco's campy Tin Angel and the gay rights movement; the American Revolution with Allen Ginsberg's poem "Howl," Lenny Bruce's obscenity trials, the Berkeley free speech movement, and antiwar protests; and Sigmund Freud with jazz clubs and the southern sit-ins that galvanized the modern civil rights movement. The force of this sociocultural field, this web of meaning, was not mysterious or metaphysical. It was historical and anthropological, the result of cultural transmission and symbolic action. These seemingly disparate historical subjects were connected through multiple ideas, people, and places, tied together like threads in a tapestry.

Pre–World War I bohemias in New York City and San Francisco were largely defined by writers and artists dedicated to cosmopolitan lifestyles that occasionally drifted toward socialism amid the Progressive Era's concerns about monopoly capitalism. The 1920s saw attention focused on the avant-garde—although still with tinges of leftism. The Depression-era 1930s witnessed the culture of the Popular Front, the alliance of communists and liberals behind Franklin Roosevelt's New Deal, and opposition to fascism. But throughout, America's urban bohemia saw many of the same individuals keeping their commitment to sociocultural criticism and personal liberation. Meanwhile, the influence of European café society flowed directly into American culture, manifested in both the imagination—through the literature of those like James Joyce—and in person, as émigrés sought asylum from Nazism, such as singers Marlene Dietrich and Lotte Lenya, each of whom had left-leaning bohemian personas.

The collision of outsider art and leftist politics within bohemian nightspots is not as surprising as it may appear at first. Both cabaret in the United States and the American Communist Party owed large debts to the flow of ideas and individuals from Europe—whether by exclusion or choice. Cultural critic Irving Howe's classic description of the Left could almost as easily describe the owners of many bohemian niteries: "Many students have noticed that a high proportion of the American party membership consisted of either first-generation immigrants or the sons and daughters of such immigrants . . . [who suffered] not absolute deprivation but a sense of social disparity. . . . It was only when a series of blows fell upon a social group—when, for example, urban immigrant workers suffered the handicap of being part of a minority ethnic group together with the frustration of being unable to live by the American values they had begun to accept—that anti-capitalist ideologies acquired a power of attraction."[3] This combination of outsider sensibilities and Depression-era disillusionment with the American dream contributed to bohemia's rejection of pure avant-gardism, or "art for art's sake," that had often defined dissent in the 1920s.

Drawing on the ideas of organizations such as the International Ladies' Garment Workers Union (ILGWU) and the Industrial Workers of the World (IWW, or Wobblies), left-wing activists sought workers' control of their own labor. This approach was matched by the Communist Party's organizing effort for groups such as the National Maritime Union and the International Longshoremen's Association, which was fundamental to the General Strike of 1934 that rocked San Francisco. Although the Popular Front was short lived—largely collapsing after the Nazi-Soviet Pact in 1939—the shared desires of leftists and liberals to end poverty and confront fascism ran through the ideas of postwar intellectuals such as C. Wright Mills, whose 1948 study, *The New Men of Power*, articulated this liberatory stance: "Classic socialism shares its master purpose with classic democracy. The difference between Thomas Jefferson and Karl Marx is a half century of technological change, during which industry replaced agriculture, the large-scale factory replaced the individual workshop, the dependent wage and salary worker replaced the independent proprietor. Left movements have been a series of desperate attempts to uphold the simple values of classic democracy under conditions of giant technology, monopoly capitalism, and the behemoth state—in short, under the conditions of modern life."[4]

If the 1930s slogan of the Communist Party (CP), "communism is twentieth-century Americanism," obscured its alliance with the Soviet Union, neither was it entirely disingenuous. The party's support of the Congress of Industrial Organizations and elements of the New Deal helped to establish workers' rights and crucial programs such as unemployment insurance. And the CP was often a lone voice calling for the inclusion of African Americans within these new institutions that supported "jobs, security, democracy, peace."[5]

Rebel Café nightspots played a particular role in Depression-era America, helping to develop relations between the working class, front-line leftists and cultural producers, bohemia, and the mainstream. They also served as key social nodes for dissidents themselves—forming some level of community among self-defined outsiders and meshing involuntary outcasts into the urban fabric of San Francisco and New York. It would be facile to suggest that these connections and social functions could not have occurred without the bohemian nightspots of the 1930s. Organizations like the Works Progress Administration and unions of all stripes were equally important. Yet the emerging Rebel Café provided a vital form of social lubrication, creating spaces in which the exchange of ideas became part of the lived experiences of radicals and bohemians. Moreover, by making this community public and attractive, it provided both a point of connection for the uninitiated and an identifiable cultural symbol of rebellion and sociopolitical opposition. The American cabaret eased down the sometimes difficult pill of dissent with a living aesthetic that blended European sophistication with artistic and personal avant-gardism, setting the scene for a new kind of nightclub to enter the American stage.

Subsequent shifts in the nightclub culture from World War II to the early Cold War period reflected the nation's changing racial, gender, and sexual norms. The Second World War brought transformation, ending the Depression through massive governmental spending and placing the United States in an unrivaled position of affluence and global influence. The nation's jazz war, ironically fought with a segregated military even as many found joy and solace in the strains of swing music, highlighted the promise and contradictions of American democracy. War production offered an opportunity for African Americans and women to transcend their previous positions in the social hierarchy, as higher wages and antidiscrimination laws supported newly independent lives in urban areas. These social openings were matched by an emerging queer culture that used bars and cafés as informal institutions, bolstering the strength and visibility of gay and lesbian communities. Coinciding with these trends, Harlem began a slow decline as the center of Manhattan's nightlife and jazz scene, marking a shift to Greenwich Village that entrenched jazz nightspots within left-wing bohemian circles. And the explosion of jazz meant that San Franciscan audiences increasingly crossed the color line. These changes were quickly followed by a conservative backlash that undercut full citizenship rights and social equality, resulting in deep tensions as the 1940s came to a close. Yet the growing number of jazz clubs laid a cultural foundation for bohemia's later support of civil rights struggles.

Between 1947 and 1949, the seismic shifts in American society placed small Rebel Café nightclubs at the epicenter of a new underground cultural geography. The boom years of military mobilization came to an end, essentially killing off the last of the large swing-jazz venues that survived the difficulties wartime rationing had placed on big bands. Without gas for buses or rubber for their tires, only the most renowned of the big bands, such as Duke Ellington's, could afford to travel; and restrictions on shellac, along with a Musicians' Union strike, had practically halted record production, leaving performers without this important promotional tool. As a result, a new, leaner style of nightclub, featuring small combos of four or five players, was most likely to survive the 1940s—another cornerstone in the Rebel Café's foundation. Jazz clubs also highlight the significance of lived experience in the growing black freedom struggle. By the 1950s, when most of the formal institutions of the Left were crushed underfoot, it was precisely the use of public space—from integrated jazz clubs to sit-ins—that proved to be the most successful in sparking change. While the evolution of America's nightclub culture followed no simple linear narrative of progress, it nonetheless suggests the ways in which subterranean venues offered platforms for dissident or progressive ideas, spaces for public discussion, community cohesion, and venues for the development of forward-looking cultural works.

In some sense, 1950s American culture was defined by the yin and yang of nightclubs and labor unions: the liberatory feeling in jazz, and a material liberation from the economic and social vagaries of the 1930s. Between these two sociocultural fields, however, the seeds of future clashes were also being sown. The roots of deindustrialization and urban crisis lay in the late 1950s, as did the demands for personal, racial, and sexual liberation that underlay identity politics. The postwar period was shaped by the sudden independence of the nuclear family from traditional urban structures that tied them to multigenerational homes and communities. Of necessity, many young people in American cities before World War II had maintained residences either with or near their parents. By contrast, in postwar sociological surveys, respondents noted that independence from their parents was one of the primary attractions of the suburbs—a trend that only increased with the expansion of colleges and universities.[6] As illustrated by psychologist Arnold Green's 1948 article, "Why Americans Are Insecure," social tensions that emerged from these trends were rooted in the nation's bureaucratic technocracy and the deep insecurity of understanding that love was the ultimate goal of personal fulfillment, even as "modern 'success' is registered only through externals: bank account, clothes, mannerisms, automobile, club memberships." Green concludes that what he calls the era's specialized conformities would lead to "dissatisfaction, frustration, and intra-family conflict."[7]

What he could not have foreseen was America's dual reaction. The dominant trend, made possible by the postwar economic boom and the affluent society of the 1950s, was to manufacture quasi-rural environments, complete with green, suburban, acre-sized lots and spiking baby boom birthrates—an embrace of the nuclear family, commonly referred to as "togetherness." The opposite trend turned the urban landscape itself into a communal refuge, a counterpart of the premodern village on the inner frontier of devalued neighborhoods. The most obvious examples of this were Greenwich Village in New York City and North Beach in San Francisco—the places that helped spawn the countercultural hippies, who put this communalist revival into wide effect in the 1960s. The Rebel Café, therefore, offered new substitutes for tradition and community, both for bohemians who reclaimed the cities and suburban tourists who explored alternative ways of life in the underground.

As scholars have recently argued, the 1950s were not a monolith of conformity and consensus, but instead were years of intense change, when popular culture sometimes drove cracks and cleavages in the calm national facade. W. T. Lhamon Jr. has offered a useful snapshot of this period, portraying an American culture of contradictions that demanded immediacy while fearing the consequences of change. The conformist 1950s was a trade off that celebrated the end of the Depression and World War II by ignoring dissent and racial inequality. Conformity was actually contentment with affluence and (relative) peace, as the nation enjoyed the most equal distribution of wealth in its history. At the same time, to Lhamon the 1950s was a decade of "deliberate speed," seen in everything from abstract expressionism to the wail of rock & roll; the Supreme Court's vacillating desegregation decisions under Chief Justice Earl Warren; Robert Frank's gritty photographs; the Beat's ecstatic language; and the folk music revival that culminated with Bob Dylan as the voice of generational protest. Deliberate speed included black culture that filled in the hollow middle of America, even as this culture itself became conflicted, with notions of authenticity and assertions of individualism that maintained racial and gender hierarchies and constricted collective action. Meanwhile, racy humor deflated the pretensions of a power elite that defined Americanism as homogeneous and hegemonic white masculinity.[8] Throughout this jumbled image, almost invisible by their ubiquity, were urban nightspots that supported oppositional performers and disseminated vanguard styles into the postwar public sphere.

This opposition points to the significance of art as a form of social criticism. Public sites affected political discourse not just through cultural content, but also their form, as the aesthetics of built environments and the organization of social space opposed mainstream norms of racial or gender segregation. Claims demanding full rights and visibility in public places made aesthetic space all the more important.[9]

As many bohemians declared, the nonrational, even absurd aspects of artistic discourse—in poetry, music, comedy—can be potent weapons to deflate pretentions and spotlight the failings of rationalized politics. Moreover, as literary scholar Tyler T. Schmidt has noted, desegregation was private as well as public, involving sexuality and intimacy, "a history located not solely in contested public institutions but in transformed homes and personal lives." He argues that interracial sex in the postwar period could be counted as part of queer history, showing the parallels between racial and sexual transgression—transformative actions that were fundamental parts of urban bohemia.[10]

The Rebel Café therefore offers a useful lens through which to examine multiple aspects of the public sphere, which sociologist Jürgen Habermas delineates as the social space that mediates between private citizens and the political realm.[11] Despite the limits imposed by social hierarchies, the function of the public sphere is to provide windows of opportunity, offering possibilities and potential solutions to social problems. Politics is the application of these ideas. While many within the Rebel Café consciously celebrated their marginal position, more arrived there through a mix of factors, including their class status, race or ethnicity, and sexual orientation. Social marginality spawned many of the compelling elements of subterranean culture. Particularly, the public function of *talk*—discussion, conversation, and debate, in a dialogue with the media—was an essential element in the Rebel Café milieu. This included performance as a kind of transformed talk, in which cultural producers and audiences interacted.

Focusing on places where cultural producers met and performed illuminates the role of public space within the Rebel Café as a left-wing bohemian "fallout shelter." To compare nightspots with the Cold War's suburban antiatomic bunkers is apt: these underground cultural venues (often literally located in basements) were commercial endeavors that provided a modicum of real protection for a few ardent leftists. Their dimly lit, windowless, smoky spaces elicited a feeling of shelter from the outside world, while their small, low stages blurred the lines of separation between performers and patrons. Yet Rebel Cafés were perhaps more important as symbols of future survival. Some victims of the Red Scare found employment in nightclubs. These venues also spawned renewed activism: club owners and performers alike gave ideological and material support to groups ranging from opponents to the witch hunts by the House Un-American Activities Committee (HUAC) to peace activists. Nightspots were therefore important places for public discussions, where ideas about the artistic avant-garde and oppositional politics were hashed out, both formally and informally.

At the level of the national psyche, these discussions took on a new urgency as the atomic age spawned a cloud of concern, hovering on the horizon. If Nietzsche and Dostoyevsky declared God dead in the previous century, this notion took on new meaning with the horrors of Hiroshima on August 6, 1945, when the instrument of annihilation became human rather than divine. At their most ambitious, subterranean radicals expounded a new apocalyptic consciousness, questioning a society that had produced the Cold War and the atomic bomb, seeking a millennial reversal of the social order. Bohemians sought individual, internal metamorphoses and used intoxicants as a way of stripping away previously received notions: a kind of creative self-destruction and a sometimes perilous form of psychic exploration.[12] These revolutionary ideas, expounded in poetry readings, art showings, and bar talk in subterranean nightspots, were then disseminated through independent media—from Grove Press and City Lights Books to Fantasy Records and the nation's first listener-supported radio station, KPFA in San Francisco.

Even as bohemian works sparked controversy, this counterpublic expanded to national proportions, becoming largely indistinguishable from the culture industry as a whole. The voice of the Beat generation, fundamental to this process, broke into the broader public sphere in 1957, when Jack Kerouac's *On the Road* hit the bestseller list. The previous year, Allen Ginsberg had come to wide notice after his book *Howl and Other Poems* was banned as obscene by the San Francisco police, leading to a high-profile court victory. The bohemians of the nocturnal demimonde became fodder for the popular press. They were now labeled "beatniks" by columnist Herb Caen, after he overheard poet Bob Kaufman in a North Beach bar playing with the words "beat" and "Sputnik" (the Soviet satellite that sparked the space race).[13] Despite their allure as colorful journalistic subjects, beatniks were simply one of many cliques in the underground community of the 1950s. But *Howl*'s celebrity made a nebulous community visible to itself, and this self-awareness coalesced it. Ultimately, the media spotlight that brightened its sheltered spaces made it impossible to maintain its focus, but not before Greenwich Village and North Beach had established themselves as alluring destinations for bohemian wayfarers across the nation— migrations that changed the histories of New York and San Francisco and had lasting effects on American demographics and politics.

Developments in these two sociological arenas were far more complicated than the cultural ones. Much work remains to be done on the urban history of the big sort, but a quick sketch is possible. The kind of bohemian (or, in today's parlance, hipster) bar and coffeehouse districts, such as North Beach and Greenwich Village, are now mainstays in American cities from Austin, Texas, to Boston, Massachusetts. Each has its own history, but each also carries the faint glow of allure that attracted postwar seekers to San Francisco and New York City. Over the past sixty years, as multitudes of people decided whether to stay in a familiar hometown or move somewhere that offered more promise, these districts were both attractive and commercially viable.[14] Among the many factors that drew likeminded liberals to places like New York and the Left Coast was the cultural capital gained by participating in hip, intellectual culture. The big sort's deeply divided political map—with America's blue coasts and cities encircling the broad red middle—is at least partially traceable to changes in the nation's urban nightlife.

Maps offer two distinct ways to view New York City and San Francisco as the most significant Rebel Café locales. The first is geographic. Both developed as excellent ports with protected harbors, which inherently contributed to their cosmopolitanism as waves of workers and visitors poured in and out from overseas during the decades before air travel. Further, San Francisco's peninsula, at around forty miles in length, essentially functioned as an island, mirroring Manhattan's long, narrow geography. These two locales confined residents to tight-knit neighborhoods but also facilitated public transportation along their urban grids. Yet physical geography alone didn't determine their cultures. Both cities had enough wealth to support elites and intellectuals who sought to display their sophistication by building a kind of literary infrastructure, ranging from institutions such as universities to cocktail parties. These relied on a transatlantic psychogeography, mental maps that sketched out the continental traditions of intellectual exchange, personified in the Enlightenment's Salon de Paris or by literary figures such as Samuel Johnson.

In a way, these two sides of urban culture were reflected and encapsulated in the dual nature of nightspots. On the one hand, they were duplicitous, promising a community that, by definition, was ephemeral and rootless. On the other hand, paradoxically, the conversations fostered by their dark spaces and the social lubrication of alcohol could remove the masks of pretense that often separate people, allowing a certain kind of truth-telling: *in vino veritas.* (It is no coincidence that the word "saloon" shares an etymological root with the French *salon*.) As historian David Hollinger has argued, the question of cosmopolitanism is also a question of solidarity, in which the engagement of human diversity fundamentally relies on the "experience of willed affiliation."[15] Nightspots were signposts in a landscape of public spaces that were vital to definitions of American democracy aspiring to the ideal of *E Pluribus Unum*.

The pages that follow present a cautiously sympathetic look at the accomplishments of people seeking not only their own liberation, but also the freedom of others, happening on a human scale, in the places where they lived and played. There is no doubt that the Rebel Café, reflecting the United States as a whole, was dominated by Euro-American heterosexual men. Yet many of these men chose to question and criticize their privileged position, revising national culture in ways that undercut their own symbolic power. In the words of Mark Twain, "It is a mighty fine thing to fight for one's freedom; it is another sight finer to fight for another man's." Nonetheless, this statement was as problematic as it was noble. It could only be made from a position of power, and it presumed to know what someone else's liberation should look like. Yet my assessment of the Rebel Café's oppositional culture suggests that closely examining sociopolitical successes holds as much value as focusing on failures, and nightspots are rich sites in which to explore consensus as well as conflict. During an era when organized political opposition seemed remote, the Rebel Café was a key site where battles over the definition of America were fought. In many cases, it served as a final redoubt for cultural expressions of democracy, political consciousness, and identity formation. As the old bartenders' saying goes, "Nightclubs aren't just places to drink, people can do that at home." Instead, nightspots represent a complex social phenomenon, sometimes destructive, but always offering possibility: the chance for connection, conversation, and—occasionally—transformation.

Marlene Dietrich (*left*) in *The Blue Angel*, 1930. Courtesy of Photofest

blue angels, black cats, and reds

Cabaret and the Left-Wing Roots
of the Rebel Café

Vinea submittit capr[e]as non semper edulis.
She goats bred in vineyards are not always edible.
Kenneth Rexroth, "On a Beautiful Bar Butterfly
in the Black Cat," 1949

Marlene Dietrich stood at the center of the Rebel Café. Not the real Marlene Dietrich, the German film actress and cabaret singer, but her star persona—Dietrich as she was in the American imagination. Nor was the Rebel Café a real place, but instead was an imagined one, an ideal that grew from hundreds of inconspicuous nightspots in American cities in the late 1940s and 1950s, most known only to the handful of local residents who went there to have a beer or a cup of coffee—and maybe a quick, cheap meal—listen to some music, and talk, often about politics. Whether they thought about it or not—and many of them did in some way—Dietrich was with them in spirit, as a ghost that emerged from the 1930 film *The Blue Angel*, which made her a star and introduced audiences to her signature song, "Falling in Love Again." In fundamental ways, Dietrich's defiant, gender-bending, sophisticated, and unconventional allure was the mythical embodiment of the American nightclub. Her image and ethos floated through the urban underground like the gauzy memories of a dream.

The nocturnal milieu of urban cabaret—the kind portrayed in *The Blue Angel*—was transatlantic, spawned in fin de siècle Paris and Berlin, both of which had absorbed American jazz into their musical social satires. Much like these twin European centers of the arts and entertainment, New York City and San Francisco claimed the most significant and infamous nightspots, which largely defined the nation's cabaret culture from the 1890s through Prohibition in the 1920s, the Depression, and the war years in the 1940s. Within these sites, politics and poetry coexisted—and sometimes conjoined—offering commentary that most often leaned leftward, expressing working-class grievances against the excesses of capitalism. Cabaret owners and performers also challenged taboos—both social and sexual—and some patrons took the opportunity to explore new identities and changing mores. Other audiences simply enjoyed the racy performances as exotic entertainment and never seriously considered crossing racial or sexual boundaries. The cabaret, therefore, established patterns that later crystallized in the Rebel Café, showing both the promise and the limits of socially conscious entertainment as a force for change.

Throughout the early twentieth century, nightspots served a vital democratic and inherently modern function: as places of public discussion. Cabaret evolved as part of a rationalized and bureaucratized world, where impersonal relations in labor and life replaced an ethos of deference and mutual responsibility. Technology offered more leisure and mobility, aiding the farm and factory production that drove urbanization, as well as new notions of time and space. In a practical sense, cars—and later airplanes—augmented the railways' compression of physical geography, while Einstein's theories quasi-mystically expanded awareness of the universe's vastness. The modern city became the new frontier for many who fled familiar rural environs, an inward turn that paralleled Freudian psychoanalysis. Cabaret owners responded to these conditions by presenting entertainment designed (however unconsciously) to alleviate this sense of urban anonymity and alienation—sometimes in spectacular fashion, but mostly by emphasizing connection on a human scale.

The line between cabarets and nightclubs was often blurry, but they were mostly distinguished by their size and style of entertainment. The cabaret featured more-intimate spaces and performances that pushed artistic boundaries. Despite hints of rebellion, however, the cabaret still enforced its own kind of orthodoxy, an exclusionary sense of outsider status. At its most effective, the cabaret freed patrons from the burdens of the past by grappling discursively with the present. Performers and patrons alike scrutinized and skewered social and political issues and coalesced into like-minded communities.

The American cabaret affected political consciousness by offering a transnational, usable past. Feeling connected to the sophistication of Europe bolstered the courage of nonconformists and heightened their nocturnal experiences. Although direct ties to political activism varied, the personal politics of opposition were a significant force, particularly for left-leaning cultural and sexual radicals. Bohemianism was also central to the cabaret, connoting the literati and the intelligentsia, the unconventional and the avant-garde. While this cultural inheritance fostered problematic notions of bohemian authenticity—leading each new generation of subterraneans to decry the next as posturing and phony, as well as reinforcing racial stereotypes—it also wove a web that interconnected people and ideas across oceans and decades. For bohemians, the dark and dangerous cabaret was a site of cultural expression that offered a more vivid engagement with the public sphere than an evening at home with the *New York Times*, a volume by Mark Twain or Edgar Allan Poe, and a bottle of Bordeaux. Part of the allure of cabaret sophistication was its implication of European decadence in a puritan nation continually flirting (increasingly openly) with prohibition. In the bohemian underworld, both real and imagined criminality and transgression lurked.

Between the Gay Nineties and the Great Depression, two distinct bohemias rose and fell in New York City and San Francisco, where the Rebel Café's roots first gained ground. While central figures such as Jack Kerouac, James Baldwin, or Susan Sontag did not arrive until the 1940s and 1950s, a collection of radical poets and artists in the 1930s laid the foundation for a significant postwar oppositional culture and community. These included Kenneth Rexroth and Shirley Staschen Triest, each of whom contributed to the blending of left-wing literary/artistic, and queer culture that later emerged, and who used San Francisco's Black Cat Café as a home base. In New York, the anarchist poet Max Gordon made his mark not through his art, but by founding the Village Vanguard—a nightclub that perhaps most fully incorporated the archetypal Rebel Café elements of literary salon, jazz club, and political cabaret. Along with another cabaret-inspired Greenwich Village club, Cafe Society, the Vanguard also prominently promoted an antiracist agenda, welcoming interracial performances and integrated audiences. This public effort was cut short, however, by accusations of communist sympathies amid the Red Scare after World War II, which led the Village Vanguard and its successors to retain a more subversive, underground style.

The Rebel Café as an ideal, much like Dietrich's star power, evolved as both a spectral projection, represented through the media, and a living entity. Each influenced and, in essence, constituted the other. Patrons of American nightspots entered with preconceived notions that mixed fact and fiction, with expectations structured by everything from the stories of friends to mass-produced novels and films. Nitery owners attempted to fulfill those expectations—maybe even exceed them—or channel them into new avenues of taste and desire. The Rebel Café formula that emerged between the 1890s and the 1930s rested on three key elements of expectation: the allure of song, satire, and sexuality; bohemianism, either as an identity or a vicarious experience; and a nocturnal, imaginary existence, an appetite whetted by evocative media representations of urban American nightlife. Patrons arrived with fantasies of titillation, subversion, and even criminality. Yet the conversations they had in the smoky confines of nightspots were real enough, as were the relationships—sexual and otherwise—and the politics that developed there. This was the elusive promise of *The Blue Angel*: within the cabaret, the ethereal might reveal itself to anyone daring enough to look at its surprising, spectacular, subversive, and sometimes sordid substance.

The Color and the Shape: The Origins of Cabaret

The title of Dietrich's film was aptly chosen, reflecting a deep history of drinking establishments in Western culture that took modern form in the cabaret, starting in the nineteenth century. European taverns and their American cousins had long used color-and-totem formulas, with their suggestions of fantasy or familiarity, to attract patrons. With monikers such as the Red Lion or the White Horse and their accompanying images, eighteenth-century tavern signs easily alerted even illiterate revelers. These sites were also fundamental to a widening public sphere, supplying newspapers, mail deliveries, and social connections. This sociocultural nexus sometimes included radical elements. As political theorist James Scott has asserted, "In

European culture the alehouse, the pub, the tavern, the inn, the cabaret, the beer cellar, the gin mill were seen by secular authorities and by the church as places of subversion. Here subordinate classes met offstage and off duty in an atmosphere of freedom encouraged by alcohol." Just as Ed Sanders's poetic formulation in "Hymn to the Rebel Cafe" suggests, the American Revolution was, at least in part, hatched in taverns like the Indian Queen.[1] But whether revolutionary or mundane, the eighteenth-century tavern was a place of participatory publicity, where patrons formulated, transmitted, and digested the news through a combination of written sources and face-to-face exchanges.

As modern communications developed in the nineteenth century, the role of the nightspot began to change. Information became more widely available through the expansion of public education and mechanized print, and trains and telegraphs whisked correspondence straight to recipients' homes within days or even minutes. The challenge was not simply to get information, but to make sense of a newly complex web of media and social relations. Those ill-suited to the demands of industrial capitalism—the artists, intellectuals, and political radicals who had an eye for the problems that accompanied progress—found that mainstream institutions, from universities to national newspapers, often failed to address their subterranean perspective. The cabaret arose as one response to these new conditions, offering commentary, criticism, and context for the modern urban citizen—all spiced with the sizzle of satire and pleasingly washed down with wine and song.

The first-known cabaret was established in Paris in 1881 by Rodolphe Salis and dubbed Le Chat Noir (The Black Cat). The name embodied a long history of French culture in which the cat was a symbol of magical and sexual mischief, signaling the social inversion of *carnivale* and caricature as seen in the bawdy satire of Rabelais and the medieval "abbeys of misrule."[2] As a member of Paris's young and rebellious artistic set, Salis began his venture with informal group performances by poets and musicians. But he soon formalized these ragtag routines for the sake of bourgeois entertainment, setting a precedent of commercializing bohemia that replayed itself on both sides of the Atlantic. By 1925, one bohemian, reminiscing about Paris in the 1880s, could proclaim, "Ah, this Black Cat, progenitor of every Black Cat, Blue Horse, Green Cow, Stuck Pig and similar temples of 'art' throughout the civilized world!" Such cabarets now dotted "every Greenwich Village, Montmartre and Mayfair in Christendom."[3]

The original Chat Noir closed in 1897, but tourist-trap imitators followed, and its style soon spread to Berlin and beyond. Cabaret performances, first at the Motley Theater in 1901 and later at Berlin's own Chat Noir, were combinations of sexually suggestive songs and skits, sometimes spiked with political critique. Absurdist lyrics were matched by the grotesque decor (epitomized by the work of Expressionist artist and cabaret designer George Grosz), with stages that were small, low, and close to the audience. German imitators of the Black Cat invoked Nietzsche's ideas of humor in which Dionysian "joy in nonsense" became an antidote to the arbitrary in the modern world. One Berlin *cabaretier* suggested that "we need every wanton, floating, dancing, mocking, childish, and blissful form of art, in order to preserve that *freedom over things* that our ideal demands from us."[4]

European cabaret also highlighted the notion that humor is able (and maybe even necessary) to question dangerous political trends. German cultural critic Walter Benjamin suggested in the 1930s that comedy is useful for introducing new ideas, stating that "splitting your sides normally offers better chances for thought than shaking your soul." Conversely, the cabaret's facetious approach to modernity also reflected Freud's views on the pleasure of jokes, which worked as a safety valve—releasing the psychic dams that result from social strictures, but also deflating the cabaret's radical potential.[5]

An ethos of absurdity was definitely at the heart of the Cabaret Voltaire, birthplace of the influential Dadaist art movement. Founded in Zurich, Switzerland, in 1916, by a small collection of French and German artists, Dadaism sought to express (on neutral ground) the nihilistic horror of the Great War that raged through the continent.[6] Cultural critic Greil Marcus has described the aims of Cabaret Voltaire in sweeping sociocultural and liberatory terms: "Dada was the notion that in the constructed setting of a temporally enclosed space—in this case, a nightclub—anything could be negated. It was the notion that, there, anything might happen, which meant finally that in the world at large, transposed artistically, anything might happen there too." Cabaret Voltaire itself was short lived, closing after only a few months. But several of its artists—in particular the poet and performance artist Tristan Tzara—remained influential through the Cold War era as touchstones for American bohemians, including the Beat generation poets and a few radical jazz musicians.[7]

Cabaret Voltaire was typical of the direct and indirect lineages that connected European nightclub culture with its transatlantic counterpart. Some links between people, ideas, and styles fall under the slippery rubric of "influence," yet they remain tantalizing hints of transnational flows. Le Chat Noir was almost singlehandedly responsible for establishing Montmartre as an area of controversial entertainment and revelry, whose romanticized image bloomed in the American imagination for decades to come. Parisian cabaret, which satirized capitalists and anarchists alike (though usually with more sympathy for the proletariat) harbored Tzara after the demise of Cabaret Voltaire.[8] While political propaganda was rare in the first two decades of Berlin cabaret, the Weimar period saw a rise in the Communist Party's propagandistic agitprop groups and venues. One included Weintraub's Syncopators, who performed the music for *The Blue Angel* and exemplified the importation of American jazz. Further, the cabaret Sound and Smoke featured a version of the proletarian play *The Weavers*, a title that provided the moniker for Pete Seeger's blacklisted folk group in the late 1940s. Most notably, Marlene Dietrich began her career in cabaret, as did composer Kurt Weill and playwright Bertolt Brecht, all of whom influenced US cabaret and left-leaning cultural producers after their exile from fascist Germany in the 1930s.[9]

European cabaret was also emblematic of the contradictions that later appeared in American nightclub culture. Cabaret lyrics offered subtle critiques of modernity and consumerism, while facing the difficulty of transmitting these ideas to a non-politicized audience. Themes of social misfits and the gutter were common. With roots in 1920s Parisian nightclubs, these tropes critiqued society by exploring the sub-proletarian regions, using prostitutes, vagabonds, and criminals to illustrate the depredations of the modern city. Yet this also aestheticized poverty, creating a proletarian picturesque that failed to address real conditions and causes, or to propose solutions. Bridging the gap between popular entertainment and pointed social criticism proved to be elusive for owners and performers alike.[10]

Berlin cabaret of the 1920s, then, was most important not for its partisan satire, but for its artistic freedom and its challenges to established notions of good art. Although women mostly remained stereotyped as apolitical objects of desire, some subversive and potentially liberating elements did appear. For instance, "The Lavender Song" ("Das Lila Lied"), published in 1920, featured brazen lyrics about gay rights. Dietrich's early work similarly included a hit about lesbian lovers, demonstrating that oppositional artistic forms could help reframe the political.[11] But while there were some workers'-movement revues presented by former *cabaretiers* (including Brecht), by the end of the Weimar Republic in 1933, many bemoaned the cabaret's embrace of the bourgeois and its loss of outsider status. Overall, the cabaret's political effects were minimal in the face of Fascism. The Gestapo closed most cabarets in 1935, and, while a few continued as liberal enclaves, they did not offer much intellectual resistance.[12] Yet a tradition of avant-gardism, satire, and belief in the social power of art survived. The lineage spawned by Le Chat Noir had already crossed the Atlantic decades before Hitler's Reichstag fire burned a clear line across European history, and the cabaret played an equally significant, if uncelebrated, role in American society and culture.

Whither (or Wither) Bohemia?: Cabaret in the United States

The absorption of cabaret style significantly affected the color and shape of American nightlife. Especially in the port cities of San Francisco and New York, elements of theatrical performance—from stages and lighting to well-rehearsed vaudeville or floor shows—began to define nightclubs, whereas taverns or saloons featured informal entertainment at most. Yet venues that embraced the label "cabaret" maintained some of the saloon's community functions—part of what later set Rebel Café nightclubs apart from the mainstream. Even as bohemians in the 1920s embraced the cabaret as social space, a swing toward jazzy routines met resistance from the previous generation of subterranean literati. San Franciscan and New York incarnations of the Black Cat illustrated these changes, as patrons ranging from radicals to rich socialites used the cabaret's atmosphere to confirm their urbanity and worldliness. Nightspot owners, meanwhile, employed its exotic allure to support their own commercial and sociocultural endeavors.

As the *San Francisco Chronicle* expounded in March 1897, "The cable from Paris saying that Rodolphe Salis, founder of the Black Cat, is dead will revive many memories of one of the most original and eccentric characters in Paris." The article reveled in details of the café's flamboyant style, describing Salis's subtle mockery of the formalities of high culture as he spoke to his customers "in the French of three centuries ago, in the language of Rabelais" amid wrought-iron gas jets shaped like cats. The article concluded by noting that the Black Cat was one of the places in Paris "to which all foreign visitors go." But by the time of Salis's demise, New York City had already enjoyed its own bohemian Black Cat Café for just under a decade, and in a little more than that same time span, San Francisco would have one as well.[13] Stateside club owners incorporated many of the elements that made Le Chat Noir a must-see boîte, from playfully improvised artists' murals to an embrace of dark humor. More importantly, several of these nocturnal entrepreneurs cultivated a clientele from the cream of their cities' literary and artistic crops, sometimes to boost their venture's renown, and sometimes to satisfy their own desires to be among the bright young lights and shining wits.

The 1910s were a kind of bohemian golden age in Greenwich Village. Djuna Barnes, whose novel, *Nightwood* (1936), later became a classic of lesbian literature, captured the atmosphere of bohemia in her pre–Jazz Age journalism. She summoned the spaces of Village nightlife, where the communist radical John Reed rubbed elbows with professional bohemian Harry Kemp, and debauched patrons drank until dawn. For Barnes, the Village was a place of youth and sex, birth-control pamphleteers, poetry, and a living past among the "memories of great lives and possibilities." Like many Euro-American bohemians, Barnes was largely insensitive to the complications of race. Yet she did not obliterate them from her accounts, in which a "colored girl on the sidewalk jostles a Japanese servant and wonders whether he, too, is colored or if he is thought to be white like 'dem dagos.'" Despite crowds of slummers, both the real and the unknown were to be found in bohemia's basements, where even a waiter could claim equal social space and therefore must be "negligent before he can be Nietzsche." Most of all, it was "not where one washes one's neck that counts but where one moistens one's throat." At the Black Cat, Barnes proclaimed, a local singer could be seen standing on a table for a rendition of "Way Down South in Greenwich Village," as the "radical pests come in with flowing ties and flowing morals . . . maintaining that Baudelaire was right when he said, 'Be drunk on wine or women, only be drunk on something.'"[14]

Even as intellectuals and elites quaffed the atmosphere of nightspots to quench their thirst for artistic adventurism, the cabaret's transgressions of racial and sexual boundaries were more than some could swallow. Jazz, with its origins in the African American cabarets and brothels of New Orleans, was still considered to be sordid and lowbrow by prominent critics in the 1910s and 1920s, even when performed by white musicians. The rise of the American cabaret was first and foremost a grassroots expression of popular tastes that only slowly commingled with intellectual circles. As

affluent patrons watched chorus girls in luxurious cabarets and lobster houses, enjoying what historian Lewis Erenberg has called vicarious bohemianism, working-class
saloons were meeting places for the underground gay community, housed prostitution, or offered live sex shows. As Chad Heap has shown, these two trends flowed into
the phenomenon of slumming, where middle-class patrons sought working-class
partners for sexual entertainment (or exploitation) and the sophisticated satisfaction
of desires not condoned by polite society. Slummers found their diversions in
Harlem's "black and tan" nightspots during the 1920s Negro vogue, bohemian "thrillage" in Greenwich Village cafés, or vicarious excitement during the 1930s "pansy and
lesbian craze."[15]

Another aspect of the American cabaret, however, also merits some emphasis. Just
as the urban saloon was an institution that maintained an autonomous alternative culture for workers—which offset poor housing by offering indoor plumbing, affordable
fare, socializing, work and union information, check-cashing, and mail—bohemian
literary cafés and cabarets served a similar purpose for writers and artists.[16] In San
Francisco, this was most notable in the symbiotic relationship between Coppa's
Restaurant and the Montgomery Block building. The four-story Montgomery
Block was built in 1853 at Montgomery and Washington Streets, on North Beach's
southern boundary, to display the city's gold rush wealth as the tallest building west
of the Mississippi. By the 1890s, it was well known as a site of affordable housing for
bohemians, who nicknamed it the "Monkey Block." To escape its spartan rooms, the
Monkey Block's poets and painters gathered at Coppa's, on the ground floor, where
they soaked up the Italian atmosphere, along with the food and wine. Coppa's attractions ranged from minstrel shows to the patrons themselves, who included Jack
London, Mark Twain, and Robert Louis Stevenson. As barter for their tabs, a group
of local artists painted an elaborate mural on Coppa's walls, featuring surreal images
of angels, devils, debauched patrons, black cats, acrobats, and a list of writers and phi-
losophers. Coppa's was a frequent hangout for socialists and anarchists, and, alongside
its reputation for revelry and racial mixing, it drew bohemians and slummers
alike until chaos in the wake of the 1906 earthquake left it without enough customers. The sturdy Montgomery Block survived, however. Along with memories of
Coppa's, the building evoked a romantic image of the Gay Nineties as a period of
freedom and excitement that anchored North Beach as a bohemian stronghold.[17]

Of the increasing numbers of American cabarets between the turn of the century
and World War II, Coppa's successor, the Black Cat, best captured the blend of exoticism and bohemian community. The Black Cat was originally located in the heart
of the prewar cabaret district, at 56 Mason Street, near the center of downtown San
Francisco. Opening the club in 1911, owners Myer P. Cohen and John F. Crowley
hinted at the inspiration provided by Le Chat Noir and signaled a new trend in Bay
Area nightlife. The aspiring nitery offered dinner and wine (both shared in continental style at a communal table), music, and dancing—all for $1—making it San
Francisco's "classiest cabaret." Within a few years, a plethora of cabarets with moni-

Coppa's North Beach mural, circa 1900. Courtesy of the San Francisco History Center, San Francisco Public Library, photo ID AAB-2650

kers such as Stack's Café and Spider Kelly's opened just north of Market Street, advertising everything from dancing and billiards to homemade tamales. The Black Cat itself promoted bohemianism, novelty, Parisian style, and a gender-inclusive ethos, with local talent, vaudeville musicians, dancers, and comedians, all lit with "serpentine" electric lights, "an effect never before staged" in San Francisco.[18]

Cohen and Crowley themselves were prototypical Rebel Café owners, with many of the nightclub underground's defining characteristics. Both were second-generation immigrants and lived near their venue, in neighborhoods that included residents of similar ethnicities.[19] These working-class qualities were underscored by the café's connection to local labor unions. Cohen and Crowley apparently only hired unionized workers, and in 1917, the AFL-affiliated San Francisco Labor Council lobbied authorities to aid the Black Cat's acquisition of a dance license. The cabaret also hosted shows to benefit local organizations, and while this certainly represented a strategy to widen the café's clientele (and perhaps ward off prosecution following the start of Prohibition), it also suggests the cabaret's role as a community gathering place.[20] Yet while Cohn and Crowley promoted the Black Cat's "highest class and most wholesome entertainments," the management's emphasis on bohemianism was a cultural code that invited adventurism and perhaps a chance for social or sexual transgression. Local news reports reveled in the cabaret's association with petty crime and adultery, as well as in the colorful antics of its performers and patrons, both male and female. Such reports betray subtle signs of slumming and the sense of thrillage that would only have been enhanced by the air of criminality—as well as the growing social prominence of the "new woman," who was beginning to assert her independence in the early twentieth century.[21]

Clouding the glimmer of their festivities, however, Cohn and Crowley featured minstrel shows, a popular form of entertainment with a troubling ambivalence toward African American culture. The addition of a tango band and its singer, a "dainty fiesta queen," may have ensured that the Black Cat had the liveliest entertainment in bohemia, but it also carried deeper racial connotations—what Eric Lott has termed "love and theft"—in which admiration and exploitation converge.[22] The inclusion of minstrelsy alongside such acts as the fiesta queen hints at the sort of commodified exoticism found in 1920s nightclub entertainment. Both the Cotton Club in New York City and American émigré Josephine Baker's Parisian performances became infamous for their art nouveau–inflected jungle themes that associated nonwhites with a dense nocturnal urban milieu of primal sexuality and decadent modernity.[23] Although less noted by historians, San Francisco nightspots also embraced this formula.

The first incarnation of San Francisco's Black Cat Café failed to survive Prohibition, reflecting a history of trouble with local authorities. City supervisors had brought charges of collusion in 1917, due to Cohn and Crowley's labor union ties, and the cabaret apparently violated restrictions against interaction between female employees and male patrons. The Black Cat closed on May 5, 1921. Cohn's subsequent arrest on a Prohibition violation ended his cabaret career, and the Black Cat's fixtures were sold by auction.[24] Meanwhile, civic groups aimed for a clean sweep of the cabaret district, in order to make it safe for the expansion of a neighboring shopping district, and other venues soon felt similar pressure. An alliance of businessmen, law enforcement agents, and moral reformers saw cabarets as a sign of compromised female virtue and, in a Progressive-era version of gentrification, forced out the very cultural institutions that had first raised the profile (and thus the value) of the area's property.[25]

In New York, a parallel process was at work. Greenwich Village's Black Cat Café opened within seven years of the original Le Chat Noir and spanned a turbulent history of over five decades before going down for good. Following the closure of the café's original site around the turn of the century, literary patrons lamented in a manner that was echoed by each succeeding generation of bohemians. As one sulking scribe wrote in 1910: "There was a time when New York held many haunts dear to the hearts of men whom the world called bohemians; now it holds places dear to the hearts of those who love to call themselves by that name—and have thereby made the title odious. . . . The places not killed by prosperity have been driven out by commerce."[26] The Black Cat reopened as a cabaret, still in the heart of Greenwich Village, and cashed in on its continental style, touting its Italian ownership as a badge of authenticity into the late 1930s before fading into obscurity.[27] The bohemians' lament for the Black Cat presaged the losses of similar sites to the steamroller of economic expansion or urban renewal. Nonetheless, rumors of bohemia's demise were always greatly exaggerated, even as its substance ebbed and flowed from decade to decade.

Drinkers with Writing Problems: North Beach and the New Deal

Early twentieth-century bohemias in the Village and in San Francisco were defined by community and a common sense of purpose, binding together progressive reformers, feminists, and political radicals. The 1920s saw diffusion as the pressures of war and the first Red Scare sent oppositional figures either deeply inward—searching for usable historical, philosophical, or political models—or abroad, as seen in Parisian literary émigrés like Ernest Hemingway and Djuna Barnes.[28] The 1930s, conversely, saw a new, more institutionalized oppositional community, forged in the fires of the Depression and formed around literary and state institutions ranging from the Communist Party's John Reed Clubs to the New Deal's Works Progress Administration (WPA). The predominant nightclub culture that emerged in San Francisco and New York between the world wars was similarly defined by the broad national contexts of Prohibition in the 1920s and the subsequent Great Depression, and it was against this shifting backdrop that the earliest examples of Rebel Café nightspots appeared.

Prohibition and the Depression had three main effects on urban nightlife. First, earlier trends, begun during the cabaret craze of the 1910s, intensified as middle-class white patrons sought entertainment that combined the glamour and glitz of modern stage productions with exoticism. Second, the rising regulation of nightspots squeezed out legal venues in Midtown Manhattan and downtown San Francisco, siphoning patrons toward marginalized areas such as Harlem, Greenwich Village, and North Beach, where their ethnic and racial demographics made authorities less likely to enforce Prohibition. In response to the Volstead Act in 1920, cabarets had the choice of either establishing themselves as legitimate by becoming restaurants or small theaters—thereby welcoming patrons *sans spiritueux*—or becoming speakeasies and balancing liquor-sale profits against their illegality. It was during the Roaring Twenties that organized crime permeated the nightclub business. Many of the most renowned clubs in New York and Chicago—from the Cotton Club and the Copacabana to "Diamond Jim" Colosimo's café and the infamous hangouts of Al Capone—were run by gangsters and continued that way through the 1960s. While San Francisco avoided Mafia control of its nightlife, the high profiles of the New York and Chicago syndicates (further enhanced by the popularity of crime fiction and gangster films) entrenched nightclubs in the public imagination as illicit sites. As a result, patrons often arrived at Prohibition-era underground clubs with the expectation of uninhibited and sexually explicit entertainment, which also loosened taboos against women in drinking establishments.[29]

Lastly, after Prohibition's repeal took effect on December 5, 1933, the Depression's deprivations fueled desires for lavish entertainment.[30] The legitimization of night-clubs and civic leaders' concerns about moral decline, however, led to a backlash against the most sexually explicit shows. In "Gotham," local boosters proclaimed the return of European-style decorum to the city's nightlife, declaring the demise of both the gloomy subterranean speakeasy and the supposed horror of the old-time, all-male open saloon. Authorities restricted cabaret licenses in residential areas, reinforcing rules that banned obscenity and the fraternization of female employees with male patrons and making arrests for curfew violations. They also discouraged middle-class slumming by increasing the arrests of white women in black neighborhoods and tainting Italian or Eastern European venues as racially precarious "gyp" establish-ments. Moreover, as venues such as the Tic Toc Club and the Greenwich Village Barn touted their chorus lines and promises of wine, dance, and romance, the nov-elty of Harlem's exotic cabarets began to wear off. The Harlem race riot of 1935 only further cemented the feeling that its venues were no longer worth the risk for white, middle-class pleasure seekers. The Cotton Club's relocation to the midtown theater district in 1936 symbolized the return of nightclub entertainment to Amer-ica's mainstream.[31]

San Francisco witnessed a similar trajectory, as clubs such as the Moderne and the Montmartre traded on the city's bohemian past and abounded with Parisian themes. San Francisco boasted of its wild nightlife with imagery that evoked carnivalesque humor, minstrelsy, and thinly veiled sexuality, as the mad atmosphere and nymph-laden adornments of nightclubs betokened their cosmopolitan style. This self-promoting tone, however, hid the darker side of Bay Area nightlife. In early 1935, municipal authorities raided local venues, seeking to quash underage drinking and prostitu-tion.[32] In general, mainstream nightclub culture flourished in line with the Depres-sion era's conservative mores: European styles no longer implied exotic and open sexuality, but rather refinement and highbrow decorum (at least as advertised).

Against this complicated backdrop, the Rebel Café began emerging as a distinct nocturnal milieu in nightspots such as San Francisco's Black Cat and Iron Pot. As bridges between 1920s bohemianism and the postwar jazz culture and Beat genera-tion, their leftist-radical habitués and cabaret styles set them apart from the bulk of American nightclubs. Rather than lavish settings with elaborate floorshows and wide dance floors, of the kind found at mob-owned boîtes such as the Copacabana, bo-hemian club owners maintained independent oases of socially conscious entertain-ment. With capacities below two hundred patrons, they emphasized conversation and performances on an intimate scale. They were equally remarkable for the number of innovative and controversial cultural producers they could claim as regulars. Depression-era bohemians established a Rebel Café tradition of political leftism infused with humanistic notions of personal liberation. Other venues in San

Francisco's bohemia eventually ingested this formula, which distinguished them from the mainstream of American nightlife.

The Black Cat best demonstrated the continuities between bohemian generations. Its second incarnation, opening in 1933, lacked the original's commitment to cabaret entertainment, yet it maintained much of its predecessor's spirit. Owners Jack Ricossa and Peter Lucchesi, both second-generation Italian immigrants, rekindled the café's bohemianism, as well as its literary connotations. Moreover, after its sale to a recent German émigré, Carl "Charlie" Haberkern, sometime between 1936 and 1938, the Black Cat maintained its radical-left patronage well into the 1940s.[33] During that time, the café commingled with the artistic colony emerging along Montgomery Street and the rebirth of literary bohemia in San Francisco's nightspots to play a pivotal role in the transition of North Beach from a primarily ethnic neighborhood to a bohemian one.

This transformation can be illustrated by a sketch of the neighborhood's interlaced residential and working spaces. Haberkern had lived around the corner from the Black Cat since at least 1935, working as a cook and a bartender. After purchasing the Black Cat, he moved to Columbus Avenue, in the middle of North Beach, and took on a partner, Letizio Bonetti, known to the regulars as "Pucci." Bonetti later joined Haberkern at the same address, which was a boarding house largely occupied by fellow immigrants, many of whom worked in local nightspots. Several café habitués, including the artist Maynard Dixon (onetime spouse of famed photographer Dorothea Lange), also lived just to the south, at the Montgomery "Monkey Block" Building, in boarding houses, or in studios in the Canessa building, which housed the Black Cat.[34] The Monkey Block's turn-of-the-century residents had found their entertainment not only in Italian North Beach or simply downstairs at Coppa's, but in the downtown cabarets along Mason Street. By the 1930s, however, the interplay between the massive rooming house and the Black Cat Café was making North Beach itself the center of bohemianism.[35] In addition to the Black Cat, cafés such as Izzy Gomez's mixed highbrow patter, radical politics, jazz, and torrid dancing. The "Beret and Smock Brigade," reported one local scribbler, went nightly to "guzzle and truck and shoot [the] intellectual breeze."[36]

Yet the transition from Italian enclave to radical bohemia was uneven. Reporters cited North Beach nightspots as locales featuring mixed crowds of artists and the upscale smart set, but as late as 1938, they just as often noted the area's ethnic flavor. City fathers planned "North Beach Nights" to promote its touristic appeal, extolling the merry strains of German folk bands or the charm of its Italian sidewalk cafés. The press also painted lurid pictures of North Beach nightlife with stories about prostitution and murder, creating a collage of the city's exoticism and politics with advertisements for Marlene Dietrich's local stage appearance in *Angel*—the story of an adulterous housewife on a European fling—nestled beside articles denouncing both the Socialists and Fascists in the Spanish Civil War as antidemocratic.[37]

The Black Cat was a microcosm of this wild medley, an embodiment of San Francisco's pluralism, playfulness, danger, debauchery, and political debate. Entertainment

Two lives of the Black Cat. *Top*, interior on Mason Street in the 1910s. *Bottom*, exterior on Montgomery Street in the 1930s. Courtesy of the San Francisco History Center, San Francisco Public Library, photo IDs AAB-2597 and AAB-2599

included jazz performed on the café's upright piano or games of pinball between pick-up lines, guzzled drinks, and poetry readings. A local tourist guidebook offered a telling description:

> The dictionary says a Bohemian is "one of a class of artists, intellectuals, etc., who adopted a mode of life in protest against, or indifference to, the common conventions of society . . ."
>
> Rebels have been flaunting convention at the Black Cat for over twenty years. Any night you can watch genuine artists, intellectuals and andsoforths boisterously protesting, or being loudly indifferent to such common social practices as sobriety and amiable conversation.
>
> Rebellious art work lines the littered, smoke-stained walls.

"Even Rebels have their institutions," the guidebook concluded. "Sunday morning breakfast at the Black Cat is one: three eggs, a quarter-pound of bacon or pork sausages, four pancakes, fruit juice, coffee, and one repeat . . . for one buck."[38] Columnist Herb Caen, writing in the 1960s, fondly remembered the café as a symbol of literary San Francisco, the place where playwright William Saroyan could be found "booming his loud dreams" to fellow patrons. With its continental style, the Black Cat offered pseudo-Parisian adventure without a lengthy sea voyage. In 1942, the *San Francisco Examiner* captured this theatricality, describing an archetypal ingénue and her coed companion slinking up to the bar and ordering "two rum cokes—in French." Charlie Haberkern, recognizing the naïf's high school accent, served the cokes sans rum and paternally watched over the pair, playing along that they were "mysterious . . . Parisian refugees" who had come to "recapture a little of the genuine European touch they left on the Left Bank."[39] Haberkern's jovial German bearing, along with a supporting cast of feminists and bohemian radicals, allowed the coeds to successfully perform their roles.

For some Black Cat patrons, the café's resemblance to its Montmartre counterparts fulfilled more than fantasy; it was a tangible reminder of past experiences. Tourists may have watched the hijinks from a distance, but for local nonconformists, the "lusty tavern of talent at 710 Montgomery Street" was a reliable institution, a true home away from home. Haberkern was renowned for supporting starving artists by adorning the café's walls with their work. More directly, for wandering souls down on their luck, he was also "good for a touch or credit."[40] Many 1930s patrons were either recent European immigrants or returning American expatriates fleeing fascism and the looming threat of war. The Black Cat's offbeat cosmopolitanism offered continuity to left-wing or Jewish artistes, for whom the Continent had become too hostile.

Of all the notable nonconformists who frequented San Francisco's subterranean nightspots, radical poet and essayist Kenneth Rexroth perhaps best embodied the spirit of left-wing bohemianism. An irascible and insightful public intellectual, the droopy-eyed, mustachioed Marxist was something of a renaissance man throughout his long career, which lasted from the 1920s through the 1970s. A self-aggrandizing and self-educated multilinguist, he was quick to tell tales of his youthful work on western cattle ranches and as a merchant marine, or to discuss Japanese poetry. Born in 1905, Rexroth grew up amid the labor conflicts of early twentieth-century Chicago. He precociously participated in the city's socialist movement in the late 1910s and 1920s, gaining a reputation as a young soapbox speaker. Like many Rebel Café radicals, he sought to reconcile social justice and psychological liberation. As a result, Rexroth rejected statist approaches, such as the Leninist Stalinism of what he facetiously called the "Russian Orthodox Communist Party," in favor of an artistic brand of libertarian anarchism.[41] In his memoir, Rexroth staked a claim to "movements which younger people think they invented in the late 1960s—sexual freedom, racial equality, militant feminism, homosexual liberation, Native America." While hindsight led him to exaggerate his liberal views on social equality, Rexroth was indeed a powerful liberationist voice throughout the 1930s and 1940s. "I believe that the field of the artist, at least of the poet worth his keep, is the moral consciousness of history," he wrote in 1941. "The artist functions truly when he devotes himself entirely to a struggle to surpass [politics as 'the art of choosing between two evils']. Such activity I believe to be truly 'permanently revolutionary.'"[42]

Rexroth's interactions with an older generation of bohemians made him a link between various incarnations of the American underground. In the 1920s, Rexroth's ambitions had found outlets in Chicago's Prohibition-era cafés, the Dill Pickle Club and the Green Mask (of which he was part owner). Each offered a venue to proclaim his poetry and political philosophy, all within a milieu that welcomed both intellectuals and working-class subterraneans. He later wrote of the Green Mask, "Around the walls were blue nudes dancing with silver fauns under crimson trees and shelves with books of free verse and books about the sexual revolution." Rexroth first met the Harlem Renaissance poet Langston Hughes in Chicago's bohemian cafés, and together they devised a form of poetry accompanied by jazz that influenced beatnik culture in the 1950s. "Here I was, living it out," he recalled, "part of the scene, just like Tristan Tzara, even if it was only on Grand Avenue in Chicago."[43]

Rexroth made a trek to Paris himself, working aboard a steamer, and, according to his own account, met Tzara while basking in the Montmartre café scene. He returned to the United States determined to construct a scene of his own, an American version of the Parisian avant-garde, but one more fully committed to both artistic and political progress.[44] Rexroth found Greenwich Village too claustrophobic, so in 1927 he headed to San Francisco. There he found a permanent haven. Rexroth connected with the city's intellectual circles and immersed himself in North Beach's bohemia, which was a tiny enclave primarily identified by Izzy's café, some young painters, and socialist newspapermen. The poet found a welcoming home at the Monkey Block and, by the mid 1930s, the Black Cat Café became his regular haunt.[45] Rexroth's activism helped turn the café into the district's social center as he launched a politically charged poetic movement later dubbed the San Francisco Renaissance.

Identifying the politics embedded in the North Beach café scene necessarily relies on circumstantial evidence: social networks, offhand and artistic statements, tangential institutional ties—in other words, "guilt" by association. Some dissidents could indeed be found on the membership rolls of left-wing organizations: Rexroth joined the Communist Party–affiliated John Reed Club, for example, and his first wife Andrée was an active CP member. Many Black Cat habitués were tied to leftist institutions by thin and tangled threads. Rexroth and the sculptors Harry Dixon and Peter Macchiarini, for example, each taught at the California Labor School, which the independently libertarian Rexroth later denounced as "the local Stalinist institute." But most others, like artists Shirley and Frank Triest, were part of a looser affiliation of Trotskyists and anarchists who urged political change through psychological and artistic transformation, rather than programmatic Marxism.[46] Anarchist-libertarians in the 1930s saw the contradictions of capitalism all around them as the Depression grew from exactly the kind of unequal distribution of wealth that Karl Marx had predicted. But, at most, they turned to unions as the first step toward autonomous, voluntary, local-production labor collectives of the kind that were betrayed by Russia's Bolshevik centralization. While anarchists differed from the CP in rejecting the USSR's brand of statism, both agreed that socialism offered the answers to capitalism's shortcomings—an agreement reflected in the alliance of leftists and liberals known as the Popular Front.

For anarchist bohemians, the most unifying organization to arise out of this broad leftist alignment was Franklin Roosevelt's Works Progress Administration. With only the faintest ideological boundaries, the WPA nonetheless was a reference point for the oppositional North Beach milieu and fostered bicoastal ties with New York. Organized in 1935, the cultural division of the WPA offered work relief for artists, writers, and theater folk, thereby promoting public art and education through murals, art classes, and publications.[47] Although left-wing networks played a part in the WPA, helping individuals to obtain positions through the kind of favoritism present in almost any large-scale enterprise, its artists and writers were anything but doctrinaire communists. Many, such as Rexroth, who worked for the WPA writing a history of California, were concerned about social justice and promoted the Popular Front as a way of achieving political, economic, and cultural democracy. But even among the most radical, the multiplicity of ideas and social connections belied any straightforward political allegiance.[48]

North Beach bohemia's web of relations is best illustrated, literally, by the Black Cat's most renowned mural, sometimes dubbed "The Regulars." Painted in 1938 by WPA artist Cornelius Sampson (in exchange for his $75 bar tab), it features seventy-eight café regulars sitting, drinking, talking, and cavorting in classic Black Cat style. Although the mural's figures skew heavily toward visual artists,

Defining the Rebel Café: Cornelius Sampson's 1938 Black Cat mural, "The Regulars." Courtesy of the Bancroft Library, University of California, Berkeley, Henri Lenoir pictorial collection, BANC PIC 2004.158—fALB, vol. 1

they also include writers, journalists, labor organizers, and other sundry characters. Two of them, artists Karl Siegel and Henri Lenoir, became notable in the Beat generation and the 1960s counterculture. Still others, such as artist-philosopher Hilaire Hiler and labor organizer George Hitchcock, were part of Rexroth's anarchist circle.[49]

Perhaps the most intriguing figure in Sampson's mural is Cecil McKiddy. Tucked away just to the left of center, the mustachioed McKiddy establishes an important connection between bohemian culture and the formal Left. A communist activist, McKiddy helped to organize the agricultural strike on which John Steinbeck based *In Dubious Battle* (1936). Steinbeck secretly interviewed the young radical while he was in hiding from the police, and McKiddy's account of the strike gave substance to the novel's characters. This connection lends support to the North Beach lore that Steinbeck raised a glass or two at the Black Cat. But whether the author of *The Grapes of Wrath* imbibed his beer there or in some other Bay Area dive is beside the point. His writing exhibited the radical café ethos, a metaphysics-meets-Marxism style that was clearly influenced by McKiddy, a North Beach regular.[50]

In this light, the Black Cat symbolizes an elusive and ephemeral world, a heady swirl of lost conversations, seedling ideas, and spontaneous art whose only vestiges lay in the memories of participants and happenstance audiences. Despite its bar-café atmosphere, it maintained elements of cabaret. Sampson's mural featured—front and center—a guitar-wielding Haberkern and a merrily dancing Pucci, hinting at the musical entertainment served up by the émigré pair. And in the early 1940s, Rexroth and the innovative bassist Charles Mingus introduced North Beach to a pioneering performance of poetry and jazz.[51] Yet the Black Cat was most significant as a literary and artistic center. Rexroth often held court among young poets there, building toward the San Francisco Renaissance. One local observer (borrowing from Truman Capote and Brendan Behan) later quipped that the Black Cat "didn't attract writers with drinking problems, but drinkers with writing problems." For the literary Left, the Black Cat was a place where they could sit and talk forever about art, politics, and where the twain should meet.[52]

Rexroth's Black Cat performances and literary salons foreshadowed 1950s North Beach, when its nightspots mixed politically conscious subcultural networks with jazz sensibilities and sexual nonconformity. Contemporary press accounts focused on the flamboyance of the artistic community more than on its revolutionary aspects, noting Chinese American artist Dong Kingman's "exotic Oriental spirit" or Henri Lenoir's shirtless rendition of "Big Fat Butterfly," performed while his accompanist on the café's piano attempted to "keep the ivories from catching fire."[53] Yet the more hidden history of North Beach queer culture occasionally rose to the surface. While openly activist gay and lesbian groups, such as the Mattachine Society and the Daughters of Bilitis, had yet to organize in the 1930s, the Black Cat played a formative role in the development of queer activism. The café did not become a predominantly gay bar until the 1950s, but its atmosphere made it a welcome home for many gay and lesbian artists and writers. The *San Francisco Examiner*, a conservative Hearst publication, sarcastically hinted at how the gay community intertwined with the café's reputation as "ultra-Bohemian—or something" when it reported that the Black Cat shared a similar telephone number with the city's chamber of commerce, "which keeps getting calls in high-pitched falsetto voices wanting to know 'if that mad, mad Audrey has come in yet.'"[54]

Charlie Haberkern's good-natured indifference to his customers' sexual and political preferences provided an early foothold for later social movements in which nightspots were fundamental for public expressions of dissident views.[55] The *Examiner* was always quick to report sexual infractions and the subsequent policing in North Beach, including B-girls (young women hired to solicit drinks from male customers) and gay patronage. Such reporting made for sensationalist copy and lent the rag an air of moral superiority. But even the communist-hunting Hearst paper missed the leftward currents that flowed together with sexual liberality at the Black Cat. Knute Stiles, a pivotal figure in the city's postwar bohemia and queer activism, noted that even after his arrival in 1949, Communist Party and union stalwarts haunted the café, alongside a growing number of gay patrons. "The Black Cat went through an evolution such as is common in bohemian bars," Stiles said. "It started out . . . [as] a hangout for bohemians; and then it gradually drifted into the radical camp. And [it] was very much a hangout for the enthusiasts for the General Strike."[56] The press's focus almost entirely on sex is explainable partly by anarchism's tendency to avoid large-scale organizational ties—making it harder to identify—and partly by the distraction of bohemia's colorful nonconformity.

Yet the presence of participants in the General Strike—the wave of dockworker demonstrations that shut down the city in 1934—attests to the multiple layers of activism ingrained within North Beach's café society. In addition to labor organizers, waterfront workers were common customers at the Black Cat, which was an easy half-mile walk from San Francisco's famous piers. While there is no detailed evidence of the café's role in the demonstrations, at least one of its regulars, Peter Macchiarini, was injured by police during the violent clashes known as Bloody Thursday.[57] Other WPA artists from the Black Cat circle participated in the 1934 strike wave, including Shirley Staschen Triest and Kenneth Rexroth, who had worked as a National Maritime Union organizer. Both were active in the local Artists and Writers Union, which organized a sympathy strike around the New Deal's Coit Tower mural project at the summit of North Beach's Telegraph Hill.[58]

These regulars signaled both the café's connection to the Left and its place in the mental geography of San Francisco's radical bohemia. "Well, there was just a tremendous amount of political discussion, and a tremendous amount of artistic discussion that could get pretty hot," Triest recalled. She described the Black Cat, along with Izzy Gomez's café (and, occasionally, the drag-show nightclub Finocchio's), as common hangouts for newspapermen and union organizers, a colorful mix of town drunks and Trotskyists. Columnist Herb Caen, in a composite profile of an archetypal "Mr. San Francisco," later intoned that "in his era at the Black Cat and Izzy's all the bohemians were fired up about something every minute, and once in a drunken moment he even volunteered for the Abraham Lincoln Brigade; sober, he changed his mind"—an apropos juxtaposition of intoxication and leftist fighters in the Spanish Civil War. Ideas about proletarian art, as promulgated by the communist press, such as in the *Daily Worker*, were audible in the conversations at the Black Cat, Triest insisted, and charged the atmosphere on Montgomery Street with the feeling of being a communal village.[59] A printer for the anarchist journal *Circle* similarly portrayed the neighborhood as a tapestry of social, political, and transnational elements. He recalled that "there were a lot of people who had gone through the Spanish Civil War—some of them Basque sheep herders" and described the confluent streams of writers and artists in the 1930s, including the left-wing Mexican muralist Diego Rivera. Emphasizing the sense of a larger community, he concluded that the Black Cat was "a very special place."[60]

Such characterizations of North Beach betoken the communal and economic strategies of urban bohemians and the role of café society. Niteries like the Black Cat paralleled the taverns and saloons of the eighteenth and nineteenth centuries, offering refreshment, communication, and camaraderie for working folks—even if their work was cultural. The federal government's steady flow of WPA funds also played a large part. Yet the WPA only had a real impact in San Francisco for four short years, from 1935 to 1939, before Martin Dies and other congressional conservatives put an end to artists' relief programs. Both before and after, North Beach nonconformists devised strategies for survival that made their anarchist principles a reality within the existing industrial capitalist framework. For both practical and ideological reasons, the Black Cat was significant, a node in a national social network that connected dissidents and artists alike. Triest emphasized the café's role in professional circles, stating that showing up at the café scene "was everything" for those seeking work in the culture industry, "because that's where everything was happening."[61]

Yet while WPA networks and anarchist circles connected the North Beach scene with some of the East Coast dissidents, Bay Area cultural producers struggled against the perception that their city was a backwater compared with New York's cosmopolitan publishing houses and galleries. Rexroth, in his typically bristly style, rejected this idea, asserting: "San Francisco stood to NYC about as Florence or Venice to Rome—that is—completely independent. It has its own writers, poets, painters, musicians, many of whom are far better known in Paris & London than in NYC." Triest concurred, writing to Rexroth during a 1936 trip to Gotham that "however pleasanter the general setup is here than in SF, I'm going to be at a hell of a pass to find any high-minded literary conversation."[62] These statements also betrayed a defensiveness about West Coast provincialism, as San Francisco had yet to challenge New York City for national cultural notoriety. Gotham's radical bohemian culture was evolving along lines paralleling that of the Bay Area, but it still outshone its western counterpart.

At the Vanguard

Like the Black Cat milieu, New York's commingling of art and politics extended into the city's nightclub culture. Two Greenwich Village clubs in particular, the Village Vanguard and Cafe Society, demonstrated the confluence of bohemian and leftist currents in the era of continued economic depression and looming war. Cafe Society became the more infamous of the pair, closing due to Red Scare accusations of communist infiltration in 1949. Yet the Vanguard actually played a more significant part in American culture, surviving up to the present day, partly because of its more circumspect politics. It was precisely its nondoctrinaire formula of socially conscious entertainment and underground allure that made it the most enduring Rebel Café nightspot.[63]

Max Gordon, later known as the dean of the Village operators, opened the Village Vanguard on February 26, 1934. In the 1950s, it developed a reputation as an excellent jazz room, and through the 1970s, hundreds of live albums were recorded there, making "Live at the Vanguard" a familiar phrase for jazz enthusiasts the world over.[64] From the beginning, the club was an extension of Gordon's left-wing orientation, conceived as a site for public discussion. Like many in the nightclub underground, Gordon had artistic aspirations: he was part of Kenneth Rexroth's extended literary circle and started out in life as an anarchist poet.[65] "I had dreamt of the kind of place I'd like to open in the Village," Gordon wrote in his memoir. "You dropped in, met your friends, heard the news of the day, read the daily papers provided by the house . . . [and] perhaps a resident poet would rise and declaim some verses he had composed for the entertainment and edification of the guests." In addition to connotations of avant-gardism, the Vanguard moniker was a code that signaled safety for radical patrons, invoking the Marxist notion of a politically conscious cadre whose leadership would spark proletarian revolt. Gordon coyly acknowledged these political leanings, saying that the name originated with his handyman, who "was always just coming off a job at the Federation of Teachers union hall . . . or the Communist Party headquarters—places seemingly in constant need of repairs." Gordon attracted more poets than painters, so his handyman recommended a set of WPA muralists who adorned the walls with "bold, defiant, marching faces of workers with placards."[66] At the Vanguard, indeed!

Max Gordon's biography is practically a checklist of Rebel Café credentials. Born in 1903 to Jewish parents in Svir, Lithuania, he arrived in the United States in 1908. The family settled in Providence, Rhode Island, before moving to Oregon. Gordon spent his youth running around the streets in Portland, selling newspapers with artist Mark Rothko, and eventually attended progressive Reed College. After a sojourn in the Bay Area, Gordon moved to New York City in 1926, briefly attending Columbia Law School. By his own account, he found law to be a predatory profession and left after six weeks to begin a bohemian life in the Village. Gordon haunted all-night cafeterias, seeking like-minded intellectuals and artists, and found the kind of camaraderie that also distinguished North Beach. By 1930, he was working as an advertising copywriter and living just blocks from the eventual site of the Vanguard.[67]

When his writing career stalled, in 1932 Gordon opened a short-lived venue called the Village Fair Coffee House. He then scraped together some funds and opened the Vanguard, first in a small place at 1 Charles Street, and then moving in early 1935 to its permanent site in a former speakeasy, a triangular basement room at 178 Seventh Avenue.[68] The club coalesced out of a mix of European cultural romanticism and a desire for bohemian authenticity. Gordon's 1980 memoir is full of wistful passages about creating "the kind of place where Sam Johnson hung out in eighteenth-century London," with a bohemian atmosphere where "the conversation soared and bristled with wit and good feeling." His partner had pressed him to open the Village Fair because their previous hangouts—the Gypsy Tavern, the Black Cat, and the appropriately named Sam Johnson's Coffeehouse—had sold out to "a fast, hard-drinking crowd of uptown tourists." This left Village locals struggling for bar space and, more importantly, easy credit for their ever-mounting bar tabs. Gordon correctly assumed that the poets who had helped to popularize these now-crowded joints, such as Maxwell Bodenheim and Eli Siegel, would follow him to his new venue. The Vanguard promised free rein to expound their verses, recompensed with food and drink.[69] While some uptown slummers came to the Vanguard to gawk at its poetic curiosities, Gordon and his cohorts were satisfied that they had maintained the integrity of their literary stomping grounds.

Even from his vantage point in the 1980s, Gordon's characterization of 1930s Greenwich Village rings true. Although his spouse, Lorraine Gordon, later stated that "Max wasn't sure what he wanted in those days," she also maintained that he was "simply an intellectual looking for a place to drop his intellect."[70] The Village was also in transition. As described in Malcolm Cowley's 1934 essay, "The Greenwich Village Idea," proponents saw bohemia as an ideal rejection of capitalist alienation from work and bodily pleasures—and critics decried it for the same reasons. Opponents declared that "the Village was the haunt of affectation; that it was inhabited by fools and fakers; that the fakers hid Moscow heresies under the disguise of cubism and free verse." Yet, as Cowley astutely pointed out, the ethos of liberty, self-expression, feminism, and psychological and sexual freedom that had made the Village controversial in the 1910s had become part of mainstream America in the 1920s. Businesses saw opportunity in rejecting the Protestant ethic of frugality and conservatism in order to sell cosmetics and cigarettes to liberated flappers, promoting consumerism's immediate gratification to all.[71] Cowley suggested that many Village bohemians, nightspot owners included, busily sold their rebellion as entertainment for slummers and tourists.

Cowley's essay captured much of this phenomenon, despite its complete erasure of racial or sexual exploitation as an element of slumming. But it also demonstrated a more overarching failure of analysis, due to its limited historical vantage point. The middle years of the Depression—amid political realignment, the repeal of Prohibition, and ever-changing cultural styles—were not simply the end of Djuna Barnes's Village bohemia, but the beginning of a new one. The year 1934 signaled, as well as any point can within a slow and gradual evolution, a generational shift, another turn in the bohemian cycle. In this respect, the Village Vanguard was both a sign of change and an active agent in the formation of a new American subculture.

The Village Vanguard fostered principles of liberty for a community of artists who espoused leftism of the anarchist variety. Lorraine Gordon has asserted that Max had a "point of view," a code common among fellow-travelers to indicate leftist sympathies, but stated that "he advertised it through the club," rather than by political activism or formal communist ties. In addition to Bodenheim and Siegel (whom one Village insider in 1933 called "the most popular man on . . . the left wing of the Village"), Gordon added the left-leaning writer Ivan Black to his core of performers, which also included dancers and singers. Black served as master of ceremonies, sometimes reciting his own verses, and also began his long-standing career as a publicity agent.[72] Black's fledgling position yielded few results, yet the early Village Vanguard's lack of press coverage only underscores Gordon's commitment to a neighborhood clientele. Among the club's scattered newspaper mentions was the awarding of "the office of Poet Laureate of Greenwich Village" to a dramatic denizen characterized as the "last of the Bohemians," on whom Siegel and Gordon himself bestowed the honors. Gordon, described by one employee as a true egalitarian, created "an atmosphere in which all were free to be themselves"—a notable parallel to Haberkern's Black Cat.[73]

The Vanguard's physical space and decor also served as a blueprint for later Rebel Café venues. From the sidewalk on Seventh Avenue, patrons approached the basement club through a steep, narrow staircase—a hint of its former life as a speakeasy. At the bottom, this corridor hooked sharply to the left, where audiences entered the Vanguard's triangular room, with a small, low bandstand at the narrow end. The tiny cocktail tables, seating two or three, could accommodate just under a hundred patrons, with room for a few more at the wide end, near the bar. The effect was precisely the sort created by European cabarets, with performers and audiences in close proximity, nearly at eye level, allowing interactions from the stage with listeners seated all the way to the club's back wall. The Vanguard's murals completed its air of aesthetic rebellion, even subversion.[74] Verbal sparring between hecklers and poets became part of the show, and the crowds grew even more vocal during breaks, which featured dance tunes played on the club's radio or its upright piano.

The Vanguard's more radical regulars tended toward a "philosophy of organism and holism in terms of Marxian dialectics"—a sort of unity-of-life-and-art humanism designed to bring the bourgeoisie's "dead soul of Puritan America back into life again," which differed from North Beach's proletarian activism. Perhaps as a result, some performers' harangues against unconverted Vanguard patrons became increasingly moralistic and bitter. By 1939, Gordon decided on a change of format (and strategy), recognizing the limits of a nightspot's affective abilities. "You don't try to straighten people out in a nightclub," he maintained. "You leave them alone and hope they'll leave you alone." Yet he continued to offer entertainment soaked in social critique, a public space for patrons to consider the roots of capitalism's crisis, even as they sipped their tonic and gin. Much as he had welcomed his muralist's portrayal of a demonstration in Union Square, Gordon now turned to a more orthodox expression of Popular Front culture: political cabaret.[75]

Hot Spots and Holidays: Jazz, Race, and Popular Front Cabaret

In November 1941, just weeks before Pearl Harbor shocked the United States into action against the Axis powers, the Village Vanguard featured a remarkable bill that encapsulated its political slant. Sharing the stage on a single night were the Popular Front blues legends Huddie "Leadbelly" Ledbetter and Josh White, as well as folk-singers Woody Guthrie, Pete Seeger, and Richard Dyer-Bennet. The next day, Guthrie wrote a lengthy letter to Gordon that offered criticism and praise in equal measure, detailing his thoughts about the show's social import. "The opening . . . of your new show featuring Josh White and Leadbelly has got all that it takes to make real night club history in New York," he wrote, "and to give the Negro people a real honest chance to bring their music and singing before the general public in such a way that will not only please your own customers, but will . . . open up a whole new field for entertainers of all colors, namely just plain common, everyday American Music." Guthrie made a few suggestions for improving the singers' stage placement, as well as the content of their material, declaring that the call for "Negro Rights, equal chance, equal pay, equal treatment" was important, but so was supporting the effort to beat Hitler. He concluded by stating that publicizing the singers was as important as presenting them onstage, declaring, "It is a whole peoples affair, and stories and articles can be slanted from all sorts of angles—all very progressive, all political at heart."[76]

The Vanguard show was emblematic of the Popular Front era, which saw the rise of a new, more prominent culture of political cabaret, sometimes tied formally to the Left but seldom directly under the banner of the Communist Party. Yet if the cabaret culture's political ties mostly flew under the radar, its challenges to the color line were about as subtle as a skywriter. Throughout the late 1930s and 1940s, the Village Vanguard and Cafe Society were the nation's most notably progressive cabarets, courting interracial performances and audiences at a time when segregation in New York's jazz clubs was common—even on famed 52nd Street. "The policy [on 52nd Street] was that they would serve a black person at the bar," recalled one scenester, "but when he finished his drink they would break the glass to let him know he wasn't welcome."[77] Jazz, blues, and folk cabaret attested to the ideological power of performances, as politically conscious entertainers from Woody Guthrie to Billie Holiday focused the attentions of diverse audiences by acting like a spotlight, shining intensely on the underside of American life. This, combined with cabaret's continental flair and transgressive atmosphere, had an acute effect on perceptions of difference, confronting the racist logic of enforced separation.

Along with a rising racial consciousness came the complex and intricate sound of bebop jazz, fitting for a war-era populace highly aware of social and psychological transformations. Adding to the significance of the moment, Max Gordon and Cafe Society's Barney Josephson widely publicized their interracial policies, intensifying the wartime discourse about civil rights. Yet as Woody Guthrie's juxtaposition of antifascism and antiracism in his critique of the Vanguard revealed, tensions existed within the emerging Rebel Café around the issue of the black freedom struggle. While white progressives supported civil rights, they simultaneously approached their black allies with a condescending paternalism, insisting on a color-blind universalism that often ignored blacks' fundamental concerns—a contradiction that extended throughout the Rebel Café's existence.

As a prototypal Rebel Café, the Village Vanguard was part of a genealogy of American political cabaret that directly linked German performers and composers to fellow-traveling New York nightclubs and the Popular Front. The first in the line was Herbert Jacoby's Le Ruban Bleu (The Blue Ribbon). Jacoby's roots in French politics and cabaret culture swayed New York nightlife, since he featured performers such as Lotte Lenya (whose star had risen, along with Dietrich's, in *The Blue Angel*) singing songs by left-wing composers Kurt Weill and Hanns Eisler. In France, Jacoby had served as an editor for Leon Blum's left-wing newspaper, *Le Populaire*, and as a publicity agent for the Dadaist Parisian cabaret, Le Boeuf sur le Toit (The Ox on the Roof). Fleeing anti-Semitism after the fall of Blum's government, Jacoby opened Le Ruban Bleu in December 1937 and, the following April, brought Lenya to New York for her first American appearance. The Popular Front's Theatre Arts Committee (TAC) followed suit, offering a series of cabaret nights that featured satirical and radical songs, including Earl Robinson's "Joe Hill," an ode to the executed IWW leader, and Lewis Allan's anti-lynching ballad, "Strange Fruit." Jacoby later joined forces with Max Gordon, opening the Blue Angel in 1943. While this uptown venture focused more on sophisticated entertainment than the bohemian Vanguard, it nonetheless carried on the tradition of cabaret satire for over twenty years. Gordon and Jacoby were therefore part of a circle of New York *cabaretiers* that also included Leo Shull, the founder of Genius, Inc., who supported left-wing performers such as Paul Robeson, as well as the political fight against Jim Crow policies.[78]

Cafe Society, opened by Barney Josephson in December 1938, has been characterized by scholars as the heir apparent to the cabaret tradition of Le Ruban Bleu and TAC. It is easy to see why historians Michael Denning and David Stowe have focused on Cafe Society as the prime example of what critic Irving Howe derisively called the "social-minded night club"—a symbol of the Popular Front's effort to wed leftist politics with American culture that Denning has termed the "cultural front." Josephson explicitly stated that he modeled Cafe Society on Berlin cabaret, describing the influence of a 1931 visit there, as he took in the socially satiric and political revues of Friedrich Hollander, the composer of *The Blue Angel*'s "Falling in Love Again." Cafe Society most likely was bankrolled by the Communist Party, through Barney

Josephson's brother Leon, an active communist who became the first to level a court challenge at the House Un-American Activities Committee, the federal body most responsible for anticommunist investigations, resulting in a year-long jail term for Leon in 1947. Barney Josephson also had close ties to Popular Front figures, such as jazz producer John Hammond and musician Teddy Wilson, who was nicknamed the "Marxist Mozart." Josephson's club, dedicated to social and racial justice, put its point of view on display with a satirical maitre d' in a raggedy tuxedo and an antifascist spoof, placing a stuffed monkey dressed as Hitler at the front door. Descending the stairs into the smoky basement venue, patrons were greeted with the rare sight of both interracial bands and audiences, as well as murals, painted by Popular Front artists, lampooning Cafe Society's wealthy namesakes. The club's motto directly summarized Josephson's political stance: "The wrong place for the Right people!"[79]

Cafe Society was where Billie Holiday popularized "Strange Fruit," and Denning devotes an entire chapter to what he calls her style of cabaret blues, which she shared with other radical protest singers, such as Josh White, Sonny Terry, and Brownie McGhee. The drama of the club's closing following Leon Josephson's high-profile HUAC disaster makes Cafe Society understandably attractive copy. Moreover, the progressive stance that Barney Josephson took in support of civil rights was significant, and the club did indeed help redefine the nation's nightclub culture. But scholarly emphasis on the club's CP ties and its role as a Popular Front institution has obscured both its historical place within New York's nightclub culture and its influence as a progenitor of the Rebel Café style of the postwar years. Denning is correct to say that Howe's condescending description of the social-minded nightclub as little more than liberal slumming—a "thrill over cocktails"—failed to note the significance of racially integrating entertainment and urban spaces.[80] Yet Josephson's effort, self-consciously and aggressively taken, was limited by its agitprop nature, not only because of the postwar Red Scare, but also because individual experiences and ideologies are not so easily manipulated.

The story of the Village Vanguard paralleled that of Cafe Society in almost every way, shy of the overt communist ties, suggesting that Cafe Society was not unique, but instead was part of a larger shift in American nightspots.[81] For instance, in the same month when Josephson's Cafe Society opened, the Vanguard began to present a revue featuring "skits and songs of satire and social significance." The Vanguard revue was hailed as part of a mild renaissance in the Village, in which "latter-day Bohemians who have seen the chestnut trees in Paris" and whose discussions "revolve around those twin imponderables—what is art? and the pathology of sex" regained some of their spirit. The source of this revival was a troupe *identified as* the Village Vanguard, but who soon dubbed themselves the Revuers, composed of Adolph Green, Betty Comden, Alvin Hammer, John Frank, and Judy Holliday. Critics lauded their skits as sophisticated entertainment that took "action against some of the more desperate phases of modern life and society," including one that portrayed the sale of scrap steel from New York's L train to fascist Japan, with bombs falling on California

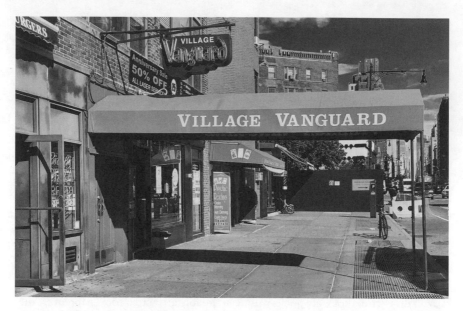

A popular front: the Village Vanguard. Photograph by the author

marked "Made in NY." This teenaged troupe, the press crowed, skewered "any one from chairman Dies to Noel Coward."[82] Holliday, in particular, had deep ties, including close family members, to socialist circles and to Barney Josephson (who first saw her perform at the communist Tamiment resort), making Gordon's Village Vanguard a suitable site for the Revuers' debut. The troupe quickly capitalized on their popularity and moved to the uptown Rainbow Room in the fall of 1939, although they also participated in TAC's Midsummer Cabaret.[83]

Inspired by Popular Front productions, such as the International Ladies' Garment Workers' Union musical *Pins and Needles*, Gordon continued to present political satire at the Vanguard. He began with a troupe called Six and Company, followed by the Bargain Basement Revue, with songs written by Popular Front figures such as Earl Robinson, the renowned songwriter of Paul Robeson's populist and antiracist "Ballad for Americans."[84] This policy of social-minded satire continued through the 1940s, including return performances by the Revuers (now promoted by Ivan Black) and "Professor" Irwin Corey, a comedian with CP roots who started at the Vanguard in 1942. Folk singer Richard Dyer-Bennet, part of Woody Guthrie's "city-billy" genre that promoted the Popular Front's notion of people's songs, also made his Vanguard debut that year.[85] Only Communist Party funding could have embedded the Vanguard more deeply in the cultural front.

Cafe Society did move ahead of the Vanguard in one aspect of Popular Front progressivism: interracial jazz performances. Josephson opened Cafe Society with a vow to overturn nightclub conventions of racial segregation, as well as to eschew what he saw as the corroding influence of mob ownership. "I wanted a club where blacks and whites worked together behind the footlights and sat together out front," he later recalled, "a club whose *stated advertised* policy would be just that."[86] The emphasis Josephson added to this statement is significant. Interracial "black and tan" nightclubs were nothing new; they were fundamental, in fact, to Negro vogue slumming in the 1920s. But these venues were often illicit, or at least secretive (even if the secret was an open one). What was new about Cafe Society was its propagandistic approach to breaking the color line, its open promotion of interracial policies to both black and white patrons.

At the same time, Cafe Society embodied the tensions between white leftist and African American goals. Josephson's communist ties, for instance, sometimes led him to overburden his performers with demands for controversial content or participation in political protest. For example, black musicians welcomed performances for inter-racial audiences (the more the merrier), but an interracial jazz group per se was not their main goal. African Americans were also happy to claim the CP as an ally in the fight for equality, even if they had no real interest in a proletarian revolution and sim-ply wanted their own fair slice of the economic pie. So Josephson's dual role as club owner and artists' manager, mostly without written contracts, alternately strength-ened and strained his relationships with black performers. Jazz pianist Mary Lou Williams, for example, fondly remembered Cafe Society in the 1940s as a place where she was "treated like a member of the boss's family" and enjoyed regular get-togethers with fellow pianist and singer Hazel Scott. "The only drag in New York was the many benefit shows we were expected to do—late shows which prevented me from running up on 52nd Street to see my favorite modernists," she recalled. Billie Holiday, how-ever, found Josephson's managerial style overbearing, on one occasion breaking her engagement with the club in retaliation after he insisted on repeated encores during a performance at the Apollo Theater.[87]

Taking these performers' views into account, it is apparent that Josephson was concerned with the *appearance* of antiracism but maintained a level of white paternal-ism when newsmen and their cameras were looking the other way. In her 1956 auto-biography, Holiday suggested that Josephson's concern for racial justice was perhaps only skin deep, recounting the audition of Hazel Scott, whom Josephson initially re-fused to hire because "she wasn't pretty—she was too dark." While it seems unlikely that Josephson was so uncharacteristically callous, when viewed in a broader context, Holiday's account bears the ring of truth. Whether or not Josephson *specifically* stated that he turned down Scott due to her skin color, he did tend to focus on African Americans as *symbols* of social injustice. Josephson's public stance was certainly well intentioned, but it betrayed the reality that Cafe Society was still primarily a site for white audiences to display their enlightened views.[88]

It would be overly simple to dismiss Cafe Society's public stand for racial equal-ity as ineffective, however, even if it was partly a product of partisanship and white paternalism. The club's open invitations to interracial bands and audiences—

augmented by the presence of African American luminaries such as Paul Robeson, Walter White, Langston Hughes, and Adam Clayton Powell Jr.—had a wide influence, elevating socially conscious nightspots in the public eye. Moreover, it is important to distinguish between Josephson's private and public positions. Racism is not simply an individual pathology, or even a historical constant, but a continually evolving part of the social structure, a manifestation of power relations ranging from culture to economics.[89] Josephson, along with his publicist, former Vanguard emcee Ivan Black, recognized that the lack of positive publicity for African Americans in the white press reinforced a structural discourse of black invisibility and racial hierarchy. To provide a widely publicized platform for interracial performances in front of mixed audiences undermined the dominant framework.[90]

Ironically, considering the Village Vanguard's later status as the nation's most revered jazz club, Gordon was slower to feature jazz performances, sticking instead to satirical revues through most of 1939. Yet Cafe Society's lead in adopting a racially progressive stance was slim. That fall, Gordon began to include African American calypso performers, making the Vanguard one of the first nightclubs in the country to do so. While calypso's popularity certainly relied on elements of exoticism— reviews in the white press tended toward cringe-inducing descriptions of "voodoo stuff" in which gaudily clad black performers "jerked at the knees" as their heads "rolled the rhythm"—the African American press also highly praised the Vanguard's new acts.[91] By 1940, the Vanguard regularly featured jazz combos. Equally importantly, the club began to partner with the black community, hosting presentations honoring African American musicians and supporting benefit concerts. Throughout the 1940s and early 1950s, Gordon helped to organize benefits for civil rights causes and organizations, such as the National Association for the Advancement of Colored People (NAACP).[92] Gordon's Village Vanguard thus quickly followed in Cafe Society's footsteps, becoming part of a newly progressive, interracial public sphere.

Of course, the growing social significance of jazz began with the musicians themselves, as modernists—such as trumpeter Dizzy Gillespie, pianists Thelonious Monk and Mary Lou Williams, and saxophonist Charlie Parker—developed the style known as bebop. Beboppers rejected big-band swing in favor of small combos, complex harmonies and rhythms, dissonance, and virtuosic solos played at breakneck speed. Bebop developed slowly between 1939 and 1945, mostly through nightclub jam sessions—including early bebop jams featuring Gillespie at the Vanguard. The style is often associated with the nightclubs along 52nd Street. But the most important site in the development of this new style was Minton's Playhouse in Harlem, where Monk and Gillespie drew the attention of likeminded players. The 52nd Street clubs—like the Onyx, the Three Deuces, the Downbeat, and the Spotlite—enjoyed notoriety (and infamy) in the 1940s, but as World War II ushered in a nightclub-business boom, and then a postwar bust, their prominence in New York City's jazz scene was relatively brief, lasting only from 1938 until a steep decline a decade later.[93] These venues, sometimes mob owned, were certainly significant, employing innovative jazz greats, introducing bebop to white audiences, and occasionally offering taboo-busting inter-racial activity. But nightclubs in the cabaret tradition could boast of a much longer history—and a greater impact on American culture.

In addition to providing locations for jam sessions, nightclubs made progressive musical statements public, blurring the line between folk and commercial art. Ralph Ellison later described Minton's in a 1959 *Esquire* article as a descendent of the Cab-aret Voltaire, stating that "it is associated with those continental cafes in which great changes, political and artistic, have been plotted." This sentiment was echoed by Sid-ney Finkelstein in his seminal 1948 study, *Jazz: A People's Music*, which similarly placed jazz within the Dadaist tradition.[94] Finkelstein, however, also challenged the notions of automatic expression and racial essentialism that bedeviled African Amer-ican music, establishing a line of thought that continued through radical scholars like Eric Hobsbawm and LeRoi Jones.[95] All three placed jazz in the social context of protests against racism, often with ties to the Left and New Deal liberalism, as a form of folk music that had a complex relationship with the public through commercial-ization, yet resisted co-option by remaining rooted in black cultural traditions.

The nightclub's function as a community institution further highlights the arti-ficial distinction often made between folk and commercial art. Musicians described clubs as schools, and jam sessions as intellectual exercises. Ralph Ellison's *Esquire* article cited Minton's aura of jazz authenticity, which later drew pilgrimages of European fans, much like the Americans who had flocked to the Café de Flore in Paris. But Ellison explained that in the 1940s, this model for later Rebel Cafés served a more direct purpose. It was an academy where individualism, democracy, folklore, black consciousness, rebellion, community, interracial exchange, and musical meritocracy were the curriculum. Ellison asserted that it was "more meaningful to speak, not of [a] course of study, of grades and degrees, but more of apprenticeship, ordeals, ini-tiation ceremonies, of rebirth." Another *Esquire* piece in 1947 likened it to a bebop salon, where musicians traded licks in the grand tradition of European intellectuals trading quips.[96] Jazzmen themselves tended to be more straightforward. Drummer Kenny Clarke affirmed that it was about teaching, insisting that the music's message was "whatever you go into, go into it *intelligently*." Moreover, women instrumental-ists, who were at a disadvantage in the masculine world of jazz, often remarked on the role of nightclubs like Minton's and the Vanguard within their community. Gui-tarist Mary Osborne, for instance, went to jam sessions at the Vanguard and at venues on 52nd Street in the 1940s and later suggested that they were the places where she felt most at home.[97]

As Harlem diminished as a draw for white patrons during World War II, the cen-ter of the jazz scene migrated southward, down Manhattan. Lucien Carr, an early member of the Beat generation, remembered the war as a turning point for the young jazz fans who frequented Harlem clubs in the 1940s. Carr suggested that changing attitudes in African American clubs were sparked by the influx of white servicemen and southern war workers, both black and white, who "brought their little prejudices with them." Whereas previously the Harlem clubs were delighted to welcome white patrons, their warmth now cooled, leading white jazz fans, such as the Beats, to revel at 52nd Street clubs.[98] When most of these Midtown Manhattan clubs went out of business in the late 1940s—amid racial violence, commercial real estate development, and oppressive policing—Village clubs picked up where Gillespie's Vanguard jam sessions had left off.

In September 1948, Minton's pioneer, Thelonious Monk, began a two-week run at the Vanguard, which was a key moment in that club's history. When Monk stepped onto the stage and announced, "Now, human beings, I'm going to play," he also unwittingly signaled bebop's fully established presence in Greenwich Village.[99] Monk's weird, angular, and dissonant piano style had been at the center of the modern movement, and his sartorial style defined hipness, with his goatee, dark sunglasses (he was a night person), and beret (an antifascist symbol of solidarity with the French Resistance and the Surrealists). Monk also had a reputation for erratic and rebellious behavior. He often showed up late for performances, sometimes drunk or high, and just months before his Vanguard stint, he was arrested for marijuana possession. The high priest of bop therefore carried an air of mysterious anticommercialism that made the neon-lit clubs of 52nd Street leery, especially given the area's increased police presence. But it made him a perfect fit for the Vanguard's left-wing, bohemian atmosphere.[100]

Monk's key ally was Lorraine Lion, who ardently promoted him for the Blue Note record label. As a young jazz fan, Lion had started her own nocturnal excursions to Greenwich Village in the late 1930s. She was part of a Jewish immigrant family with artistic left-wing ties and began coming to the Village Vanguard in order to hear Leadbelly's protest blues and Irwin Corey's "political mumbo-jumbo routines." But she later remembered that the greatest attractions were the club's Sunday afternoon jam sessions. Max Gordon must have held some attraction as well. In 1950 she became Lorraine Gordon when the pair married.[101]

Lorraine booked Monk at Max's club for both practical and ideological reasons. Monk's arrest had resulted in the suspension of his New York cabaret card, the license required by the city's police department for live performances in any venue serving liquor (and a controversial source of corruption).[102] The Vanguard's low profile allowed Gordon to bypass police oversight, providing Monk with much-needed income. Equally importantly, Lorraine recognized that the Vanguard's bohemian tastes could give Monk's eccentric style a firm footing, an insight that proved to be pivotal for his career. Monk continued to use the Vanguard as a home base as he wound a serpentine path through the jumble of jazz nightclubs, record labels, press, and festivals in the 1950s, earning a dedicated following of nonconformists.[103] Once again, the Vanguard had earned its moniker, setting a Village precedent by regularly headlining beboppers.

Bebop's arrival in the Village was significant in the context of rising black consciousness and individualistic bohemianism. In 1947, the NAACP had delivered a report to the newly formed United Nations, calling for the harsh treatment of African Americans to be declared a human rights violation. Beat writer Jack Kerouac proclaimed 1947 as the year "bop was going like mad all over America," beginning his famous westward journey on the road while "listening to that sound of the night which bop has come to represent for all of us." Saxophonist Norwood "Pony" Poindexter recalled that while serving in the navy during World War II, listening to bop records was a statement that challenged white authority. Confronted by white sailors complaining that the music disturbed their morning church services, Poindexter retorted that the ship's arrival off the African coast had had an emotional impact on him and his compatriots: "So now we're celebrating. You should be able to understand this. You celebrate St. Patrick's Day. . . . You feel something beyond the festivities. And in the same way, we Africans feel something beyond the merriment."[104] While Poindexter's 1985 memoir was certainly filtered through a post–Black Power lens, it nonetheless captured bebop's part in postwar political consciousness.

While black beboppers maintained claims on their style—its very origin being an attempt to create music that whites "can't steal, because they can't play it"—they seldom complained of white audiences' enthusiasm. The Vanguard's V-shaped room became the very symbol of such musical connections, with the "justly famous interaction between audience and performer that is generated down there."[105] But the Vanguard was also part of a larger national discourse around racial integration and jazz that made Greenwich Village a central locale of postwar progressivism. As early as 1946, Langston Hughes wrote of seeing the Village as a historic, nineteenth-century, African American neighborhood that was being reclaimed by black artists and writers. Citing the Village Vanguard and Cafe Society as part of this process, Hughes stated that "now a number of our folks till the fields of the arts or live the life of Bohemia in or near the Village." Make no mistake, the Village was no racial utopia. That same year, several racially motivated attacks occurred, some specifically targeting entertainers from Cafe Society, and the black press continued to call for more police protection in the area through 1947.[106] African Americans' perseverance despite such violence also attests to their determination to claim their full rights to urban spaces—an effort that was often backed by jazz's antiracist slant.

White Villagers' embrace of bebop was part of an intellectual sensibility found most notably among bohemians and radical writers, such as Norman Mailer. Intellectuals saw the music as an authentic expression of alienation appropriate to the start of the atomic age and the Cold War. While this view certainly stumbled over its own kind of racist essentialism—the figure of the black jazzman as a natural representative of free creative and sexual expression—it also demonstrated a white desire to participate *in* black culture, not simply to exploit it as entertainment. John Clellon Holmes's *Go*, the first published work by the Beat generation, offered a fictional account of New York nightclubs that captured the experiences of young jazz fans in the 1940s. "In this modern jazz," he wrote, "they heard something rebel and nameless that spoke for them, and their lives knew a gospel for the first time."[107] Holmes's novel not

Jam sessions at the Village Vanguard. The club's murals are visible on the far right of the photograph. *Top*, Maxine Sullivan at the Vanguard in 1947. *Bottom*, Miles Davis (*upper left*) on stage in 1958. *Top*, courtesy of the William P. Gottlieb / Ira and Leonore S. Gershwin Fund Collection, Music Division, Library of Congress; *bottom*, copyright © Dennis Stock / Magnum Photos, STD1958003W00007/05 only evoked the ecstatic American lament that jazz represented, but it also illuminated how nightclubs manifested this zeitgeist, allowing subterranean sensibilities to become publicly visible.

Fallout: The Red Scare and the Rebel Café

As the Cold War fostered an increasingly inquisitive Red Scare, however, this visibility could become a liability. The story of Cafe Society's closing was a prime example of the Red Scare's effect on left-wing musical culture. McCarthyism was not a monolithic phenomenon led by its namesake, but rather a patchwork of anticommunist efforts. Some had official ties to the government, such as the HUAC hearings in the House of Representatives and Joseph McCarthy's investigations in the Senate. Each of these carried the threat of jail time for uncooperative witnesses or of prosecution under the Smith Act, which effectively outlawed the Communist Party as a treasonous organization. McCarthy's tactics also included smear campaigns in the press, aided by Hearst newspaper columnists and the newsletters *Counterattack* and *Red Channels*. Simply being called to testify before HUAC could be enough to taint one's name in the culture industry, making the blacklist an elusive threat.[108]

In March 1947, Leon Josephson was summoned before HUAC. He was called to testify about his role in acquiring a fake passport for communist leader Gerhart Eisler, the nation's "no. 1 Red." The Eisler case was an outgrowth of Josephson's longtime involvement in CP activism and espionage, which included everything from projects to establish fair housing for African Americans to his arrest in Denmark after a failed attempt to infiltrate Nazi Germany and assassinate Hitler in 1935. Josephson refused to testify, instead offering a written statement that denounced HUAC for perpetrating a "well-planned program to create a national psychological basis for a domestic brand of Fascism" and asserted that the hearings were "repugnant to the provisions of our Constitution." "I am an American," he stated. "I believe in democracy, in government of the people, by the people and for the people. . . . I am a Communist. Like all Communists, and like most Americans, I am also anti-Fascist." In October, Josephson was convicted of contempt of Congress and sentenced to one year in jail. America's "no. 2 Red," the press reported, "showed no emotion."[109]

From late 1947 through 1948, conservative columnists, such as Walter Winchell, waged an innuendo campaign against Barney Josephson's nightclub, highlighting Leon Josephson's arrest and communist ties. In response, Barney Josephson ran advertisements in the press defiantly declaring that he would struggle on, stating, "My head is bloody but not bowed." Yet in the Cold War's atmosphere of suspicion, this proved to be a last-ditch effort to keep his customers. Winchell's syndicated society column unleashed a backlash that cascaded through New York's nightclub underground. Cafe Society's business dropped precipitously, and the club closed on March 2, 1949. Throughout the 1950s, Josephson wrote, he was "out of the nightclub business and flat broke." He was even denied a passport, scuttling his plans to open a new club in Paris.[110]

Within a few years of Leon Josephson's imprisonment and the club's closing, Cafe Society and Village Vanguard performers Zero Mostel, Judy Holliday, Pete Seeger, Josh White, and Hazel Scott were subpoenaed by congressional committees, as was publicity agent Ivan Black. The various strategies that these nightclub leftists adopted represent the paths taken by hundreds of others during the blacklist era. The entertainment field is enormously fickle, and many a performer's career has tanked quickly enough without McCarthyist sabotage. Yet the career trajectories of blacklisted Rebel Café performers suggest that the Red Scare had rapid and noticeably detrimental impacts on their success. For instance, when Seeger and Mostel were each listed in *Red Channels* in 1951, this effectively put an end to their popularity. As Seeger recalled of the Weavers' blacklisting, "Instead of singing in the Waldorf Astoria or Ciro's in Hollywood we were playing in Duffy's Tavern in Cleveland."[111] Despite having won the Best Actress Academy Award in 1951, Judy Holliday never again starred in a major Hollywood hit. Mostel would not appear in another film until 1966.[112]

When Josh White and Hazel Scott were called to testify, they were well aware that as African Americans, racial prejudice would most likely worsen their fates, so they testified as "friendly" witnesses (as did white folksinger Burl Ives), recanting their leftist affiliations and naming names. (If Paul Robeson's fate is any indication, their assumptions were correct: his "unfriendly" repudiation of HUAC resulted in a ban on his travel abroad and persecution at home.)[113] In 1951, Scott was listed in *Counterattack* and *Red Channels*, specifically due to her ties to Cafe Society. During her testimony, Scott bravely read a statement denouncing red-baiters as totalitarian "profiteers in patriotism." But she also repudiated Josephson, insisting that he "often lent my name and time to affairs without consulting me" and stating that "managers send their talent to appear at various benefits and we go because our managers tell us it builds our audience." Whether White and Scott would have gone on to wider acclaim if not for the taint of their HUAC summons is open to speculation. What is certain is that their careers stagnated from that point on. Neither appeared in any more feature films, and they remained mainly nightclub performers through the 1960s.[114]

Mostel's, Seeger's, and Ivan Black's 1955 testimonies took a strictly unfriendly stance against HUAC, ridiculing the committee's methods and denouncing them as unconstitutional. Black suggested that HUAC violated the First, Fifth, Sixth, Tenth, and Fourteenth Amendments. When Representative Gordon Scherer retorted, "All Commies think so," Black replied, "That's what Hitler said, Congressman Schnorr."[115] The circumstances of their testimonies, however, were decidedly different from Holliday's or Scott's. Joseph McCarthy had already fallen out of favor by late 1954, having overstepped his bounds by accusing military officials of subversion, and Mostel had little to lose, as his film career was already over, due to the blacklist. But the effects of the Red Scare remained very real. Black's publicity work had included Hollywood films in the early 1950s, and he headed New York's Publicists' Guild of Broadway. Both positions ended after his first HUAC subpoena in 1953. Moreover, his ability to take a stand against HUAC relied on the Rebel Café. After losing his more prominent clients, Black returned to work as the press agent for New York nightclubs, particularly those with socially conscious entertainment.[116] This gave him a source of income largely outside the reach of the blacklist—a strategy others would follow in the 1950s.

The Red Scare also marked the end of the Rebel Café's formative period. While those like Pete Seeger and Zero Mostel were able to eke out a living in the 1950s by mixing nightclub appearances with theater shows and concerts, African American singers such as Josh White, Sonny Terry, and Brownie McGhee relied heavily on Rebel Café venues. As a result, these nightspots were known for their "authentic" folk performers, while also meeting jazz audience expectations by pairing these musicians with sophisticated, modern bebop groups. Although some satirical performers, including Irwin Corey, escaped HUAC scrutiny—in part because their material was as much absurdist as political, thereby hiding it from prying congressional eyes—the overtly political cabaret that had proliferated in the 1930s came to an end by 1950. The collapse of the Popular Front stranded left-wing theaters such as TAC, leaving them without institutional support, while Cafe Society closed and the Village Vanguard felt pressure to minimize its satirical content. Until the darkest days of the Red Scare began to lift in 1954, social protest in American nightclubs was limited to the more oblique form of jazz/folk performances.

Moreover, while government-sponsored arts projects like the WPA had helped democratize and disseminate cultural productions, their limitations were clear to participants. Any state-run project is subject to the whims of politics—and no less so in a democracy. With the end of the Popular Front, and in lieu of a more enlightened (or utopian) alternative, the neo-artisanal creations of nightclub performers provided the most direct and progressive public entertainment in the midcentury United States. The social meaning of folk forms (broadly defined) from Guthrie's city-billy ballads to Gillespie's bebop became part of an emerging alternative-culture industry. Jazz was particularly intertwined with other cultural forms within the nocturnal underground. As the left-wing, bohemian novelists and poets of New York City and San Francisco absorbed bebop as an expression of postwar rebellion, they also gathered in bars and cafés, adopting them as the institutions of a literary revolution. The political stakes were also clear. With the Cold War pressing down on nonconformists and civil rights activists alike in the late 1940s and early 1950s, the rebellious ethos of the Black Cat and the Village Vanguard extended into a mushrooming number of nightspots.

subterranean aviators

Postwar America's Literary Underground

Neal—
We're all at the Pink Elephant
Allen, Holmes, Bill, Al, Jack
undated note, circa 1948

"At 'The Pot,' passionate, tireless artist-debaters mill about the bar," proclaimed the midcentury tourist guide, *Where to Sin in San Francisco*, describing North Beach's Iron Pot. The café's menu, the guidebook noted, captured its bohemian sense of playfulness and exploration with the disclaimer "We are not responsible for lost articles or customers." Even more slyly winking at its commodified artistic allure, the menu advised customers that the "bohemian atmosphere is strictly phony. For genuine bohemian atmosphere, go to the Black Cat."[1] As these passages suggest, between World War II and the fall of the red-baiting Joseph McCarthy in 1954, the nightspots that collectively made up the Rebel Café welcomed a new generation of bohemians, as aspiring artists and intellectuals connected with Depression-era dissidents—or simply claimed the promise of personal and artistic freedom. One small group of novelists and poets that formed around Jack Kerouac and Allen Ginsberg recognized this trend and dubbed themselves the Beat generation. But they represented just one clique within a larger cohort that gathered in literary nightspots like San Francisco's Black Cat and New York's White Horse Tavern. Moreover, the long-standing but tenuous links between the two coastal bohemias became firmer, both through oppositional social networks and shared cultural sensibilities. This vanguardism added to San Francisco's allure as an entertainment alternative to Hollywood—a bohemian challenge to mainstream mass media. The mirrors that hung behind the bars of underground nightspots metaphorically reflected a carnivalesque, funhouse image, exaggerating the warps and curves of experimental outrageousness (especially when caught in the sights of conservative critics or the distortions of intoxication). But they also enabled some Americans to take a good hard look at themselves and the nation.

While bohemia certainly exhibited many of the racial, sexual, and gender inequalities that broadly afflicted society, it nonetheless was a key liminal site, a doorway to new identities. For scores of young writers, artists, and dissidents drawn to Greenwich Village or North Beach, "it was the kind of scene [they'd] dreamed of."[2] Nightspots played a vital role in radical communities, providing neighborhood institutions and the foundation of a new public sphere that challenged many of the assumptions of mainstream America. During the direct and indirect oppression of the Red Scare, the Rebel Café was a fallout shelter for left-wing cultural producers and intellectuals, offering protected places for discussions and social connections. Further, it was an experimental space for the more daring subterranean aviators to flight-test their flamboyant public personas. As the Village poet Max Eastman once said, suggesting the mix of art and life that energized the nightclub underground, "We wanted to *live* our poetry."[3]

Mad to Talk: Communication and Liberation in North Beach

At the core of the Rebel Café's emergence as an oppositional institution was a deceptively simple activity: talk. Admittedly, it has become a cliché to quote Jack Kerouac's declaration that its subterraneans were "mad to live, mad to talk, mad to be saved," a phrase tossed out almost reflexively as shorthand for youthful exuberance and the romance of the American road.[4] Yet it is equally true that this remark's literal central meaning—the sociocultural role of talk—is often taken for granted. Bohemians and progressive thinkers in part developed their ideas through intensive sessions of bar talk. Moreover, while many nocturnal conversations hinged on the innocuous or the inane, even these can't be completely dismissed. Nightspots were places to blow off steam and escape the pressures of modern society. Even the most playful bar talk could have profound meaning for those seeking liberation from social, sexual, or racial norms.

Rather than the cool, almost formalized cocktail conversations that have long characterized private gatherings in the urban apartments of artists, academics, and writers, bar talk brewed up a desultory mix of social ambitions. Cocktail-party talk is the result of invitation, where participants more or less know that they are part of an identifiable group with whom they can mingle. Such interactions were important to dissident social circles—enough so that the intellectual Mary McCarthy once quipped that radicals ended up as either communists or socialists, "depending on what cocktail party you went to."[5] A bar, on the other hand, is for searching, for navigating multiple social streams in hopes of finding a suitable landing, the place where an invitation is finally obtained. As the writer John Gruen said of his booth-hopping conversations with painters and publishers at New York's Cedar Tavern, "we did not go to the Cedar simply to be seen; we also wanted to belong."[6] Literary bar talk guided the construction of new social networks arising from the disruptions and constraints of World War II and its aftermath. Therefore, the *spaces* in which these conversations took place, in terms of both physical places and social relations, had a significant impact on the evolution of Cold War culture.

North Beach's Iron Pot was just such a place. Taking up the slack where the support of the WPA had left off, it functioned as an avant-garde gallery and, along with the nearby Montgomery Block building, as a haven for artists, leftists, and other nonconformists. Many local artists garnered the meager incomes needed to live at the Monkey Block with sales from the café. *Where to Sin in San Francisco* offered a colorful description of the Iron Pot that hinted at its dual role as a community center and as a part of San Francisco's commodified bohemia, including its potent mix of radical talk, artistic daring, and transgressive sexuality:

> Eager tourists, bored card-players, cab-drivers (ardent collectors) and rapt, sometimes wrapped lovers jam the oilcloth-covered tables. . . . And often you'll find an authentic S.O.S. tacked up: 'HELP! Being EVICTED again. Desperately need something CHEAP and EMPTY.'
>
> Armchair psychoanalysts enjoy the Men's Room. Here unknown artists have covered the walls . . . with inartistic, venomous, very red symbols of political, sexual and aesthetic frustration.[7]

Such descriptions illustrated the atmosphere that regulars and tourists alike expected from North Beach and Greenwich Village nightspots, but they also underlined the spatial relationships that often characterized Rebel Café sites: open areas up front, relatively welcoming to initiates and furnished with tables for face-to-face interactions, and deeper recesses that intimated more subversive activities.

While a night out in bohemia meant adventurous entertainment for the uninitiated, with only the *possibility* of participation in the underworld, for dissident cultural producers, nightspots were bound up with the process of creative self-expression and community formation. "We would do the grand tour," recalled radical artist Knute Stiles, discussing his early experiences in San Francisco. "We covered the Black Cat, the Paper Doll, and so on in North Beach, and then on down to the bars south of Market Street." Stiles arrived in 1949, where he joined his friend, photographer Leo Krikorian, a fellow alumnus of the experimental Black Mountain College in North Carolina, and "the first night that I was here—he took me to the Black Cat." Stiles's anarchist leanings also led him to Kenneth Rexroth's loquacious Libertarian Circle, where conversations often went on well into the night at various North Beach cafés. Stiles remembered: "There were a lot of people whom I had first known as Marxists who quarreled with me a lot. And so it was a genuine dialogue; it wasn't a monologue."[8] This kind of talk, intertwined with increasingly visible gay and lesbian communities, continued to be labeled as bohemian by Bay Area commentators as new arrivals—such as the radical gay poets Jack Spicer and Robert Duncan, and the young surrealist Philip Lamantia—also joined Rexroth's anarchist circle. "Above all, I was attracted by his inexhaustible and encyclopedic way of conversing," Lamantia recalled. "Sometimes we'd talk [for] a whole weekend." For radicals such as Lamantia in the ever-more-conservative 1940s, "bars like the Iron Pot and the Black Cat, where intellectuals went to talk," were "islands of freedom."[9]

Another central figure in the North Beach scene was the jazz musician, painter, and occasional Dadaist performance artist Henri Lenoir. Born Silvio Velleman in England, he began his career as a drummer in European nightclubs in cities ranging

from Paris to Budapest. In the mid-1920s, Lenoir reinvented himself, moving first to
New York, and then Los Angeles, before arriving in San Francisco around the time
Charlie Haberkern purchased the Black Cat. Lenoir started off selling silk stockings
to sex workers in North Beach and then picked up work as an Old Gold cigarette
salesman. He became a café regular and a familiar face on the Montgomery Block,
although he was soon fired from his job for supplying too many gratis packs to cash-
strapped smokers. Lenoir then applied his talent for self-promotion to become a kind
of mobile art dealer, arranging showings for local painters at both the Black Cat and
an ailing café across the street, the Iron Pot. Starting in 1941, Lenoir offered raffle
tickets to Iron Pot customers, giving away a painting by a local artist at the end of
the evening—and tripling the bar's receipts in the process. For his trouble, Lenoir was
paid $1 and had $2 removed from his extant bar tab per day.[10] Lenoir's satirical flair
was soon stamped on the café's paraphernalia. Menus contained price lists for paintings, alongside proclamations that "Male customers who need a hair cut are not artists" and "No credit extended to editorial consultants, advertising agency account
executives, radio continuity writers, newspaper men or other bums."[11]

The Black Cat/Iron Pot hub became the nucleus of North Beach bohemia, giving artistic rebellion a public platform. While the Black Cat maintained a measure
of infamy in the press as a "menace to public morals" because of the occasional arrests there for drugs, fistfights, or lewd behavior, reporters also heralded it and the
Iron Pot as "one of the last vestiges of S.F.'s Bohemia."[12] As North Beach nightlife experienced a wartime expansion and postwar contraction, scenesters and journalists
mistook the generational shift as a decline. This led Lenoir to wage a sort of artistic
public relations campaign, promoting avant-garde art showings while snapping
photographs to document nonconformist patrons. Iron Pot regulars spanned across
those in the WPA and laborite crowds of the 1930s, such as Rexroth, to a younger
generation, like Peggy Tolk-Watkins, who later opened her own nightclub—the
campy Tin Angel—in 1948.[13] Lenoir's photos even captured interactions across the
color line, still relatively rare during this period. Images of interracial couples and
black artists such as Sargent Johnson, whose work was influenced by the Harlem Renaissance, were prominent in Lenoir's collection—although his captions' references
to various African Americans as an unnamed "wandering musician" or a "piano player
from Club Alabam" also betray an element of jazz/hipster exoticism.[14]

Cafés were also sites of psychosexual experimentation that invoked romantic notions of a cosmopolitan, bohemian past. One free-spirited actress remembered North
Beach cafés as the places in the early 1950s where she "tried peyote and listened to a
lot of writers and musicians and anarchists." Turning a jaundiced eye toward her
youthful exuberance for a milieu that included nudist parties and sexual encounters
of all stripes, she continued:

> Once a woman got furious about some pictures in the bathroom: some vaguely
> Asian prints of a fornicating couple. . . . There were these little flames all around

their genitals. I thought the bland looks on their faces were supposed to be funny, but the woman who got furious stormed out of the bathroom and gave the painter and his friends hell because she didn't think such pictures should be in the *bathroom* where people could look at them while defecating, because that put sex in the toilet, lowered it to the level of a bodily function. . . .

[The Iron Pot] was on Montgomery Street, but I felt as if it might be on the Left Bank with the last of the Lost Generation. Everything suited my imagination, except the people. I couldn't get them to fit. I thought being bohemian meant being yourself, and I thought being yourself meant being happy.

The collision between liberationist ideals and commercialized bohemia could indeed be disillusioning. "I expected to look up and see Gertrude Stein walk in with Alice," the actress concluded. "I didn't know Gertrude Stein had moved to Paris because it was *cheaper* than San Francisco."[15]

The rising rents in North Beach were indeed an outcome of the bohemian influx (an effect that was even more pronounced in Greenwich Village), but the gradual proliferation of literary cafés was another sign of the area's radical reputation.[16] In 1948, in the wake of the Iron Pot's success, the café's owners decided that Lenoir's art-brokering services were superfluous and handed him a pink slip. Lenoir quickly moved his operations, first to the gay bohemian bar 12 Adler Place, and then to "a jernt of his own," the Vesuvio Café. Opening in July 1949, the bar was another attempt to wed tourist-friendly publicity with the kind of creative atmosphere found at the Black Cat. Vesuvio marked what one local artist called a "new era in North Beach bohemia."[17] Lenoir displayed local art in his new café, as he had at the Iron Pot, including pieces by Hilaire Hiler, with whom he had performed in Paris cabarets during the 1920s. He had purchased the ailing bar from an immigrant family ("nothing but Italian spoken in the joint," remembered Lenoir's first bartender), and he now began to promote his latest venture as "Bohemia's last stand!" After first calling the bar Lenoir's, he cast about with the locals for a new name, testing out such monikers as the Blue Beret and the Last Stand before caving in to its patrons' preference simply to keep the original one, Vesuvio.[18]

Lenoir imported much of the political slant—and many of the regulars—from the Iron Pot and the Black Cat. He hired former WPA artist Luke Gibney as a bartender, whom a coworker remembered as "very leftist in his attitudes" but also artistically cosmopolitan: "He had been in Paris as a young man and he kind of carried that tradition here, and so did Henri. . . . And [Vesuvio] was a little extension of what Paris must have been."[19] In a letter to Kenneth Rexroth in 1964, Lenoir revealed hints about his radical literary approach to Vesuvio—as well as the misogyny that sometimes suffused bohemian nightspots. After praising Rexroth's recently published autobiography and admitting that he "had no idea of the many fantastic experiences you have had, nor your incredible devotion to study, painting and pussy," Lenoir reminisced about their prewar days at the Black Cat and the Iron Pot, placing Vesuvio in a tradition going back to Rexroth's Green Mask:

> With my limited experience I tried to make the Vesuvio interesting but it was a far cry from your Chicago joints. In the beginning with the sawdust, candles and beer and wine license, it attracted every penniless chess-player and militant left-wing guitar player and folk singer in Northern California. I had no capital reserves, in fact was in debt, so after putting up with alot of unprofitable bullshit and FBI surveillance, I finally got fed up and kicked alot of those people out. One day I was so exasperated that I put a big sign in the window which said "This establishment is positively non-bohemian."

Lenoir was typical of immigrant nightspot owners who balanced their artistic or social standpoints with the exigencies of commerce. Yet his attempt to clean house, however seriously he took it, could not stem the left-wing bohemian tide. Noting a news rack placed in front of the bar, he quipped, "It says IWW, and has 'The Industrial Worker.' I don't know who put it there."[20]

One habitué later recalled the importance of Vesuvio for San Francisco's changing postwar bohemian community: "Vesuvio has never been just a bar. It's true that booze sales pay the bills but the place is also an art gallery, a museum, a living room for those of us in cramped apartments, a community meeting place, a support group headquarters, a literary Mecca, a mandatory stop on a tourist's agenda, and a place to try and get laid."[21] Lenoir further boosted the site's bohemian feel with printed signs over the bar and matchbook covers sporting ironic catchphrases, such as "MODERN DANCING and IMMODEST DRESS STIR DESIRE: leading to Lustful Flirting, Fornication, Adultery, Divorce, Disease, Destruction and Judgment," and "The customers in this bar are entirely fictitious. Any resemblance to actual, living persons is purely accidental."[22] The conservative *San Francisco Examiner* jovially heralded Vesuvio as a "hangout for the illiterati," describing men's room graffiti that included the opening passage from Virgil's *Aeneid*—"in Latin, yet." The café was also the San Francisco drinking destination of Welsh poet Dylan Thomas, after Knute Stiles brought him there during Thomas's first visit to the United States in 1950. If, as one local magazine suggested, Vesuvio represented North Beach's answer to Greenwich Village, Thomas's visit certainly made it the West Coast counterpart to New York's White Horse Tavern, where the doomed poet ultimately drank his last beer three years later.[23]

It is not surprising that Thomas took a liking to Vesuvio, with its narrow, street-level barroom and a balcony with carved wooden railings and balustrades. The bar's Old World roots were still visible underneath the contrived carelessness of the poetic paraphernalia that cluttered its walls—including pages from Freud, a life-sized effigy of Lenoir in beret and sunglasses, and a Victorian-era magic lantern projecting slides of nudes and impressionist paintings, as well as a direct invocation of North Beach's esteemed bohemian past: the door from Izzy Gomez's café. With a seventy-five

Flight of the bohemian butterfly. *Top*, the Iron Pot. *Bottom*, Henri Lenoir and the exterior of the Vesuvio Café. Courtesy of the Bancroft Library, University of California, Berkeley, Henri Lenoir pictorial collection, (*top*) BANC PIC 2004.158—fALB, vol. 1, Iron Pot scrapbook, (*bottom*) BANC PIC 2004.158—fALB, vol. 3, Vesuvio scrapbook

person capacity, much like that of the Iron Pot and the Black Cat, Vesuvio's close quarters encouraged intimate talk among familiars and between-table talk among strangers.[24] Yet a sort of spatially reversed hierarchy also formed, which helps to explain the bar's success. Regulars capitalized on their insider status, squeezing themselves in at the bar or in tiny ground-floor alcoves, while tourists took the more exposed spaces, such as the balcony. This allowed visitors to imbibe both the atmosphere and their cocktails to their hearts' content, while locals kept a sense of

exclusivity, a fictional distance from commercialism that underlay Vesuvio's bohemian credibility. One regular later divulged how hip artists playfully enjoyed this
arrangement, saying, "I can remember many times sitting with them in Vesuvio . . .
and they remarking that all those people over there looking at each other are tourists and they think they are looking at artists, but here the artists are over in this
corner."[25]

These multiple levels of public presentation, conversation, and group play set Vesuvio alongside the Black Cat and the Iron Pot at the center of North Beach bohemia, even as it gained a reputation among insiders in the 1950s as a tourist trap. For
many who had to fund their social exploration with day jobs, these sites satisfied their
need to unwind from the mundane world.[26] Especially for new arrivals to the area,
North Beach bars offered personal connections in an otherwise large and impersonal
city. In the early 1950s, for instance, Jack Spicer went to the Black Cat to overcome
his bewilderment at city life and to meet area poets after departing Berkeley's university enclave. One member of Spicer's circle remembered the literary connotations of
the café's clientele, which also evoked hints of European cabaret: "Intellectuals;
painters; it was very 'modern,' in that sense, because you had everything from transvestites to businessmen to girls out on dates with young boys. It was the sort of place, you
know, to start an adventure . . . almost like an existentialist hangout . . . [where]
everybody was reading Sartre and Camus." Leo Krikorian later described the libertine ethos of Vesuvio, which had regulars that included a heterosexual transvestite and
a young woman who stood on tables and stripped each time her favorite song played
on the jukebox. In 1953, Krikorian and Knute Stiles started their own bohemian bar,
The Place, which shared similar patrons, because "we used to hang out in Vesuvio's
and the Black Cat, so we knew all the artists already." What was the attraction? "Well,
the Black Cat and Vesuvio's, you could almost do anything."[27]

Nocturnal New York, Leftist Literati, and the Beat Generation

In Greenwich Village, a similar mix of Black Mountain College alumni and budding
writers from New York's Columbia University and the city's left-leaning New School
composed the new generation that populated rebel nightspots. The most significant
hangouts were the San Remo Café, the Cedar Tavern, and the White Horse Tavern.
Each attracted some of the twentieth century's most notorious artistic and literary
iconoclasts. Although there was much overlap among bar patrons, the San Remo and
the White Horse mainly hosted writers and poets, including Norman Mailer, James
Baldwin, Judith Malina, and the Beats. The Cedar was primarily a hangout for painters
and claimed Franz Kline, Willem de Kooning, and Jackson Pollock. As a result,
these sites gained quasi-mythical reputations that are sometimes difficult to disentangle from their actual histories. Because of New York City's status as the national
(even global) center of postwar publishing and the arts, American readers were often
privy to offhand mentions of these Village bars. From the 1960s through the 1990s,
they appeared in a multitude of novels, memoirs, and articles focused on the 1950s

scene, as writers and journalists placed their accounts in now-familiar settings—and grasped the prestige that came with situating themselves in renowned nightspots.

In reality, many other lesser-known places fulfilled the same function within New York's nightlife scene. The Minetta Tavern, Café Reggio, Goody's, and Louis's Tavern in the Village; the West End Bar near Columbia University; and numerous other bars and clubs along Times Square or 52nd Street were spaces in which to explore the underside of American life. Beat writer William Burroughs, working as a bartender during World War II, expressed his fascination with the characters of the underworld by keeping an annotated list of bars along Eighth Avenue in Midtown Manhattan.

The West End Bar was the most significant Beat generation site in the formative years of the late 1940s. Beat writer Joyce Johnson later described it as a "plain bar of dark wood and no particular charm, bottles lined up on mirrored tiers." The West End Bar was one of New York's "nondescript places . . . that for some reason always made the best hangouts." Along with the pads of local hipsters, she recalled, these bars were like a "psychic way station between the Village and Times Square, or between Morningside Heights and the Lower Depths, in the mental geography of those who came together there."[28] It was at the West End that Jack Kerouac was introduced to compatriot Lucien Carr by Edie Parker (Kerouac's first wife), who went there between Columbia University classes with the socially conscious German artist George Grosz. Carr then introduced Kerouac to Burroughs, a friend from his native St. Louis. The West End was also where Allen Ginsberg first met Neal Cassady (the model for Dean Moriarty in Kerouac's *On the Road*). In addition to these literal introductions, the West End also provided literary lessons. It was the place where Kerouac and Ginsberg had some of their most fervent early discussions about writing, which Ginsberg fictionalized in an abandoned novel he variously titled "The Radical Café" and "The Rational Café." "The trouble with you, Bliestein, is that you don't write about your own environment," penned Ginsberg in one scene.[29] In these early West End conversations, the Beat concern with immediacy, "the real," and a sense of place had already begun to surface.

Harlem also claimed a share of important nightspots, most notably Small's Paradise, where a seventeen-year-old Malcolm Little became "Detroit Red"—the first stop on his path from the underworld to leadership in the black freedom struggle as Malcolm X. Like so many other ambitious newcomers, he sought to put his small-time past behind him. "Within the first five minutes in Small's," he later declared, "I had left Boston and Roxbury forever."[30] But few of the transformations experienced within New York City's nightlife were as dramatic and significant as that of Malcolm X. Most passed unremarked and unrecorded. So, although many accounts of Small's, the Cedar, the San Remo, and the White Horse probably misidentified their locales, they are nonetheless useful as collective memory, symbols that represent many more numerous, nameless, and ephemeral moments within the nocturnal demimonde.

For Village bohemians and cultural producers, literary bars served much the same function as the Black Cat or Vesuvio in North Beach. The owners of the New York bars, however, tended not to be bohemians, but instead paralleled the Iron Pot model, in which immigrant families simply welcomed any crowds willing to spend their dollars. Both the Cedar and the White Horse Taverns originally opened in the nineteenth century, with the Cedar possibly as early as 1866. The White Horse opened in the 1880s, serving the largely Irish immigrant community that swelled the West Village. German émigré Ernest Wohlleben took over its ownership by 1917, and the White Horse continued through the 1950s under his stewardship. Ernie, as his loyal patrons called him, persevered through Prohibition by serving bootleg beer on the sly, and by the 1930s he had attracted a varied mix of left-wingers, labor organizers, local Irish patrons, and a smattering of bohemians. In 1925, the Santini family opened the San Remo Café, which also survived Prohibition. The Cedar didn't, but it reopened in 1933, just before Prohibition's repeal, under an incorporated ownership that reportedly included a WPA sculptor, which may help explain its connection with painters such as Pollock.[31] Otherwise, there were few significant ties between Greenwich Village bar owners and the culture industry.

One habitué suggested that the Cedar's cultural tabula rasa was precisely its attraction for artists, "because it wasn't handicapped by possessing any character." The Cedar's identification with painters was established by 1948, the year critic Clement Greenberg assigned as the start of the abstract expressionist scene—although it was probably Jackson Pollock's regular haunt for a couple of years previously. Greenberg, who hated the notion of identifiable art movements and insisted that "a scene kills," absolutely detested the artists' tavern. "At the Cedar," he recalled, with its "studiedly proletarian" ambiance of booths and rickety tables, "*everybody* looked unattractive."[32] The San Remo contrasted similarly with the flamboyant decor of the Black Cat or Vesuvio. Yet, like their North Beach brethren, each was small, with a capacity below a hundred people, a bar along one wall, and separate sections for face-to-face conversation. At the San Remo and the Cedar, this meant booths opposite the bar, which became gathering points for small groups, while the White Horse had two successive rooms, each with small tables, giving patrons a sense of sheltered descent as they moved down into the back room. And, like North Beach, these bars had deep roots in the Greenwich Village working class. Before World War II, they frequently served longshoremen who worked nearby, as well as the neighborhood's first- and second-generation Italian immigrants.

By 1948, however, the journal *Commentary* could blithely describe one long-forgotten bohemian hangout as "the ancestor of the San Remo today." The San Remo's literary origins are obscure, but poet Harold Norse reported having gone there as early as 1942 with bohemian labor organizer Harry Hershkowitz. Norse also recalled that, after an evening of drinking at the bar, he met a teenaged James Baldwin in the street outside it the following January. Baldwin himself became a San Remo regular by 1945.[33] A future *New York Times* restaurant critic who moved to the Village in the 1940s remembered the bar as fundamental to her early bohemian experiences, as her defiance against her parents' warnings about the neighborhood's interracial couples and communists became wrapped up with bohemia's literary image. By the time leftist activist Michael Harrington arrived in 1949 and innocently wandered into the lesbian Café Bohemia, seeking local left-wingers, he was quickly told: "You don't belong here, buddy. You're a San Remo type."[34]

It is clear that by 1950, when Norman Mailer began to host a writer's group in the White Horse Tavern, the Village's cultural bar scene was already established. The artist and critic Elaine de Kooning, spouse of painter Willem, called it the booze explosion, as rebellious originators sought authentic experiences through intense and often sodden interactions with working-class or underworld characters.[35] This producerist aspect—which espoused both the value of neoartisanal economic independence and the right of all laborers to fair wages—began in isolated pockets of discussion, such as Norse's wartime East Village bouts with Harry Hershkowitz and other radicals in an apartment building courtyard, nicknamed "Paradise Alley." Norse noted that, at the same time, "unknown to us," the young Beats were "doing their job of making a new sound in the spoken word in New York" as Ginsberg and Kerouac began their explorations in the West End Bar. These clusters slowly absorbed each other into a single scene that was psychologically, if not always geographically, set in the Village. While Norse admitted that the eccentric Hershkowitz "talked much and wrote little," the literary circle in which they and Kerouac "traded drunken insults" at the San Remo or the MacDougal Tavern proved to be a creative wellspring.[36] Over the course of the 1940s and 1950s, it provided fertile soil not only for the Beat writers and their publishing houses, Grove Press and New Directions, but also for the *Village Voice*, Norman Mailer's New Journalism, and groundbreaking texts of social criticism that laid the foundations for the sweeping changes of the 1960s, such as Paul Goodman's *Growing Up Absurd* (1960) and Michael Harrington's *The Other America* (1962).

The poetry and literature spawned by the creative competition in these largely masculine sites also grew from New York City's notoriously close quarters, with its cramped apartments, its neighborhoods that mixed working-class denizens and intellectuals, and its diverse political viewpoints. "At one time in 1945–6," Ginsberg wrote in a 1948 journal entry, "Jack and I had spent a lot of time together, even sharing the same small room around Columbia, and we had no money, and no place to go at night to continue talking after the bars closed." Ginsberg's "intellectual" friend Lucien Carr introduced him to both "low-life" bars like the West End—where conversations about Cezanne and Oswald Spengler alternated with jazz and marijuana—and the Village scene at the Minetta Tavern.[37] Norse spent his nights with fellow poets like Paul Blackburn, when they would "drink in the Village and talk about [Ezra] Pound." Norse reported that Blackburn's group included several "ardent disciples of the great lunatic," and even counted one "niggerlynchingsonofabitchmotherfuckingbastard" who embraced Pound's fascist politics.[38]

Pound's anti-Semitism or Spengler's theories of Western civilization's decline made appropriate bar talk fodder for a generation disillusioned by World War II. Norse, for example, had witnessed the lynching of an African American worker while serving in a sheet-metal production plant in Alabama. The feeling of helplessness from his inability to stop the attack shattered the optimism kindled during his experiences in the WPA. He was haunted by the incident, which augmented his sense of outsider solidarity with blacks and women that, in itself, was at least partly rooted in his own gay Jewish identity. As Norse recalled, "Perhaps, because we were young and struggling for liberation from oppression, we shared a community of feeling that gained intensity because we could entertain little hope, realistically, for improvement of our condition."[39] Despite his subtle nod to the naiveté of such an overly simple idea of coalition, Norse nonetheless captured the contradictions of the postwar years, in which the victory over foreign fascism often rang hollow for those still marginalized at home.

Mailer's *The Naked and the Dead* (1948) was the first major literary monument to postwar distress, with its Tolstoyesque view of human fallibility in war and politics. Like Norse, fellow New Yorkers such as Paul Goodman, Michael Harrington, Anatole Broyard, and John Clellon Holmes shared his discontent. Each thought that writers and intellectuals could effectively critique society, and they gathered at the San Remo and the White Horse to hash out their ideas.[40]

Heterosexual writers like Mailer, Broyard, and Holmes, who stylistically tended toward the center of the dissident spectrum, had served in the military during the Second World War. (Harrington, younger than the others, volunteered for the Army Medical Reserve during the Korean conflict, as a compromise between his pacifist convictions and his family's patriotic pressure.) The journalist and critic Broyard, and the Beat novelist Holmes, both noted the social dislocation of wartime chaos. Each described the "nighttime wilderness of a nation at war," populated by "young people torn up at the roots . . . who searched in bars and movie balconies and deadend streets for home and love, and, failing to find them, forgot." Broyard recalled that the war "had broken the rhythm of American life, and when we tried to pick it up again, we couldn't find it," as if "a great bomb, an explosion of consciousness, had gone off . . . shattering everything." As the forlorn walked the streets of the Village and filled the bars, it was "loneliness that made it seem such a lively place." In response, writers looked to literature to tie up the loose ends of disjunction and desire. "If it hadn't been for books, we'd have been completely at the mercy of sex," Broyard recalled. "Books enabled us to see ourselves as characters—yes we were characters!—and this gave us a bit of control."[41]

This performativity should not be dismissed as vacuous. As Harrington later insisted, the San Remo and White Horse patrons "postured about the first-rate, about Proust and Joyce and Kafka, the later Beethoven quartets and Balanchine choreography, Marx and Lenin," suggesting that "our phoniness had high standards." Moreover, he saw the emergence of San Remo types like himself and Ginsberg as a more adventurous extension of Village bohemia in the 1930s, when it was populated by intellectuals such as Irving Howe and Dwight Macdonald. This, Harrington argued, culminated in their own effective literary works, since "the proof is in the production."[42]

The more bombastic stylists—such as Kerouac, Norse, Goodman, Ginsberg, and Burroughs, whose eccentricity or homosexuality made the military an ill fit, and who therefore worked in the merchant marine or sat out the war among anarcho-pacifists—were mainly attracted to the nonconformity of Village bars.[43] With more experimental (and experiential) approaches than the observational ones of Holmes and Broyard, their accounts were peppered with mentions of "visions" and "madness," of beauty, the "fidelity of memory," and "unashamed desire." Kerouac, for instance, in an August 1945 letter to Ginsberg describing a night out in Times Square after Japan surrendered, focused mostly on the ensuing drinking and charming madness, but also on his inability to pick up women, since it was a night for servicemen. Kerouac ended the evening by sleeping with a friend's wife as her husband lay passed out beside them. Burroughs, Ginsberg, and Goodman, meanwhile, found places to explore their homosexuality in literary sites like the San Remo (despite the homophobia of its owner) and other bars that locals recognized as gay.[44]

In a Freudian world, talk was as important to sex as sex was to experience, all of which was fundamental to intellectuals' nocturnal explorations of identity and group dynamics. As an academic already in his thirties, Paul Goodman's approach was sometimes clinical, applying his theories of Gestalt psychology during discussions at the San Remo with participants such as Judith Malina, founder of the influential and avant-garde Living Theatre. She, in turn, soon developed the inner strength to reject aspects of Goodman's therapy, which she found misogynistic.[45] Parisian émigré Anaïs Nin, who had become a legendary symbol of Greenwich Village's sexual liberation during the 1940s, claimed the White Horse as her favorite café in the early 1950s. Embracing it as truly Irish, replete with "old-fashioned mirrors . . . and dark wood panels, mugs of dark beer and a mixture of artists and the underworld of the docks," Nin found its working-class roots still intact:

> A workman in workmen's clothes with a giant poodle, who looked sad and innocent watching his master drinking. Artists in house painters' uniforms. Beards, mustaches, corduroy trousers, soldiers, Negro jazz players, a Chinese girl out of a Chinese print. And the rapid machine-gun talk. Directness like a thousand arrows and utter freedom. We can say anything. There are no pauses, no examination of what we are going to say, and no effort of sequence. It is elating and invigorating. Euphoria comes from the freedom of improvisation and the fact that we never judge each other. We have set no moral, social, or realistic limits. All we ask is the electric charge of vital life dynamics, and the next day, as after listening to jazz, no hangover, no backtracking, no censorship, no malaise.

Much like her contemporaries Henry Miller and Kenneth Rexroth, Nin found liberation and authenticity in this exoticized mix of transnationalism, jazz, and unfettered talk, making her another bridge between the bohemias of the 1930s and the 1950s.[46]

Similarly, feminist Simone de Beauvoir, whose existentialist discussions with Jean-Paul Sartre at the Café de Flore in Paris symbolized the very height of European sophistication for American bohemians, frequented New York's nightspots as a way to experience the postwar United States. Chronicling her 1947 visit in *America Day by Day*, de Beauvoir used bars as a doorway into a foreign culture: "I don't like the taste of whiskey. . . . Yet until three o'clock in the morning, I drink scotch docilely because scotch is one of the keys to America." She found hotel bars too genteel, like "tearooms for old ladies," and she noted disappointingly that "it's not customary here to do work where people drink." Her visit offered self-reflection and an opportunity to view the city's glittery promise with a newfound identity as a European—a word "I never use in France." Yet de Beauvoir suggested that New York did not support bohemianism, since "there are no cafés or salons where intellectuals meet; everyone leads separate lives." She saw attempts to recreate Parisian styles as inadequate: "I go down to Greenwich Village with my friends. Near Washington Square they show me a charming café, the Jumble Shop, which looks almost European with its red tiled floor and its quiet little tables arrayed along the walls. You can eat and drink there all night. . . . During years of exile, French writers and painters tried to resuscitate Les Deux Magots and Le Café de Flore here, but they failed; their get-togethers were always too contrived. For one reason or another, New York doesn't have the right atmosphere for café life." Yet it was also in the city's bars that de Beauvoir found "places [that] are open to the world," where patrons "are living out the real moments of their lives."[47]

European sensibilities like Nin's and de Beauvoir's provided both inspiration and psychological resources for the burgeoning feminism of American bohemians, serving as a public presence in the company of other rebellious women and offering new horizons of experience. Judith Malina, for example, was a regular at the San Remo and the White Horse throughout the early 1950s. She found the San Remo to be like a Paris café, where she talked about anarchism with sophisticated patrons and explored the "possibilities radiating from the present." In a different vein, Alice Denham painstakingly carved out a career writing and modeling, which allowed her to resist family pressure to marry and forgo her work. The "desirably seedy" San Remo, "with a plateglass view of its own hip corner," was Denham's first destination in New York City when she left home in 1951 to "seek my intellectual freedom."[48] For these pioneering women, Village bars were pathways to independence, key points in the mental geography of personal liberation.

The Beats, still in their teens and twenties, sought personal and artistic transcendence through a tapestry of lascivious and loquacious encounters, mixing intoxication with similar invocations of de Beauvoir's native milieu. Ginsberg wrestled with the feeling of an intellectual divide between himself and a lover he met at the San

Remo, yet he also wanted to recapture "the feeling of pure wonder and joy" of their meeting. Amid subterranean explorations in Bowery bars, he found "likker kicks similar to marijuana—same corridors; same drive to metaphysics and concretion." Kerouac opined that drinking Pernod in a "Parisian" bar in the Village allowed him to see people through new eyes and in a new light, like "that Cezanne light of the day" or "the light of Lucien's intelligence." Bar talk offered the chance to probe the "possibilities of each other." If a bar marked the start of Kerouac's evening in a search for female companionship, failure to find "love" meant a late-night return with male cohorts, where bar talk just might lead to "perfection of understanding."[49]

The Beats' adventurism amounted to a naively optimistic, if sincere, search for a single source of both happiness and creativity. Yet Kerouac's admonition to live more and write more, and his mantra that life's joy lay in "good food, and drinks, and many women all around, the interplay of the sexes, and much happy meaningless talk" fit snugly alongside Goodman's anarchist psychological theories, as well as the hypermasculine antics at the Cedar Tavern, which frequently involved fistfights between Pollock and other abstract expressionists. Each found representational language inadequate and emphasized what they referred to as "action" as a healthy antidote to the neuroses of modern life and the atomic age. Each also found liberation, in Goodman's words, in "concentrated sensation and in the playful manipulation of the material medium."[50]

While the teetotaling Goodman most often psychoanalyzed patients in the privacy of their apartments, his frequent presence at the San Remo also suggests his recognition that drinking lifted inhibitions in both word and deed—a common notion among the Beats and the abstract expressionists. Alcohol and drugs played a role in Villagers' attempts to live life as art, a kind of creative self-destruction. For instance, within the painters' concept of drinking as prowess—a test of masculinity that was often accompanied by (sometimes playful) violence—"booze was the talisman," Elaine de Kooning noted. The Beats simply factored language into this art-as-life equation, echoing Goodman's admonition that making common speech poetic was one solution to social problems stemming from the false stimulation of the mass media.[51] True enough, the Beats' outrageous alcohol- and drug-fueled behavior—their "quest for the unusual, the 'real,' the crazy"—smacks dangerously of automedicated self-psychoanalysis. But the postwar generation that Holmes decried as "everywhere wild, everywhere lost, everywhere loveless, faithless, homeless," was also conscious of bar talk as a path to social criticism. "Booze was a social thing," recalled one Villager. "The bar scene wasn't just to get drunk. It was like the public square in a town or a sidewalk café in Paris—comradely meeting and talking."[52]

This point was colorfully illustrated in Ginsberg's aborted novel, which portrayed his bohemian clique along the lines of Holmes's *Go*. In a letter to his father in 1948, Ginsberg described his intent to write a "naturalistic-symbolistic" account of a whole community in its own terms, in which the characters and literary devices acted as symbols of society. The novel's climax, set in the fictitious "Rational Café," personi-

The White Horse Tavern, inside (*top*) and outside (*bottom*). Photographs by the author

fied the kind of social disease that resulted in Nazism by contrasting the actions of
the avowedly decadent poet Arthur Rimbaud with the social sadism imposed by the
"'normalcy' of the café patrons—sailors, farmers, wives, bourgeois businessmen." It
is clear that this was a microcosm of the postwar West End, San Remo, Cedar, and
White Horse scene, replete with eccentricity, "crucial [i.e., obscene] language," and

iconoclasm, in opposition to the sexual repression and "emotional imbalance" of America's bourgeois intellectual attitude.[53] Ginsberg's "Rational Café" was a spatial representation of the Greenwich Village ethos, the mental geography of social liberation, and a dialogue between modernity—with its rationality, militarism, and bureaucratic economy—and the primal human desire for free expression, sexuality, and unfettered liberty. Or, as another bohemian regular at the White Horse put it simply, there was "drinking in the front room if you wanted to get laid, drinking in the back room if you wanted to talk politics."[54]

Poetics and Politics

In 1950, Kerouac sent Ginsberg a clipping of an article by syndicated columnist Westbrook Pegler. Pegler suggested, in no uncertain terms, that Mark Van Doren, Columbia University's respected literature professor, was a communist dupe. The clipping, along with Kerouac's tongue-in-cheek note saying he wished he could get such widespread publicity so that he could "sell my books and get married and be happy in Havana," speaks volumes about the ambivalence of Cold War culture. Pegler's column was unabashed red-baiting, attacking Van Doren for nothing more than having joined the Society for the Prevention of World War III, which opposed the anti-Soviet strategy of German rearmament. While Van Doren's position at Columbia was secure, the Red Scare forced thousands of less renowned professors, school teachers, and government workers from their jobs for far less cause.[55] Even Kerouac's flippancy betrays a hint of concern for his and Ginsberg's former mentor—otherwise why send the clipping at all? Yet Kerouac's dispassion was also symptomatic of a postwar generation who rejected both the USSR's collectivism and the USA's conservative repression. *On the Road* later made Kerouac the very symbol of American rebellion that claimed unconventional individualism as its only ideal.

The Rebel Café continued to nurture leftism, although not in the same institutional form as the 1930s. Conservative congressmen had begun to shut down the WPA in 1939, but HUAC, along with J. Edgar Hoover's FBI, really went into high gear with the start of Cold War tensions in 1946. By the time Joseph McCarthy gained notoriety in 1950, prosecutions of Communist Party members under the Smith Act and purges of CP loyalists from unions, civil rights groups, and liberal organizations had already decimated left-wing institutions.[56] The Rebel Café harbored a compact but committed core of the anti-Stalinist Left. Identifying themselves variously as Trotskyists, anarchists, and Libertarians, their ideas withstood the Cold War winter and, through a process of cultural evolution, eventually branched out and bloomed into significant social movements.

Anarchist-libertarian networks formed a motley composite of social relations, little magazines, and loose political affiliations that organically overlapped with artistic bohemian communities. Although Rebel Café nightspots did not make up the bulk of this leftist fabric, they did serve as patches that covered the institutional holes torn by McCarthyism and the nation's rightward turn. By the official end of the WPA in

1943, cultural left-wingers could no longer rely on its formal channels and federally funded offices for social connections. Instead, they began to fill this vacuum by using informal institutions such as the Black Cat, the Iron Pot, Vesuvio, the San Remo, the Cedar, and the White Horse as nodes in their social networks.[57] Moreover, World War II had further disrupted these connections, as pacifists like Kenneth Rexroth and Frank Triest worked stateside and were imprisoned as conscientious objectors, or, like Paul Goodman, simply laid low. The Allied victory offered them a chance to reorganize, as well as to refine their ideas.[58] They formed new Libertarian groups in both San Francisco and New York that proffered an intellectual alternative to the Manichean militarism of the United States and the USSR, confounding the Cold War logic of conservatives and Communists alike.

Anarchist-libertarians had never fit easily within the American Communist Party. Their antistatism made them frequent targets of purges that sought to maintain a pro-Soviet party line. New York City Libertarians, such as Paul Goodman and the radical poet Jackson Mac Low, never relied on the party's facilities for meetings, and instead were comfortable with small gatherings in private apartments or Village nightspots. San Francisco, farther from Gotham's CP center, offered opportunities for public meetings in the Longshoreman's Hall and the Workman's Circle meeting room, where Rexroth's Libertarian Circle gathered between 1946 and 1949. This difference may have led Rexroth, always defensive about San Francisco's junior position in the Left's hierarchy, to refer disparagingly to the "American Stalinoid of the Cafe Society Downtown Set" and the "wishful grand strategies of the habitués of New York coffee shops."[59] But even his Libertarian Circle came to an end after infiltrations and disruptions by both the FBI and the CP, leading him to host more of the circle's artistic gatherings in his home and at the Black Cat by 1950.[60] In any case, small, less formal meetings suited anarchism's antibureaucratic ideology. During the early years of the Cold War, East Coast and West Coast anarchist-libertarian circles became more intertwined, both through the exchange of ideas in print and the movement of individuals within a developing bicoastal oppositional community.

The conversations that took place among dissidents in Village and North Beach nightspots can never be fully recovered, but a semblance can be reconstructed in bits and pieces from their personal journals and correspondence, which reflected, at least somewhat, the content of their café chats. For instance, during their visits to San Francisco, Rexroth shared thoughts with Paul Goodman or his old Chicago friend Lawrence Lipton about topics such as pacifism, the intricacies of Marxism, alienation, ethnic identity, jazz and folk music, HUAC hearings ("that American version of Kafka's *TRIAL*"), the relationship between culture and psychology, Dadaism, social planning, marriage, and sexuality—which were also fodder for Goodman's conversations with Jackson Mac Low and other New York anarchists.[61] Meanwhile, bohemian poets like Allen Ginsberg, Robert Duncan, and Tram Combs conversed with anarchists such as Knute Stiles about religion, poetry, and participatory democracy ("the feeling that true country is the promise within the tyranny of the 'nation'").

They mulled over industrial capitalism, existentialism (the typical New Yorker feels "he really shouldn't be an existentialist but then 'it is important'"), and the ties between bohemianism, surrealism, and the Left. They also discussed community, racial equality, and gay culture (John Gielgud's "campy" 1944 production of *Love for Love*, a revival of William Congreve's Restoration comedy, was rivaled only by the drag queens at Finocchio's nightclub). "If I sound a little bitter," wrote Stiles to Combs in 1952, after detailing the horrors a friend had relayed from the Korean War, "put it down to the fact that I always feel a little bitter and revolutionary when I'm broke— besides it's appropriate to feel a little bitter on May Day when one realizes that one is almost alone in one's revolt against the square world which is more clearly dedicated to permanent war each day."[62]

Stiles and Duncan also reported clashes during private family functions that demonstrated their distance from the postwar mainstream. Stiles described a visit by his brother, who was shocked by his North Beach bohemian life. His brother's navy buddy threw a cocktail party that Stiles attended. "I was astonished: such respectable, bourgeois philistines I have never met," Stiles quipped of the veteran and his friends. "He stood on a chair to demonstrate its strength, he talked about chairs, tables, the war, commodes, the war, chairs and tables, the Episcopalian church, the navy, the war, the navy, chairs and tables . . . and wanted to know, did I do portraits and altar pictures? I made it quite clear that I was a pacifist, an anarchist, an atheist, and an abstractionist; I too stood on the chair just to make sure that it was really sturdy; it cracked." Besides betraying Stiles's own inverted elitism concerning middle-class values, this scene sits squarely beside Duncan's description of a dinner with a friend and her racist father, who aroused his ire by continually referring to "niggers" and left them feeling "as if we had been trampled for two weeks by some gross monster created by the bourgeoisie's Frankenstein."[63]

While Duncan's primary vocation as a poet has left him largely ignored by historians, he was nonetheless a gifted social critic and an influential figure, both within North Beach's bohemian community, as a mentor to young intellectuals, and nationally, as an early gay rights activist. His groundbreaking 1944 essay in Dwight Macdonald's *Politics* magazine, "The Homosexual in Society," was a demand for gay liberation that neatly encompassed the Rebel Café's most egalitarian ideals. In anarchist terms, Duncan wrote that a just society required "devotion to human freedom, toward the liberation of human love, human conflicts, human aspirations." He continued:

> To do this one must disown *all* the special groups (nations, churches, sexes, races) that would claim allegiance. . . . It must always be remembered that one's own honesty, one's battle against the inhumanity of his own group (be it against patriotism, against bigotry, against—in this special case—the homosexual cult) is a battle that cannot be won in its immediate scene. The forces of inhumanity are overwhelming, but only one's continued opposition can make any other order possi-

ble, will give an added strength for all those who desire freedom and equality to break at last those fetters that seem now so unbreakable.

As he wrote more succinctly to Rexroth in 1946, "We will find our strength more and more, our intellectual strength, our erotic strength, our creative strength in the flesh, in the actual." He concluded, "Only the individual can experience or express fraternity of freedom or justice."[64]

This eloquence and fortitude brought Rexroth past his own admitted homophobia, declaring his admiration for Duncan, who had "lived thru, past & beyond Jewish Xian [Christian] queer guilt."[65] Such statements show a path less taken in the gay rights movement: not a call for identity politics, but instead the absorption of sexuality into a larger liberatory program. Both men's views suggested that if a moral code demands equal respect for oneself and for others as individuals—including the acknowledgement that such empathy means working for the collective good—then one's sexuality cannot, by definition, be a source of guilt. Rather the reverse: such guilt can only undermine individual and collective dignity.

Ideas about how to achieve these goals differed wildly within the bohemian underground. Some, like Rexroth and Lipton, continued their opposition to bourgeois life as part of the class struggle, emphasizing organization and cultural movements. The Beats were a more ambivalent reflection of this, as Ginsberg carried forward an alternative form of organizing through his personal correspondence and social networks, which demonstrated his grounding in Marxism, despite Kerouac's overt rejection of formal politics (and eventually even the notion of the Beat generation itself).[66] The common thread through both camps was a rejection of statism and the espousal of individual liberty, as well as notions of an authentic self, which applied to both queer and bohemian identities and stood in tension with leftist collectivism.

On a practical and personal level, bars offered opportunities for homosexual encounters. This was particularly important for the bisexual Goodman, who (in a reversal of the 1950s cliché) protected the privacy of his traditional family life while publicly embracing a gay identity. In 1953, Goodman fictionalized the San Remo in a short story that showed "how a scene really is," capturing a snapshot of the Village's radical literary circle, with its mix of intellectual competition, ambivalent valorization of the working class, and transgressive sexuality.[67] His characters hop from booths to tables, arguing about psychoanalysis and poetic affect, while also eyeing an attractive pair of sailors at the bar. The sailors, in uniforms "cut for public love," symbolized the inherent conflict between community and individual desire at the heart of Goodman's libertarian dialectic. Although the San Remo crowd "thinned out to its mean size and it was my community," the tension between sex and love, between a hotel room at "magical two o'clock" and home with "my bed and wife," made fulfillment of the communal ideal impossible. Yet for Goodman, it was the promise of *communitas* that underlay the potential political function of the bar scene:

to talk, to strive for connection, to recognize that community is not a static entity, but a process continually reformed by interaction.[68]

Ginsberg, conversely, still struggled with making his homosexuality public, but already he was inching toward the open revelations that would make his 6 Gallery reading of "Howl" a landmark in gay liberation. Despite concerns about his "preoccupation with queerness, dope, vice & bop, apocalypse of Subterraneans, dispersal of attention to practical affairs," Ginsberg, in his journal, reveals how each new encounter in a Village bar steeled him against the fear of "being discovered on the block as a queer."[69] This kind of atomic-age identity had developed partly through a process of *self-reflection*—sometimes metaphorically, through social mirroring, but also literally, in Village bars. Here Ginsberg met older gay poets, such as W. H. Auden (fictionalized in Goodman's San Remo story), who soothed his concerns with stories of their own experiences. One night, Ginsberg might gleefully converse with a group of Village lesbians, with an especially vocal woman pronouncing that hypocritically uptight academics were "Freudian on campus and freaks in bed." On another night, he could reflect that "I don't like my own looks in the bar mirror—my image of floating city slicker, disillusioned, somewhat of an empty heel or a middle-class intellectual con artist . . . as I once saw myself through [psychotherapist] Dr. Cott's eyes."[70]

The penultimate scene of John Clellon Holmes's *Go*, in which his bohemian crew mourns the accidental death of one of its own by going on a bacchanalian spree through the bars of the Village and the New Jersey riverfront, similarly ends with an image in the men's room mirror. As Holmes's alter-ego protagonist flees his friends' drunken antics, which for him have become a scene out of Dante's *Inferno*, he catches "a dark glimpse of himself in the shattered mirror over the sink: a drawn haunted face." Always more pessimistic about the promise of bohemian rebellion than his fellow Beats, Holmes continues: "The fumes of chlorine, urine and vomit rise from the slippery floor. . . . Defaced telephone numbers, obscene drawings, and humorless epigrams were scrawled on [the wall] with that desperate and precise crudity of which men are capable only in the privacy of a latrine . . . blunt confessions of longing, words as would be written on the walls of hell." Holmes's protagonist, not daring to look at himself again, bolted from the bar, heading toward the lights of New York City. The novel concludes by asking, "Where is our home?"[71] For Holmes, the bohemian bar scene represented the dystopian mirror image of Goodman's *communitas*. Yet both expressed a yearning to belong amid the foreboding senses of dislocation and disillusionment that characterized the late 1940s.

As World War II's promise of lasting peace gave way to the Cold War's darkening of world events, the nightclub underground balanced ominous visions with an embrace of the carnivalesque, as a method of empowerment and cohesion. Invoking the medieval and Rabelaisian ritualistic social reversals of charivari, bohemians claimed a liberation from social norms through outrageous behavior. By 1948, Kerouac declared that his letters had become apocalyptic, "full of 'frightening' and inescapable predictions, scatologically smeared with an evil leer sometimes." Commentators proclaimed that Dylan Thomas's visits to Third Avenue bars, "loud with Rabelaisian reminiscence" and "pubroom ribaldries," matched the Cedar's carnival atmosphere of macho performativity.[72] This outrageousness played a part in sparking a national sociocultural change as underground sites and their antics gained visibility. In 1949, Jackson Mac Low, in his journal, recorded an exchange that highlighted the tensions around radical authenticity in sites that also required considerations of commerce: "Had an arg[ument] w[ith] 'Jackson,' bartender at the Remo who wanted me to be in some shots *Life* was taking of the Remo—for picturesqueness. I refused & he became angry. Besides not wanting my picture taken, I felt it inappropriate that I should be in a Remo picture, being so seldom there. Besides I'd rather not be so strongly associated w[ith] the Remo in that *Life* magazine way!" Indeed, Mac Low's concerns seem justified by *Life*'s demeaning description of the San Remo's corner, at the junction of Bleecker and MacDougal Streets, as "a center of infamy"—a phrase that implied both gay and interracial encounters.[73]

Since the days of Rodolphe Salis's Chat Noir, bohemia's nonconformity always existed symbiotically with commerce. Kerouac bewailed such associations in the 1940s, suggesting that Village scenesters were too self-conscious, "like a professional group, almost. The way they foregather at bars and try to achieve some sort of vague synthesis between respectability and illicitness."[74] Meanwhile, the Minetta Tavern hired a down-on-his-luck poet, Joe Gould, to sit at a window table and scribble in his notebooks, in order to advertise its bohemian atmosphere—as likewise happened with North Beach poet Hube the Cube at Vesuvio in the 1950s.[75] Wider exposure was also part of the uneven process of making gay and bohemian life visible, and thus something that could be claimed publicly, as well as advertising potentially liberating sites for hopefuls in the hinterlands, more of whom flocked to Village nightspots every year.[76]

These issues also underlay changes in North Beach in the early postwar years, as proletarian struggles gave way to personal politics. During World War II, Black Cat owner Charlie Haberkern, weary of running a bustling (and controversial) business and perhaps in bad health, sold the café to his accountant, Sol Stoumen.[77] Meanwhile, Rexroth's pacifism, Libertarian Circle organizing, and his readings tour in Europe had kept him out of the late 1940s North Beach café scene. Following his divorce in 1950, he returned to the Black Cat as a way of reconnecting with this local bohemia and found that under Stoumen's stewardship, the café had also become "a hangout for militant homosexuals."[78] This characterization actually proved to be more prescient than Rexroth could have known. In 1949, police raids against gays in the Black Cat led Stoumen to challenge California state law, resulting in a state supreme court decision in 1951 that banned arrests of homosexuals for simply gathering in public.

While historian Nan Alamilla Boyd has documented that case as an early salvo in the gay liberation movement, it was also intertwined with bohemia's more general opposition to Cold War social norms. The homosexual prosecutions were just the most recent in a series of police raids dating back to World War II, *before* the café became a primarily gay venue. As late as 1949, Stoumen continued to insist that the café was one of the few remaining colorful bohemian sites in the city. Stoumen himself was straight, with social ties to the Black Cat that went back to the 1930s.[79] The Black Cat maintained a reputation as both a bohemian *and* a gay hangout until at least the mid-1950s. Following a second attempt by local and state authorities to close the café in 1956, Stoumen explicitly tied his defense of gay rights to bohemianism. "My patrons are merely members of the bohemian intelligentsia who gather at the Black Cat to discuss art and semantics," he asserted during a court hearing. Bohemianism was "a way of life, a way of thinking. It has no reference whatsoever to moral or immoral conduct." Calling the prosecutions a "witch hunt," he insisted that his patrons' sexual activities were "none of my business." Stoumen's chief ally throughout his legal battles was prominent local attorney Morris Lowenthal—a civil rights advocate and opponent of the University of California's loyalty oath requirement— and it seems certain that while *Stoumen v. Reilly* was an important milestone in the gay liberation struggle, it cannot be divorced from the café's bohemian and leftist history.[80]

Bicoastal Bohemia and Cold War Community

The Black Cat's postwar clientele did include a younger generation of gay bohemians, such as Knute Stiles, but it also consisted of hipsters and radical poets who began crisscrossing the country in search of both kicks and community as San Francisco's and New York City's bohemias overlapped. While Kerouac's *On the Road* would not be published until 1957, it was between 1947 and 1949 that he made the legendary cross-country trips with Neal Cassady on which the novel was based. This overall journey, Holmes wrote in *Go*, was a quest for the real, an antidote to what the Beats saw as the emptiness of bourgeois existence.

Bars were often the doorways to such experiences as Kerouac motored from one end of the continent to the other. In response to Holmes's report that Kerouac had hit the road and "searches out the good bar (or Life) in Denver," in 1949 Ginsberg wrote, "Life as Jack (and other writers) says is basically irrational because we live in a world of thoughts, and . . . the difference between absolute thought and absolute feeling is something that can only be known, by experience."[81] A central moment in *On the Road* is an argument between Kerouac's alter ego, Sal Paradise, and Old Bull Lee (William Burroughs) over the continued existence of the ideal bar in America. Responding to Paradise's desire for a night out in nearby New Orleans, Lee responds: "It's a very dull town. It's against the law to go to the colored section. The bars are insufferably dreary." Furthermore, as Lee cantankerously (and nostalgically) insists:

> An ideal bar is something that's gone beyond our ken. In nineteen ten a bar was a
> place where men went to meet during or after work, and all there was was a long

counter, brass rails, spittoons, player piano for music, a few mirrors, and barrels of whisky at ten cents a shot together with barrels of beer at five cents a mug. Now all you get is chromium, drunken women, fags, hostile bartenders, anxious owners who hover around the door, worried about their leather seats and the law; just a lot of screaming at the wrong time and deadly silence when a stranger walks in.[82]

Hidden within this declaration's masculinist assumptions and homophobic language (which always sat conspicuously next to Burroughs's real-life homosexuality) were Kerouac's own idealistic notions of the American bar: a site of authentic community, uncorrupted by considerations of commerce, free from policing by a powerful state, welcoming to any intrepid stranger ready to embrace its rough-hewn and nonalienated way of living. Old Bull Lee was half right—such an ideal not only was impossible in 1949, but it also had never been fully realized—yet this did little to temper Kerouac's quasi-utopian longing.

Kerouac was not alone. Other bicoastal seekers during this period included New Yorkers such as Gerd Stern, who began his connections with bicoastal bohemia through the San Remo and the Black Cat; bohemians Bill and Betty Keck, who left San Francisco for Ginsberg's San Remo circle (and subsequently offered him his first peyote trip); and Philip Lamantia, who returned to San Francisco in 1946, after working with Gotham's surrealist émigrés. As a budding fifteen-year-old poet, Lamantia had contacted the surrealist André Breton in 1943 and, after garnering some quick advice from Rexroth, departed for New York to work as an assistant editor for the journal *View*. Interactions with European refugees such as Breton had a pronounced influence on Lamantia's art and politics, as did American left-wing activists like Dorothy Day, with the Catholic Workers. Lamantia also noted that the formal artistic and literary world was intertwined with jazz nightlife, as his New York sojourn was defined by "weekly gallery openings, jazz on Fifty-Second Street, endless parties, and almost daily invitations to lunch and dinner."[83]

A falling out with *View*'s editor soon led Lamantia back to the West Coast. He rejoined a scene that Rexroth now called the San Francisco Renaissance, but which was rapidly becoming a bicoastal underground. "There were parallels to what was going on in New York at the same time," Lamantia recalled. "Here [in San Francisco] it was after-hours jazz in the Fillmore district and rhythm-and-blues at the Little Harlem off Folsom and Third Streets, both scenes celebrated by Kerouac in *On the Road*. Those of us, like Gerd Stern [he was "Jack Steen" in *The Subterraneans*], who knew Birdland and Fifty-Second Street in New York and Jackson's Nook here, were living these connections."[84] Robert Duncan's move to San Francisco to join the Rexroth orbit, along with Jack Spicer, completed the core of poetic radicalism that defined North Beach in the early 1950s as both a gay and a bohemian haven.

This period also marked the arrival of another Jewish anarchist poet who, like Ginsberg, had studied under Mark Van Doren at Columbia University, Lawrence Ferling, who adopted a nom de plume (or *nom de guerre*) appropriate for the city's

Latin Quarter: Lawrence Ferlinghetti. Introduced to the bohemian scene at the Black Cat, Ferlinghetti met left-wing activist Peter Martin, who had begun publishing a magazine called *City Lights*. "I discovered North Beach around this time, about 1952," he recalled. "The Black Cat was the first place I ever went to and then the Iron Pot. I met Pete Martin around then." The two partnered up, but the magazine failed to support itself, so in 1953 Ferlinghetti opened a bookstore across the alley from Vesuvio. City Lights Books became an anchor in the bicoastal bohemia, serving as an "unintentional non-profit" that only gradually made money from publishing after the success of Ginsberg's *Howl, and Other Poems* in 1956.[85]

City Lights was simply one of the many independent publishers that appeared in the postwar period, several of which had symbiotic relationships with local night-spots, either financially, socially, or creatively. City Lights' bookstore business fed off of Vesuvio (and vice versa), while the Village's 8th St. Books and Barney Rosset's Grove Press drew both their artistic content and their staffs from patrons of the San Remo and the Cedar Tavern. Less successful, yet still highly influential, was *Neurotica* magazine, published by Jay Landesman, a St. Louis nightclub owner (and hometown comrade of Michael Harrington). Although *Neurotica* folded in 1951, after only three years, it gave some of the first national exposure to budding poets, writers, and intellectuals like Allen Ginsberg, John Clellon Holmes, Anatole Broyard, Judith Malina, and Marshall McLuhan.[86] These bohemian publications were complemented in the political sphere by left-leaning publications such as the *Partisan Review*; the anarchist little magazines *Why?* and the *Catholic Worker* in New York, and *Circle* in San Francisco; and, perhaps most importantly, *Liberation*. The latter's editor, Bayard Rustin, used it as an institutional foundation to help organize the 1963 March on Washington, but he also maintained ties with radical and gay liberation writers like Jackson Mac Low, Tram Combs, and James Baldwin in the late 1950s. These outlets, along with James Laughlin's New Directions Publishing, gave a voice to the postwar demimonde, drawing directly from the unconventional rebellion of North Beach and Greenwich Village literary bars.[87]

Their publishers also reveal the limitations of Rebel Café liberation during this period. Whether in the pages of *Neurotica* or *Politics*, few voices of women or African Americans were heard. Women certainly maintained a forceful presence in the anarchist world—Marie Rexroth's organizing, for instance, practically held the Libertarian Circle together during Kenneth's travels in the 1940s, and Harrington's introduction to antipoverty campaigns was through Dorothy Day's Catholic Workers, where he joined forces with several women activists.[88] But women rarely claimed positions as spokespeople. Rather, they remained largely in supportive, even domestic roles, ignored by publishers. As Elizabeth Pollett, spouse of *Partisan Review*'s Delmore Schwartz and a successful author in her own right, later stated in an interview: "I didn't have much sense of a career. What I wanted to do was write, which was an essential part of my being. Delmore handed my novel to James Laughlin at New Directions with no name on it. Laughlin liked it a lot. If my name had been on it, maybe he wouldn't have liked it so much."[89] Pollett's experience was distinctly echoed in the art fraud case of Margaret and Walter Keane (dramatized in the 2014 film *Big Eyes*), which began when Walter claimed Margaret's paintings as his own when they were on display in a North Beach nightclub. In both instances, Pollett's and Keane's identities as working artists came in conflict with their gender status, a friction that would come to the fore in the women's movement of the 1960s.

While left-wing bohemians had begun the tentative work of overcoming racism (including their own) long before, the color line remained largely unbroken by the early 1950s. James Baldwin was the first of the postwar generation of black writers to follow the trails blazed by Langston Hughes, Ralph Ellison, and Richard Wright. His San Remo experiences encapsulated the place of black writers in the postwar literary underground. Baldwin left Harlem for the Village in 1943, hoping its gay scene would offer the sexual freedom denied him uptown. But his skin color made him the target of local Italians, who, "egged on by the cops, thought it was great fun to bounce tables and chairs off my head." In an oft-repeated tragedy of the American melting pot, these ethnic Villagers, defensive of their white status that was only one generation removed from the stigma of immigration, saw the presence of blacks as a threat. This included Joe Santini, the owner of the San Remo, who refused to serve the struggling young writer.

Baldwin, however, soon made friends with an Italian living in the Village, whose threats of retaliation apparently stopped the beatings. Moreover, by 1945, Baldwin was being courted by Harper Publishing's president, Frank S. MacGregor, who took him to the San Remo for dinner at Baldwin's request. "We entered, and they seated us and we were served," Baldwin recalled. "The San Remo thus began to attract a varied clientele, indeed—so much so that Allen Ginsberg and company arrived there the year I left New York for Paris [in 1948]." Soon, Santini was actually *defending* the young writer against a racist crowd of tourists who were offended by the bar's interracial patronage. For Baldwin, the San Remo became a public declaration of his acceptance into the republic of letters: "Once I was in the San Remo, for example, I was *in*, and anybody who messed with me was *out*—that was all there was to it. . . . And no one seemed to remember a time when I had not been there."[90] Baldwin's Village experiences powerfully informed his work, including the novel *Go Tell It on the Mountain* (1953), the essays in *Notes of a Native Son* (1955), and, particularly, *Another Country*, which he published amid his vocal civil rights activism in 1962.

Baldwin's examinations of the social fiction of race and the human distance it creates evocatively reveal that, even among dissident intellectuals, the drive for experience and sexuality often carried hints of exoticism. Anatole Broyard, who passed as white throughout his time in New York (from the 1940s through the 1960s), recounted a story that spotlighted the contradictory layers of radical intellectualism, exoticism, and masculine authenticity that suffused postwar bohemia. As a young writer, Broyard was pleased to find himself in a booth at the San Remo, talking with Delmore Schwartz, Clement Greenberg, and Dwight Macdonald about primitivism in works by Picasso and Hemingway. But as the author of a recent *Partisan Review* article, titled "Portrait of the Hipster," Broyard "didn't want to be typecast as an aficionado of the primitive." Even as he sought to avoid exoticization, however, he used the eroticized thrillage found in nonwhite nightclubs as a pathway to establish and explore his bohemian intellectualism:

> Like many other New York writers and intellectuals of his generation, Delmore . . . still thought of ordinary people as the proletariat, or the masses.
>
> I wanted to be an intellectual, too, to see life from a great height, yet I didn't want to give up my sense of connection, my intimacy with things. . . . I talked about Spanish Harlem . . . that I'd seen a man killed [in a dance hall there] . . . so we jumped into a taxi and went straight up Fifth Avenue. . . .
>
> I offered to find partners for our group. Delmore, who never hesitated to play the crazy, impulsive poet, had a blank look on his face. Clem was sliding his eyes around—not like an art critic, but a tourist. Only Dwight, who was a permanent revolutionary, wanted to dance and appeared to be at home. . . . He wasn't standing outside the culture looking in. He was in the thick of it. He felt its rhythm.[91]

Broyard noted the nightclub's radical potential, but he also betrayed many of bohemianism's unconscious assumptions: conflation of "the real" with violence among society's marginalized denizens, male privilege, and faith in the liberatory power of sex.

For those more firmly on the Left, this kind of sociosexual exploration was divorced from political aims, even while recognizing the revolutionary aspects of oppositional culture. James Laughlin, for example, in response to Rexroth's query about his glamorous life in New York's publishing sphere, replied in a manner that suggested the kind of phony revolution in the cocktail set that the genuinely radical Rexroth deplored. "I assume you are joking when you speak of my having a 'hell of a time,'" Laughlin quipped. "I have to spend my evenings dancing in places like El Morroco [*sic*], the Stork Club, Cafe Society. And for what? Because I have a necessity to be in love. Oh hell. Harold, hand me the hatchet, I's'll cut the things off."[92] But eroticism aside, the chief function of nightspots for such cultural figures was to make their rebellion public. For some, this was as ambitious as social revolution: the end of capitalism and the start of a brand of anarchism that was, in the words of Walter Lowenfels, "the world as poem," a society in which "poems will be acted out in the daily living realization of the earth and man's socially productive processes."[93]

While the Rebel Café certainly fell short of this lofty vision of truth and beauty, it did provide sites in which chosen identities and community were formed. Dylan Thomas's performative visits to the San Remo, Vesuvio, and, momentously, the White Horse Tavern were examples of this process. During his stateside visits (between 1950 and 1953), Thomas confirmed his poetic fame by holding court in local pubs, pontificating and punning the crowds into adoration or, when he became too drunk and belligerent, annoyance. This also confirmed the position of those present, bolstering their insider status. It was Thomas's death after a night of drinking at the White Horse that firmly established the tavern as a literary site for regulars, and one of pilgrimage for tourists. Little did it matter that Thomas's drinking binges were largely the product of trying to live up to his own legend, and were limited to his American tours, as well as that the actual cause of his death most likely was a failure to properly treat his diabetes. Thomas's host and biographer, John Brinnin, sold more books by ignoring the fact that Thomas drank only three beers during his final night. Instead, Brinnin repeated the apocryphal tale that the poet quaffed "eighteen straight whiskies," thus cementing the White Horse's part, and his own, in the Dylan Thomas mythology.[94]

Identification as a San Remo type—being known at bars such as the White Horse or the Black Cat—was a badge of bohemian literary authenticity that confirmed this inclusion. Conversely, drinking at a Rebel Café bar without gaining some level of public recognition meant risking the label of being a hipster poseur.[95] Yet this sort of subcultural elitism should not be entirely taken as shallow exclusivity. Reputations were made or broken not only on frivolous criteria, such as fashion sense, but also on creative and verbal ability—on wit, eloquence, and wordplay—as the Village and North Beach formed a kind of meritocratic literary community. As more of its members began achieving wider fame in the 1950s, the attraction of the Rebel Café would only increase for new arrivals seeking a place to belong.

The poet and activist Maya Angelou, who started her own career in the nightclubs of North Beach, once said: "The ache for home lives in all of us. The safe place where we can go as we are and not be questioned."[96] While "safety" is certainly a relative term when discussing bohemian nightspots, Rebel Café sites nonetheless offered some shelter from the cold winds of America's social norms. The nocturnal underground's informal institutions aided new social networks. And bar talk paved the way—however unevenly—for sexual experimentation and cultural challenges to American assumptions about race, militarism, domesticity, and homosexuality. The molecular processes of conversation and critique, fundamental to public discourse and increasingly disseminated through print culture, slowly formulated opportunities for further, more visible demands for both individual and collective liberation. As the Cold War deepened, this liberationism became entwined even deeper with the ethos of jazz, making nightclubs such as the Village Vanguard part of the bicoastal bohemia.

bop apocalypse, freedom now!

Jazz, Civil Rights, and the Politics of Cross-Racial Desire

In this country, for a dangerously long time, there have been two levels of experience. One . . . can be summed up in the images of Doris Day and Gary Cooper: two of the most grotesque appeals to innocence the world has ever seen. And the other, subterranean, indispensible, and denied, can be summed up, let us say, in the tone and the face of Ray Charles.
James Baldwin, 1964

We are musical anarchists.
Nick LaRocca, of the Original Dixieland Jass Band, 1957

On February 17, 1951, the *New York Amsterdam News* reported that the glamorous Josephine Baker would begin a short run at the Strand Theatre. The engagement was part of Baker's sensational return to the United States after nearly three decades in France, where she had redefined Parisian cabaret, as well as fought in the Resistance against the Nazis. She planned to follow the Strand booking with a more permanent cabaret gig—but only on her own terms. "At least three night club operators are now dickering for her services," the *Amsterdam News* reported, "but one thing certain she will not accept any night club engagements unless there is no discrimination whatsoever." Baker's civil rights stance was not new. She had previously worked with *Ebony* magazine and the NAACP's Walter White to desegregate audiences during her stint at the Copacabana in Miami Beach. In October 1951, Baker and White spearheaded protests in New York City, this time against the swanky Stork Club's racist policies.[1]

As historian Martha Biondi has shown, the Stork Club protest was a vital symbol of the black freedom struggle early in the Cold War—with typically contradictory results. While the protest sparked widespread publicity and a new state law banning discrimination in public accommodations, Baker's leftist associations put her on the blacklist and hardened the NAACP's resolve to purge communists from its ranks, for fear of a media backlash. The protest, which featured luminaries such as Thurgood Marshall on the picket lines, also successfully undermined the prominence of the Stork Club and its media mouthpiece, Walter Winchell. Yet while this was an important turning point in the integrationist phase of the civil rights movement, Baker's stand had even deeper roots in nightclub culture. Over a year previously, the *New York Amsterdam News* had reported that the city's "café society crowd [is] snubbing Broadway spots that use discriminating tactics in the seating of patrons" and gave a "list of the OK spots" that were exempt from the boycott, including the jazz clubs Bop City and Birdland, as well as Cafe Society, Herbert Jacoby's Le Ruban Bleu, and Max Gordon's Village Vanguard.[2] Baker's high-profile protests were actually part of a longer effort to resist racial discrimination, in which activists used nightclubs to gain public visibility and black patrons displayed their claims to social space, leisure, and affluence.

If black culture in cabarets in the 1920s was almost entirely exoticized entertainment, and Cafe Society's presentation of Billie Holiday and "Strange Fruit" represented cabaret entertainment's shift toward white liberalism, the cabaret in the late 1950s and early 1960s was where African Americans laid full claim to their place in the public sphere—especially given the period's integrationist impulse. This also meant that jazz was absorbed into left-wing bohemian culture, with contradictory, even paradoxical, results. While white bohemians embraced jazz as a hip doorway into primal, authentic expression, its intellectualization made it less accessible to the broader public. Country music, rock & roll, and rhythm & blues (R&B) soon became the music of the masses. Even as proponents proclaimed jazz to be democratic—a dialectic between the individual and the group—it was gradually becoming the possession of cultural elites. Yet many of these sophisticated jazz fans were also spurred to speak out about southern racial segregation as a symbol of boorish backwardness. Jazz and folk music promoted universalism and contributed to the national conversation about civil rights, despite this discourse's partial reliance on racist assumptions about "natural" black abilities.[3]

Moreover, at the start of the 1950s, the word "press" began to take on an even more expansive meaning. With new recording industry technology, long-play vinyl records (LPs) were being pressed by the tens of thousands. Previous formats could carry no more than about five minutes of recorded sound (and typically only three), while LPs could contain an entire album's worth, almost thirty minutes per side. This transformed the way Americans listened to music at home, allowing a closer simulation of long pieces, such as one would hear at a symphony or a nightclub. Live recordings of improvised jazz club performances became hot commodities. But instead of replacing nightclubs, albums worked in symbiosis with them, introducing new fans to modern styles and increasing their aura of artistic prestige. At a discursive level, these mediated interactions became their own kind of conversation. As a result, a new generation of nightclub patrons and performers arrived in the boîtes of New York and San Francisco, armed with new, more nuanced language about both race and music that helped to reshape the meaning of America.

Meanwhile, as Kenneth Rexroth promoted his poetry renaissance in the Black Cat and the Iron Pot, his vision of San Francisco as a rival cultural center to New York

City was becoming a reality.[4] While still a lesser star than Gotham, the Bay Area scene developed rapidly. Bolstered by San Francisco's growing bohemian reputation and the continual influx of revelers through the city's ports, jazz outgrew the African American Fillmore District and expanded into North Beach. In the intimate subterranean nightclubs on both coasts, cultural artisans crafted unique performances that were all the more vital, since audiences experienced them interactively—art on a human scale.

As the postwar civil rights movement grew to its peak, nightclub culture and politics entwined more intricately than Popular Front *cabaretiers* could have envisioned when bebop was in its infancy. Throughout the course of the 1950s, Rebel Café nightclubs contributed to racial politics in three ways. First, they enacted the integrationist imperative that dominated the movement through the mid-1960s. Jazz clubs were sites of cross-racial exchange and helped to foster communities in Greenwich Village and North Beach that were among the most integrated in the country. Second, the universalist ethos of many jazz performers, club owners, and patrons promoted the movement's call for racial justice and social equality that it encapsulated as "freedom." Third, and perhaps most importantly, many in the jazz/folk community directly participated in the black freedom struggle, either as activists or as financial supporters of organizations such as the Congress of Racial Equality (CORE) and the Student Nonviolent Coordinating Committee (SNCC)—the young advocates of participatory democracy whom Howard Zinn famously dubbed the "New Abolitionists."

Jazzmen Charles Mingus and Dave Brubeck were particularly noteworthy for their contributions to the black freedom struggle. Also significant were the bohemian poets and writers, whose experiences as nightclub patrons informed their work. For the Beat generation, jazz musicians, and audiences alike—in dialogue with each other and the wider public—nightclubs were laboratories of democracy, complete with all of the contentiousness attending that form of politics.[5] But at least in part, this jazz sensibility provided cultural roots for a commitment to universalism among both blacks and whites. Jazz clubs offered more than simply the soundtrack of rebellion. Their ethos, and the cross-racial interactions they encouraged, contributed to a slow and tentative erosion of racial caste in America in the 1950s.

On the Spot, into the Cellar, and through the Gate

In 1949, as Cafe Society was closing its doors in Greenwich Village, owner Barney Josephson packed up one of its satirical murals and shipped it to WPA artist Anton Refregier, who was then teaching at San Francisco's California Labor School.[6] Josephson could not have known it at the time, but in a way, he was passing a torch. Even as his symbol of Popular Front defeat arrived, one of the most significant venues in the history of the Rebel Café opened across town. The Black Hawk, run by Helen Noga, broke away from the Bay Area's previous nightclub culture. It challenged dominant nightlife norms, became a key site in San Francisco's jazz/bohemian scene in the 1950s, and helped to solidify the city's bicoastal connections to New York. In the 1940s, San Francisco's jazz clubs mostly featured Dixieland, evoking nostalgia for the Gay Nineties and the Jazz Age of the 1920s as mythical eras of decadence and cheer. With the exception of the Fillmore District's club scene around Bop City and Jack's Tavern, very little modern jazz was heard in area nightspots until the Black Hawk opened at the corner of Turk and Hyde Streets, in the heart of the old Tenderloin cabaret district. Avoiding flamboyant decor, Noga and her partners—her husband John and fellow bartender Guido Cacianti—instead focused on musical virtuosity and avant-garde jazz. Bringing culture to the people, they opened a spare, rectangular venue, soon to be infamous almost as much for its ability to trap cigarette smoke as for its musical acts.[7]

Before the Black Hawk, for most jazz bands, particularly the modernists, touring was less a circuit than a one-way trip. Heading out from the center of the jazz world in New York City, their sole West Coast destination was usually Los Angeles, where they sought contacts with Hollywood producers. But Noga and her partners brought in prominent modern acts, including Billie Holiday and Dizzy Gillespie's protégé, Miles Davis. Moreover, the Black Hawk completed the jazz circuit by offering a viable export: the ambitious young pianist Dave Brubeck, who, for the first time, gave the jazz players in Chicago and Gotham a run for their money. Brubeck debuted at the Black Hawk in 1950, the same year another California jazzman, Charles Mingus, moved to New York.[8] Both established considerable reputations in the jazz world, with Brubeck defining what came to be known as the West Coast "cool" style.

Mob-owned venues in San Francisco were uncommon, but the few that did exist were mostly jazz clubs in the Fillmore or the Tenderloin. The Black Hawk therefore became another key link in a developing network of progressive venues that challenged organized crime's control of American nightlife. While left-leaning nightclub owners such as Barney Josephson and Max and Lorraine Gordon have been generally (and understandably) tight-lipped about any pressures they felt from organized crime, the few references they have made to the mob are suggestive. For example, in her memoir, Lorraine Gordon contrasted the sophisticated Village Vanguard and Blue Angel to mob-tied venues like the Stork Club. Josephson was more outspoken, describing gangsters' efforts to muscle in on Cafe Society with strong-arm tactics, such as taking "ownership" of the coatroom and then demanding a monthly payment for "rent." Josephson's resistance to organized crime played a part in establishing progressive nightclubs as a legitimate business—part of a larger process of jazz respectability and racial integration in the American mainstream (as well as a likely tactic to avoid attention from hostile authorities).[9] Although the Nogas and Cacianti had no significant ties to the political Left, Brubeck and his band (in particular, saxophonist Paul Desmond) were part of Rexroth's extended circle of bohemian anarchist-libertarians. This later made the club an important site for Beat generation writers, as well as for Rexroth's explorations of jazz and poetry. Other clubs, such as San Francisco's Jazz Workshop and New York's Five Spot, soon widened this circle even more.

Other developments changed the shape of New York's jazz scene. Following the demise of 52nd Street clubs in the late 1940s, bebop's center of gravity moved southward, down Manhattan, as the Village Vanguard became its anchor (along with Birdland holding the fort in Midtown). More jazz clubs also sprang up in Greenwich Village in the early 1950s, such as Café Bohemia and the short-lived Open Door. But the Five Spot Café, near the Bowery at 5 Cooper Square, became the main locus for leftist bohemian jazz after it opened in 1956. Originally known as the Bowery Bar when Sicilian-born Salvatore Termini purchased the place in 1937, it served the neighborhood's working-class men, sometimes providing respite from the cold for local transients. Salvatore's sons, Joe and Ignatze ("Iggy"), rechristened it the No. 5 Bar when they took over in the late 1940s. The influx of bohemians to the East Side in the mid-1950s led them to jazz. With a new decor featuring art show and jazz concert posters, and a cabaret license in hand, the bar was refashioned as the Five Spot.[10]

The Five Spot solidified the Village jazz/bohemian scene when it began hosting jam sessions with neighborhood regulars. Seeing the growing audience for this kind of small music room, the Village Vanguard cemented its all-jazz format in 1957—the same year the Beat generation broke into the mainstream.[11] While the Vanguard relied on mainstays like Dizzy Gillespie, the Five Spot attracted John Coltrane and Ornette Coleman, who pushed the boundaries of jazz improvisation. "By the time Monk and Trane got there," Beat poet and activist LeRoi Jones (later writing as Amiri Baraka) recounted, "the Five Spot was the center of the jazz world!" For the musicians, the club offered not only a job, but also the chance to test their ideas and innovations. Jones later remembered Joe and Iggy Termini as "two of the nicest guys in the business," and the Five Spot ran advertisements in his *Yugen* magazine, the text of which spoke volumes about the club's atmosphere and jazz/bohemian appeal: "Home of Thelonious Monk—Home of Jazz-Poetry—Home of America's Leading Painters, Sculptors, Composers, Actors, Poets, PEOPLE."[12]

One of the first jazzmen to perform there, David Amram, who would soon collaborate with Jack Kerouac on a short film, *Pull My Daisy*, described the club as "a funky bar in the Bowery that . . . welcomed everyone—artists, moving men, postal workers, winos, and off-duty firemen." "Late at night," he continued, "poets and actors would sometimes join us, reciting poetry or improvising verse with music. . . . Our era was always *in*-clusive, not *ex*-clusive. Jazz was about sharing and spontaneity." As historian Robin D. G. Kelley has noted, most of the early Five Spot habitués were, like Amram, white males, and they included many of the Cedar Tavern's crowd, such as Franz Kline and Willem de Kooning. White writers and poets like Jack Kerouac, Allen Ginsberg, Gregory Corso, and Frank O'Hara also joined the fold, along with black musicians, such as Ted Joans and avant-garde jazz pianist Cecil Taylor. Taylor's classically trained style also embraced the influence of Dave Brubeck and Thelonious Monk, who began playing at the club in mid-1957, as did Charles Mingus. The Five Spot's audiences therefore reflected the Village's changing demographics: mostly white, but increasingly including African Americans. The area's tastes were moving further away from its Italian and Jewish ethnic past. "The Terminis didn't know who the artists or musicians were—the scene was self-made," recalled the club's hat-check attendant, Helen Tworkov. "It was all underground word of mouth."[13]

The Five Spot's bohemian coterie also contained a growing number of women—such as writers Anne Waldman, Diane di Prima, and LeRoi Jones's soon-to-be spouse, Hettie Cohen—who challenged the norms of the 1950s in various ways. For this new generation of nonconformists, the Five Spot was a literal point of connection and a landmark in their mental geography. Waldman later recalled that Amram would take her around to clubs such as the Five Spot, where she met painter Larry Rivers and others in the Beat scene. When Kerouac published works such as "Mexico City Blues," Waldman saw the underground life it represented unfolding before her eyes: "What I appreciated as a young teen girl growing up on MacDougal Street in Manhattan's West Village, was this poem's . . . obvious relationship to jazz, to dharma. . . . These very tangible 'Beat' literary poets were now walking my streets."[14] The Five Spot became so entrenched in the Beat imagination as a radical mixed-gender site that Ginsberg found it materializing in his sleep. "I look, sometime in the same dream, to see what's playing at the Five Spot, Jazz Reichian revival hall," he wrote in his journal in 1957. "See woman dressed like hermaphrodite in dancing fancy dress . . . that's what became of the old time Trotskyite girls." Memoirist and model Alice Denham similarly associated the club with the visceral impact of music and interracial romance. "Down into the low roar of the Five Spot to hear the great Thelonius [*sic*] Monk," she wrote. "[My date] and I sat at a tiny table for two in the dark urban forest beneath a pinpoint lamp. . . . The new innovative jazz, bebop or modern, charged me up like Bartok's scintillating dissonances."[15]

For Hettie Jones, too, Five Spot jazz was, in her words, "another, new language," one that offered the chance to jell an untried kind of community. "I suddenly knew a score of new people," she recalled. "I think of us trying to laugh off the fifties, the pall of the Cold War, the nuclear fallout—right then, the papers were full of it—raining death on test sites in Nevada. I think we were trying to shake the time. Shake it off, shake it up, shake it down." She continued with a long view of jazz/bohemia's interracial terrain:

> In the United States white people have historically made their way to places like the Five Spot in times like the late fifties. . . . But it's important to the particular history of what would later be called the New Bohemia that going to the Five Spot was not like taking the A train to Harlem. Downtown was everyone's new place. . . . The jazz clubs were there among all this. And all of us there—black and white— were strangers at first. . . .
>
> However, I entered the Five Spot, and all these other new doors I opened with Roi, as another image. . . . That summer *Dissent* magazine published Norman Mailer's essay "The White Negro." There I read that jazz was orgasm, which only

blacks had figured out, and that white "hipsters" like me were attracted to the black world's sexy, existential violence. But the only violence I'd ever encountered, the only time I'd heard bone smashing bone, had been among whites in the South. The young black musicians I met didn't differ from other aspiring artists. . . . All I wanted to do at the Five Spot was *listen*.

The following year, after moving farther uptown to the Chelsea neighborhood, Hettie Jones began to pine for the East Village and insisted that LeRoi find them a place where she could feel connected with friends, longing for "the Five Spot and the Fourth Avenue bookshops."[16]

Hettie Jones's reminiscence certainly oversimplifies the interracial history of American nightclubs, and perhaps she idealized her experiences, using jazz as a way to authenticate her own bohemian sophistication. But it also indicates the importance

Charles Mingus at the Five Spot. Copyright © Dennis Stock / Magnum Photos, STD1958004W00158/10

of Village nightspots as public spaces, both for community formation and as landmarks on the maps of memory. Concluding her 1990 memoir, Jones described going to the roof of her building to survey the neighborhood, as she had just surveyed her own past. "The view from up there is changed," she lamented, "A fourteen-story building looms in the sky where the Five Spot used to be."[17] The fact that the Five Spot was singled out in multiple memoirs was doubtless the result of selective memory, but it is a useful representative of dozens of similar places. Village nightclubs, such as the Jazz Wagon and the Half Note, prospered in the late 1950s, and patrons had comparable experiences to those at the Five Spot. In 1956, Charles Mingus wrote to Langston Hughes in terms that showed both the difficulty of maintaining a jazz community and the everyday role that nightclubs played. "Sorry I'm so long in getting this to you but I've been out of town with my group," he wrote. "I'm opening at the Cafe Bohemia. . . . Hope you get a chance to come by." More directly, Thelonious Monk found his first steady gig in years at the Five Spot. The club became a de facto home away from home for him, with his spouse and other family members attending almost every night, and the club's kitchen serving almost as a living room, where Monk and his fellow musicians talked art and politics between sets.[18]

As journalist Nat Hentoff noted in his 1961 survey, *The Jazz Life*, nightclubs offered opportunities for both personal and social transformation. "When you walk into a jazz club," he wrote, "you never know what combinations of emotions, some perhaps long dormant, will be reawakened and reset before the night is out." While Hentoff was justifiably cautious in his praise for jazz's racially progressive potential, he nonetheless observed that "it is one of the very few areas in American life where whites and Negroes, otherwise residentially segregated, have been able to form relatively casual friendships." He continued: "Even full-time white liberals still seldom know Negroes apart from their roles in committees or Negro organizations. As for the average American, I expect a wide sampling might indicate that a revealingly huge majority have never had a Negro, other than a domestic, inside their homes. Jazz clubs, however, have become islands of at least acquaintanceship between Negroes and whites."[19] In retrospect, Hentoff's language seems problematic, with its assumptions of average Americans as white and its integrationist aims, which tacitly discounted autonomous black institutions in favor of assimilation into the nation's proverbial white home. But in 1961, Black Power was still five years away from taking hold, and the dominant strategy of activists, both black and white, was integration. Perhaps nowhere in the United States did this ideal find its most notable application than within the jazz/bohemian community, where racial politics was the stuff of daily life.

Despite the fact that integration often fell short of more-radical goals, such as the restructuring of economic resources, it was still decidedly controversial in the 1950s—a period when, according to Chief Justice Earl Warren's memoirs, President Eisenhower could blithely suggest to him that southern segregationists "are not bad people" but simply concerned "that their sweet little girls are not required to sit in school alongside some big overgrown Negroes."[20] For those in the oppositional underground, jazz was intertwined with a deep commitment to interracial relations. The jazz world has long been one of the few American social spaces in which interracial marriages and partnerships flourished without much condemnation. Relationships such as Charlie and Chan Parker's, or Billie Holiday's with Benny Goodman, were not uncommon, even as a majority of states maintained laws prohibiting what was referred to as "miscegenation," or interracial sex. Declaring the "soulfulness" of Kenneth Rexroth's Chicago cohort Dave Tough, Dizzy Gillespie suggested that the drummer's interracial marriage had political implications: "Dave Tough married a black woman and took her everywhere he went. . . . I think that period was the beginning of this current age of civil rights." Parker reportedly had similar (if more visionary) ideas about his own marriage, proclaiming it was "my way of showing the world that there's no such thing as white and black."[21]

Jazz life was also fundamental to LeRoi and Hettie Jones. Longtime friend Joyce Johnson later declared that when Hettie deviated from the traditional path laid out by her suburban parents, her new passion was jazz. Johnson asserted, in terms that reveal both the problematic nature of racial construction in the 1950s and the jazz underground's potential for identity transformation, that "black came to seem the color of a great deal more that was realer than what she'd known, some purer definition of experience, some essential knowledge that the white suburbs denied their children." The jazz community eased the couple's way forward, despite the fact that their marriage left Hettie "orphaned" by the rejection of her parents. "The following summer at the Newport Jazz Festival," Johnson wrote, "she'd see the children of other interracial couples and think Yes, she and Roi would have children; all that was possible, too." LeRoi Jones, writing as Amiri Baraka after adopting Black Nationalism and ending his interracial relationships in the mid-1960s, also remembered the era's social complexities and the significance of the bohemian community. "We both took up marriage like hesitant explorers on the shore of some unknown country," he recalled. Although Baraka admitted that "we were unprepared for the inner conflicts that such a union portends in America," he noted that they, as a couple, were "shielded to some extent by residence in the Village."[22]

Writing to an aunt in 1961, Hettie Jones conveyed both the social pressures on her marriage and the role the jazz community played in legitimating it. The aunt's visit to their home showed that "you still feel I exist as a human being," Hettie wrote. "You see, Roi and I are really not a unique phenomenon. There are hundreds of interracial marriages in this country and abroad." Concluding that "we both realize that without the other neither one of us would be quite *real*," Hettie defended LeRoi and the couple's jazz/bohemian milieu by mobilizing the language of traditional gender roles. Insisting that he was "a very great man," she asserted, "even now, at 27, he is the 'darling' of all the so-called 'avant-garde' of painters, writers, musicians" and that "right now he is trying to wake up enough to meet someone interested in making jazz records—it's nearly Midnight and the man wants to go hear some music at one of the downtown clubs—so you see he works at night, too."[23]

North Beach was less notable for interracial partnerships in the 1950s, but Bob and Eileen Kaufman's exemplified those of many lesser-known couples. For the Kaufmans, jazz at the bohemian Coffee Gallery was a fundamental part of their public life as writers and poets. "When I met Bob Kaufman, King of North Beach," Eileen declared, "my values changed overnight." Evoking the nightclub's social spaces, she continued: "There was no partition for the entertainment section, and jazz was played throughout the place any time the musicians fell by. Spontaneity was the key word in our life style in North Beach. This is what made it 'the scene.'" Bob highlighted this Beat fabric in "West Coast Sounds—1956," as he intoned, "San Fran, hipster land, / Jazz sounds, wig sounds . . . / Rexroth, Ferlinghetti, / Swinging, in cellars." While many relationships like the Kaufmans' were admittedly stormy—with some African American rebels prone to the same violent hypermasculinity as Euro-Americans like Norman Mailer—successful ones would have been almost impossible without the shelter of a sympathetic community. "Well," Eileen later recalled, "I felt at home with the Beat Generation."[24]

North Beach's jazz/bohemian community found several new homes in the mid-1950s. The area's reputation for jazz grew from two simultaneous phenomena. Several older clubs, such as the Say When and Ciro's, closed down, due to charges of prostitution, underage drinking, and other offenses, opening the door to more cutting-edge music venues.[25] Meanwhile, Kenneth Rexroth and Robert Duncan attracted a new generation of radical writers, who flocked to bohemian nightspots. This cohort's craving for modern jazz was sated by the sounds emanating from venues such as the Jazz Workshop and the Cellar.

In 1956, attorney Art Auerbach opened the Jazz Workshop at 473 Broadway, extending the hip modern jazz scene from clubs such as the Downbeat and the Black Hawk into North Beach. His appearance as a conservative family man belied a desire to present provocative productions, and the Jazz Workshop quickly became a favorite among jazz enthusiasts in search of bleeding-edge bebop.[26] Hailing from New York and Chicago, Auerbach had come to San Francisco to attend law school and purchased the club a year before his graduation. While he still considered civil law his primary vocation, Auerbach was dedicated to promoting jazz, bemoaning it as "an art that too many Americans overlooked." Auerbach himself was far from bohemian and often emphasized that the club's success was due to his sound business principles. Yet he also became a devoted fan: "I now book groups largely according to what kind of jazz sells, but some of my favorites are those on whom I took a chance. John Coltrane, for example, or Mingus. I really get involved in what they play. . . . We are in the jazz business, and for me that means sticking to the point—music . . . and the emphasis is on listening."[27] The club's atmosphere attracted a wide range of patrons, including local artists, jazz devotees, and Beat poets.

The Cellar, however, perhaps more than any other San Francisco nightspot, embodied the connections between hip street sensibilities and bebop bohemianism. It also opened in 1956 and was run by a group of jazz musicians: Wil Carlson, Jack Minger, drummer Sonny Nelson, and pianist Bill Weisjahn. The Cellar became the city's chief site for jazz and poetry. Following a trend started by the German émigré Ruth Weiss, Kenneth Rexroth and Lawrence Ferlinghetti held "Jazz and Poetry Nights" and subsequently released Fantasy Records' now-legendary *Poetry Readings in the Cellar* in 1957. While the style, noted at the time as "a kind of Wild West legend on the eastern seaboard," soon became a beatnik cliché, it nonetheless cemented the relationship between Beat writing and live improvisation.[28]

Far more important than the jazz poetry craze specifically was the social role played by nightclub culture as a whole. Modern jazz gave the New Bohemians a common focal point and an immediate form of shorthand communication. If someone could demonstrate fluency in its language, they could quickly find a place within the underground community. Jazz's social codes were fundamental to bohemia as its denizens traversed the continent from coast to coast. For its young writers like Joyce Johnson or LeRoi Jones, jazz clubs offered destinations and spaces for self-reinvention, points that marked their physical and artistic arrival in the Village or North Beach. In the midst of her affair with Kerouac in 1957, Johnson pined to join him in San Francisco, where "he'd take me out to all the jazz joints that very night, and introduce me to everyone." For Jones, who came to the Village in 1957 seeking to escape both racism and his parents' staid middle-class life in New Jersey, bebop meant "another kind of life that existed that somehow I had access to." Jones's partner at *Yugen*, Diane di Prima, recalled jazz as a structuring poetic element, asserting that "the things in my words" were informed by "Miles Davis at the Cafe Bohemia."[29]

Community connections in jazz clubs ranged from the personal to the professional. In his autobiography, Jones recalled the Five Spot as one of his entry points into the Village literary scene, where he went to hear Langston Hughes and the "great populist" Jack Micheline read poetry, backed by Charles Mingus. Following his estrangement from Hettie Jones, it was also a place where he reconnected with African American love interests. Charles Mingus also met his spouse Sue at the Five Spot, making them another of the Village jazz scene's interracial couples. The writers who formed the Black Nationalists' Umbra Workshop in the 1960s also first met in the coffeehouses and jazz clubs of the East Side. Like Hettie and LeRoi Jones, the Umbra poets drew inspiration from the Five Spot, both as a site for jazz poetry and as a respite from the racism that still sometimes marred the Village. Umbra member Tom Dent further noted the importance of jazz bohemia in the late 1950s, during the group's formative years: "We also reveled in the jazz that we brought with us—Archie Shepp, Cecil Taylor, Thelonius [*sic*] Monk, Bill Dixon, Eric Dolphy, Sunny Murray, Elvin Jones, and John Coltrane, in the Old Reliable bar, in Slugs, and in the Five Spot, which was already in the neighborhood before we arrived."[30] Such scenes were paralleled in San Francisco. "So there I was in the Cellar," wrote poet Peter Orlovsky to his partner, Allen Ginsberg. "Came in with Ferlinghetti, we were talking for 3 hours . . . the music blasting loud, rock an' roll type excitement music . . . [Michael] McClure there behind Rexroth . . . [and] we were digging the music, the Silent drummer who sits there playing, with tilted head and eyes rolled up toward heaven."[31]

As the jazzy New Bohemia developed, the New York club that most wholeheartedly seized the socially conscious cabaret tradition was the Village Gate, opened at 160 Bleecker Street in 1958 by former journalist and concert promoter Art D'Lugoff. The Village Gate was an attempt to bridge Popular Front sensibilities with the Beat generation. D'Lugoff, the son of a Russian-born father and a mother who emigrated from Jerusalem, was born in a Harlem hospital in 1924. He grew up in the Jewish community of Brighton Beach, where, he recalled, the synagogue and the local Communist Party headquarters shared the same building and "were always vying for our souls." After serving in the army during World War II, D'Lugoff attended New York University, studying English literature and political science on the GI Bill. The universalist thinker Norman Corwin was also an early influence, and D'Lugoff admired his antiracism and his humanist stance as a "one-worlder." Coming from a well-educated liberal Jewish family, D'Lugoff was attracted to campus politics, participating in both the Young Democrats and the 1948 Henry Wallace campaign, but he later insisted that the less structured bohemian circles in Greenwich Village truly radicalized him. Like many of his generation, he rejected formal Communism (finding any group that sat gazing at "Stalin's picture" to be "sort of fishy"), but he was active with the Left-linked United Electrical Workers Union (UE) and considered himself a bohemian anarchist. In the early 1950s, D'Lugoff also worked at *Compass* (the successor to the left-wing newspaper *PM*) and was impressed by the leftist-liberal journalist I. F. Stone. He continued his own journalistic bent at small papers in the Catskills and wrote for the African American *California Eagle*, where he expressed his concerns about McCarthy's anticommunist methods.[32]

In 1955, D'Lugoff's interest in music and the bubbling popularity of folk singers led him to book a series of performers at the Village's Circle in the Square theater, starting with Pete Seeger and later including Sonny Terry and Brownie McGhee. He continued with "ethnic" performers like the Clancy Brothers, and by 1956 he was booking jazz concerts featuring Dave Brubeck, Louis Armstrong, and Duke Ellington. During Billie Holiday's cabaret-card suspension in 1957, D'Lugoff promoted her at the Sheridan Theater, one of her legendary last performances. In 1958, D'Lugoff continued his connection with the cultural front of the 1930s by orchestrating the return of Paul Robeson to Carnegie Hall, after nearly a decade of blacklisting.[33]

Described by one friend as "a left-wing Jewish atheist," and "very proud of it," D'Lugoff gave the Village Gate a radical point of view. He opened his new venue in the basement of a flophouse, the Greenwich Mills Hotel. The club fit in snugly among the coffeehouses of Bleecker Street—it was modeled after "Italian and Austrian coffee shops, with a place to sit down, enjoy pastry and conversation"—as the scene picked up steam. D'Lugoff had felt at home in the Village since his New York University years, and the Gate was one part concert hall, one part restaurant, and one part bohemian bar—"something of an unofficial headquarters" for folk singers and radicals, said the *Village Voice*, where "formal folk concerts will supplement the casual entertainment provided by the customers." As folk music's popularity waned in the mid-1960s, D'Lugoff shifted to jazz (due to its "history"), featuring Thelonious Monk, Miles Davis, and John Coltrane, but also blues and jazz/folk singers like Nina Simone and Odetta. D'Lugoff considered Barney Josephson to be a role model and continued Cafe Society's approach, warmly welcoming integrated audiences and making the Village Gate its heir apparent.[34]

The Village Gate was part of a cabaret milieu in which the visibility of black culture gave voice to African American concerns. This jazz/folk scene featured Popular Front performers and a younger generation of politically conscious musicians. In particular, Nina Simone, whose haunting piano ballads epitomized the jazz/folk style, noted that the Gate was a central part of her life in the Village. Simone found a vibrant public space there, along with fellow musicians and intellectuals such as John Coltrane, LeRoi Jones, Langston Hughes, James Baldwin, and *Raisin in the Sun* playwright Lorraine Hansberry (who based the titular character of *The Sign in Sidney Brustein's Window* on D'Lugoff). "Politics was mixed in with so much of what went on at the Gate that I remember it now as two sides of the same coin, politics and jazz," Simone wrote in her autobiography, *I Put a Spell on You*. "Comedians like Dick Gregory, Bill Cosby and Woody Allen opened for the players and it was all part of the same thing—the music and the comedy, the jazz and the politics, it all went together."[35]

Simone's jazz/folk sensibility even had a thread connecting it to the roots of radical cabaret, as she made Kurt Weill and Bertolt Brecht's "Pirate Jenny" from *The Blue Angel* one of her standards. But "Mississippi Goddam" was probably the most significant piece in her repertoire, a civil rights anthem that was a descendent of Holiday's "Strange Fruit," yet devoid of the latter's undercurrent of silent suffering. Instead, it was an outspoken claim to the dignity of black womanhood. "The name of this tune is 'Mississippi Goddam' / And I mean every word of it," she sang in 1964 to a New York audience:

> Alabama's gotten me so upset
> Tennessee made me lose my rest
> And everybody knows about Mississippi Goddam . . .
> Picket lines
> School boycotts
> They try to say it's a communist plot . . .
> Yes you lied to me all these years
> You told me to wash and clean my ears

And talk real fine just like a lady
And you'd stop calling me Sister Sadie . . .
I don't trust you anymore
You keep on saying "Go slow!"
"Go slow!"
You don't have to live next to me
Just give me my equality . . .
Everybody knows about Mississippi Goddam[36]

While nightclubs were sometimes untrustworthy sources of support (both morally and financially) for such an uncompromising performer, Simone found a steady ally in D'Lugoff. "I was always treated properly at the Gate," she recalled. "Art treated performers as equals, as people worthy of respect. . . . Art became a friend and invited me over to his house for dinner many times. He understood that respect was important: when it was due he gave it, and got it back in return." D'Lugoff later maintained that he introduced Simone to Lorraine Hansberry, who had a profound effect on the singer's political views. Simone remained outspoken about racial justice throughout her career. And she frequently beamed with pride that her music, which developed within the Village Gate's cabaret atmosphere, was a sort of unofficial soundtrack for SNCC organizers, noting that "everywhere they went to meet fellow workers they found my records."[37]

Although disseminated through mass media, the jazz/folk style remained rooted in particularities of place and space. Greenwich Village and North Beach communities experienced social interactions and cultural productions made concrete by the Rebel Café's contours, its physicality and its sensuousness—a highly contentious process, all the more so because of the enigmatic nature of musical messages. The tensions around race and gender could not simply be washed away by waves of sound. But jazz/folk performances sometimes cracked the transparent wall of these divisions. In his 1962 novel, *Another Country*, James Baldwin described the debut of fictional black jazz singer Ida Scott at a Village nightclub, writing that the music was infused with "a quality so mysteriously and implacably egocentric that no one has ever been able to name it." Baldwin then conjured the dialectic of live performance and social transformation, a quality that "involves a sense of the self so profound and so powerful that it does not so much leap barriers as reduce them to atoms—while still leaving them standing mightily, where they were; and this awful sense is private, unknowable, not to be articulated, having, literally, to do with something else; it transforms and lays waste and gives life, and kills."[38] Despite its elusive qualities, music could be a powerful, transformative tool to break those social barriers. And given the importance of sound, acoustics, and party-like mingling to any jazz club's success—in other words, nightlife's version of the conditions needed for freedom of speech and assembly—its physical spaces also played a role.

Recasting the cabaret: Nina Simone at the Village Gate in 1965. Sam Falk /
New York Times / Redux, image 4274040

You Become the Object You Came to See

Nightclub spaces shaped the interplay between performers and patrons, ranging from the Five Spot's intimate 150-person capacity to the Café au Go Go's gargantuan cellar and the Village Gate's spartan seats. Despite some differences, all of these venues were small enough that a close connection between audiences and performers was the rule—so much so that the performers' common complaint was that audience conversations interfered with the music. It is understandable that musicians sought the stricter decorum of concert halls, but this says little about cabaret's social function in the 1950s.[39]

Patrons actively sought the combination of talk and mellifluence, sociability and entertainment. Their presence in a nightclub and their displays of appreciation for artistically ambitious styles were a kind of social currency, but these also gave them an opportunity to ease into novel social relations and identities, to explore sexuality, and to publicly address conflicts. One North Beach journalist, steeped in the Coffee Gallery's "atmosphere of more or less near-anarchy," lamented that an evening in most nightclubs meant too many tourists and drunks and not enough careful listeners. Yet he continued to seek his nocturnal ideal: "A house of jazz. Jazz! With its cloak of colors. A sound painting of feelings and emotions! Inspired! Uninhibited! And above all, happiness!" The reality, of course, was that on some nights the clubs were so packed, it was impossible to appreciate the music. As critics on both coasts observed, jazz spots enjoyed a varied patronage, from the "pseudo-jazz intellectuals who see a weird motive in the playing of every note" to "beards, bulky sweaters, and Brooks Brothers suits . . . shuffling around the room, table-hopping, mens-rooming, and telephoning."[40] Such comments were also typical of the milieu's masculine social coding, as female jazz fans frequently were unnoticed.

Jazz club decor was often bohemian. The Cellar cultivated a modern laissez-faire atmosphere, as did the Five Spot's dimly lit room, with its red-painted walls. As captured in Martin Williams's 1964 article, "A Night at the Five Spot," interactions in these spaces were layered with meaning among the club's motley crew:

> Roland Hanna, looking like a kindly but officious banker who is about to explain an overdraft to a befuddled dowager, enters the clubroom through the kitchen . . . and chats with his bass player. . . . He sits down on the piano bench and warms up. . . . The crowd continues to buzz and chat. But when Hanna is interpolating a phrase from "Solar" . . . the banker is a forgotten person. There is applause as the pianist segues into a bass solo, and it is followed by a sudden burst of irrelevant laughter from someone enjoying a private joke at the bar. . . . [Then] a long drum solo, has the eyes and ears of the crowd. At the end of the bar, a middle aged woman looks on admiringly, as if she knew exactly what was happening. She has a copy of the *New Yorker* and a half-empty martini glass on the bar in front of her. To her right, her escort looks noncommittal. . . . A few feet down the bar, a young man who has been nursing a beer for about an hour says to his companion, "How about that rent strike in Harlem?"

The Five Spot's small capacity guaranteed that this jumbled mélange—the simultaneously brilliant and blasé stuff of American democratic culture in action—could be boiled down into a single concoction, a unitary experience of sight and sound.[41] Such an overly simple display of social complexity was comforting to young audiences, who were seeking spaces where they felt they belonged to something or someone. Meanwhile, the labor of the jazzman (symbolically evinced by his entrance through the kitchen) was easily missed amid the din.

Especially creative or powerful performances intensified the trend toward unified audiences, offering the possibility of transcendence. The astonishing style of Thelonious Monk, the "high priest of bop," could focus the attention of even a diverse mixture of patrons. "Monk comes through the kitchen door and moves toward the stand," wrote Williams. "A burst of hard applause covers his opening notes, but almost immediately the room is silent." For Hettie Jones, the language of jazz was best captured by Monk at the Five Spot, where, through the club's open door, "the music rushed out, like a flood of color onto the street." Monk's music "explained" her nonconformist longings as she "heard a new sound, or heard sound in a new way." She then continued, connecting this visceral-aural experience with the desire for community: "One night, after the last set was over, someone—not Monk himself—began to play 'Greensleeves' on the piano. He played tentatively at first, and then, as the harmonies settled, with chords that took the simple line into an elegant statement, a hymn. . . . A hush fell over the emptying club, and on either side of me spaces opened, and I could see the same feeling in all of us, at once both apart and together, absorbing the clear, absolute notes."[42]

John Coltrane and Charles Mingus similarly affected their audiences—expanding consciousness, even as they potentially inflamed the libido. When bohemian activist Jerry Kamstra arrived in San Francisco in 1955, he recalled the sociosexual effects of hearing Coltrane at the Black Hawk: "I had a girl and I was on leave from the Air Force and we sat in the back row until the cocktail waitress came over and threw us out. She said it wasn't right that we were dry humping while serious musicians were up there on the stand doing their licks. I was a little amazed that anyone could see us since the club was so dark, and was also incredulous that dry humping wasn't allowed, since the music emanating from the stand really turned me on. . . . I was rather proud that I'd been initiated in the Black Hawk while listening to John Coltrane." Kamstra eventually returned to the club to hear Charles Mingus. While he was "sitting out in the cool dark audience . . . Mingus wrapped himself around his bass and thundered hate and anguish in waves out across the floor. It was my first taste of anger precipitated through a musical instrument and it left its mark on me, realizing as I did that horns and basses and drums speak in a language you have to study to understand."[43]

Amiri Baraka also recognized jazz's shift in consciousness, "a new tongue and vision for a generally more advanced group in our generation" of politically active African Americans. "Blues is the basic pulse and song, the fundamental description and reaction. . . . Jazz, as Langston says, is the child, the blue/black prodigy of the earth mother/father . . . Jazz, the most advanced music of the African American people . . . wants to describe the whole of this society, its multinational reality, to that society itself, and propose alternatives." Reflecting the spirit of the rising civil rights movement, Baraka connected jazz club sounds with political struggle: "The power and beauty of that music was something again. And now there was so much of it coming out and everybody was talking about Freedom."[44] San Francisco journalist Ralph Gleason concurred, saying of the Beat-inflected jams in the Cellar, "It is the language of youth—the language of the real jazz age." As Baraka argued in his classic 1963 study, *Blues People*, the inclusion of improvisation in professional performances, rather than only in private settings, was fundamental to the formation of a visible African American public. White audiences and performers, Baraka argued, had to acknowledge their debt to black culture.[45]

It would be naive to assume that audiences absorbed progressive notions about democracy and community simply by listening to live jazz, although jazz/folk lyrics sometimes overtly carried those messages. But within a larger discursive process, in which performers like Charles Mingus and Dave Brubeck publicized their sociopolitical views in articles and interviews, audience identification with them could have noticeable effects. When fans wrote to Brubeck saying that a show at the Black Hawk or at Basin Street East converted them to the cause, they—perhaps unwittingly—declared themselves allies in his project to make jazz a force for liberation. One such supporter, a YMCA director, sweepingly declared, "Jazz effects [*sic*] every facet of our daily lives including religion, politics, work, expressions of the human personality, etc."[46] In 1960, one journalist crystallized this ethereal communal and ideological mix. Describing a visit to the Black Hawk to hear the Modern Jazz Quartet—renowned for their dignified dedication to their music as "erudite . . . serious art"—he declared, "This was us, modern America, being portrayed to ourselves, by ourselves on the very best terms."[47] Such intense identification could indeed transcend the barriers of both ideology and geography, challenging racial and cultural stereotypes.

As an embodiment of jazz's musical and social rebellion, Charles Mingus loomed large. He was a physically imposing man, known for both his quick temper and his capacity for tenderness. Mingus's music, with its aggressive rhythms, time changes, complex forms, and soulful expressionism, encapsulated both the muscular side of the jazz/folk style and what scholar Eric Porter refers to as a Romantic approach that insisted jazz "was the product of one's spirit and emotions," in opposition "to the marketplace."[48] Born in 1922, Mingus grew up with a complicated relationship to race in America. His mother was of Anglo, black, and Chinese descent and his paternal grandmother was white. (Family legend had it that she was a cousin of Abraham Lincoln.) Mingus's father, a career military man, was light skinned and blue eyed, and thus passed as white through much of his adult life. Biographer Brian Priestley suggests that Mingus's darker skin was a source of tension, and that his father discouraged him from associating with even darker "blacks" during his youth in Los Angeles. The bassist's ambivalence about World War II reflected this turbulence. Mingus rejected the nation's internment of Japanese Americans, but he patriotically tried to enlist in the army, although he did not serve, due to a failed medical exam. Throughout his travels and travails in the jazz world, Mingus was involved in conflicts, because of his skin color. According to saxophonist Tony Scott, he lashed out—sometimes physically—to prove his "negritude." This concern was palpable in Mingus's 1971 autobiography, *Beneath the Underdog*, in which an antagonist refers to him as a "half-yella schitt-colored nigger"—a phrase that he originally proposed as the book's title.[49]

The pressures of subterranean life, beneath the underdogs, drove Mingus to address the injustices of American society in his music. Beginning in October 1955,

Converts to the cause: Dave Brubeck (*left*) and fans at the Black Hawk, circa 1950. Brubeck Collection, Holt-Atherton Special Collections, University of the Pacific Library, copyright © Dave Brubeck

Mingus featured socially conscious material, such as "Haitian Fight Song," which he recorded live at the Café Bohemia with Max Roach on drums, later saying that it could have been called the "Afro-American Fight Song." In 1956, he published a poem, "Suite Freedom," in which references to McCarthyism underscored calls for civil rights:

> This mule ain't from Moscow;
> This mule ain't from the south,
> But this mule's got some learning . . .
> Mostly mouth-to-mouth . . .
> This mule could be called stubborn—and lazy
> But in a clever sort of way,
> This mule's been waiting and planning . . .
> For a sacred kind of day . . .
> That burning sticks—
> Or crosses—
> Is not mere child's play . . .
> But a mad man
> In his bloom.

During a Café Bohemia show in 1957, Mingus improvised the seed of perhaps his most powerful protest song, "Original Faubus Fables," the centerpiece of his 1960 album, *Charles Mingus Presents Charles Mingus*. In response to the bassist's impromptu query about who was "ridiculous," drummer Dannie Richmond shouted back, "Governor Faubus"—a denunciation, around which they structured the song, of Arkansas's segregationist leader.[50]

Mingus therefore makes a fascinating counterpoint to his fellow jazz activist, Dave Brubeck. Each espoused jazz as liberation, but while Brubeck saw this as a positive freedom—freedom *for* pluralism and self-expression—Mingus demanded freedom *from* economic and racial oppression. In *Beneath the Underdog*, Mingus illustrated the conflicts between artistic integrity and paternal responsibility in the narrowed avenues of African American opportunity:

> "But Mingus, how about them crumb-crushers of yours when their little stomachs get to poppin' and there ain't nothin' in their jaws but their gums, teeth and tongue, what you gonna do? Play for money or be a pimp?"
>
> "I tried being a pimp, Fats. I didn't like it."
>
> "Then you gonna play for money."

Yet he still sought to demolish traditional barriers. "There is no jazz, there is no classical," he told the *New York Times* in 1962, "there is only music."[51]

Over the course of his career, Mingus performed in his share of mob-owned clubs and sometimes cultivated their associations as a part of his persona, a form of street cred. In reality, however, he mostly courted relations with independent club owners in New York, such as Mike Canterino of the Half Note Café on the Lower West Side, who offered him a standing invitation. Mingus described the Half Note (fictionalized as the Fast Buck in his memoir) as "a musical home, a place to play for people who really seem to want to hear," where the owner "calls [me] son and his two sons call [me] brother." In 1957, Mingus backed up Langston Hughes's poetry reading at the Village Vanguard, and Art D'Lugoff included him in Billie Holiday's famous Village concert in Loew's Sheridan Theater. His appearances at the Five Spot completed his immersion in New York's bohemia. All of this, however, was not without conflict. Mingus famously engaged in multiple physical confrontations, including a fistfight at the Café Bohemia in 1958, and one of his appearances at the Vanguard ended in an argument with Max Gordon over money, during which the bassist brandished a knife and smashed a light fixture.[52]

Yet this volatility was backed by ambition and a gregarious side that garnered him faithful (and sometimes useful) friendships. During a brief stint at San Francisco's Bop City in 1950, Mingus's displeasure over an interview with Ralph Gleason led him to write an angry letter in *Down Beat*, denouncing the critic. By 1955, however, Mingus and his wife Celia were regularly corresponding with the Gleasons, who discussed their kids, music, and jazz festivals, with hopes that they could visit the Mingus family and "make the Newport scene." After settling more or less permanently in

New York in 1951, Mingus also started a close friendship with Nat Hentoff, whom he described as "one of the few white guys you could really talk to"—a rare word of praise from the bassist, who otherwise skewered music critics as talentless hacks.[53]

Mingus's reputation as an irascible performer who berated fellow musicians and audiences in equal measure was so entrenched that some nightclub crowds went away disappointed if the bassist simply played politely, denying them the opportunity to participate in the show. Taken alongside his autobiography, which infamously recounts numerous sexual exploits of preposterous proportions, Mingus's persona betrayed more than a hint of a put-on. His memoir is unsettlingly misogynistic, reflecting the trend of hypermasculinity within the jazz world. But it is also a complex work of modernist literature, a kind of jazzy Joyce, clearly calculated to confront the reader with social transgression, to create the effect of dissonance that paralleled his musical work, which he insisted must be seen as a form of composition at the highest level.[54]

An oft-repeated episode during a Mingus show at the Five Spot contained many of the contradictory elements of the bassist's social role, spotlighting sources of strain within the Rebel Café, with various threads of put-on, racial tension, performativity, misogyny, homophobia, and even improvisational composition. Beginning with Mingus's demand that a woman in the audience stop talking, he then berated the entire crowd:

> You, my audience, are all a bunch of poppaloppers. A bunch of tumbling weeds tumbling 'round, running from your subconscious. . . . Minds? Minds that won't let you stop to listen to a word of artistic or meaningful truth. . . . You don't want to see your ugly selves, the untruths, the lies you give to life. So you come to me, you sit in the front row, as noisy as can be. I listen to your millions of conversations, sometimes pulling them all up and putting them together and writing a symphony. But you never hear that symphony. . . . All of you sit there, digging yourselves and each other, looking around hoping to be seen and observed as hip. *You* become the object you came to see, and you think you're important and digging jazz when all the time all you're doing is digging a blind, deaf scene that has nothing to do with any kind of music at all.

Mingus then turned his tirade back to the gossiping African American woman at the front table, hissing facetiously that "I might dedicate to the mother who brought along a neighbor and talked three sets and two intermissions about the old man across the hall making it with Mrs. Jones' son . . . giggle giggle." The woman, however, refused to be cowed and retorted that she "has to listen to jazz all day long" and "lives on [the stuff]," therefore earning the right to talk through the performance if she wished.[55]

Mingus's exchange with this "jazzy mother" revealed how music was woven into the fabric of daily life—including the nightclub as a gathering place for community, and the storytelling that helped to string it together. Equally importantly, however, was Mingus's accusation that Five Spot patrons had "become the object you came to see," a phrase that had a dual meaning within the nightclub underground. First, and most obvious, was the club as a social space, where one's position as an aficionado or bohemian scenester was on display, overshadowing its role as a musical space. Yet Mingus's rant was met with shouts of approval, as the audience called out, "Bravo!," "Tell 'em Charlie!," "Someone has been needing to say that for years!," and "Most of us want to listen." This response highlights the participatory undercurrent of live jazz, in which community aspects and self-revelation became fully intertwined with the act of improvisation. Mingus himself wrote about this esoteric interaction in an un-published draft of his autobiography, suggesting that informed audiences knew that "if I didn't begin to write at the moment of my creative urgency I'd be no more."[56] At this secondary level of meaning, the division of subject and object blurred into a unitary process of becoming, which carried liberatory potential for this interracial milieu.

The nightclub's dark spaces were central to this process. Much like movie-theater audiences, nightclub patrons were able to project their own layers of meaning onto the performers. As they gazed through the cigarette smoke and remained hidden from the musicians' view in the contrast between the stage lights and the darkened club, audiences could inscribe their desires onto the players.[57] The racial implications of this are clear and present: for white audiences, black jazzmen were often symbols of un-fettered sexuality, prowess, spontaneity, and mystery. Yet musical improvisation is an aural process. The sound of an audience/performer interaction (or its silence) is just as important as its spectacle. Therefore, this subject/object relationship became, for many musicians, mutually constructive—even allowing for a reversal of social hier-archies (at least temporarily).

Perhaps the most striking illustration of this was the cross-racial identification de-scribed in Jack Kerouac's *On the Road*. In his depictions of jazz clubs—alongside his protagonists' ecstatic shouts for black jazzmen to "Blow for me, man, blow!" and to take their solos to new heights, to "Go, go, go!"—are pauses in which Sal Paradise and Dean Moriarty identify different instrumentalists, according to their resem-blance to various Beats. "It's Carlo Marx!" announces Moriarty about a bookish saxo-phonist who shares the appearance and demeanor of Allen Ginsberg's bespectacled alter ego. Yet this trope is not reducible to race. Rather, it represents identification as a way of rendering the new as familiar, even within the very act of rebellion. "It's Old Bull Lee!" shouts Moriarty as dawn breaks, seeing a fidgety white man resem-bling the fictionalized William Burroughs.

Later, Paradise aches to shrug off his troubles, "wishing I were a Negro, feeling that the best the white world had offered was not enough ecstasy for me, not enough life, joy, kicks, darkness, music, not enough night," wishing that he could be "a Denver Mexican, or even a poor overworked Jap, anything but what I was so drearily, a 'white man' disillusioned."[58] This problematic passage has rightly drawn reams of criticism for its assumption of white privilege and its erasure of racial oppression, portraying "happy, true hearted, ecstatic Negroes of America" in a style uncomfortably close to minstrelsy or southern myths of the contented plantation slave. Yet Kerouac's novel was also a sign of slow, uneven, but significant historical change: the gradual erosion of social hierarchy, a rejection of the Kiplingesque white man's burden as an ideology that sustained American racial caste. Kerouac signaled this by identifying himself, in quotation marks, as a "white man," suggesting the fluidity of racial identity. The jazz club was where this fluidity took on a new form, as a coalescence of sight, sound, and identity transformation.

Cultural critics have argued that Kerouac's representations of jazzmen created a one-dimensional, patronizing view of African Americans' "nature." But this criticism fails to recognize the multiple levels of meaning within the jazz nightclub, seen as a historical phenomenon. Minstrelsy, for instance, relied on a racial discourse that only allowed for the gaze of white spectators. Yet Kerouac's *The Subterraneans*, in which the 1958 roman à clef's protagonist takes his African American love interest, Mardou, to hear Charlie "Bird" Parker at the Red Drum, describes Parker watching the couple from the stage, with the saxophonist "digging Mardou several times." Blessing the new union with his eyes and his music, Bird was "the kindest jazz musician there could be." Kerouac thus invests the black viewpoint not only with agency, but with authority, suggesting that the jazzman's beneficence toward their transgressive relationship was worth more than the era's dominant view—a complete *reversal* of the social hierarchy in the 1950s. Furthermore, critics often ignore the reciprocal process of jazz improvisation. As Kerouac effused, "The king and founder of the bop generation . . . digging his audience digging the eyes, the secret eyes himself watching, as he just pursed his lips and let great lungs and immortal fingers work." Throughout *The Subterraneans*, references to the eye and to vision imply seeking, longing, desire, and passionate intellect.[59] It was the *communication* between an audience and a performer, which so many jazz greats have noted as fundamental to live improvisation, that underpinned these representations of musical virtuosity.

Whatever shortcomings Kerouac's fiction may have had in its portrayal of Parker's full humanity offstage, the historical fact remains that he *was* one of the few white fans to follow the early beboppers at Minton's—which, at least according to one fellow musician, earned him the admiration of players like Dizzy Gillespie. Doubtless, both Pony Poindexter and Slim Gaillard noted Kerouac's presence at their shows, welcoming him as a great listener. "Jack showed up every night," recalled Gaillard, "and stood with his back against the wall and while he listened, all the girls would cruise by and admire him. Between sets, I'd stand there right next to him."[60] Although Parker's personal life is never explored in Kerouac's novels, the lives of *other* less-known musicians are given fuller and more sympathetic treatment, integrated into Kerouac's subjective "mad" world.

On the Road includes one such scene. At daybreak, after a late night in a San Francisco jazz club, Moriarty and Paradise accompanied their African American friend Walter back to his apartment, where they "sat around the humble table to drink the beer and tell the stories." Kerouac's portrayal of black life was problematic, with Walter's "tenement" being part of a bohemian nocturnal picturesque that contrasted with the staid white world: "Holy flowers floating in the air, were all these tired faces in the dawn of Jazz America." (Not to mention that his admiration grew in part from Walter's domination of his wife, who "never said a word.")[61] Yet Kerouac's inclusion of these conversations, in spaces suggesting social equality and intimacy, drew the faint but visible outlines of a cross-racial community in the 1950s that was decidedly uncommon elsewhere, but which sometimes took shape in Greenwich Village and North Beach. While Kerouac claimed a more privileged position in this process for the Beats than they were due, he nonetheless represented the audience's perspective in a dialectic that most jazz musicians understood as fundamental to improvisation: the synergy between players and listeners.[62] Kerouac celebrated this interaction, blurring the (color) line between jazzmen and their audiences, claiming interracial alliances (however illusory), and questioning American assumptions of racial caste (however erratically).

The "roots and routes" (to borrow Paul Gilroy's inimitable phrase) of jazz as a cross-racial cultural production were certainly not linear and neat. They ramified and tangled, branching in reaction to new environments, to modernity and countermodernity, to racism and antiracism, twisting back on themselves, attracted by difference and novelty, by affinity, by tradition, and by familiarity.[63] Mingus's novel illustrated these roots and routes, depicting an all-star jam session in ecstatic style, but with an insider's sense that often eluded Kerouac and captured the multilayered meanings of jazz improvisation:

> "When are you motherfuckers going to stop talking and start playing, instead of Dodo and Stan over there jacking off?"
>
> "Miles, you're so vulgar."
>
> "I want to hear Bird blow, not all this dumb-ass conversation."
>
> "So gone. One, two, three, four."
>
> "Yeah, Bird. Play, baby! Go, man!"
>
> "Hooray!"
>
> "Ladies and gentlemen, will you all shut up and just listen to this motherfucker blowing!"
>
> "Miles! Careful, man, you can't say that."
>
> "Schitt, man, I put my hand over the mike on 'motherfucker.' Remember Monk calling the club owner in Detroit a motherfucker seven times on the mike 'cause he didn't have a good piano?"
>
> "He had it next night though. If he'd called him 'sir' he'd of had the same old clunker."
>
> "Who's this Buddy Collette, Mingus? . . ."
>
> "He plays flute, clarinet, everything—just like the white man says you're supposed to play and a little fuller."

"Cat named Paul Desmond up in Frisco plays like that. You heard him? . . ."

"Go on, Dodo! Man, that ofay sure can play! And that drummer too. What's his name?"

"Stan Levy [*sic*]. He's a Jew. You know them Jew boys got soul and gone."

"Gone. Take it out. . . . Hooray! Yeah!!"

Such praise for "ofays," a slang term for "whites," was uncommon among black jazzmen, yet Stan Levey and a handful of others were continually singled out by those such as Gillespie as excellent musicians—to the extent that black bandleaders were sometimes willing to test the bounds of segregation on tours in the midwest or the south, despite a greater risk than that for their white counterparts.[64]

The jazz underground was no utopia, however. Despite its many communal aspects, nightclub culture had its divisions. Not all musicians agreed that audiences participated in jazz club improvisation, instead insisting it was merely "practicing in public" and that musical technique and preparation were primary. Along similar lines, Kenneth Rexroth criticized the Beats' romantic primitivism, calling them "debauched Puritans" who "embrace the false image [of the American Negro] which their enemies the squares have painted." He then illustrated his point: "As Charles Mingus once said to me, 'We didn't evolve the new forms of modern jazz in dirty cellars full of dope peddlers. We worked it out in people's homes, which we didn't call pads either. And our families stood around and listened and approved.'"[65] Lines of gender and sexuality further separated performers and audiences. The misogyny in Mingus's memoir was more extreme than most, but its homophobia was fairly typical in the jazz world, associating homosexuality with weakness, filth, or criminality. Jazz musicians and Beats—including those like Billie Holiday and Jack Kerouac, who were bisexual—routinely spoke in derogatory tones of "faggots" and "dykes."[66]

Yet tensions and controversies over race remained at their most contentious in the jazz world. For instance, Dave Brubeck's meteoric rise drew a major outcry from black musicians, who saw the media's preference for this white performer, despite his more watered-down cool style. Conversely, journalists condemned blacks' rejection of white jazzmen as racist "Crow Jim." Indications of racially divided audiences were common, such as Art Blakey's famously exaggerated pronouncement that Bird held no allure for black audiences who "don't even know him" and had "never heard of him and care less."[67] Pony Poindexter expressed dislike for white slummers who came to San Francisco's Bop City, bringing police raids in their wake. And African American critics frequently decried the predominantly white audiences in jazz clubs, reflecting the feeling that jazz was an authentic black art form "which 'we' are largely responsible for." Most significantly, black musicians resented the preponderance of white nightclub ownership. Black-owned clubs remained in segregated areas, such as Small's Paradise in Harlem or Bop City in the Fillmore District, but the mass media largely ignored these venues, forcing musicians to perform in the Village or North Beach if they wanted to advance their careers. Nightclubs were first and foremost businesses, with mostly slim profit margins, and owners often became antagonists. To musicians, in the words of Orrin Keepnews, owners were "not exactly the *enemy*," but "at least the *opposition*."[68]

Rexroth concurred, privately complaining that "nightclub owners & bookers *etc are* really about the worst people there are." Poindexter was even more blunt, betraying an undercurrent of anti-Semitism by singling out Jewish proprietors and stating that white-controlled clubs and media offered "jazz directed at white audiences and presented in such a manner as to exclude most of the black players." Mingus's admiration for Stan Levey belied a similar streak of anti-Semitism, although the bassist also declared solidarity with Jews as fellow sufferers under white supremacy.[69] Jazz scholars have rightly argued that white understandings of jazz often relied on notions of "color blindness," which made the social and political histories that informed black music invisible. Moreover, this blindness paved the way for white liberal resistance to the kind of collectivism that might have offered deeper solutions to economic and social inequalities. Even Brubeck's and Gillespie's universalism, most notably displayed during State Department–sponsored global tours, carried shades of American cultural imperialism, with jazz used as a pawn in the larger Cold War game of wooing nonaligned African and Asian nations and opening new markets.[70]

Yet alongside these conflicts were acknowledgments of interracial solidarity—even from those like Poindexter, whose memoir was steeped in Black Power sensibilities. He noted that the Black Hawk was a "favorite hangout for those so inclined—black and white," where "we had a ball" playing with the Brubeck Quartet, until the media inequitably raised Brubeck's star (and salary). Poindexter also praised the Coffee Gallery and the Cellar's "pure bop" and "beatnik" patrons, who came to hear him back Rexroth's and Ferlinghetti's poetry readings. While he was a sharp critic of Rexroth as "a performer," with "no sense of drama" and, worse, "no sense of rhythm," Poindexter nonetheless praised the "substance of his poetry [that] spoke of the depth of his being turned on by a black woman," which he read "with a sort of passion and this got him over." Poindexter reveled in North Beach's interracial community, where "everything was swinging." This unity was marred only by police harassment of mixed couples and the occasional racist "cracker" in the audience, for whom the scene "defied all their ideas of what life should be in America."[71] These transgressive spaces could be culturally effective—even if patrons were not always conscious of their underlying politics.

Currents of jazz universalism in no way canceled out the racism that haunted nightclub culture. But while patrons came mostly for the music and merrymaking, undercurrents of social critique did occasionally surface. Given that interracial relations were so rare in the 1950s, these conversations were all the more poignant. Poindexter, for example, remembered the political discussions during breakfasts that followed all-night jams at Bop City, in which the Korean War, immigration policy, municipal corruption, and the "fact that racism is so ingrained in the United States" were topics du jour. He recalled the whole San Francisco jazz/bohemian scene as being intellectual, because "cats understood about poetry, they understood about sculpture—and they understood about jazz."[72] Players like John Coltrane often spoke of jazz as a "force for unity," while his nightclub audiences—which one journalist estimated to be just under half black—were described as a miniature United Nations. Coltrane continually emphasized the style's universalism, insisting (even in the Black Power era of the late 1960s) that there was little difference between black and white audiences (or, strikingly, musicians), asserting that jazz had "nothing to do with questions of skin color." It seems somehow appropriate that when a friend who headed the Interracial Jazz Society in Baltimore wanted to send Coltrane a Christmas card in 1957, he sent it to the Five Spot Café.[73]

Give Me Liberty!: Mingus, Brubeck, and the Freedom Struggle

Throughout the 1950s, Rebel Café nightclubs fermented a potent concoction of racial integration, black self-determination, urban cosmopolitanism, and left-wing cabaret sensibilities. This often included folk music in addition to jazz. Despite the relative invisibility black women suffered in the 1950s, reflected in nightspots having long been coded as masculine, women increasingly claimed these sites of social, cultural, and sexual expression. Even as the media focused primarily on male performers, a key group of audacious entertainers, including Maya Angelou and folk singer Odetta, fought for a place in the spotlight.[74] Both came to prominence within the queer world of San Francisco nightclubs, at the Tin Angel and the Purple Onion, respectively. Angelou, in particular, having started as a nightclub calypso singer and dancer, followed threads of connection through the nightclub underground of the 1950s and 1960s and established herself as a national figure who blended her art with activism, becoming one of the most prominent and eloquent voices for racial justice in America. Similarly, calypso singer Harry Belafonte became a major figure of outspoken black self-determination. Starting at the Village Vanguard, he grew to be a massively popular recording and movie star who demanded control of his own career and dignity for all of black America. Alongside folk music's tradition of social protest, going back to Woody Guthrie and Leadbelly, this progressive musical approach became part of a critical social discourse that joined national discussions about the most recent phase of the black freedom struggle. As the modern civil rights movement heated up in the early 1960s, Angelou, Odetta, and Belafonte each backed their socially conscious cultural work with political action, participating in benefit concerts for organizations such as CORE and SNCC.[75]

Nonetheless, despite the national popularity of Angelou's, Odetta's, and Belafonte's African American folk styles, the most potent musical expression of social protest in the nightclub underground of the 1950s was jazz. Why? Because it spoke to those alienated from the norms of Cold War America. Jazz represented mystery, which could only be unraveled by those in the know, those who were hip. But it paradoxically also invoked black self-determination and democracy, with its dialectic of the individual voice working within a group. This medley of meaning perfectly suited an oppositional underground that was still inchoate but reaching toward a new kind of American Left—one that could both reject Soviet totalitarianism and embrace a "beloved community" of collective economic and racial justice. Rock & roll's impulse was similar, but in the 1950s it appealed mostly to teens and was dismissed by critics as the silly stuff of school dances. While rock's brand of cultural rebellion sold at a record pace, it was not the soundtrack of political rebellion until the 1960s. In the meantime, jazz filled the Cold War void. As the din of geopolitical saber rattling clattered over calls for universalism—and wide-eyed confrontations with the atomic threat bred nihilism in the American psyche—the dissonant, contrapuntal, antiphonal, harmonic, and sometimes atonal sound of modern jazz was a perfect musical vessel for postwar oppositional consciousness.

The interracial community fostered in New York and San Francisco nightclubs participated in a groundswell of support for African American civil rights in the late 1950s and early 1960s that, in part, rested on white liberal associations between cosmopolitanism and sophistication. These associations fortified indignation toward the vulgarities of southern Jim Crow laws and racial violence. But the universalism within jazz circles themselves, which was sometimes expressed in the activism of performers and club owners, was also significant. Since the end of World War II, New York City had been established as a global center of the arts, jazz, and print culture, what Nat Hentoff called "the most sophisticated city in the country" and Kerouac termed the "Nation of People . . . [where] Paper America is born." But San Francisco now shared its East Coast counterpart's jazzy cosmopolitan connotations—so much so that Herb Caen declared it a truism, with "the good jazz of Cal Tjader filtering out of the Black Hawk and getting lost under the stars that shine down on Turk Street," enlivening the "Pearl of the Pacific" as a "port of call for half the world and beloved landmark for the other half."[76] Jazz artists—from Dave Brubeck, Dizzy Gillespie, Chet Baker, and Billie Holiday to Charles Mingus, Miles Davis, and Gerry Mulligan—anchored themselves on both coasts at the Black Hawk, the Jazz Workshop, Birdland, and the Five Spot. But they also toured the national club circuit, stopping at Chicago's Blue Note, Detroit's Flame Show Bar, Kansas City's Orchid Lounge, and innumerable roadhouses and concert halls across the midwest and the south.[77] With each show, in combination with publicity and protests, they signaled to the nation that jazz's artistry stood out as opposed to racial discrimination.

These networks had political implications, connecting a new generation of musicians with Popular Front activists and civil rights organizations. After an early New York appearance by the Brubeck Quartet, Paul Desmond wrote excitedly to his father that John Hammond and Judy Holliday were in attendance. Hammond recruited Brubeck for a series of benefit concerts, solidifying the piano man's place in socially conscious entertainment circles well into the 1960s (when Hammond would similarly work with Bob Dylan and Aretha Franklin).[78] Brubeck did not need much convincing. He soon became an outspoken voice for racial equality, who cemented his role in the black freedom struggle through a series of events in the 1950s and early 1960s. In

1957, Brubeck canceled a concert in Dallas when promoters refused his demand to integrate the audience. Similarly, after African American bassist Eugene Wright joined the group in 1958, Brubeck turned down shows in Athens, Georgia, as well as in South Africa during their State Department tour, when local officials insisted that he replace Wright. And in 1960, all but three out of twenty-five college concert dates in the quartet's southern US tour were canceled as segregated schools spurned the "mixed group" and Brubeck again refused to replace Wright.[79]

As Brubeck challenged the social-spatial divisions of segregation, it was significant that he, a symbol of jazz sophistication since his 1954 appearance on the cover of *Time*, had increasingly moved from nightclubs to college concerts.[80] His cancellation of the Dallas show in 1957 coincided with the tumultuous integration of Central High School in Little Rock, Arkansas, during which federal troops were used to overcome Governor Faubus's staunch opposition. "This racial aspect of American life is at best tragic," wrote an African American friend to Brubeck in the wake of these events, adding that racism "interferes with my effectiveness to act as an individual citizen . . . [so] thank you for taking such a stand." Expressly tying inclusion to liberty, this friend continued: "Some people feel that they have the right to draw lines that exclude people and/or groups from the human family. . . . Once freedom is denied further denials of rights become easier." He concluded on a hopeful note, echoing the highest aims of the civil rights movement by stating, "Our greatest salvation as Americans is that we are making greater strides in human relations than any other country in the world."[81]

The canceled 1960 tour sparked a firestorm of publicity, as Ralph Gleason's coverage was picked up by African American newspapers and the Associated Press just days before the famous sit-ins, calling for integrated lunch counters, began in North Carolina. Yet racially mixed groups had long performed in southern nightclubs without much notice—an indication of the divide between nightlife experiences and the politics of institutionalized racism and state power. The difference was that Brubeck was bringing this nightclub sensibility to the surface, as implied in the title of his breakthrough 1954 album, *Jazz Goes to College*. Following the dean of Southeastern Louisiana University's notification to Brubeck's agent that "we would not take a mixed group," the University of Mississippi, Millsaps College in Jackson, Mississippi, the Georgia Institute of Technology, and a host of other schools likewise cancelled their bookings. "The trouble is not with the students," Brubeck insightfully (and tactfully) stated. "It's the state college officials, who do not want to be cut off from state funds over this matter." Desmond concurred, adding a satirical jab that invoked Cold War civil rights: "I feel sorry for the kids down there, but maybe all is not yet lost. The State Department could always send us on a tour through the south!"[82]

Added to this mix was a financial component that ignored questions of structural inequality but fit progressive liberal notions of shared sacrifice in the name of social justice. Brubeck forfeited $40,000 in profits from the tour, rather than replace Wright. Out of this, Desmond earned a percentage, while the rhythm section, including

Wright, received a set salary. Letters of support, including one from the NAACP, praising Brubeck's insistence that the "group is interracial and will remain so" and stating that "we do not underestimate the financing loss incurred nor do we overestimate the very valuable and tangible contribution that you have made to the fight for human rights." By choosing "friendship and craftsmanship" over money, Brubeck had "given us all an example of what is at the beating heart of our American life: human honor."[83] Throughout the episode, Wright remained upbeat and above the fray, stating that if southerners "ever do get themselves together, they're in for a treat," and that "my feeling is, You don't lose when you know in your heart you're right." But he also betrayed his disappointment at a deeper sociocultural level, telling a reporter, "Wherever I go, I'll be playing the blues, the good old 100-year blues." As Gleason put it, "Brubeck's next Columbia LP is called *The Southern Scene.* On it, Eugene Wright plays a bass solo in 'Nobody Knows the Trouble I've Seen.'"[84]

By 1960, the nation could hear the sounds of African American protests that were more unmistakable than Wright's solo. It is no coincidence that the first sit-ins took place in college-town eateries. SNCC's founders, like many young Americans, were familiar with the Rebel Café milieu, so the idea of claiming public space in places of refreshment and discussion must have seemed obvious, albeit dangerous. As one of the organization's original members, Julian Bond, wrote poetically in the *Student Voice*, expressing the nightclub underground's jazz/folk sensibility and the ability of bebop virtuosos to inspire action:

I too, hear America singing
But from where I stand
I can only hear Little Richard
And Fats Domino. But sometimes,
I hear Ray Charles
Drowning in his own tears
or Bird
Relaxing at Camarillo
or Horace Silver doodling.
Then I don't mind standing a little longer.[85]

Two recordings that year reflected this claim on black visibility and public equality: Max Roach's *We Insist!: Freedom Now Suite* and *Charles Mingus Presents Charles Mingus.* The more notable was *We Insist!*, which, in addition to Abbey Lincoln's politically charged vocals, used a photo of a sit-in for its cover. Roach and Mingus had previously gained more control over their careers by founding their own record label, and Roach stated that *We Insist!* was originally conceived as musical theater, "commissioned by the Junior League of the NAACP in honor of the 100th anniversary of the Emancipation Proclamation."[86] The album's sensibilities were rooted in a Harlem community of cultural producers that included Maya Angelou. Songs like "Driva' Man" and "Freedom Day" were classic civil rights statements. With lyrics that compared modern racial oppression with slavery, the album's style drew on hard bop, blues, and even musical theater, with hints of *Porgy and Bess* and Duke Ellington's cultural front piece, *Jump for Joy*. Perhaps most significantly, given the context of its times, *We Insist!* channeled the sounds of gospel, invoking the churches that were fundamental to black political organizing—much like Ray Charles, who also gained widespread acclaim in 1960. The LP captured these elements most fully in the sound poem "Triptych: Prayer/Protest/Peace," while the percussion instrumental, "All Africa," stood as a pan-African statement and a musical precursor to the Black Arts Movement, led by Black Nationalists such as Amiri Baraka.

Mingus Presents also insisted on black public visibility and self-determination. Recorded for the same label as *We Insist!*—Candid Records, with Nat Hentoff in an advisory role—the album was part of a conscious effort among cultural producers to give the freedom struggle a voice. While *We Insist!* had slender ties to the nightclub scene (Roach and Lincoln met, for example, at Chicago's Black Orchid in 1957), *Mingus Presents* grew directly from the Rebel Café milieu. As described in Hentoff's liner notes, the songs evolved during a stint at Greenwich Village's Showplace Club, and the album's recording session was designed to "set a mood that might resemble a night in the club." This included dimming the studio lights and, most remarkably, recording the faux stage banter heard on the album, in which Mingus announces song titles and warns nonexistent patrons to refrain from talking and rattling cocktail glasses. "I finally realized," Mingus asserted, "that a lot of jazz records don't make it because guys almost unconsciously change their approach in a studio from what they do every night. I finally wanted to make an album the way we are on the job."[87]

As Mingus's gendered language suggests, the record is a testament to the muscular jazz that predominated in nightclubs of the 1950s. It also evoked the experimental and participatory aspects of nightclub culture, as suggested by the ambitious "All the Things You Could Be by Now if Sigmund Freud's Wife Was Your Mother," whose "title probably came from the way the audience was reacting one night." The song rested heavily on antiphony—call and response among instruments—and the wails, grunts, and cries of Eric Dolphy's saxophone, in conversation with Mingus's serpentine bass, signified an escape from culture-industry commercialism, a refusal of the demands of musical convention and the marketplace. Meanwhile, "Folk Forms, No. 1," with its aspects of jump-blues and R&B, forcefully reclaimed jazz as an expression of the African American community. Moreover, *Mingus Presents* embraced integration more fully than *We Insist!* This was most apparent in "Original Faubus Fables," which decried and satirized the Arkansas governor's obstructionism with its call-and-response shouts between Mingus and drummer Dannie Richmond, who shouted: "Nazi fascist supremists! He won't let us in his school—then he's a fool!" The song's dual refrains feature the two musical compatriots singing in unison, "Oh Lord, don't let them shoot us; oh Lord, don't let them stab us," and, deliberately echoing the chants of a determined crowd, "Two, four, six, eight, they brainwash and teach you hate!"

As the *New York Amsterdam News* reported in 1962, both Mingus and Roach, along with Miles Davis, gained dual reputations in the African American community as virtuosos and as jazz's angry men, refusing to kowtow to white tastes. That September, after finishing a run at the Five Spot, Mingus announced he was leaving the United States. A friend told the *Amsterdam News*, "Charlie is a little tired of our brand of democracy."[88] Although Mingus later abandoned this plan, he had made his point: black life in America must be lived on its own terms.

Mingus was not shy in pointing out pay discrepancies between himself and Dave Brubeck or Chet Baker—whom he considered weak imitations of Thelonious Monk and Miles Davis—which he expressly tied to black exploitation by the white culture industry:

> Jazz is big business to the white man and you can't move without him. . . . He owns the magazines, agencies, record companies and all the joints that sell jazz to the public. If you won't sell out and you try to fight they won't hire you and they give a bad picture of you with that false publicity. . . . Then if some honest club owner tries to get hold of you to book you, they tell [him] you're not available or you don't draw or you'll tear up the joint like you was a gorilla. . . . But if you behave, boy, you'll get booked—except for less than the white cats that copy your playing and likely either the agent or owner'll pocket the difference.[89]

While Mingus's critique finessed Davis's position as the highest-paid jazzman of the period (not to mention his own well-deserved reputation for tempestuousness among both white and black acquaintances), he nonetheless convincingly connected economic and political liberation.

Writing to a friend who was helping to collect royalties from a British record company, Mingus put his thoughts into characteristically direct and volatile terms: "Give me liberty or give me death. Yeah that's how I feel. Paul Revere style. . . . How did you get mixed up with such phoneys? Man that Crow stuff is all shot to hell, it's Freedom Day." His autobiography, *Beneath the Underdog*, recapitulated this sentiment in terms of armed self-defense and revolution. Like a jazzy reflection of radicals such as Huey Newton and Robert Williams, Mingus proclaimed that black musicians should follow the example of the American Revolution's founders and load up on "some heat, guns, cannons, and be willing to die like *they* was." He concluded by placing the tradition of American independence in the service of African American liberation: "That's all I heard when I was a kid, how bad they was and not afraid to die—to arms, to arms, and all that schitt. . . . Show me where that atomic power button is and I'll give them cocksuckers some liberty!"[90]

While *We Insist!* and *Mingus Presents* were not huge sellers by the standards of popular music (although Roach would later assert that the former "sold more copies than any record I've ever made"), they were nonetheless important cultural statements, serving as flash points of social commentary that ignited the protests rising from the nightclub underground.[91] As Farah Jasmine Griffin has argued in her study of Billie Holiday, black performers, aware of the invisibility of their lives to white society, cloaked themselves in a mantle of mystery. Nina Simone, painfully familiar with this tactic, explicitly rejected the racist assumptions that underpinned the myth of the mysterious jazz singer, recoiling from comparisons with Billie Holiday: "And I deeply resented it because the comparison had nothing to do with our musicianship and everything to do with the fact that we were both black . . . [because] in American society a black woman's talents are never truly seen for what they are."[92] The music of Roach, Lincoln, Mingus, and Simone demanded the recognition of their humanity, making the African American community visible and echoing the most vocal phase of the freedom struggle.

Few people enjoy being disabused of their pleasurable illusions, however, and many, if not most, white fans were loath to relinquish the allure of black mystery.[93] Yet the integrated spaces of jazz clubs offered openings that allowed white patrons a chance, for those willing to take it, to peer past received notions of race. Joyce Johnson's description of Billie Holiday's famed impromptu Five Spot performance, just before her death in 1959, illustrates this tentative shift:

> I remember one night when a middle-aged, sad-faced black woman stood up beside the table where she'd been sitting and sang so beautifully in a cracked, heart-broken voice I was sure I'd heard before. There was silence when she finished, then everyone rose and began clapping. It was the great Lady Day, who had been deprived of her cabaret card by the New York police and was soon to die under arrest in a hospital bed—subject of the famous poem by Frank O'Hara, who also heard Billie Holiday sing that night:

> Leaning in the john door in the 5 Spot
> While she whispered a song along the keyboard
> To Mal Waldron and everyone and I stopped breathing,[94]

With its references to Holiday's heartbroken voice and her death amid legal wrangling, this passage was a tenuous symbol of the move from black jazz as a picturesque form of noble suffering toward its recognition as a protest against institutional racism. Moreover, Frank O'Hara was a staunchly antiracist participant in the Village scene, described by Baraka as a friend whom he "admired [for] his genuine sophistication." O'Hara also offers one of the few ties between New York's gay and jazz scenes. His ode to Holiday was part of a larger movement to infuse jazz into poetry, as an impetus for social change—what one literary scholar has explicitly called "democratic symbolic action." Baraka viewed this as a way to break from Eurocentric aesthetics, stating, "It would be better if such a poet . . . listened to the tragic verse of a Billie Holiday, than be content to imperfectly imitate the bad poetry of the ruined minds of Europe."[95]

Many in the jazz world went beyond art and engaged more directly in political action. And Rebel Café nightclubs were often sites in which aesthetics and politics became publicly coupled. Max Roach's first public performance of *We Insist!* was at a Village Gate benefit show for CORE, the organization that supported the Freedom Riders' fight to desegregate interstate buses in 1961.[96] It is no surprise that Roach debuted his politically charged work at D'Lugoff's nightclub. The Village Gate was frequently the site of civil rights benefits—particularly for SNCC—that featured folk singers such as Pete Seeger and Theodore Bikel alongside jazzier fare, including by Thelonious Monk. D'Lugoff was quick to aid the southern sit-ins and their supporting organizations. For example, in 1960, the Village Gate featured four stand-alone civil rights benefits, plus the weekly *Cabaret for Freedom*, which supported Martin Luther King Jr.'s Southern Christian Leadership Conference (SCLC). Maya Angelou recalled becoming directly active in civil rights through connections she made at the Gate when starring in *Cabaret for Freedom*. The public commitment to social justice that shone through her performances convinced Bayard Rustin to offer her a position with the SCLC. Along with Roach's and Lincoln's Village appearances— echoing the blazing speeches of Malcolm X—Angelou recalled that during this period, "the world was on fire." Continuing to carry the torch for freedom, in 1965 Simone and D'Lugoff, along with Langston Hughes, traveled to the civil rights demonstrations in Selma and Montgomery, Alabama—which were largely responsible for pressuring Lyndon Johnson to push through the Voting Rights Act—where she, Odetta, Harry Belafonte, and Dick Gregory performed for the marchers.[97]

In San Francisco, the Cellar and the Jazz Workshop raised $2,200 for the Freedom Riders in June 1961, presenting performers such as Dizzy Gillespie and Pony Poindexter. In a more populist vein, Ray Charles benefitted the NAACP, appearing at the Longshoremen's Auditorium. Ralph Gleason praised Charles's gospel and soul as the sound of the folk, calling him "an artist who spoke for the people." Gleason may have been hyperbolic when he suggested that this signaled America's moral reawakening, but he was correct in stating that these shows contributed to a groundswell of public opinion supporting civil rights.[98] In other large venues, jazzmen from Monk to Mingus also supported SNCC, most memorably at a Carnegie Hall concert in February 1963. Brubeck lent his name as a sponsor of the event. Despite the warnings of his agent that "I hate like the devil to see you take these kinds of dates," due to the loss of revenue, Brubeck agreed to another SNCC benefit in November. He also personally donated to both SNCC and the Highlander Folk School, which trained activists in nonviolent civil disobedience. Brubeck specifically earmarked revenue derived from southern performances, feeling that he was "putting Southern money to good work conquering the civil rights problem."[99]

Both fundraising and the rising public profile of the civil rights movement drew on long-existing social networks. John Hammond helped to connect Brubeck with the Highlander school, as he had with earlier benefit shows. Ivan Black, Theodore Bikel, and Lorraine Hansberry were among those who kept the pianist in contact with SNCC's organizing needs. Black, whom D'Lugoff had "inherited" from Cafe Society's Barney Josephson—and whose vocal opposition to HUAC had made him reliant on nightclubs as a source of income—was a key liaison between Village nightclubs and SNCC. Black organized civil rights benefits throughout the early 1960s, including a 1963 concert supporting CORE at the Five Spot, with Thelonious Monk and Bill Evans.[100]

These benefits used the networks of the jazz underground to help establish an independent source of funding for civil rights organizing. Yet they also showed the limits of white liberal support. For instance, Brubeck began to turn down benefit shows in 1965, claiming that despite his "sympathy with . . . 'the cause' . . . the time has come when we are besieged with so many requests for free appearances for worthy causes that we are forced to decline most of them, simply to maintain our value on the concert circuit." Brubeck still remained vocal about racial justice in 1968, however, declaring that, although the movement had "won" the battle for school integration, the United States had failed to live up to its "basic guarantee which is equality of man to our citizens."[101]

At the grassroots level, the effect of Rebel Café culture on a new generation of subterraneans was equally fundamental to change in the 1960s. Paul Krassner—the radical satirist, publisher of the *Realist*, and cofounder of the Yippies, with the infamous Abbie Hoffman—began his career doing standup comedy at the Five Spot. Similarly, the poet and activist Ed Sanders first found his main inspiration for action in leftist poet Lawrence Ferlinghetti's 1959 reading at the Village Gate. By 1961, Sanders was participating in the freedom struggle and peace marches; the next year, he was jailed in the south for civil rights organizing. Throughout the 1960s, Sanders stayed active in both New Left politics and the artistic counterculture.[102] Sanders and Krassner were singular examples, becoming countercultural celebrities. Yet they represented the experiences of thousands of others whose views were guided by, and sometimes formed within, the Rebel Café. As late as 1965, well after the Beatles' arrival in the United States made jazz less than synonymous with young radicals, San Francisco activists continued to associate the civil rights scene of CORE and SNCC with Rebel Café clubs. Even as the nation's attention turned toward antiwar demonstrations and the free speech movement's protests, the city's emerging countercultural press routinely promoted benefits at the Coffee Gallery featuring jazz, folk, and experimental films; shows at the Jazz Workshop with activist jazzman John Handy; or the "sensitive and arresting" music of Horace Silver.[103] Like SNCC's Julian Bond, they, too, heard America singing.

beatniks and blabbermouths, bartok and bar talk

New Bohemia and the Search for Community

> Every act of rebellion expresses a nostalgia for innocence and an appeal to the essence of being. . . . Human rebellion ends in metaphysical revolution. It progresses from appearances to acts, from the dandy to the revolutionary. . . . Beauty, no doubt, does not make revolutions. But a day will come when revolutions will have need of beauty.
> **Albert Camus, *The Rebel: An Essay on Man in Revolt*, 1951**

> Perhaps the only reason they survived . . . was that they were not alone. God knew how many more there were with a hothouse sense of time, no knowledge of life, and at the Mercy of Fortune.
> **Thomas Pynchon, *V.: A Novel*, 1963**

"Now the lowly saloon is seldom praised in our society," wrote San Francisco jazz critic Ralph Gleason in 1961. "So let us here for a moment say a few words in the defense of this democratic institution."[1] As an advocate for the egalitarian potential of jazz nightclubs, Gleason had good cause for championing the lowly saloon. For over a decade, Rebel Café nightspots in North Beach had fostered a community of cutting-edge literary figures and intellectuals. In much the same way as the urban working-class saloons of the nineteenth century had provided information and support for social networks, unionization, and employment, in the 1950s, bohemian literary bars served the material and psychological needs of their poetic patrons. The result was a particular kind of nightspot, a New Saloon that fed the minds and bodies of the New Bohemians who frequented them. Throughout the 1950s, the jazz/folk sensibility that had helped transform identities and create communities was also intertwined with the evolution of American bohemianism. As the Beat generation's literary and social movement gained momentum, and a renewed conversation about oppositional activism heated up in the radical bars and cafés of North Beach and the Village, the Cold War's public sphere was revitalized.

Similarly, the spirit of the 1930s left-wing cabaret survived into the 1950s. Yet this ethos was transformed by hot and cold wars, losing its more partisan aspects. Rebels and cultural radicals often soaked up the anarchist principles of those such as Paul Goodman or Kenneth Rexroth, invoking *communitas* but also focusing inward on their own consciousness. As the poet and antiwar activist Denise Levertov later put it, the goal was to seek liberation for the individual within group action, "to realize how much the apparently external problems have their parallels within us." She asserted that in "dialogue with himself," the artist clarifies "not answers but the existence and nature of questions." Levertov openly channeled a current of thought that ran underground in bohemia: that oppositional culture could outline new ways of living, and that the "peculiarly human" act of artistic creation was "in the most profound sense, a 'social' or 'political' action."[2] While debates certainly raged among bohemians over how obviously political their work should be, by the 1950s, even the most open of the activists saw themselves less as *members* of political institutions than as individual *participants* in social movements—a shift away from the collectivist ideology of the Old Left.

With the Red Scare underway, bohemian opposition blended a changing leftism with avant-garde artistry and transgressive social norms. A prime example of the challenges facing rebel artists was the cancellation of revered poet William Carlos Williams's Library of Congress post in 1953, due to his marginally leftist past, which marked a low point in America's public support for dissident arts. Although some of the academic posts that many writers relied on remained available for those like Lawrence Ferlinghetti, the owner of City Lights Books, it was only when "there was no wafer to be eaten [i.e., a loyalty oath] to get the job." This says nothing about the frequently open restrictions against gays and lesbians, exemplified by the Lavender Scare purge of homosexuals from federal jobs during the Truman and Eisenhower administrations. Within these narrowed economic opportunities, Rebel Café sites offered both moral and financial support through bartending, poetry readings, or sales of little magazines. While San Francisco law (and, usually, New York custom) prevented women from bartending, nightspot ownership bypassed this prohibition, opening opportunities for a host of entrepreneurs within the bohemian and lesbian communities, such as Ann Dee of Ann's 440 and Peggy Tolk-Watkins of the Tin Angel.[3] Yet women's often-muted public voices testify to the resistance they faced as cultural producers, both in society as a whole and within the Rebel Café. Only slowly, as a new generation arrived in North Beach and the Village in the late 1950s, would women claim a more equal place in the national public sphere.

In the meantime, members of the San Francisco–New York bicoastal bohemia—labeled as the Beat generation, New Bohemia, or, dismissively, beatnik—found ways to live outside the mainstream of American consumerist society. Haunted by the mythical "man in the gray flannel suit" of the 1950s novel and film by that name, bohemians rejected the postwar affluence that came with US domination of the global economy and mass unionization as little more than a path to mechanized regimentation, whether in a factory or its corporate offices. Whatever inverted elitism was present in this rejection of bourgeois comforts, the Beats rightly noted that the

Korean conflict, the oppression of minorities, and a looming nuclear apocalypse darkened the supposed dawn of a new, industrial Golden Age. Individual tactics varied, but almost all bohemians relied on Rebel Café nightspots for mutual support. Across New Bohemia, nightspots were extensions of urban pads, the cheap lofts and cold-water flats furnished with little more than cinder-block-and-plank bookshelves that were filled with used paperbacks, a bare mattress, an "unpainted wooden chair," and "a scarred drop-leaf kitchen table."[4] Equally importantly, sites like the Cellar, the Coffee Gallery, and the Coexistence Bagel Shop in North Beach, or the San Remo, the White Horse Tavern, and the Cedar Tavern in the Village, connected underground networks—literally and literarily.

Nightspots were ports of call for subterranean wayfarers in a pre-digital age, where letters were received and phone messages relayed to restless young seekers who seldom kept a steady address. Within these left-wing bohemian spaces, transgressive talk was common and traditional boundaries were blurred as bohemians developed aesthetic affiliations that replaced the private sphere of the family with hip cosmopolitan alliances. The result was a fully functioning, if ephemeral, intentional community, an interregnum between the utopian experiments of the nineteenth century and the counterculture hippie communes in the 1960s.[5]

The most important part of this development occurred in North Beach, particularly in a literary bar simply called The Place. While North Beach has become popularly associated with Jack Kerouac, Allen Ginsberg, and other Beat generation writers, in the 1950s it was populated by a host of lesser known poets and painters who celebrated the underside of modern America. New Saloons nurtured an interracial, queer, and bohemian culture that the Beats entered and used to solidify the literary style they had been crafting since the 1940s. North Beach was a platform from which the Beat movement was launched, most notably with Ginsberg's reading of his poem "Howl" at the 6 Gallery in 1955.

The Beat movement was the final link that firmly connected North Beach with Greenwich Village dissidents. Yet its popularity also disrupted the bicoastal bohemia's previous isolation. What had been a mutually supportive (albeit artistically snarky) community—often described by its denizens as a kind of therapeutic, alternative school of aesthetic anarchism—quickly became public. The New Bohemia therefore took on a function that could be described as socially Freudian, raising America's underlying, unconscious, instinctual drives to the surface, where the pleasure principle and the death instinct were examined freely, often through the lens of dark humor and satire—a sort of national talk therapy. Conversely, the expansion of the Beat ethos into the American mainstream by the 1960s obscured its place in the history of the 1950s.

Ultimately, bohemia was less revolutionary than simply rebellious. Rather than replacing the old order, it became a Rabelaisian politics of opposition. Its carnivalesque critique was a performative stage for the more active social shifts that followed. Instead of attempting to overturn capitalism or level class divisions, à la the

Bolsheviks, bohemians simply refused to participate, instead forming mutually supportive communities as liberatory pockets within the larger system. This should not be dismissed as unimportant, however. New Bohemia was a significant social space for dissenting women, African Americans, gays, and lesbians years before the rise of second-wave feminism, the March on Washington, or the Stonewall Inn revolt. Changes were continually contested from within and without, and some participants used the privileges of whiteness or masculinity to aid their ambitions. For women, the threat of misogynistic violence posed a continual challenge, as did the social and medical risks of sex in a pre-pill, pre–*Roe v. Wade* world. Nonetheless, while bohemian antimaterialism and its claims on urban public spaces didn't turn American society on its head, they did set a significant precedent. They established the Rebel Café as an outpost of possibility for a new wave of personal politics that focused as much inwardly, on the relationship between freedom and identity, as on social or economic structures.

The New Saloon and The Place

Just as 1953 was a pivotal year for the Cold War, with the death of Stalin, the end of the Korean War, and the beginning of McCarthy's slide into disrepute, it was also momentous for the bicoastal bohemian community. That year, The Place opened in North Beach, at 1546 Grant Street, a few blocks north of Broadway. Owners Knute Stiles and Leo Krikorian—alumni of the experimental Black Mountain College— opened the bar as an extension of their anarchist politics and aesthetic ambitions, that is, as a space for public discussion and art. In its seven-year run, The Place probably defined the tone of New Bohemia more than any other nightspot, with its jazzy mix of radical bohemian, literary, and queer cultures.

Stiles and Krikorian had solidified their friendship in left-wing bohemian circles during the late 1940s. After they both left Black Mountain College, Stiles attended the New School in Manhattan, and they roomed together in Krikorian's "commune in the Bronx"—a shared space that welcomed other Black Mountain alumni. Stiles attended anarchist meetings and connected with radical West Coast poets such as Philip Lamantia, Tram Combs, and Robert Duncan (who had also taught briefly at Black Mountain). He then followed Krikorian to San Francisco in 1949. Both Stiles and Krikorian flourished in North Beach's Black Cat / Vesuvio scene, yet each embodied a different aspect of subterranean nightlife. Stiles, a writer and painter, was gay and politically active, while Krikorian was straight and largely apolitical, a photographer and a libertine.[6] Their differences complemented each other, and the tiny bar's atmosphere attracted a dedicated core of patrons.

In many ways, Krikorian was the archetypal Rebel Café owner, a real-life echo of the fictional saloonkeepers concocted by playwright William Saroyan, whom he once met as a youth. Krikorian's parents, fleeing persecution by the Turks in Armenia, immigrated to the United States in the 1910s and settled near Fresno, California, where Leo was born in 1922. Like many of his generation, the New Deal was a daily reality in his household, with a brother and a sister each working as clerks for the WPA. Drafted into the army during World War II, Krikorian trained as a photographer and studied with Ansel Adams after the war. The GI Bill allowed him to continue his education at Black Mountain College, but after his move to San Francisco, he shipped out as a merchant marine, hauling military equipment to Japan. Krikorian first opened The Place by partnering with a fellow seaman, who was prevented from owning the bar because of a police record. Krikorian paid $1,500 to buy the space, including its beer and wine license, but the bar did a poor business at first. Stiles borrowed the money to buy out Krikorian's partner in March 1954.[7]

Krikorian went into the bar business to support his artistic interests, making enough to pay the $40 rent for a room he shared with Stiles in the Montgomery Block, where fellow artists garnered income from doing custodial work or growing cannabis. Throughout The Place's run, Krikorian showed a penchant for mutual aid and community. He offered cheap food and drinks (beers cost 25 cents) and extended a $2 per month credit to locals. "They used to call me 'The Godfather of Beats,' because I used to help a lot of people out," Krikorian said. "I'd give them money, I'd feed them, buy them drinks." Krikorian's bartenders described North Beach as a community where denizens "lived in little hotel rooms like the Monkey Block or the old Italian hotels, but they spent all their time at The Place, or the other bars," and there was "a spirit of sharing." The bar opened at 9:00 a.m. and, throughout the day, was a hub for patrons that Stiles characterized as "poets of all sizes and ages, some painters, some photographers, some merchant seamen, some radicals, some conservatives." Despite customers passing a series of bad checks, the bar's popularity allowed Krikorian and Stiles to eke out a living. As Stiles bluntly reported to Tram Combs, he at least made "as much money as some floozie clerking at the dime store."[8]

Stiles's entrepreneurial motivation grew from his politics, as "the anarchists were the only revolutionaries that interested me." Writing to Combs in 1954, Stiles expressed his concern about maintaining North Beach radicalism, complaining that Vesuvio was becoming a tourist trap and that "12 Adler is now a dike bar, so I feel that another bohemian spot is a much needed thing." Stiles had attended Kenneth Rexroth's Libertarian Circle meetings in 1949, which set him on his activist path. "Actually I only got in on the last two meetings," he recalled, "but it was a meeting, largely, of poets; and their attitude was that political resistance was impossible in the McCarthy period. And that they were looking for ways to bring about cultural changes in lifestyle . . . that was really my motivation at The Place, in going into the bar business."[9]

A bar was a fairly logical extension of the anarchist circles that, Stiles noted, proposed to alter bourgeois consciousness through various methods, which included introducing weed and peyote to the middle class. More importantly, "there was a general feeling there had to be a change about sexual relationships," with "greater candor about homosexuality" and "experiment even in heterosexual relations." Underscoring his cultural politics, Stiles recalled that he and his fellow anarchists initiated a project of "introducing the ladies to swear words," thinking that by undermining the "specialized language of the male-oriented society . . . it would be possible to have the liberation of women." Stiles recognized that his sociopolitical efforts would have to be matched by artistically confrontational performances, "so when I went into the bar business in 1954—April 1st, 1954—we started with the Dadaists."[10]

In this case, the Dadaists were artists organized by poet Jack Spicer into what he called the Cacophony Band. Stiles and Krikorian had met Spicer through the San Francisco Art Institute, where he taught art and literature. By this time, Spicer and Robert Duncan, along with Kenneth Rexroth, had already become the center of the San Francisco Renaissance. Friends since their days together at the University of California, Berkeley and in the Libertarian Circle in the 1940s (Spicer sought out Duncan after reading his article on homosexuality in *Politics*), they organized poetry workshops and literary salons. With Spicer's, Duncan's, and Rexroth's patronage, The Place became a "meeting place of the 'out'-groups." The bar's clientele, Stiles recalled, included "lesbians and queers and revolutionaries . . . who were interested in poetry . . . [and] pacifism."[11]

The Place was the epitome of an intimate American literary café: a storefront venue with one plate-glass window, a bar with about a dozen stools, walls adorned with "daub-and-swab school" modern art, an upright piano, and a cramped balcony. Stiles and Krikorian consciously designed it as a headquarters for cultural revolt and public discussion. "The Place was small enough, so that if you got three or four people, why the fifth person could come in and immediately get into the dialogue, even if he was unknown to the other people," Stiles said, "and in fact Krikorian and I had that in mind . . . [with] the bench running all the way along the wall so that people sitting at a table would be also sitting at the next table. . . . In other words . . . there wouldn't be any single-tabled people. . . . As a matter of fact if you really wanted to be alone, they went up in the balcony." In true subterranean style, its spatial connotations were playfully cosmopolitan. As bartender John Allen Ryan recalled, "There was poetry in 14 languages in the toilet, pasted, written, painted on the wall."[12]

In 1955, Stiles sold his interest in the bar, moving to an anarchist colony in Oaxaca, Mexico, and then back to New York City, which he deemed to be necessary in order to "make my living as an artist." But he maintained ties with Krikorian—who provided him with a monthly stipend—and when Stiles returned to San Francisco in 1958, he bartended at his old haunt. This sort of personal touch was typical of Rebel Café venues, where owners and staff created a welcoming atmosphere of nonconformity, assuring patrons of relatively safe spaces in which to explore transgressive ideas—although The Place was more openly radical than most. "I was really standing behind the bar just blathering anarchist propaganda," Stiles admitted, chuckling. "Somebody else might have thought I was doing something else, but that's what I thought I was doing."[13]

Stiles's comment exemplifies another important aspect of literary cafés: the role of bartenders, who set the tone and guided patrons through sociopolitical experiments.

Top left, Knute Stiles. *Top right*, Leo Krikorian. *Bottom left*, The Place. *Bottom right*, a crowd outside The Place. *Top left and right*, courtesy of the Leo Krikorian 1997 Trust; *bottom right*, *Look* Magazine Photograph Collection, Prints & Photographs Division, Library of Congress, L9-58-78425-FR-19, job 58-7842-VV, contact sheet image #20; *bottom left*, courtesy of the San Francisco History Center, San Francisco Public Library, photo ID AAB-9643

This was particularly the case in North Beach, where venue owners tended to be participants in the art scene, although, to varying degrees, it was also true of New York sites such as the San Remo, the White Horse, and the Figaro Café.[14] As Stiles stated in a letter to Combs, running The Place was "like being host to a party which is never over." The conservative *San Francisco Examiner* reported in 1958: "The joint is self-consciously shabby but comfortably relaxed. Filled with young people deep in talk, with the peculiarly tripping improvisations of the progressive piano style serving as background music."[15] Literary bars, entwined in the social fabric of San Francisco and New York, became a sort of public home.

Pivotal to The Place's public function was Blabbermouth Night. Bartenders Jack Langan and John Allen Ryan borrowed the idea for it from a Chicago watering hole that was in the tradition of Rexroth's Green Mask. Blabbermouth Night, held every Monday, was an open forum. One scenester later remembered that, based on the crowd's reaction, "a magnum of champagne went to the best bullshit artist," contingent on the "wit and verbal persuasion of the contestant."[16] Some presented prewritten pieces, but the expectation for bohemians and tourists alike was to talk extemporaneously on topics that could be either serious or satirical—although the tendency was toward the latter. Yet this was no free-for-all. Instead, Blabbermouth Night was a supreme example of countercultural public discourse. The proceedings followed meticulous rules, which an area sociologist recorded in 1959: "The participants, leaning on a box labeled 'Soap [for Cultural Sanity],' address the audience from a balcony. The 'official' themes are posted on a blackboard behind the bar. Each speaker is allowed three minutes in which to present his ideas. More commonly, the themes serve as a takeoff point for more immediate personal interests. The 'formal' address is followed by a question period and a rebuttal, and a winner is declared. Sometimes the debates are real and even violent." In addition to the champagne, winners were awarded a "Blabberlistener" certificate, which stated that the recipient could sit on The Place's "panel of experts."[17]

Krikorian insisted that "the speech-making on Blabbermouth Night was political in nature." But discussions were mostly informed by mainstream news sources, underscoring the satirical label "experts."[18] Topics ranged from the surreal to the profound. On a given Monday, you might hear speakers rail against Nixon or General Motors; ask "Was Macbeth Beat?"; or discuss "the superiority of the bagel as a contraceptive," "American imperialism," and "the Iraq Rebellion." The Place's emcee created an atmosphere not altogether different from that of a comedy club, with routines that were reminiscent of the Bay Area's New Comedians, such as Mort Sahl and Lenny Bruce. At times Blabbermouth Night slipped into hip exclusivity, as speakers spouted self-referential jokes and put-ons to "tourist squares." One Berkeley professor, for example, presented a spoof of Robert Duncan and the Spicer circle, which affably caricatured them as "Archbishop Drumcan" and "Lady Superior Spice."[19] On the whole, however, The Place met the test of inclusiveness, although the continual use of the word "fuck" (especially

Blabbermouth Night. *Top*, a speaker. *Bottom*, listeners. *Top*, courtesy of C. R. Snyder; *bottom*, *Look* Magazine Photograph Collection, Prints & Photographs Division, Library of Congress, L9-58-78425-FR-19, job 58-7842-UU, contact sheet image #14

by women) must have offended some sensitive patrons. Police shutdowns were frequent.

Such psycholinguistic controversy only highlights the Rebel Café's socially Freudian function. Existentialism and the death drive were also common fodder. In both private conversation and to the press, flippant statements that "Beach chicks surround themselves with death symbols," wearing "long black stockings, black shirts, and black sweaters," sat alongside earnest suggestions that authentic nonconformity entailed "wanting—sometimes desperately—to die." One Place regular insisted that "everything that's wild and beautiful about N. Beach people" included "the death-wish down-to-the-bottom urge."[20] Such invocations of unconscious recesses paralleled bohemia's rejection of the traditional family and society—a kind of voluntary social death.

Bohemia's death-wish fixation was more than a symptom of mass suicidal tendencies. It informed the community's dark sense of humor, a useful defense mechanism in the new age of atomic threats. Blabbermouth Night offered the opportunity for sardonic self-expression to all comers. Reporting on a scene soaked with Freudian elements, from the neurosis of repressed desire to the dark humor that released it, columnist Herb Caen wrote that "at last Mon. night's session, a girl with matted hair and glasses to match arose to announce: 'I really don't have anything to say, I just came here to be humiliated.' Out of the ensuing silence, a voice bellowed: 'Siddown!' 'Thank you,' she said meekly, 'now I've been humiliated.' She looked quite relieved." One more transgressively satirical Blabbermouth identified herself as "Big Cyn" and offered an account of arriving in North Beach's "utopia" with "three strikes against me": "I'm German, I'm a virgin, and I'm a secretary." After patrons responded with broad laughs and suggestions about how to solve her so-called problems, they voted her that night's winner. When Big Cyn stood up to accept her award, however, she announced that she had a confession to make: "I happen to be French, a whore, and a painter."[21] Even such satirical moments demonstrated the Rebel Café's mix of continental flair, sexual liberationism, and artistic expression.

Non-Ghettoizing Gay: North Beach Queer Culture and the Beats

Following its 1951 state supreme court victory, allowing openly gay patronage, North Beach's Black Cat Café began to feature drag shows starring the future political activist José Sarria. As a result, the ambiance changed, with more-formalized entertainment that was less welcoming for extended literary conversations. Nightspots such as The Place, the Coffee Gallery, and the Coexistence Bagel Shop gradually replaced the Black Cat as bohemia's main literary locales. In particular, Jack Spicer's writers' circle, known to insiders as the Spicerkreis, essentially headquartered itself at The Place—to the extent that Spicer began to receive his mail there. The Place soon proclaimed itself "Where the Literati Linger in Bohemia's Hall."[22] Yet this did not mean a clear separation between gay and literary crowds. Instead, queer San Francisco venues—including the Black Cat, the Paper Doll, the Anxious Asp, the Mr. Otis bar, Gino and Carlo's, Ann's 440, 12 Adler, and Miss Smith's Tea Room (which became the Coffee Gallery in 1958)—were intertwined with bohemia's social scene.[23] In the 1950s, the notion of identity was in transition, with chosen labels such as artist or bohemian mixing with and supporting more "essential" sexual or racial ones. Similar to the jazz/folk sensibility, which functioned as a currency that eased exchanges across the color line, bohemianism was a medium through which gay identity could be more safely expressed in public. Although its roots ran much deeper, the fully formed idea of queer identity did not become dominant in gay America until the late 1960s.[24]

Narrowly "Beat"-en views of North Beach have obscured these continuities between the Black Cat's queer bohemianism of the 1940s and left-wing radical artists of the 1950s. Most notably, Nan Boyd's groundbreaking study of queer San Francisco draws a solid line between bohemia and the decade's emerging gay public sphere, especially after a 1956 moral reform campaign by Mayor George Christopher and the Alcoholic Beverage Control Board once again put the Black Cat in legal jeopardy. Boyd argues that by the time of the crackdown, the café was divided from a bohemia defined by the Beats, whose "mystic and masculine culture" had little direct connection with the "gender-transgressive quality of queer culture."[25] Yet this contention is problematic, for two reasons. First, it misconstrues the relationship between the Beats and North Beach, in which gay activists like Stiles, Spicer, and Duncan were prominent—a connection not explored by Boyd. Second, it relies on a reductive definition of gay as an identity, manifesting itself in "flamboyant and effeminate" personas, to the exclusion of sexuality and affiliation—an ironic counterpoint to the California law that recognized the rights of gays and lesbians to publicly gather, as long as they did not participate in sexual behaviors, premised on the idea that they were otherwise impossible to identify.

The Beats were part of a gay bohemian community that often, though not always, celebrated masculinity, but also asserted its own range of homosexualities. As the controversial publisher Irving Rosenthal—whose early 1950s stint in San Francisco included taking closeted friends to the Blue Angel, "a very gay bar" where affectionate patrons eased their "opening up"—later wrote to Allen Ginsberg, "'Howl' is an angry poem, we have a right to our anger." He concluded emphatically, in the Freudian parlance of his times: "I do not care whether Allen Ginsberg thinks there is a connection between his own cocksucking activities and his mother's parasitism. . . . But I know *I* am a homo which my mother manufactured, and I am perfectly willing to blow any not too repulsive male on the floor of the United Nations to prove it."[26] The younger poets of the Spicerkreis, which included The Place habitués George Stanley and Russell FitzGerald, were equally vocal about their homosexuality. Stanley recalled that their stance was tied to class consciousness, describing the Spicer circle's confrontational antibourgeois approach as one that, at the same time, avoided gender transgression: "We suck cock, take it or leave it! And the next comment would be about baseball—traditionally masculine." Stanley did, however, note divisions between the Spicer group and the Beats: "The beatniks themselves, I think, were quite heterosexual. . . . [Ginsberg] was famous enough to get away with it . . . but among the followers of the beatniks it was *not* OK to be homosexual at all." Yet the beatniks of North Beach in the late 1950s included those like FitzGerald, who occasionally cross-dressed and once boasted that "I have sucked over fifty different cocks since last Easter" without raising an eyebrow among his compatriots.[27]

Stanley added that anarchist scenesters rejected the notion of gay identities as being separate from artistic and political ones, asserting, "It was OK to be homosexual . . . but non-ghettoizing, you know, it was the bohemian tradition, and we were more that way." Robert Duncan had long been publicly outspoken about his homosexuality and privately used his poetry to process ideas about universality and community. "Christianity tries to persuade that we can love more than one—love our fellow men—and at the same time makes it immoral," he wrote to Spicer. "If I am free from the Christian blight in any way, it's not in that, 'I have many Gods' [as] I tell myself in the poems. But [that] I can't realize it." Writing publicly about North Beach in 1959, Duncan declared that he sought a "community of values," a "kinship of concern and a sharing of experience that draws us together," thus avoiding the peril of a "sinister affiliation offered by groups with whom I had no common ground other than the specialized sexuality."[28] The notoriously surly, sardonic Spicer (whose persona clearly inspired the better-known Beat poet Charles Bukowski) was less effusive about his sexuality, being prone to terse statements about his "prideful love" and describing the local scene as "all very depressing." Spicer nonetheless recognized the need to mobilize politically and was an early organizer for the Mattachine Society, a gay rights group founded by former communists whom Spicer knew through Berkeley's leftist social networks.[29]

Kerouac's disdain for effeminate "faggots" that was apparent in *On the Road* (despite his own bisexuality) was also real enough in beatnik circles, much as it was in the jazz community that inspired them. A 1959 sociological study of North Beach found several instances of bohemians who rejected gays as "very putrid, weak, and offensive," while a tourist guidebook that a friend jokingly gave to Jack Spicer similarly denigrated the blending of bohemia and queer culture. "One of the most colorful places for a real drunk in other days used to be the Black Cat," the author complained. "The place changed hands and the new owner encouraged the fruit[s] and the place went to hell." (In response, Spicer's compatriot simply scrawled on the cover of the pamphlet, "Bull Shit.")[30] But use of the term faggot reflected concerns about gender transgression and effeminacy, rather than simply sexual behavior. Gay bohemians like FitzGerald, for instance, often referred casually to the "faggot table" at the Coffee Gallery or The Place, a spatial delineation that represented an identity based on style rather than on sexuality.[31]

North Beach's predominant mood was tolerant, and it commonly celebrated unorthodoxy. As one African American scenester later asserted, homosexuality just "didn't matter," while activist Jerry Kamstra noted the nightclub underground's erotic fluidity, suggesting that "many of the artists were bisexual—or just sexual." "The fact of the matter was, you could have sex any way you wanted it on the Beach if you were patient enough," he declared, "and homosexuality was one preference that was accepted by the bohemian crowd." As Beat poet Gary Snyder wrote to Allen Ginsberg in 1959 about Robert Duncan, "He has totally accepted his homosexuality & there is nothing schizoid about him coming on faggoty & campy one minute or straight & intellectual the next; I get the feeling he has gotten himself pretty integrated & self-accepted."[32] Even as this statement reflected a problematic emphasis on masculinity, it equally showed a concern for both the full expression of sexuality and intellect as fundamental to Beat consciousness.

Rather than the Black Cat marking the separation of gay and Beat scenes, North Beach nightspots served particular roles for intertwined social cliques. For example, Stiles recalled that various social spaces affected his relationship with Spicer. Things were amiable when "we would see each other at The Black Cat . . . [or] meet on the bus going to North Beach," where they would sit together and talk. "On the other hand, I would say that we did not have good conversations at The Place. In fact . . . I was anathema." George Stanley noted that when he joined the scene in 1958, The Place set the standard for new bars, such as Mr. Otis, the Anxious Asp, and Gino's. But he also frequented the Tower Café, the Coexistence Bagel Shop, Vesuvio, the Coffee Gallery, and "the gay bars" like the Black Cat. "If there was, quote, 'nobody in the bars,'" he said, "we would go to Paper Doll's." Similarly, in October 1957, Russell FitzGerald wrote in his diary that his usual haunts had left him depressed, so he walked up Telegraph Hill, seeking solitude among the murals that adorned Coit Tower. On the way, however, he ran into Spicer and "turned back to the Beach and conversation at the Anxious Asp."[33] Given the centrality of talk in literary bars, the Black Cat's shift to cabaret-like *performances*, rather than its gay *patronage*, better explains the usurpation of its cachet by the New Saloons.

While the most serious discussions of poetic tradecraft took place during the Spicer-Duncan workshops at the San Francisco Poetry Center or the San Francisco Public Library's meeting rooms, the city's bohemian mental geography—which included the former WPA project, Aquatic Park—was fundamental to exploratory talk. "Either Aquatic Park, or a bar, might be a place for the serious discussion of literature," Stanley recalled. He added, noting Spicer's competitiveness, "The poetry meeting was . . . more like a bull ring." Poet Joanne Kyger also remembered bars as particularly welcoming spaces for Spicer's verbose, Marxist-inflected writers' salons: "How he talked. . . . This is where his poetry politics took place, a two-block long avenue [with] Vesuvio's, Mike's Pool Hall."[34] Disproving Stiles's contention in 1954 that North Beach's bohemia needed to free up the social space taken over by lesbian bars, Vesuvio and 12 Adler were absorbed into a growing scene that included both artistic and queer cultures. Artist Nemi Frost recalled the variety of nightspots that made up North Beach's nonconformist geography: "We used to go to Mike's Pool Hall, and we used to go to Vesuvio's—that was our little circuit. . . . It was home, it was where everything was happening." As one "Beat Madonna" told a local sociologist, "her social life was 'almost entirely centered about the Bagel Shop.'"[35]

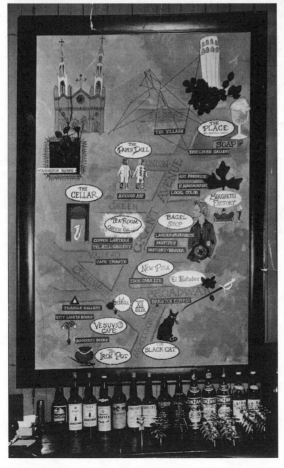

North Beach bohemian geography. *Top*, the Coexistence Bagel Shop. *Bottom*, a map of North Beach, highlighting popular Beat generation establishments, in the Coffee Gallery. The map was created by the wife of the owner, Paul Naden, circa 1958. *Top*, *Look* Magazine Photograph Collection, Prints & Photographs Division, Library of Congress, L9-58-78425-FR-19, job 58-7842-T, contact sheet image #18; *bottom*, Gordon Peters, photographer, Mark Green papers, 1954–1991, bulk 1954–1978, Archives of American Art, Smithsonian Institution.

Like The Place, the Coexistence Bagel Shop was an informal institution, complete with a massive bulletin board filled with fliers, letters, and notes from wanderers, to the extent that Beat scholar Bill Morgan called it a bohemian news center. It was not uncommon to see a scruffy poet engage the crowd with various aesthetic or political rants, standing atop its upright piano—which sat across from the bar in the narrow, dark wood, shotgun-style room—eliciting spirited responses from the interracial patrons seated around small tables covered with beer glasses and chess sets. Other drinkers—men with goatees, and women with heavy Egyptian-style eyeliner—carried on their conversations or turned to a variety of reading material, from James Joyce to *Mad* magazine, and, sometimes, to the sound of Pony Poindexter's saxophone. At the nearby Coffee Gallery, men with mustaches and beards talked in front of a sign advertising "famous bands, singers, comedians." Illustrating nightspots as places of out-group unity, in 1958 Nemi Frost reported to Joanne Kyger about a recent night at the Coffee Gallery, proclaiming that "it was a tableau of loveliness, with . . . everyone singing in a community sing."[36]

Lesbian-owned nightspots like the Anxious Asp were also mainstays of the bohemian scene. Originally opened in 1955, the Anxious Asp began as a cabaret. But Arlene Arbuckle bought the venue in 1958 and pivoted toward the queer bohemian crowd, sharing both staff and clientele with bars such as Vesuvio and The Place. A local magazine described the Anxious Asp's "casual atmosphere," while customers noted its sexual undertones: the restrooms were "papered with [pages from] the Kinsey Report." According to newspaperman Herb Caen, the Anxious Asp was a "true pillar of North Beach bohemia . . . with a mixed bag of patrons."[37]

The Place was a key anchor, both in North Beach's queer community and in the bicoastal bohemia, as well as a hub of oppositional networks and information. In 1955, when John Allen Ryan spent a season studying art alongside Knute Stiles in Oaxaca, Mexico, he exchanged poems by mail with Allen Ginsberg, who had recently arrived in North Beach. "If you would like to see more of my scribbles," Ryan wrote, "see Ed Woods at The Place." After Ryan's return the following year, he wrote to Jack Spicer, who was planning to come back from a short stint in New York and was casting around for a job, telling him that "your notice has been posted at the 6 [Gallery] and The Place," adding that the local "crew were in The Place Sunday as I was tending bar, and gave me to understand they would do what they can."[38] Joyce Johnson later described a letter she received from Jack Kerouac just before *On the Road* was published. He pleaded with her to join him in San Francisco and ebulliently hyped The Place: "You will love this mad joint. Nothing like it in New York." The bar, Johnson noted, "had clippings about 'Howl' on the bulletin board as well as paintings by local artists and phone messages and letters that the bartender held for his customers."[39] Yet, due to the later prominence of the Beats, its public image became filtered through Kerouac's lens. He claimed The Place as "his" bar in *The Dharma Bums* (1958) and *Desolation Angels* (1965), praising its "brown lovely bar made of wood," the "sawdust, [the] barrel beer in glass mugs," and its "old piano for anybody to bang on"—descriptions that revealed its hip-literary reality less than his own nostalgia for the classic American saloon.[40]

Although Kerouac waxed ecstatic about The Place's incomparability, many regulars, such as Stiles and Spicer, routinely traversed between North Beach and Greenwich Village, finding similar environs in the San Remo or the Cedar Tavern. "Just when I was so eager to abandon New York," recalled Joyce Johnson, "it seemed to turn before my eyes into a kind of Paris. The new cultural wave that had crested in San Francisco was rolling full force into Manhattan, bringing with it all kinds of newcomers—poets, painters, photographers, jazz musicians, dancers—genuine artists and hordes of would-be's."[41] Far from being isolated cases, the Beats' San Francisco sojourns instead were part of the larger trend toward a bicoastal bohemia.

San Francisco's New Saloons were crucial to the formation of this oppositional community—even when a focus on their own small social circles and the divisions between cliques blinded them to the bigger picture. For instance, George Stanley used the local psychogeography to express another artist's aesthetic distance from the Gino and Carlo's crowd, saying that "he's as far away from us as The Coffee Gallery."[42] Yet Stanley himself later acknowledged the largely false division between queer bohemians and the Beats, saying, "We were all beatniks, but we didn't know it." Much of this confusion grew from petty disagreements among Bay Area poets, whose bruised egos in the face of the Beats' popularity after 1957 drove them to seek an independent artistic identity. As Kenneth Rexroth, an early ally and mentor of the Beats, famously stated in 1958, invoking the bicoastal bohemia's nocturnal geography, "Those two [Kerouac and Ginsberg] aren't from San Francisco, they're from the San Remo."[43]

This short-term revisionism, however, denied a reality that was both broader and more nuanced. While Rexroth and the Spicerkreis ostensibly rejected the Beat writers as interlopers or as being intellectually sloppy, the two groups intermixed more than they cared to admit. Even as Spicer discouraged his young followers from being influenced by the Eastern mysticism of Beats such as Ginsberg and Snyder, they nonetheless shared poetry readings, as well as mutual friends, like libertarian-anarchist poet Philip Lamantia. While Spicer favored political critique based on an American approach to what he referred to as poetry's "magic," he and the Beats both challenged repression in the United States from a position of left-wing anarchism. Poet James Broughton described this dynamic, asserting that the Spicer group was "a more disciplined and more lyrically conscious group than the political publicity-busy invaders from the East Coast," but he conceded that "there were mergings and overlaps and we all knew one another."[44] What was basically a rear-guard turf war waged by the San Francisco poets became a moot point when bohemians on both coasts shared publishers, such as New Directions and Grove Press, as well as ideas about poetry and politics. More importantly, the Beat movement developed a national (and international) following that knew little and cared less about distinctions between Greenwich Village and North Beach. Yet without examining the North Beach bohemian

The "magic" of poetry at The Place, with a young poet reading by candlelight.
Courtesy of C. R. Snyder

community's influence on Jack Kerouac and, especially, Allen Ginsberg, any depiction of the Beat movement's literary power is incomplete.

"Howl" at The Place

Scholars have widely recognized the significance of Ginsberg's "Howl" as an early salvo in the battle for gay liberation, as well as for its influence in the 1960s on the New Left and that era's counterculture. But few have traced its effects from the ground up within the queer bohemian communities of North Beach and the Village, perhaps as the ultimate expression of the Rebel Café milieu. While the Beats themselves, in the words of historian Howard Brick, certainly were "a marginal literary subculture in the mid-1950s," "Howl" expressed a much deeper and broader urban sensibility that mixed jazz/bohemianism, European cabaret, anarchism and the Left's organizing tradition, nostalgic romanticism, queer culture, Freudianism, globalism, creative self-destruction, and atomic-age apocalyptic consciousness.[45] Ginsberg endeavored to spark a socioaesthetic movement, working at times like a literary agent for his fellow Beats and maintaining a mobile archive of their manuscripts and letters.[46] He infused his desire for artistic revolution with political potential, an extension of the postwar notion that change required a new consciousness. As UNESCO had declared in 1945, "it is in the minds of men that the defences of peace must be constructed." In many ways, Ginsberg adapted the Old Left's organizing methods, developing social networks and ad hoc institutions but fitting them into a Cold War context. Beginning in 1957, Beat publications made the bohemian underground nationally visible, and they were key mechanisms in the construction of a new American public by 1960. But "Howl" was also deeply rooted in the subterranean spaces of Greenwich Village and North Beach nightspots, demonstrating the relationship between local politics and national (even global) issues.

Kerouac's and Ginsberg's different relationships with the Rebel Café illustrate two aspects of the Beat movement's significance. Kerouac used saloons as transient places, vehicles that carried him along the road of literary and psychosexual exploration. His life and novels unmoored the Beats—and eventually their followers—from previous traditions and expectations, but lacked contemplation. Ginsberg, on the other hand, recognized and used bohemian nightlife's sense of *place*. Moving to San Francisco in 1954 and immersing himself in the North Beach scene allowed Ginsberg to see his previous experiences in Greenwich Village anew, as well as bohemia's and America's relationships with capitalism, which he portrayed in his poem "Howl" as the all-devouring Moloch. In many ways this was a conscious reiteration of the literary past, since San Francisco functioned for Ginsberg much like Paris had for expatriate writers in the 1920s. Ginsberg was the brains of the Beat operation, the movement's conscience, and "Howl" was an intense meditation on the nature of postwar marginalization, as well as the desire for liberation and community, which required both detachment and rootedness.

The literary connotations of San Francisco's cafés and existentialist places like the Tin Angel and the Coexistence Bagel Shop—paralleling the Blue Angel and the San Remo in New York—satisfied the Beats' nostalgic vision of bohemia. This usable past appeared in their frequent references to Balzac, Rimbaud, Baudelaire, and Rabelais—mixed with mentions of Proust's places of memory, Dostoyevsky's underground ruminations, Céline's subversion, and Spengler's apocalyptic, metaphysical philosophy of history. These literary forebears signified forlorn love and intoxication, as well as the symbiosis of travel and experience, all of which were fundamental to bohemian identity. "Right now I'm damned," wrote the lovesick French poet Arthur Rimbaud. "My country appalls me. The best course of action: drink myself comatose and sleep it off on the beach." In a chapter of *Remembrance of Things Past* titled "The Place," Proust celebrated "those marvelous places, railway stations" as "tragic places also, for in them the miracle is accomplished whereby scenes which hitherto have had no existence save in our minds are about to become the scenes among which we shall be living." And Céline, disillusioned by World War I and denouncing the Jazz Age's vacuity, found New York City to be "an insipid carnival of vertiginous buildings," as he wandered its "monotonous surfeit of streets, bricks, and endless windows, and businesses and more businesses, this chancre of promiscuous advertising. A mass of grimy, senseless lies."[47]

This literary mix of intoxicated romanticism, wanderlust, and dark social critique suffused urban sensibilities in the nocturnal underground after World War II. It was commonplace for 1950s journalists to refer to black-clad women with "enormously weird eye makeup" and men with "belt-in-the-back caps and downy cheek fuzz" who "sip beer and talk about Bartok and Baudelaire" in the bars of North Beach and the Village. Kerouac, with a similar blend of bookishness and boozy existentialism, wrote to Ginsberg in 1954, celebrating a "vast O what the hell Live It Up-ness . . . like Holmes at old parties raising [a] beerglass." "It doesn't matter, all's the same," he concluded. "Our Balzacs and Dickenses and Holy Dostoyevskys knew that." An entry in Ginsberg's journal was perhaps the ultimate encapsulation of this cultural medley, as he speculated that "Baudelaire would have liked Billie Holiday."[48] Seeking this sensibility, Ginsberg's bohemian literary quest led him from Gotham to San Francisco, "a very cultured city the rival of New York for general relaxation and progressive art life," as well as the place where he would write his most expansive indictment of Cold War America. Appropriately, he would choose to first publicly read "Howl" at North Beach's left-wing bohemian headquarters, The Place, where he "tested it out" on familiar crowds before its momentous debut at the 6 Gallery on October 7, 1955.[49]

Like The Place, the 6 Gallery connected key behind-the-scenes players in bohemia. Located at 3119 Fillmore, it was founded by a group of six poets and painters: Jack Spicer, John Allen Ryan, Wally Hedrick, Deborah Remington, Hayward King, and David Simpson. The building was converted from an auto garage, and its back room featured a stage for poetry and jazz performances, including Remington's close friend Dave Brubeck. Ryan, a bartender at The Place and a poet who was prominent in the city's radical queer culture, was a major influence on Ginsberg and fellow Beat poet Michael McClure. Spicer formed the center of this scene, with his politically charged literary workshops. Without recognizing this queer bohemian community— who often represented the beatniks in the national press—it is impossible to fully understand the cultural evolution of the Rebel Café or the Beat movement.

In both direct and indirect ways, Ginsberg's legendary 6 Gallery reading grew from his experiences in North Beach. The Place was a nerve center for the 6 Gallery group, which artist and gallery owner Wally Hedrick described as "a social place where you could meet anybody, almost, any time of the day." In conjunction with a local exhibition in 1955, Hedrick asked the budding poet McClure, whom he met through Spicer's workshops, to organize a reading, which soon included Ginsberg, along with Philip Whalen and left-leaning Philip Lamantia. Kenneth Rexroth, appropriately, was the master of ceremonies.[50] But as Ginsberg's journals and letters from that time period show, more than the reading's concrete connections were formed in North Beach nightspots. The very sensibility that gave "Howl" the power to stoke controversy was a reflection of the poet's nocturnal wanderings in America's jazzy, queer bohemian underground.

In 1952, Ginsberg had written to Rexroth, expressing his desire to come to San Francisco and get help reaching his poetic goals. "I have written a lot of stanzaic rymed [*sic*] poems and miss a certain kind of sensuousness of incantory ryme, though it is almost always abstract," he announced, "but I never developed accentual prowess to the splendor of jazz freedom."[51] On his arrival in May 1954, Ginsberg shared a room with subterranean poet Al Sublette in a cheap hotel, where he could see the Vesuvio Café from his window. Amid a blur of nights on "bohemian Broadway" with locals like Sublette and Neal Cassady, making what he called the North Beach rounds in Vesuvio, Tommy's, the Tin Angel, and The Place, Ginsberg began to compose a spate of new poetry. He wrote to his siblings that "I also hit the North Beach bars— their Village—and found more life even than NYC." He met "the same people as NY or their spiritual cousins" in a scene full of "art shows, jazz bands, hipster's parties, cellar lounges filled with hi fidelity Bach," and "communist murals in the [Coit] tower."[52]

By this time, Spicer had already established The Place as an institution where new arrivals, such as Ginsberg and McClure, could get a foothold.[53] Both of these Beat poets came to San Francisco seeking artistic opportunity, as well as love interests. McClure pursued his spouse-to-be Joanna, and Ginsberg—like Kerouac before him—panted after Neal Cassady. McClure found The Place to be the very embodiment of North Beach bohemianism, which now rivaled Paris's Left Bank as a center for the avant-garde. "The first beautiful show of San Francisco art that I saw was in the North Beach bar—The Place," he later recalled. "I had the sense at that moment that I was in the right place at the right time. It was 1954 and I knew for sure that I wanted to be in cowtown Frisco smelling the dark, salt smell of the Pacific and hearing the Chinese and Italian voices on the streets and not in Paris drinking in the last drops of existentialism."[54] Although its patrons were certainly not immune to existentialism's nihilistic tendencies (or undercurrents of romantic exoticism), The Place's mix of dark humor and outspoken social protest was alluring to peripatetic poets after their transcontinental wanderings or their arrivals from ports abroad.

Ginsberg's move to the West Coast, in fact, largely followed a trail blazed by Kerouac, the culmination of three year's worth of goading. In a flurry of letters full of references to San Francisco's art scene and hallucinogenic mystery, its radical literary and political past of Saroyan-style heroes and the International Longshore and Warehouse Union (ILWU), with its "tough white seamen / Scrapping snow white hats / In favor of iron clubs / To wave in inky newsreels," captain Jack exhorted Ginsberg to join the merchant marine and make the city his home port. "You must shuttle between New York and Frisco the rest of your life," he wrote in 1951, "just wait and see; the cats are all here, the artists are all here, LaMantia is very polite and is coming over soon to show us how to eat peotl." In May 1954, Kerouac once again wrote to Ginsberg, who had stopped in Mexico to visit William Burroughs, as well as a radical artists' colony, exhorting Ginsberg to connect with North Beach's subterraneans: "NOW LISTEN ALLEN, do not FAIL to look up, if possible, Al Subleetee, at the Bell Hotel at 39 Columbus St." Kerouac placed Sublette alongside Rexroth and Lamantia, insisting he was "maybe the first hep Negro writer in America," a "wordslingin fool" whose vision made him "a real POET in the sense in which it was known in Elizabeth's time," but whose drug-inspired spirituality was undercut by his penchant for "all the countless anxious intoxications of the jazz age and the machine."[55]

Kerouac decamped for New York just before Ginsberg's arrival, but he continued to recommend avenues of experience within the bohemian mental geography. Couching North Beach sites in familiar Village terms, he wrote in August that the "queers of Remo as you know are in the Black Cat there, on Kolumbus at Montgomery." Through the summer and fall of 1954, Kerouac related sometimes misogynistic accounts of his often interracial sexual exploits and his nocturnal escapades in the San Remo, the West End Bar, and the Bleecker Street Tavern with subterraneans such as Alan Ansen, Helen Parker, Gregory Corso, Gore Vidal, Paul Goodman, Judith Malina, Anatole Broyard, and Alene Lee (who waited tables at the bohemian Rikers Café). "I've been getting sillydrunk again lately in Remo and disgusting myself," Kerouac wrote, even as he enthused about talking with jazz pianist Cecil Taylor at a "great new bar . . . the Montmartre." Kerouac poured his late-night musings into his prose (which later took shape as *The Subterraneans*), insisting that "it would be a shame to waste all that experience." His missives also detailed the mystical and aesthetic insights of subterranean bar talk, with Buddhist notions that "the mind imagines all things which are but visions" alongside discussions of Dylan Thomas and Dave Brubeck.[56]

Ginsberg's letters similarly detailed the kind of bohemian bacchanalia that informed the more salacious passages in "Howl." But he also insisted on the need for a political perspective that Kerouac avoided. Reflecting both the solidification of Ginsberg's gay identity and his abhorrence of capitalism's dehumanizing tendencies, he called for a revolution in global consciousness that charted a liberationist path between American inequality and Soviet totalitarianism. Writing to Kerouac in September 1954, Ginsberg invoked "traditional dissenters" like Tom Paine, while insisting that he didn't "favor revolution or conquest of the United States by Red-East." But he then continued: "As for the American Revolution it *was* a revolution wasn't it? . . . All I am saying is that the United States is in the hands of people like the publishers you hate and they are fucking us up in the rest of the world's Spenglerian schemes. We should be feeding Asia not fighting her at this point. And if we actually do (for some mad reason) fight, it'll be the end. The Reds are what Burroughs thinks they are—evil—probably." While he never fully defined this view politically, Ginsberg did occasionally adopt the mantle of anarchism and insisted that he wanted to raise the "Lamb of America," proclaiming that "big trembling Oklahomans need poetry and nakedness!" While Ginsberg's Marxist-inflected replies were an occasional source of friction, Kerouac looked forward to his friend's brief return to New York for a wedding. Kerouac arranged for them to meet and talk over his new worldview, signaling the function of nightspots for both practical planning and deep discussion: "The profound ignorance of the modern world is Horrible.— 'The Horror'—is why I'll have to take refuge in The Apocalypse of the Fellaheen, which I'll explain to you come Dec. 15th when we meet at 8 P.M. in the Remo."[57]

On the West Coast, Rebel Café venues provided Ginsberg with a fertile milieu of culture and social connections. By November, he had become familiar with both the "Frisco Negro jazz" of Bop City and the cafés of North Beach. Collapsing the bar circuit into a single quasi-Joycean proper noun, Ginsberg wrote in his journal about a friend's "Jewish sentimental love verse of Broadway and the BlackCatPlaceVesuvio's Mikes12Adler." Ginsberg's journal entries and poetry during this period reflect the role nightspots played in the formulation of his signature oppositional composition. Working as a marketing researcher by day, Ginsberg chafed under the regiments of business. "Anger at boss," he wrote in February 1955, soon after a "Célinish" row with Cassady. "Depression. Speculation. Desolate loves. . . . I am a madman angry at self—2 selfs. . . . Alone in San Fran—enough. . . . God damn the false optimists of my generation." Nightspots such as The Place, he found, were a remedy for the alienation of modern life, as well as for lovesickness. Falling in with the North Beach crowd, Ginsberg took on a series of new lovers, including Sheila Williams (a singer in the cool jazz scene) and John Allen Ryan.[58]

A poem in Ginsberg's journal called "In Vesuvio's Waiting for Sheila" offers an evocative snapshot of this period: "Here at last a moment in foreign Frisco / Where I am thoroughly beautiful / Dark suit—dark eyes no glasses . . . / Toward an evening of fucking and jazz . . . / anticipating leaning on the bar." Vesuvio had recently come under surveillance by the Alcoholic Beverage Control Board for narcotics violations, which may have added to Ginsberg's anticipation. In October, he had recorded his impressions from a peyote trip with Sheila Williams and Neal Cassady, replete with a vision of the fog-bound Sir Francis Drake Hotel as "the Death Head—The building an evil monster," which became the basis for the Moloch stanzas in "Howl."[59] In the summer of 1955, Ryan put Ginsberg up in his Bay Street house and later insisted that the newcomer's style was lifted straight from his own, asserting, "One night at Gino and Carlo's . . . there was a reading by Ginsberg, and I suddenly realized that I was listening to my own poetry." Just before the 6 Gallery reading, Ginsberg himself made a similar acknowledgment, comparing "Howl" to Ryan's "SF recollections in tranquility."[60]

Another San Francisco bohemian area was Polk Gulch, south of North Beach. At its heart was Foster's Cafeteria, a late-night hangout for subterraneans like Lamantia and the site of a serendipitous meeting that set in motion an important series of events. At Foster's, Ginsberg met the painter Robert LaVigne, who introduced the poet both to his current exhibition at The Place and to Peter Orlovsky, who became Ginsberg's life partner. Taking a North Beach apartment with Orlovsky at 1010 Montgomery Street, Ginsberg continued to write furiously, inspired by love and art. He described LaVigne's paintings as a point of rupture in an otherwise bounded existence ("First! The Flower Inside, burst out"), all the while placing his nightlife experiences in literary terms. "Balzacian appearance going out with Sheila baldly appearing at The Place to back up her prestige in the desert colony of North Beach," he wrote. On another night he arrived home with "Tin Angel trumpets splashing in my eyes," followed by dreams of a poetry reading in a bar with "smoke, people, booths (Vesuvio cafe-like)." At The Place, Ginsberg also met Robert Duncan, whose disrobing performance in the play *Faust Foutu* at the 6 Gallery deeply influenced Ginsberg to take seriously the "principle of nakedness."[61]

Passages about The Place stand in stark contrast to the tenor of dissatisfaction with American life expressed in Ginsberg's poetry. In "Conversation 3rd Street to The Place," he rhapsodized about Kerouac's recent return to San Francisco, which he proclaimed in anarchistic, antimilitaristic, libertine verse:

> O Sherman Tanks of Mexico
> Your troubled sages shifting together
> on uneasy feet . . .
> I'm too young to die.
> Ma Rainey kissing together under the bar . . .
> Goodnight Mrs. Dedalus . . .
> I've never seen such imaginary beauty
> riding out of eyes—Allen
> He was made out of blue license plates and white wine.—Jack."[62]

Amid the themes that saturated Beat writing—allusions to James Joyce, connotations of free sexuality in African American blues—these lines clearly presaged the spirit that flowed from "Howl" in the following months. But equally present is the culture of North Beach, oozing out between the cracks like a predawn glow.

The 6 Gallery reading was the culmination of this moment. Kerouac was too shy to read that night. Instead, he acted as a sort of subterranean zealot, described in one report as a "Greek chorus," encouraging the audience and channeling jazz club energy with wine-fueled shouts of "Go!" Playwright Jack Goodwin was keenly aware of the performative communal significance of Ginsberg's reading, which he captured the next day in a letter to John Allen Ryan:

> He shouted at the top of his voice for upwards of half an hour, and he had the common touch and the audience was with him all the way, he actually whipped them up into hysteria . . . aching for some kind of release. This Carrowac [*sic*] person sat on the floor . . . slugging a gallon of Burgundy, passing me the bottle now and then, and repeating lines after Ginsberg, and singing snatches of scat in between the lines; he kept a kind of chanted, revival-meeting rhythm going. Ginsberg's main number was a long descriptive roster of out-group pessimistic Dionysian young bohemians and their peculiar and horrible feats, leading up to a thrilling jeremiad at the end. . . . There was a lot of sex and language of the cocksuckingmotherfucker variety in it. The people gasped and laughed and swayed, they were psychologically had, it was an orgiastic occasion.[63]

In this moment of out-group unity, "Howl" captured the bicoastal bohemian sensibility with its now-famous lines: "I saw the best minds of my generation destroyed by madness, starving hysterical naked, / dragging themselves through the negro streets at dawn looking for an angry fix, / angelheaded hipsters burning for the ancient heavenly connection to the starry dynamo in the machinery of night, / who poverty and tatters and hollow-eyed and high sat up smoking in the supernatural darkness of coldwater flats floating across the tops of cities contemplating jazz." But equally significant were lines about the political implications of a new consciousness, set within Ginsberg's Greenwich Village bohemian experiences, its "marijuana hipsters peace peyote pipes & drums" amid "storefront boroughs of teahead joyride neon." Ginsberg celebrated those "who distributed Supercommunist pamphlets in Union Square weeping" as the "sirens of Los Alamos wailed them down" and they were hauled off "waving genitals and manuscripts."

His queer cosmopolitanism declared solidarity with those who "let themselves be fucked in the ass by saintly motorcyclists, and screamed with joy, / who blew and were blown by those human seraphim, the sailors, caresses of Atlantic and Caribbean love" to the sounds of "nostalgic European 1930s German jazz." He juxtaposed his compatriots who "threw potato salad at [City College of New York] lecturers on Dadaism" with capitalism's "Moloch whose love is endless oil and stone! Moloch whose soul is electricity and banks! Moloch whose poverty is the specter of genius! Moloch whose fate is a cloud of sexless hydrogen!" And the only available response to such monstrous madness? A revived sacrament, in "Footnote to Howl," dedicated not to the dusty god of ancient west Asia, but to the sublime within the American urban underground: "Holy the groaning saxophone! Holy the bop apocalypse! . . . Holy the supernatural extra brilliant intelligent kindness of the soul!"[64]

Although "Howl" was an obvious descendent of the cultural front and the jazz/folk tradition, it was no simple reprise. As an expression of sentiment and guilt, an individualistic lament for lost days and lost loves, it did not fit neatly in either the Left or the jazz idiom. Its shortcomings were characteristic of its time; to expect otherwise would be to assign a mystical-transcendental power to art that unmoors it from history. The Beats' casual racism and misogyny are clear enough to twenty-first century eyes. But in its time, "Howl" was a brave and liberatory proclamation of resistance and solidarity. "Ah, Carl," Ginsberg exclaimed to the poem's dedicatee, Carl Solomon, embodying this ethos, "while you are not safe I am not safe." And "Howl" resonated with untold thousands—men and women, black and white, gay and straight.[65] Moreover, the poem was rooted firmly in *place*, in the bohemia of "Holy New York Holy San Francisco," even as it expansively encompassed the national and transnational: "Holy Peoria & Seattle Holy Paris Holy Tangiers Holy Moscow Holy Istanbul!" Biographically, Ginsberg's imagery was almost entirely drawn from New York, conjuring the tragicomic antics of Village subterraneans.[66] But he had to establish the *sense* of place he found in North Beach in order to look back, eastward and through time, to capture these impressions and then transcend them.

Re-Membering the Mother: Life, Labor, and Love among the Beatniks

Jack Goodwin's assessment of "Howl" as a jeremiad was insightful. Ginsberg's declaration of New York, San Francisco, Tangiers, Moscow, and Istanbul as holy was more than mere praise. It was a modern prophet's proclamation, backed not by a wrathful, omnipotent deity, but by the power of print. His prophecy was self-fulfilled by publicity. The poem marked a flash point, the moment when a disparate and divided bohemia became a recognizable community—soon to be an American social bête noir under the Beat generation banner. When *Howl, and Other Poems* was published in late 1956, along with a publicity blitz in New York supporting Ginsberg's ambition to "build the big united front" of Beat literature, this moment enveloped Greenwich Village as well as North Beach. Village poets like LeRoi Jones and Diane di Prima, who soon partnered to put out the magazines *Yugen* and *Floating Bear*, wrote to Ginsberg, praising his honesty and seeking connection. "I was moved by this poem so much because it talked about a world I could identify with and relate to," recalled Jones. "It was a breakthrough for me." Jones sent a letter to Ginsberg, by then in Paris, mixing sincerity with satire by writing on toilet paper and asking if he was for real. Ginsberg replied, also on toilet paper, saying, according to Jones, that "he was sincere but that he was tired of being Allen Ginsberg." That was the point at which Jones decided to publish a magazine.[67]

This scenario illustrates the role print culture played in establishing the bohemian community, which Paul Goodman captured in a 1951 essay, "Advance-Guard Writing, 1900–1950." It was an influential text for poets like Jack Spicer and New York's Frank O'Hara, as it described the relationship between print culture and "occasional poetry" (to use Goodman's term) that is integrated into everyday life, even as its avant-garde ambitions challenged previous norms.[68] Goodman asserted that the "essential present-day advance-guard is the physical reestablishment of community." He continued:

> This is to solve the crisis of alienation in the simple way: the persons are estranged from themselves, from one another, and from their artist; he takes the initiative precisely by putting his arms around them and drawing them together. In literary terms this means: to write for them about them personally. . . . But such personal writing about the audience itself can occur only in a small community of acquaintances, where everybody knows everybody and understands what is at stake; in our estranged society, it is objected, just such intimate community is lacking. Of course it is lacking! The point is that the advance-guard action helps create such community . . . and yet creatively imagining something, finding something unlooked-for.

Literature's fundamental role in *communitas*, Goodman concluded, "is to heighten the everyday" by bathing the world in the "light of imagination and criticism."[69]

The Beats in a New York café booth. *Clockwise, from far left,* Larry Rivers, Jack Kerouac, David Amram, Allen Ginsberg, and Gregory Corso (*in hat*). John Cohen / Getty Images, PMA 72955232T

Spicer similarly saw this in North Beach, with nightspots serving an alternative *private* sphere, homes for family-by-choice, with whom he could wage his "war on God" of poetic anarchism and gay liberation. Declaring that pride isolated from *communitas* becomes madness, Spicer insisted that it had to be "something we could build together."[70]

This was exactly the kind of mutual support that the 6 Gallery reading envisioned. "It was an *ideal* evening," Ginsberg later recalled, "and I felt so proud and pleased and happy with the sense of . . . 'at last community.'" From 1956 through 1958, "Howl" and Kerouac's *On the Road* became models on which a younger generation of aspiring nonconformists based their ideologies and aesthetics, giving impetus to the North Beach scene in the late 1950s at the Cellar, the Coexistence Bagel Shop, and the Coffee Gallery, as well as intensifying the Village scene at the White Horse, the San Remo, and the Cedar Tavern.[71] Equally importantly, Beat writing was the final link in a chain of people and places that fastened the bicoastal bohemia. The Rebel Café, in turn, expanded and became absorbed into the national culture as its publications spawned a fascination with an alternative underside of America, and its nightspots connected curious tourists with subterraneans.

Beat notoriety, however, began with a decidedly local conflict: the prosecution of City Lights Books for publishing and selling "Howl." Lawrence Ferlinghetti, impressed by the 6 Gallery reading, published the poem in paperback, initially selling it in his store without incident. But Ferlinghetti used a British printer, and the publication was therefore subject to confiscation and to obscenity charges by customs officials, who held back the book's second edition of 500 copies in March 1957. The California district attorney declined to press charges, but the attendant publicity piqued the interest of the San Francisco police. The police department's juvenile division arrested City Lights manager Shig Murao in June and filed obscenity charges against Ferlinghetti under the assertion that "the books were not fit for children to read." The subsequent trial in September and October was a cause célèbre, with a fierce defense by Al Bendich of the American Civil Liberties Union (ACLU), who called in Kenneth Rexroth, English professor Mark Schorer, and other literary notables as expert witnesses. Taking this testimony and the poem itself seriously, Judge Clayton Horn ruled in favor of the defense, declaring that "Howl" "cannot be held 'obscene.'"[72]

The significance of the *Howl* verdict went beyond merely allowing Murao and Ferlinghetti to avoid fines or prison time. The trial shifted the function of the poem from one of community cohesion to a *public* statement of opposition. "I never thought I'd want to read 'Howl' again but it would be a pleasure under these circumstances," Ginsberg wrote to Ferlinghetti as the trial was pending. He then stripped away the poem's multiple layers of meaning, surmising that state action would change its public function and infuse it with political potency: "It might give it a reality as 'social protest' I always feared was lacking without armed bands of outraged gestapo. Real solid prophetic lines about being dragged off the stage waving genitals and MSS. . . . I wonder by the way if the communist propaganda in America will further confuse the issue, the police, the judge & even ACLU. I really had some such situation as this in mind when I put them in, sort of deliberately saying I am a communist to see what would happen . . . burning bridges (not Harry) you might say." Ultimately, Judge Horn's decision relied on the same logic, stating, "'Howl' presents a picture of a nightmare world . . . [and] is an indictment of those elements in modern society destructive of the best qualities of human nature." He addressed the operation of language itself within social conflict and hinted that authenticity was also a factor: "Would there be any freedom of press or speech if one must reduce his vocabulary to vapid innocuous euphemisms? An author should be real in treating his subject and be allowed to express his thoughts and ideas in his own words."[73]

The *Howl* case therefore illustrates the problem with Goodman's notion of *communitas*, which inherently demanded that a community be *exclusive* in order to remain voluntary. The poem's protest, for example, conveyed little to the broader San Francisco population, as represented by the police, who were at best ambivalent about North Beach bohemians. Goodman's notion of community failed to address the conflicts *between* various groups, when a wider collection of fractious communities recognize themselves as a public.[74] The *Howl* trial, and the release of *On the Road* in September 1957, thus functioned on two separate but related levels: to solidify the North Beach / Village bohemia, and to interpellate a national public that had varying amounts of interest in, or *opposition to*, this community.

The trial was quickly followed by Gilbert Millstein's *New York Times* review of *On the Road*, which further expanded Beat publicity. Sales of Kerouac's novel unsurprisingly dwarfed *Howl, and Other Poems* (prose generally being more popular than poetry), as a careful editing of offensive language and explicit sexual content allowed Viking Press to distribute the book widely. Yet the City Lights edition of *Howl* sold 50,000 copies by 1960, mostly at poetry readings and counterparts to Ferlinghetti's store, such as 8th St. Books in the Village. It became transnational, with reprints in Europe, and was further disseminated by Grove Press's *Evergreen Review* magazine, which printed the poem and established its publisher, Barney Rosset, as a free-speech lightning rod. One of Ginsberg's readings was released as an LP by Fantasy Records, and slick national magazines (such as *Look* and *Life*) ran stories on the Beat movement in North Beach, with the obscenity trial and *On the Road*'s San Francisco settings leaving the impression that this was mostly a West Coast phenomenon.[75]

Life's coverage in November 1959 exemplified public disapproval. Its sneering, condescending article (complete with a staged photo of a so-called well-equipped pad featuring bongos, bebop records, beer cans, and a "Beat baby, who has gone to sleep on floor after playing with beer cans") careened from backhanded praise of Ginsberg and Burroughs to the valid criticism that the movement's "unplanned and unorganized" rebellion against materialism lacked the political force of Tom Paine or the Wobblies. While the piece was hobbled by myopic views on race and outright misinformation (stating, incorrectly, that a sociological study found 80 percent of beatniks to be mentally ill), it acknowledged the widespread appeal of bohemian critiques. *Life* recognized that what it referred to as the Beats' nonpolitical radicalism rested on the fact that "their verse is written to be read aloud before audiences," while "talk—endless talk—forms the warp and woof of Beat existence." Noting that the movement had spread to unexpected locales like Dallas and Atlanta—and even as far as Paris, Athens, Manchester, and Prague—*Life* concluded that, in what it dubbed the age of supermarkets and togetherness, the Beats offered the "only rebellion around."[76]

Both the nature and effectiveness of this rebellion was at the heart of debates about sociopolitical change in the 1950s. In *Eros and Civilization* (1955), theorist Herbert Marcuse compared bohemia's social role to a museum, preserving the notion that art "links Nature and Freedom, Pleasure and Morality"—thus presenting a challenge to America's technocratic society and military-industrial corporate state. Marcuse sought to "eliminate the distortion of the aesthetic attitude" by releasing it from the unreal atmosphere of bohemia, in other words, to infuse beauty into everyday life. This move, he suggested in both Marxist and Freudian terms, could meliorate the ills of modernity—exploitation, alienation, and the sublimation of sexual instincts—freeing the social Eros by establishing institutions that recognized sexuality and aesthetics as commonplace. Paralleling the libertarian-anarchism of Rebel Café radicals, Marcuse asserted that in a "truly free civilization . . . 'the will of the whole' fulfills itself only 'through the nature of the individual.'"[77]

If Marcuse overestimated the liberating potential of aesthetics, he also under-estimated bohemia sociopolitically. Acting on their desires to make beauty, play, and liberated sexuality a part of daily life, North Beach and Village bohemians created a model for the rest of society. What *Life*'s reporter could not have foreseen in 1959—understandably puzzled as he was by the bohemians' rejection of hard-won postwar affluence—was how deeply the ethos he tried to dismiss resonated with American youth. By the thousands, men and women in their late teens and early twenties headed for North Beach or Greenwich Village to join the movement—including a teenage Tom Hayden, who two years later helped to write one of the founding documents of the New Left, the Students for a Democratic Society's "Port Huron Statement." After reading *On the Road*, Hayden had headed to North Beach. Soon someone in Berkeley put a political leaflet in his hand, sending him on a path toward radical protest and political leadership.[78] Few Beat converts achieved such notoriety, but many were nonetheless transformed by their subterranean experiences in ways large and small.

Bohemian nightspots were central in changing notions about community, as a new kind of voluntary association blurred the lines of social class and of private versus public. For bohemians, psychic considerations trumped economic ones, and the boundaries between the private sphere of the family and the public sphere of commerce and politics faded almost beyond distinction. As a 1959 sociological study of North Beach concluded, its milieu acted as a therapeutic community, intertwining the global rise of psychoanalysis with a tradition of nonconformity going back to the nineteenth century.[79] Literary scholar Anne Dewey has noted that Robert Duncan articulated this concept in a series of essays and poems, which proposed art as a communal kingdom, rather than an individual creation, where "ideal community locates agency in a power and authority independent of the individual and the historical family." The poet, Duncan wrote, replaced biological parents with "the Mother of those who have destroyed their mothers [and] . . . created their own mothers" and the "Father of roots and races, / Father of All, / Father who is king of the dream palace." Poetry, he argued, was "re-membering the Mother," an act that reclaimed the individual from the mass democratic state through "the community of a mystery within the larger society."[80]

Duncan, who more readily accepted the Beats than Jack Spicer, proposed that the structure of bohemia rested on two strata: urban café life, and the bohemian household, with its "immediacy to all the arts" and constant flow through a "network of people."[81] Again, The Place best illustrated this dynamic, even eroding the distinction between the two halves. Leo Krikorian considered customers to be like family, and on Thanksgiving in 1958, he even offered a free dinner. "Sure we had our squabbles," said John Allen Ryan, "but it was one big family. It was artistic, intellectual—and boozy. The bars in the Beach were people's living rooms."[82]

Greenwich Village bohemians were less effusive in their descriptions, yet a similar familial ethos existed there in the 1950s. Bohemian café life was part of the urban fabric. As Village Gate owner Art D'Lugoff recalled, "I used to make the rounds of the bars—Julius's for those fat hamburgers on toast, the San Remo, the Kettle of Fish, and the White Horse." Judith Malina, who spent nearly every night in the San Remo as she and her spouse, Julian Beck, struggled to establish the Living Theatre, relied heavily on credit extended by bar manager John Santini. "If we lost our credit at the Remo," she confided in her journal in 1952, "what would become of us?" Malina further confessed that, after meeting left-wing activist Michael Harrington at the White Horse, the tavern's intense political discussion left her longing for her San Remo family. For regulars, echoed Ronald Sukenick, "the Remo was really like the living room hearth," but with "a lot of heavy drinking going on." These sentiments and social networks also reached far beyond the borders of North Beach or the Village, or even the nation. "We were like an extended family," recalled the Beach's Eileen Kaufman, "from coast to coast and all thru Europe and certain grapevine isles and countries throughout the world."[83]

Beat generation publicity expanded bohemia, even as it raised the threat of disunity. Krikorian recalled that The Place was often a landing pad for new arrivals in North Beach. "When they published *On the Road*, that started guys to try hitchhiking, you know. They'd come in with their suitcases and they'd check them in until they found a place to stay. First stop in San Francisco was the bar," he said, chuckling. Hinting at the joint's community function, he concluded, "A lot of them didn't have any money—but then I didn't buy The Place to become rich. I opened the bar to socialize."[84] Just weeks after the *New York Times* review of *On the Road*, Joyce Johnson wrote to Ginsberg that New York was seeing a similar influx in the wake of the Beat brouhaha: "Allen, three months ago there was a wild rumor that you had returned and were living secretly in New Jersey. HOWL is being sold in the drugstores now and the West End is full of young, would-be hipsters who laugh and say 'Well, I'm on the road,' or 'Think I'll go to Frisco today.'"[85]

Kerouac had previously written to Ginsberg about the same phenomenon in North Beach, reporting that there were "big rumors around town here that you were seen several times on the street and in The Place, as tho you were Hitler."[86] Kerouac excitedly continued his account, revealing the bar as a community institution whose social dynamic was now bedeviled by publicity. He described the City Lights arrests, denouncing the local "dumb fat Irish cops" for making America "like Germany, a police state." Although he boasted about himself and fellow poets Philip Whalen, Gregory Corso, and Gary Snyder being published, he declared with equal enthusiasm that he first read his poems at The Place, in order to establish his bohemian bona fides. On a different level of celebrity, John Allen Ryan sardonically (and scatologically) wrote to the peripatetic Jack Spicer, "You are famous and Legendary here, and are referred to often in the can at The Place."[87] Even *Life* recognized this dynamic, proclaiming North Beach the "capital of Beatdom," next to a photo of the Coffee Gallery. *Life* also unconsciously echoed C. Wright Mills's notion of power-elite nightspots, calling the Coexistence Bagel Shop and The Place its Stork Club and 21 Club.[88]

North Beach bars were more than the subjects of *Life*'s articles; they were the points of access into a community that was wary of squares—and was also happy to deliver put-ons to hapless journalists. In 1959, Joanne Kyger wrote to Gary Snyder about a recent interview with a *New York Post* reporter: "He used the entire conversation which Mike McClure and Bob Levigne [*sic*] had at The Place after you had left us that day and after we had turned on at my house. It is Putrid. He doesn't use names but the characters are obvious. He calls me a Faggot's Moll."[89] When the *San Francisco News* sent reporter George Murphy to The Place, Jack Spicer, George Stanley, and poet Ebbe Borregaard were less than cooperative, resulting in a portrayal that was typically condescending (if also tongue-in-cheek):

MURPHY: Tell me about Bohemia. . . .

BORREGAARD: This conversation stinks. . . .

MURPHY: How about some more ale. It's on the expense account.

STANLEY, SPICER, BORREGAARD: Okay.

MURPHY: Okay. (*orders*). Now, what's a Bohemian?

SPICER: A man who thinks what he's doing creatively is the only thing in his life.

BORREGAARD: It stinks, but it's right.

MURPHY: Is a Bohemian somebody who doesn't conform?

SPICER: No. If you didn't conform, you wouldn't be a Bohemian.

STANLEY: Sure, look at you. You're wearing a necktie—the only one here. You don't conform. You're not a Bohemian.

MURPHY: Are you proud of being a Bohemian?

BORREGAARD: It stinks.[90]

This kind of press coverage unveiled North Beach in multiple ways. It displayed this insular community to the public, leaving its denizens feeling discomfortingly uncovered, fearful of ridicule or persecution. But such reports also exposed the myth of beatnik nihilism, revealing bohemia's own norms and expectations as *alternatives* to mainstream norms—anarchism in a sociopolitical sense, not the brute lawlessness imagined by shrill critics.

The local press was usually more sympathetic. One North Beach intimate compared the Beats to the Okies in Steinbeck's *Grapes of Wrath* (1939): "They were hated because they were guilty of the most unforgivable sin of all. They were un-economic." He then noted mainstream patrons' paradoxical attraction to bohemian nightspots: "How can a barren, dimly lighted bar with battered furniture and nothing to offer except beer and wine compete with the plush uptown clubs . . . and win? . . . Men toot horns, read poetry, give you interesting conversation, and it's all for free. . . . You have nothing they could possibly want. It is sort of humiliating, isn't it?" Unsurprisingly, given the Rebel Café's literary bent, press accounts sometimes came from within the scene. Mark Green, who wrote variously for the *Village Voice* and the *Denver Post*, was a bartender at the Coexistence Bagel Shop until it closed in October 1960. He covered North Beach in a local paper and characterized its nightspots in positive terms, depicting the Anxious Asp's "atmosphere," the Coffee Gallery's "ad-libbing" actors and jazz, and Vesuvio's "intellectual longshoremen, Beat poets and psychiatrists."[91]

A dual role as artist and local laborer was more common than not in bohemia, and Green's experiences underscore nightspots as de facto mutual-aid societies. The notion was widespread that a beatnik's highest aim was, in the words of sociologist Ned Polsky, to "avoid work." By 1959, even network television portrayed this image through the character Maynard G. Krebs on *The Many Loves of Dobie Gillis*, who responded to any suggestion of employment with an alarmed, "*Work*?!" Yet the bohemians' main goal was to balance necessary employment with artistic endeavors and the quality of what they called their lifeways.[92] The issue was confused by the manner in which critics like Polsky framed this sociological problem: only writers, musicians, or artists who were *already* widely known were counted among the legitimate Beats, while those employed casually (or not at all) in order to *develop* their skills and careers (which any artist knows is a full-time job) were dismissed as unproductive shirkers.

Most commonly, beatniks went through intense periods of work, saving their funds, and then followed this with time dedicated to the arts. As Green wrote to his sister in 1959, "I have lined up a Xmas job at the Emporium . . . as a salesman in the book dept. That along with what I'm making at the Bagel Shop should give me $100 a week for a brief period which should help me finally catch up financially." His letter showed a preference for his chosen community over career advancement, yet it expressed ambition and dedication to his craft, noting that he had turned down a newspaper job offered by the combative writer Budd Schulberg because "I am just beginning to start and find myself . . . and besides I am growing very fond of this town." Meanwhile, he waited on word from the *Village Voice* about a proposed column called "West Coast Beat," insisting that "it would be a good deal if they o.k. it, prestige wise anyway."[93]

As the *Village Voice* itself demonstrated in a 1955 poll, such occasional work was paired with disciplined frugality. While income from "picture sales, parental subsidies, and odd bookings" amounted to less than $50 a week, "many of the interviewees spent less than two dollars a day on food." Enterprising artists were able to find apartments as cheap as $50 a month. In an extension of the Popular Front tradition, New Saloons also helped artists fill in the financial gaps. Willem de Kooning, for instance, whose curriculum vitae included both the WPA and teaching at Black Mountain College, enjoyed the common practice of running a tab at the Cedar Tavern during the lean years before becoming fully established in the art world.[94]

Shipping out as a merchant marine was also a frequent tactic, and bohemians relied on social networks to pave the way for them with the maritime unions, which offered both employment and subterranean status. As Kerouac wrote to Ginsberg in 1951, "Don't sail with the NMU [National Maritime Union] . . . carry your ass over to the Marine Cooks and Steward's Union at 148 Liberty street, New York . . . and you will have [a] great Negro and radical union. . . . NMU and SUP [Sailors' Union of the Pacific] are all trying to swallow it up because they're jealous; so the charge of Communist is leveled at MCS: while they're only the most powerful little union in America and on the West Coast and Harry Bridges is solid a mile behind them out there, and everybody on the Coast blows [like a jazzman]." After *Howl* was first published Ginsberg did indeed ship out, which funded his subsequent trip to Europe and North Africa.[95]

Along with work in nightspots, itinerant labor maintained bohemia's self-sustaining economy. This tactic, sufficient to support thrifty lifeways, was a real-world application of the anarchist-libertarian schemes of Paul Goodman and Kenneth Rexroth's Libertarian Circle. Anarchists called for workers' control of production, which itself would be geared toward meaningful work and quality of life, rather than a consumerist standard of living.[96] Such ideas had an obvious appeal for bohemians and artists, who frequently applied its principles, albeit unevenly. Gaps in the overall bohemian economy were filled by tourist dollars, while individuals used a patchwork of governmental support, from unemployment insurance to the GI Bill. "But there have always been rent parties, too," insisted the *Village Voice*—recalling the area's tradition of mutual aid, print culture, and pluralism—"and headlines, and homosexual bars, and bearded magazine vendors touring the bars with back issues of esoteric literature."[97]

In New York, work at various small presses directly supported bohemian lifeways and intertwined with nightlife. LeRoi Jones, for example, published freelance articles on jazz before completing his foundational study of African American music, *Blues People*, in 1963, while his spouse Hettie helped to support their family by working as a subscription agent at the left-leaning *Partisan Review*.[98] According to radical poet Ed Sanders, the Grove Press offices at 759 Broadway, just north of Washington Square, were also part of the Village street scene. Beats like Ginsberg often dropped by, and Grove publisher Barney Rosset hung out at the Cedar with the abstract expressionists and his first wife, painter Joan Mitchell. Following Rosset and Mitchell's breakup in 1952, bohemian writer John Gruen introduced him to another young woman at the Cedar—a recent arrival from Germany, with "a Dietrich look about her"—who became the second Mrs. Rosset. In return, Gruen was hired as Grove's publicity agent, allowing him to move up from his job at Brentano's bookstore.[99]

This cross-pollination included other Village bars, as well. Scenester Ronald Sukenick, blasting cultural critic Mary McCarthy's infamous 1950 *New York Post* article on the San Remo, which "simultaneously popularizes it and puts it down," asserted that she missed the bar's cutting-edge cultural vitality:

> The San Remo underground . . . besides being a new generation, which is always difficult for the preceding wave to make out, just may have been too low for a high intellopol like McCarthy to see clearly. If she could she might have spotted, for example, Paul Goodman in the Remo, musicians John Cage, George Kleinsinger, and Miles Davis . . . artists William Steig and Jackson Pollock, Julian Beck and

Judith Malina of the Living Theater, social activist Dorothy Day, and writers as diverse as James Agee, Brossard, Broyard, Ginsberg, Corso, Kerouac, and many others who . . . were doing something, even if it was something Miss McCarthy wasn't aware of.[100]

Similarly, journalist Dan Wakefield recounted that the White Horse Tavern was where he met Michael Harrington, James Baldwin, and Norman Mailer, who all talked about Marxism and about "being no part of the Eisenhower world or life." In *Desolation Angels*, Kerouac enthused about the effect this scene had on him, including Mailer, "sitting in the back talking anarchy" at the White Horse.[101] Village nightspots thus connected oppositional stalwarts and fostered community for those on the margins. "There is a kind of communality down here after all, the good side of tribalism," said Sukenick. "The underground provided a place where they could survive." As a San Remo regular, Goodman saw the Village's anarchist ethos firsthand while focusing his ideas for *Growing Up Absurd* (1960), a highly influential text for the New Left.[102]

One of the New Left's failings, like that of Goodman himself—and saloon culture as a whole—was inattention to gender equality. It is no coincidence that the Beat generation's most notable names were men. Women simply had less access to the culture industry. Scholars such as Barbara Ehrenreich are correct to point out that male Beats often took women's supportive labor for granted. Yet, as she also rightly suggests, this male revolt against the breadwinner ethic was intertwined with feminism in the 1960s. Moreover, such criticism often suffers from too much attention to Kerouac's misogynistic fiction, missing the historical reality that—in comparison with the mainstream—bohemian communities were relatively progressive when it came to gender. While solid data are hard to come by, late 1950s studies by Ned Polsky and by Francis J. Rigney and L. Douglas Smith offer some quantitative support for impressionistic views of beatnik egalitarianism. Rigney and Smith found that bohemian men and women worked at almost identical rates, and in largely the same classes of work. (By comparison nationally, 38 percent of all American women and 83 percent of all men worked outside the household.) Tellingly, nearly half of the bohemians worked in nightspots. Those who weren't employed were evenly split between receiving funds through governmental assistance programs or support by a partner or family. Rigney and Smith's study coincides with accounts that suggest this form of financing was mutual and shifting, with income earners taking turns when opportunities arose, allowing partners to pursue artistic or family interests.[103] Their blind spot toward queer culture meant that they offered no data comparing hetero and gay couples, but the trend among those like Michael and Joanna McClure also held true for Robert Duncan and Jess Collins, or Allen Ginsberg and Peter Orlovsky.

Single women also used the Rebel Café's artistic and intellectual milieu to redefine themselves and gain a sense of belonging. Greenwich Villager Alice Denham, for instance, after a divorce in the mid-1950s, became a writer despite the gender discrimination in literary circles. She found inspiration in continental sensibilities, and a place for herself in the literary bohemian community, comparing New York to Paris of the 1920s and quoting Simone de Beauvoir, who asserted, "Art is an attempt to found the world anew on a human liberty: that of the individual creator." Denham also mixed existentialism and Freudianism, adding that, among her clique in the late 1950s, "we were all busy creating ourselves." Yet Denham struggled to support herself solely by writing and often had to fall back on modeling for *Playboy* and other magazines between journalistic assignments, appropriating male-dominated norms for her own ends. Denham demanded that *Playboy* accompany the photos with one of her short stories. Sexual liberation also carried particular risks, as an unwanted pregnancy could threaten a woman's tenuous economic independence. Many chose abortion as a solution, even though it was both medically and legally risky. Elsa Gidlow, Joyce Johnson, Elise Cowen, Honey Bruce (spouse of comedian Lenny), Bob Dylan's paramour Suze Rotolo, and jazz singer Anita O'Day are among the many who reported stories of back-alley abortions that were often full of pain and danger. Denham herself concluded one harrowing description by resignedly saying, "I'd almost killed myself to regain my autonomy."[104]

While women frequently tackled these crises alone, partners and friends sometimes shared the burdens, as seen in a haunting account Joanne Kyger related to Gary Snyder in 1959:

> All sorts of emotional upheavals the past week. Mertis, the dummy decided to have an abortion . . . and got sick and infected and finally had to be sped to the hospital where they said she would have died but for them. And it also seems that Mertis had told Lew's Dr. who had visited her that day earlier that she had had an abortion . . . and he reported it. So after having saved her life the hospital sent detective[s] in . . . and she told me aside that Lew's Dr. had told her to save the largest part of the foetus when she was passing it . . . and would I please get rid of it because she was afraid of what she called Circumstantial evidence . . . and Christ what a mess in this jar of blood and I kept flushing and flushing the toilet to get all the blood rinsed down the toilet and out of the jar and kept gagging and retching and thinking this SHOULDN'T have happened. . . .
>
> House like a tomb, every time the door bell rang we thought it was detectives. . . . Lew says he is sick and lonely. And he cries a great deal and drinks a great deal.
>
> Smell of blood all over the house for days. She left a trail when they moved her from the house. . . . Mertis is back now and better. But she has to see a lawyer.

Similarly, Alice Denham's experience left her both permanently ingrained with an aching memory of loss and determined to support the legal right to terminate a pregnancy. "Wounded in the battle of the sexes, I felt like a gaping foot soldier, dying in the mud, in fury as well as pain," she declared. "To be so used, to be meat to society. No one should have to endure this."[105]

Further, bohemia was not immune to violence, including the physical and psychic violence of rape. In 1957, Russell FitzGerald wrote in his diary: "Incredible drunk last night. John Ryan's pad with Harvey Harmon and Bob Koffman [*sic*] and 'Pete'. . . . Irene Tauemer [*sic*] was almost raped and very much beaten." Although such overt cases were rare, the threat of sexual assault lurked in both North Beach and Greenwich Village, an aspect of the impersonal nature of the modern city. Further, alcohol could fuel masculine aggression, as seen in North Beach resident Sue Marko's recollection of "Bad Talking Charlie," a sculptor known for his tendency to "terrorize the neighborhood." "He nearly raped me one night," she attested. "He walked me home from The Place and into the bushes I go, and if I hadn't been a strong person . . . he almost succeeded, but I fought him off and screamed. It was awful." The San Francisco streets, with their itinerant seafarers, could be dangerous at night for lone wanderers, as seen in the murder of Connie Sublette, estranged spouse of poet Al Sublette, in 1958. Although the perpetrator was a psychotic seaman, the newspapers sensationalized the tragedy as a "beatnik" killing.[106]

Also perilous, and probably more common, was rape after a date or a bar pickup. Kerouac had admitted such an incident to Ginsberg soon after they met in 1945: "Once I was in bed with a girl. . . . I had picked her up in a bar and she promised me she would come across. When we got to bed she fell asleep and couldn't be awakened. . . . I spent the whole night wrestling around with her limp rag of a body, as she snored. It is a horrible experience. . . . You feel remorse the next day, ashamed of your desire." Kerouac further recognized that the hypermasculine climate of urban nightlife simultaneously fostered his betrayal and made it verboten to discuss it openly: "There was no one I could tell the story to who wouldn't in return blow a lot of hot air my way. . . . It's almost as though my neurosis were not ingrown, but that it was the result of the air, that atmosphere around me."[107] As Kerouac's admission indicates, these crimes were seldom reported, making their frequency a matter of some speculation, since silence increased the likelihood of their repetition and, therefore, the danger of urban nightspots.[108]

Yet for women who learned the cultural codes of urban life, the public nature of bars and cafés could offer shelter, as well. Maya Angelou recalled her favorite New York boîte, Tony's Restaurant and Bar, as a sanctuary in the late 1950s—not too dull, "nor so boisterous as to promise company combined with danger to unescorted women." Angelou relied on advice she had received as a seventeen year-old who was out on her own, "A strange woman alone in a bar could always count on protection if she had treated the bartender right."[109] It is a testament to the liberating potential of bohemian nightspots that, despite the challenges, a vast majority of women's accounts seem to recall Rebel Café sites with fondness.

Such examples indicate bohemia's ambivalent feminism, as misogyny was matched by women's determination to claim an equal public position, clear support for what Joanne Meyerowitz has called the 1950s bridge between first- and second-wave feminism. Meanwhile, as Wini Breines and Richard Cándida Smith have argued, Beat notions of male authenticity raised fears of family responsibilities, which they equated with bourgeois conformity and limited freedom—the "dark side of a philosophy that stressed personal vision and connection with the abstract forces of the cosmos over social relations."[110] Even as male Beats envisioned women as both mysterious muses and stabilizing forces, women themselves contested this containment, mobilizing their own notions of authenticity that rejected the mainstream.

Joanne Kyger wrote to Gary Snyder during his first trip to Japan to study Zen Buddhism, continuing a courtship that had begun at The Place in 1958 and illustrating the uneven process of bohemia's changing gender norms: "You don't know how much I would like to Indulge in being feminine & having a house and home. . . . But I've realized, men & women shouldn't compete but fit together." Kyger's correspondence reveals her concerns about social pressures, punctuated by characteristically colorful demands for autonomy and self-expression: "I wanted to indulge in just simple woman's emotions. . . . Well, it's pretty damn hard in this day and age. . . . God knows what women thought they were doing when they demanded the right to vote . . . and [then] I thought fuck you Gary if I have to hide what I feel."[111] Snyder responded with a mix of gendered flattery ("Kyoto is pretty & so are you") and recognition of Kyger's full social status, as well as his own internal conflicts over traditional male dominance, encapsulating his thoughts in a page-long list:

> I want you to cook & sew & keep house & I'll work too . . . / I want you to write poems & read them in your voice aloud / . . . I want you to have a baby & nurse it . . . I want you to make love to everybody you like / I want you all to myself / . . . I want you to learn things & love your own intellect / . . . I just want you to be & me just be & not demand anything of each other—I want us to live together & get along a long time.

"As for Gary Snyder," he wrote, "it probably wouldn't bug you that he seems to want one that talks, walks, & lives like a man," tacitly recognizing this socially fraught tangle. "These transformations work both ways."[112]

Despite their critiques of American bourgeois ideology, open acknowledgement of female labor's value by male bohemians was rare, and their lack of attention to structural inequality shortsighted. For instance, even if women and men were *employed* at the same rate, that did not ensure equal *pay*—an important factor for a population that lived on a financial knife edge.[113] As many of the period's critics pointed out, however, beatniks could often turn to parents or other family members for help in desperate times. Only 32 percent of Rigney and Smith's subjects and 35 percent of Polsky's were from working-class backgrounds, so the notion of bohemia as a middle-class phenomenon of New Poverty is mostly correct—a relatively privileged population choosing lifeways that were simply ways of life for working people. Yet even this critique had its limits. As Polsky's study showed, many of the late 1950s beatniks were young, from their middle teens to their middle twenties, making an apt comparison to college students.[114] Through this lens, occasional work and a focus on the development of a craft or vocation would be within the norm. This view of bohemia as a formative life stage was nearly ubiquitous among its denizens, who saw its streets and nightspots as alternative institutions of learning.

In the context of the Cold War, especially given the radicals' refusal to sign university loyalty oaths (Jack Spicer, for example, chose not to sign when he taught at Berkeley in 1950, thus propelling him into the subterranean milieu), the idea of bohemia as a radical academy bore more than a hint of left-wing anarchism. "Black Mountain was always an undercurrent," recalled Ebbe Borregaard about interactions at The Place. Kyger, further emphasizing the role of nightspots, replied: "I went to North Beach practically every night—it was like a school. . . . Poetry and jazz was happening down in the Cellar. . . . Some kind of dialogue between Jack and Robert, with us as a student audience." Even Leo Krikorian declared that running The Place was "quite an education." One New York transplant, noting North Beach's leftist leanings, multicultural influences, and sexual freedom, remembered it simply as a place of "learning and liberation."[115]

The Village, suggested Mary McCarthy, also "had all the earmarks of a student quarter." As LeRoi Jones later attested, "My adolescence extended through bohemia." This aspect of New Saloon culture had a particular impact on Michael Harrington, who recalled his first politicizing experiences in the late 1940s, "in the back of the room at Little Bohemia," a bar in his native St. Louis, "where they talked about art and psychoanalysis and the motherland of Greenwich Village." When he arrived in New York in 1949, his introduction to the city's leftist intellectual community of "voluntary exiles from the middle class" was through the San Remo and the White Horse Tavern—what he called the "united front of the Village." The scene had what he referred to as the atmosphere of a campus, where he developed his political views through the process of bar talk with a spectrum of nonconformist interlocutors who were "straight and gay; black, white, and interracial; socialist, Communist, Trotskyist, liberal, and apolitical; literary, religious, pot-smoking, pill popping, and even occasionally transvestite."[116] For Harrington, the diversity and intellectual stimulation of the Village's bar culture was fundamental to his political activism with the Catholic Workers and the League for Industrial Democracy—yet another bridge from the Old to the New Left.[117]

Russell FitzGerald—whose diary of North Beach life in the late 1950s reads like a laundry list of Rebel Café traditions, culture, social networks, and sensibilities, with references to F. Scott Fitzgerald's *The Great Gatsby* (1925), the death wish, subterraneans as family, and New Poverty—also yearned to blend his artistic ambitions with progressive politics. In 1957, FitzGerald recorded in his diary that "in the last few weeks I have tried to absorb and analyze the 'SF Renaissance' literature by reading and talking and drinking and looking." He found the *Howl* trial "rather inspiring . . . due only to the fact that I am still remotely hopeful that howling loudly enough may wake up enough people to help." Throughout, New Saloons were touchstones. "Recognition was the fun in reading *The Subterraneans*," FitzGerald wrote about Kerouac's novel in 1958. "If, though living in community, 'the Subterraneans' remain homeless, loveless and faithless, doesn't this make The Place in which they live a spiritual 'house.' . . . The picture presented is (like homosexuality though *actually* profound) an image of the human condition in its American incarnation. My work is my home." Combining artistic musing with a search for a new social consciousness, Fitzgerald infused the left-wing libertarianism that flowed through New Saloons with insights from Beat literature. He concluded that the personal was the political, and that liberation rested on continual resistance to the broader, dehumanizing aspects of mass society and the state: "The hated subject of politics begins to seem agonizingly important. Politics in the sense of social ethics and not organization. . . . The sight of a nation leading the world into an ever deepening hell of materialism and greed and unholiness, dwarfs personal problems. . . . It presents itself finally as a 'cause'—anarchy."[118] For FitzGerald, like many other bohemians, the search for identity became fused with visions of sociopolitical change.

In New York, taverns like the White Horse and the San Remo contributed to the emergence of broader and more-direct politics in the late 1950s. Politically conscious writers like Michael Harrington, Dan Wakefield, and Mary Nichols gathered in the back rooms of these haunts—the "center of community life" for left-wing bohemians in Greenwich Village—for a mixture of talk, impromptu folk songs, and sexual connection. Formal politics were always an undercurrent, as Villagers mixed bohemianism's personal rebellion with the antipoverty outreach of Dorothy Day's Catholic Workers or CORE's civil rights activism. Nichols remembers drinking at the San Remo, the Minetta Tavern, and the White Horse, mingling with patrons as varied as NMU organizers and future senator Daniel Patrick Moynihan. "That was part of the scene," concurred Catholic Worker and pacifist Eileen Fantino Diaz, "not just the Village, but the literary world. A lot of the literary types at the White Horse." Wakefield illustrated these social networks and their role in the public sphere, describing the start of his own journalistic career. "I remember somewhere I ran into Mike," he told Harrington's biographer, "probably at the White Horse." There they discussed the Emmett Till lynching trial, the subject of Wakefield's first piece for the *Nation* in 1955.[119]

For bohemian seekers, this milieu linked transgressive talk and sexuality with working-class authenticity. Gary Snyder explicitly made these connections in 1960, suggesting that New Bohemia was producing the "only true proletarian literature in recent history—because actual members of the working class are writing it." This group of what he referred to as "proletarian bohemians" had "chosen to disaffiliate itself from 'the American standard of living' and all that goes with it—in the name of freedom." Snyder noted that Old Left critics decried the Beats' brand of psychopolitics, to which he retorted that the "class struggle means little to those who have abandoned all classes in their minds and lives." This, he insisted, was the *real* revolution. Citing Friedrich Engels, Snyder linked the male breadwinner ethic to militarism and called for the disavowal of both "patrilineal descent" and the "idiocy" of nuclear armament by "keeping out of jobs that contribute to military preparations, staying out of the army, and saying what you think without fear of anyone." "There will be no economic revolution in this world that works," he declared, "without a sexual revolution to go with it." Sociologist Ned Polsky, while deriding the effectiveness of bohemian withdrawal, nonetheless recognized it as a "virtuous error" and the heir to class politics. In the face of "America's inequitable distribution of income *and* its increasing depersonalization of work and leisure *and* its racial injustices *and* its Permanent War Economy," he wrote, "the beats have responded with the Permanent Strike."[120]

Despite the Beats' assertions, however, there were very real divisions between their liberated consciousness and the concrete concerns of many workers—a whole generation of whom had finally clawed their way into the middle class through struggles for labor protections and unionism in the 1930s and 1940s. These conflicts sometimes played out in bars, as humorously captured by *Village Voice* journalist J. R. Goddard, who offered an account of his first night in the White Horse, with his elitist naiveté indicated by the moniker "Dartmouth":

> A stocky, red-faced type, with shirt sleeves rolled over his knotty, proletarian arms, frowned and muttered . . . "You wanna know sumpin'? Used to be guys like you never come in here. Now you're on the joint like flies. You're ruinin' the place. Why don't you go back uptown?" Dartmouth was getting mad. Which was unfortunate. "Hey," the scowler persisted. "*I'm* the kina guy belongs here. I belong in this part [of] Green-wich Village, not you." Suddenly his face beamed with pride. "You know why? I'm a sailor. A ship's engineer." "A ship's *engineer*," Dartmouth grinned coldly. "Well, where's your engine?" Good night sweet Dartmouth. When flights of Sixth Precinct cops have borne you to your rest at St. Vincent's you will be glad to learn the jaw was not broken—only badly bent."

Noting the bumpiness of these urban social shifts, Goddard concluded that "the West Village could still brawl . . . and the longshoremen, truck drivers, or white-collar folk . . . whose families had lived around there since the 1870's and 1880's, just didn't take to outsiders." Beat affinity for seedy joints and flophouse districts like New York's Bowery and the Mission in San Francisco exhibited similar doses of sardonic humor.[121]

Such vignettes shed light on the Beats' disregard for the working class's bread-and-butter issues, which was related to the bohemian aestheticization of poverty—a cultural lineage running back through Parisian cabaret. But it also reflected their correlation of unionism with a monolithic, oppressively impersonal technocracy. "Bureaucracy!" complained Old Bull Lee, William Burroughs's alter ego in *On the Road*. "Tain't nothing but bureaucracy. And unions! Especially unions!"[122] Jazz musicians regularly clashed with their unions, which had little patience for setting aside minimum pay in the interest of either a foot in the door or benefit shows. Similarly, the Black Cat's legal troubles in 1949 were first sparked by a labor dispute between the owner and the conservative, AFL-affiliated Waiter's Union. And, while it was rare in California, the Chicago and New York branches of the bartenders' union were tainted by organized crime.[123] Illustrating these tangled threads within the Rebel Café, one episode at the hungry i, easily misread as union overreach, was actually an extension of the Red Scare. In 1963, the mob-tied and HUAC-friendly International Alliance of Theatrical Stage Employees (IATSE) forced the club to fire its light and sound man, the Hollywood Ten screenwriter Alvah Bessie, since it insisted that the job was a union position. IATSE rejected Bessie's application, which included questions about communist party membership, with him answering that he had been a press agent for the left-wing ILWU.[124] While Bessie easily recognized McCarthyism as the source of his dismissal, more-casual observers in the nightclub underground would probably have missed the ideological chasm between IATSE and the ILWU.

At the end of the 1950s, the kind of activism that defined the 1930s had disintegrated, while the New Left and the identity movements of the 1960s were still in an embryonic stage. But New Bohemia was more than a precursor to the counterculture. It also had deep roots in the past as well, representing a vague nostalgia that went far beyond a longing for Depression-era solidarity, or even nineteenth-century bohemianism. While it was certainly hyperbole (or satire) to call it "utopia," the New Bohemia was a quasi-return to a preindustrial barter economy of the kind found in the late eighteenth-century American northeast, before the desire for manufactured goods drew farming families into national markets. It was also a revision of the artisan ideal and its public sphere, in which reclaimed manufactured household items—the detritus of the affluent society—replaced homemade ones, and voluntary public families replaced private patriarchal ones. Bohemian artists, focused on the development of their craft, relied on a complex mix of commerce and mutual support, all within a neo-Freudian framework that maintained a *social* mother/father as the new fountainhead of identity. Black Mountain College writer and Cedar Tavern habitué Fielding Dawson later penned an impressionistic memoir that captured this ethos, describing nighttime revelers as brotherly comrades and recounting the public affirmation he felt from them, such as the attendance of fellow Villagers LeRoi and Hettie Jones at his wedding. When he referred to the Cedar Tavern, Fielding said simply: "I know this place. It's my home."[125]

five

rise of the "sickniks"

Nightclubs, Humor, and the Public Sphere

Eavesdropping on human nature is one of the most important parts of
a comedian's work.
Bert Williams, circa 1909

[Humor] heightens our sense of survival and preserves our sanity.
Charlie Chaplin, 1964

"We are living in a culture of conformity, the sociologists keep telling us as they pore
over statistics that indicate college students are conservative this year," wrote jazz critic
Ralph Gleason in 1958. "That may be. But sometimes it seems as if the sociologists
miss a few points such as Bob and Ray, jazz musicians and the well-honed wit that
is bringing the Comedy of Dissent these nights to various clubs in the person of Lenny
Bruce."[1] Unknowingly, Gleason had announced the start of a cultural American
revolution and a new period in the history of jazz. While jazzmen's argot had long
informed hipster posturing, its verbal message rarely reached the public's ears un-
altered. Of course, the true language of jazz—the wail of saxophone solos, the blare
of trumpets, the syncopation of kick and snare drums—still came steaming up
from the Rebel Café. But for many white listeners, this only diverted the social
message of those like Dizzy Gillespie and Charles Mingus, since the complexities of
the African American experience were transposed into exoticism, sensuality, and libertine expression. Jazz's aesthetic was audible in Beat poetry. But the most popular
manifestation of that underground style was not in those mystical mumblings,
but rather in the prickly monologues of nightclub comedians. In particular, the
jazzy social satire of Mort Sahl, Lenny Bruce, and Dick Gregory gave a public voice
to the Rebel Café's liberatory ethos.

Numerous scholars and generations of journalists have tackled the subject of these
New Comedians (as the press dubbed them) and their challenges to notions of public propriety in the early Cold War period. Mostly they have spotlighted Sahl's West
Coast liberalism as a satirical chisel that chipped away at McCarthyism, or Bruce's
anticlerical, profanity-laden rants as salvos in the sexual revolution and the fights
against censorship.[2] Both comics were retrospectively hailed as trailblazers who significantly changed American culture. This was especially true for Bruce, a paragon

of questionable taste whose work became a free-speech litmus test for the hip set, while his obscenity prosecutions and premature death from a drug overdose in 1966 made him a countercultural martyr.[3] But scholars' generally top-down perspectives lose sight of New Comedy's cultural function. These performers did not simply emerge from the nightclub underground. In many ways they were its most salient expression, and the only new cultural form to survive the period intact. While jazz poetry, and even bebop itself, fell away from mainstream American tastes by the end of the 1960s, the style of the New Comedians visibly persists today. A close examination of their humor helps to reveal the Rebel Café's broader cultural role. It also exposes the very makeup of the underground itself, along with the complexities and contradictions of race, gender, and identity.

This point is underscored by a brief glance at the careers of Sahl, Bruce, and Gregory, as well as the performers who followed in their wake. All three came to notoriety through Rebel Café nightclub performances and live albums, as opposed to radio, theater, or television, as was the case for Steve Allen, Mike Nichols and Elaine May, or George Carlin. Moreover, each displayed an inability to adapt their humor to mass media. Compared with other New Comedians, such as Bob Newhart and Woody Allen, or with three of the African Americans that came to renown after Gregory broke the comedic color line—Bill Cosby, Redd Foxx, and Richard Pryor—neither Mort Sahl, Lenny Bruce, nor Dick Gregory developed mainstream success in film or television.[4] As such, their historical significance must be understood within the context of the nightclub underground—the site from which they launched their assault on the wider culture.

While variations existed between clubs, performers, and locations, nearly all nightclub patrons arrived expecting some level of social engagement that was greater than that of a more passive medium like film. In a nightclub, the physicality of tables and the stage, the shared spaces and conversations, and the sounds of shifting seats and clinking glasses mixing with the performance inherently went beyond the surface effects of mechanical arts like television. Audiences experienced fresh perspectives in a direct and tactile way, undetached from the actions and language in the club's urban environment—an experiential sphere with the listener at the center.[5] At the same time, a verbal craftsman forged a unique work of art in a manner impossible for mass media to replicate. As much as comics may have perfected their bits prior to the show, the very possibility of improvisation—oftentimes fulfilled in the New Comedians' case—denied any ability to mechanically reproduce a truly live performance. This active engagement served the era's desire for authenticity, while it also opened a public dialogue.

Moreover, within the national psyche, a socially conscious comedian such as Bruce functioned as a kind of holy fool—a traditional figure whose chief characteristic was to mock the intellect's ability to know truth. Like a court jester, the holy fool's clowning allowed him to jab at the powerful elites in ways that that would have seemed treasonous from more-sober critics. Concomitantly, the holy fool comedian performed a communal ritual that some commentators identified as "shamanistic": conjuring and casting out society's collective demons by ridiculing their absurdities. Humor therefore worked as an unmasking tactic that relieved social tensions, a safety valve for common frustrations. "The satirist," said the *New York Times* in 1959, "is out to deflate the stuffed shirt, prick the pompous, twit revered institutions and clichés." This was recognized by Cold War critics, who noted that if the New Comedians' performances had not been "couched in humor, their ideas might be serious indeed." In this way, the nightclub functioned as a liminal space where patrons could explore new identities with relative impunity, encountering the unexpected through both social mixing and the performances themselves. By adding in the frequent factor of intoxication, the result was a scenario that was able to stretch audiences' previous boundaries of acceptable behavior. As Norman Mailer argued, such existential challenges to established social codes could "open the limits of the possible."[6]

The Village Vanguard's cabaret satire and the early nonconformist comedy of Irwin Corey and Richard "Lord" Buckley had laid the fertile ground in which Rebel Café comedy flourished in the 1950s. While Corey's humor was more vaudeville style than New Comedy, he nonetheless introduced themes and approaches to American satire, from routines on Freudian psychology to rapid-fire delivery, that the New Comedians adopted. Corey's "mumbo-jumbo" routines and Lord Buckley's "hipso-matic" jazz lingo launched a brand of comedy that embraced the social role of the holy fool, who was labeled "sick" by the 1950s press. Within the walls of the Village Vanguard, the hungry i, and other bohemian nightspots, comic satirists crafted what was arguably the Rebel Café's most forthright view of America. Sometimes by presaging changes, and sometimes by driving them, they raised a carnival mirror to broader society, in order to expose the absurdities of the Cold War era. Some audiences flinched at the grotesqueries they saw; others burst out laughing at the crudities of the burlesque. But those with the courage of conviction, or a fiercely skeptical eye, saw past the facade of caricature and recognized the social critique lurking underneath.

Left-Coast Liberalism: Mort Sahl and the hungry i

At first blush, Mort Sahl's biography belies his role as the prototypical atomic-age humorist. Born in Montreal in 1927 and raised in Los Angeles by left-leaning liberal Jewish parents, Sahl grew up in an environment, shaped by his civil-servant father, that emphasized social responsibility and Democratic Party loyalty. But the Cold War's conservative turn sharpened Mort's political edges. "My father and mother gave me a very radical orientation," Sahl later asserted. "They are people who refused to watch America turn 180 degrees after FDR." A stint in the Army Air Forces just after World War II provided a firm education in liberalism, as he related in a 1959 interview: "I suddenly got the message. I matured in that idealistic time in the Nineteen Forties when Franklin Roosevelt was president, there was a war on [in] Nazi Germany, and the Democratic Party's social philosophy reigned. All these had an effect—probably still do—on my thinking."[7]

Sahl attended the University of Southern California on the GI Bill, studying public administration and statistics. ("Well," he later quipped, "how else can you document prejudice?") Sahl dropped out of the graduate program at Southern Cal, however, after falling in love with jazz clubs—and a young woman named Susan Babior, whom he followed to Berkeley when she began college.[8] Like many other young arrivals, Sahl found the Bay Area to be revolutionary. "Berkeley had three shifts of people who were forever talking politics in coffeehouses," he facetiously reminisced in his memoir. "There was a cadre of left-wing oriented Jewish kids with fervor. I just wandered around and listened."[9] In Los Angeles, he had occasionally performed under the name Cal Southern, styling himself as a humorist in the mold of Will Rogers, since "ruminating on the human condition" to him "seemed rural." His observational jokes and impersonations of movie stars and politicians proved unsuccessful, however, and after three years of showbiz failure, he put Cal Southern out to pasture.[10]

Sahl's experiences in the Bay Area's charged atmosphere sparked a comedic transformation. Either Babior or, as North Beach lore had it, bohemian Hube the Cube suggested that he audition at the clubs in San Francisco. After a series of rejections, Sahl approached Enrico Banducci, owner of a North Beach cabaret called the hungry i.[11] The standard comic's "equipment" at that time was a tuxedo, which was deemed necessary to give performers a hint of respectability and "class," but Sahl lacked the proper accoutrements. Wearing a suit and tie given to him by musician Stan Kenton and punctuating his jokes with a big cigar, Sahl auditioned for Banducci. By all accounts the act was less than stellar, but Banducci put Sahl on the bill to cover a last-minute cancellation on December 22, 1953. Sahl enticed his friends from campus to attend and, concealing notes for his routine in a newspaper to stave off stage fright, proceeded to crack up his ready-made audience. Banducci was impressed enough to keep the young comic on for a week's run, launching his journey into oppositional satire.[12]

Sahl's sojourn was not a solitary one. His metamorphosis from tree-stump ruminator to pioneering satirist was undertaken in close partnership with Banducci and was embedded in the Rebel Café milieu. The hungry i was first opened in 1950 by Eric "Big Daddy" Nord, later dubbed "King of the Beatniks" by the press and recognized as a West Coast originator of the bohemian lifestyle associated with the Beat generation. From the start, he envisioned the club as a site of provocative discussions and psychic explorations—the "i" stood for either "id" or "intellectual," depending on whom you asked.[13] Nord failed to make a splash, however, and six months later he sold a controlling interest in the club for $800 (reportedly to stake the purchase of a large quantity of cannabis). The new owner was Banducci, a flamboyant impresario whose mustache and beret became a North Beach trademark, invoking Old World style and an artiste's flair. He was initiated into bohemianism by having lived in the Monkey Block as a teenager in the late 1930s and 1940s, hoping for a career as an opera singer and concert violinist. But fame eluded him, and Banducci now envisioned a nightspot that would welcome nonconformists of every stripe, from North

Beach bohos to Berkeley brainiacs. The club's early clientele was similar to the Black Cat's mix of bohemian and gay patrons, and its entertainment consisted primarily of folk musicians, such as Josh White and Stan Wilson.[14]

Most press accounts focused on the hungry i's appeal to the "Bohemian intelligentsia" or the "high IQ crowd" in North Beach. In 1955, the club featured the long-running musical satire *The Pizza Pusher*, starring Vesuvio bartender Guy Wernham and The Place's John Allen Ryan. Lawrence Lipton, author of the renowned 1959 treatise on the Beats, *The Holy Barbarians*, performed jazz poetry there (backed by Eric Nord on congas) as late as 1960.[15] But this artistic eccentricity veiled a deeper leftist streak that ran through the heart of the hungry i. In addition to hiring White when the singer was blacklisted in *Red Channels*, Banducci brought in White's fellow Popular Front protest singers, Sonny Terry and Brownie McGhee.[16] Perhaps most strikingly, in 1956, Banducci hired the blacklisted Hollywood Ten screenwriter Alvah Bessie as the club's light and sound man, following Bessie's prison term for a HUAC conviction. Bessie worked at the hungry i for the next seven years as he struggled to return to Hollywood, later telling Banducci that he had "always been grateful to you for hiring me at a difficult time."[17]

Despite Josh White's performances and Banducci's roots in left-wing bohemia, the hungry i never launched the careers of any notable Cold War–era protest singers. The only folk acts that emerged from the basement venue were the edgy Limeliters, who gained only moderate renown, and the somewhat bland Kingston Trio, who, despite massive popularity in the early 1960s, did little to challenge the status quo.[18] Instead, Sahl's hungry i stint marked the start of the club's main claim to fame: comedians who performed politically tinged routines in front of the stage's signature exposed-brick wall. Banducci's bohemian persona evolved into a reputation as "the Billy Rose of North Beach," with the hungry i touted as "the most influential nightclub west of the Mississippi." Yet he maintained a free spirit and a dedication to interaction between patrons and performers. "I gave people artistic freedom, allowed them to express themselves as they wished, without any interference from me or anybody else," Banducci recalled. He certainly extended this openness to the young Sahl— who reportedly had been told by the unimpressed club owner for whom he first auditioned: "Go across the street to the hungry i. Enrico Banducci will talk to anybody."[19] The partnership that was formed between the comic and the club defined each one's place in American culture, as Sahl's iconoclasm and the hungry i's subterranean populism became inextricably linked in the public mind.

The rapport between Sahl and nightclub audiences, both at the hungry i and in New York venues such as the Village Vanguard, was fundamental to the development of his satirical brand. Sahl was the hungry i's first comedian, but the beatnik and avant-garde ambiance Banducci had cultivated over the previous three years encouraged experimentation. Sahl quickly jettisoned any traditional comedy trappings. Instead of impressions or Borscht Belt setup-and-punch-line routines, he presented stream-of-consciousness monologues drawn from his lone prop, a rolled-up newspaper. The United States was sure to win the Cold War, Sahl assured audiences, since "every time the Russians threw an American in jail, Nixon would throw an American in jail to make sure they didn't get away with it." He savagely satirized the "I Like Ike" phoniness of mid-1950s politics, bringing to the nightspot the sensibility of a subterranean Holden Caulfield (the rebellious teenage central character in J. D. Salinger's 1951 novel, *The Catcher in the Rye*). Eisenhower had better watch his step, Sahl warned, or "General Motors may become vindictive and cut the government off without a cent." These largely improvised lines also included shots at the controversial but then still politically potent Joseph McCarthy. Sahl jived listeners that there was now a Joe McCarthy jacket, just like an Eisenhower jacket, but with "an extra flap that fits over the mouth."[20] While the televised Army-McCarthy hearings from April to June 1954 undoubtedly delivered the final blow, Sahl's sarcasm added power to the discursive punch that finally knocked America's most famous anticommunist out of the limelight.

While Sahl ultimately benefited from having been ahead of the political curve, his remarks made him the target of some early, savage reactions from among the "[Fortune] 400–type socialites" or "crew-cut fraternity boys" and tourists who arrived to sniff out the wild climes of bohemia. Sahl later recalled the early resistance to his material, as "guys would come by and yell 'Communist,' and . . . wait upstairs to beat me up after work, and Enrico would walk out with me and take them on." Sahl's memoir and press interviews show that, even seen through the gloss of nostalgia and (often self-serving) memory, theirs was a joint effort. "It was the Eisenhower fifties and everyone was going along with the lie, so Enrico and I were betting that the audience was smarter than that," Sahl asserted. Those who discouraged them "were our good friends and they were frightened. They said, 'You can't say that, he's the president.' . . . The act [was] a daring rescue mission for America." As the show became more prominent, conservative patrons, often attending shows as part of Gray Line bus tours, sometimes grew hostile, and even violent. One night the wife of John Foster Dulles's pilot, angered by jibes that she felt demeaned the secretary of state, burst onto the stage and slapped Sahl. "It was really a battle," Banducci noted, invoking an image of not-so-cold warfare. Sahl similarly relied on brothers-in-arms language when he discussed Banducci's role: "Enrico is really a demonstration of how powerful an idea can be. You know, Fidel said . . . 'An idea is more powerful than an army.' Well, the club is an idea; the club existed between his ears."[21] Sahl's invocation of bewhiskered rebels tramping through the mountain jungles above Havana, mounting a muscular challenge to Batista's right-wing touristic heaven, only underscored his Cold War oppositional myth making.

As the winter of 1953/54 warmed into summer, Sahl's original one-week stint extended into months, and his new style of intellectual comedy began to catch fire with audiences. By fall, Herb Caen and other local columnists began praising Sahl and his "high IQ"—if "jaded"—humor.[22] Sahl's success relied heavily on the kind of face-to-face interactions found in small nightspots such as The Place—with many of the same cosmopolitan connotations. Banducci later insisted that the hungry i "wasn't just a nightclub, it was a place for people to come and express themselves . . . [with] the intimate atmosphere conducive to lovers of Piaf and Sartre and all the existentialists."[23] The process of challenging the prevailing satirical winds, Sahl suggested, was dialogic: "We found out things too, and you find it out by listening to the audience." He often compared the evolution of his act with jazz improvisations, with the audience acting as fellow band members, adding that "if they don't laugh you're playing a cappella."[24]

With the hungry i firmly rooted in North Beach bohemia, the club's transformation into an entertainment space required some adjustment as its circle of patrons widened to include more who were just casual visitors. Attempting to maintain an environment of rational exchange, one that was friendly to his performers, Banducci told drunks who "wanted to get in on the act" to be quiet, enforcing respect for ideas over mere uninhibited outbursts.[25] Banducci even stopped serving cocktails during the show, "so the entertainer didn't have to fight waiters pushing steaks or pushing drinks." Such a radical nightclub policy had very real implications for the dynamic between satirists and audiences. "Mort Sahl could take the lingering pause," Banducci later stated. "You could hear a pin drop in the whole damn room. Then he'd whap ya and the whole room would just break up."[26] The hungry i's distinct performative space was later illustrated in a 1961 article in *Holiday* magazine. "The spotlight is on the performer," the writer noted, "who stands with his back to a brick wall, facing the audience in a setting which suggests the working area of a Cuban firing squad." One entertainer, echoing this authoritarian tone, stated, "It's a great room because of the discipline that's forced on the audience."[27]

This emphasis on audience attention sits in uneasy tension with the 1950s cabaret as a site of discussion. Although Banducci's policies certainly discouraged a completely open dialogue of the kind found during The Place's Blabbermouth Nights, they did fit within liberal notions of a rational public sphere and reasoned debate (however uncomfortably those may sit within an often-raucous democracy). In his memoir, Sahl discussed the social conventions, cradled within the jazz idiom, that underpinned nightclub discourse:

> Jazz musicians were saying that, as Lennie Tristano put it, my newspaper was my ax and I improvised within a chord structure, which was my thematic material. They . . . seemed to know that what I had to say was innovative in the same sense that Marlon Brando's work was at that time. Marlene Dietrich said to me once in 1957, "Brando's secret is that he acts like a human being, and most actors act like actors." Well, I acted like a human being and talked about those things that affect human beings, rather than talked like a nightclub comedian. My secret was in the public domain—that the audience has just as much stake in what happens to America as I do.

For Sahl, his lack of rehearsal before a show was, in itself, part of this dialogue. Otherwise, it would have felt "like rehearsing a conversation."[28] Recognizing the commercial aspect of these exchanges, Sahl insisted that his monologues were not a lecture, but rather a "point of view" that audiences "subsidize."[29] According to Sahl, Dietrich declared that the hungry i was "the only place she'd seen political cabaret outside Berlin," recognizing Banducci's aim to foster an atmosphere of discussion and controversy, if only to swell the size of the crowds.[30]

The hungry i's crowds did indeed expand, and in the spring of 1954, Banducci opened a new, larger location, raising his seating capacity from 83 to over 200. The decor reflected the Rebel Café's sensibility, with both European sophistication and American no-nonsense populism. During the renovations, Banducci removed the decorative plaster and left the venue's load-bearing brick walls exposed. While sarcastically suggesting that the end result "looked like the ruins of Frankfurt," Sahl clearly admired the club owner's work ethic, detailing how he "poured the concrete foundation and built the bar, by hand, and worked around the clock sandblasting." Whether out of instinct or shrewdness, Banducci's innovative upgrade became a symbol for the rejection of slick, commodified facades—à la the beatniks—while simultaneously inviting patrons to envision themselves sitting in a Montmartre cabaret. "The motif of simplicity is maintained scrupulously," the *New York Times* enthused, before making a prediction that soon proved to be prescient. "If this country's offbeat tastes are spawned in such uninhibited spots as the bistros of this city's North Beach district, look out for a wave of Bohemianism combining the chi chi of Paris and the breeziness of San Francisco."[31]

This formula—combining European mystique with an American journeyman ethos, and earnest earthiness with theatrical formality—struck a nerve with the public, which craved this dual notion of authenticity. The best productions of the mid-1950s, crowed one San Francisco critic, originally "rose out of the English music halls of the early eighteenth century in which ale was served with thesping, just as it is today at the hungry i and Purple Onion."[32] Sahl's public image further cemented these associations. Banducci had encouraged Sahl to discard the comedian's traditional attire in favor of an open-collared shirt and V-necked sweater, giving him the appearance of a thoughtful graduate student "straight from the campus at Berkeley." Sahl insisted that the switch was his idea, but the intended effect was largely the same: to avoid looking "like any member of the society you're criticizing."[33]

This sartorial statement spoke to Cold War audiences on multiple levels. First, the rejection of the classy clothes normally required for comic acceptability appealed to patrons who sought to escape the conformist pressures of mass-produced consumer culture. Equally, however, Sahl's sweater, like the beatnik's sweatshirt, suggested that the transcendence of bourgeois tastes was the prerogative of *members of that class*. According to this cultural logic, those who had access to the trappings of middle-class affluence were the only ones who could truly claim to have voluntarily rejected them. Further, the mention of Berkeley highlighted the association between middle-class status and a college education, which was increasingly within the reach of those like Sahl, who qualified for the GI Bill, yet was largely withheld from African American veterans (not to mention women and gay men, who were deemed to be outside the realm of standard military service).[34] Thus Sahl's sweater was a subtle form of self-congratulation for his fans, since they saw reflections of themselves in his image—intoning the social authority of the educated, along with the authenticity of informality—and complimented themselves that their very presence at the hungry i distinguished them as connoisseurs of a new American culture.

Through the mid-1950s, as the press reported on Sahl's popularity with bohemians, college students, and jazz fans, he gained the attention of Dave Brubeck's saxophonist, Paul Desmond.[35] This led to Sahl having the opening slot on a Brubeck concert in 1955, which was recorded and later released by Fantasy Records as Sahl's second album, *Live at Sunset*, in 1958. As Sahl's first-known recording, the performance suggests the shape and appeal of his early material at the hungry i. Sahl peppered Brubeck's crowd with snappy patter, alternating between light-hearted vignettes about young, middle-class, masculine culture—with coffee tables made from doors placed on top of bricks, expensive hi-fi systems, and European sports cars—and satirical looks at 1950s politics: the push for socialized medicine, America's role in the United Nations, the plight of unions, racial discrimination, and the architects of the Red Scare. Sahl elicited boisterous responses with cracks that the American Medical Association was "against any cure that is rapid," such as "artificial insemination," and that British sports cars bought to impress girls were constantly under repair, leading to the conclusion that "neither one of them is worth it." Meanwhile, the Cold War and America's new global hegemony were never far from the surface. On US-Soviet competition for the allegiance of emerging nations in Asia and Africa, Sahl quipped, "Are they our neutrals or are they theirs?" Stabs at FBI agents, the military-industrial complex, and conservative efforts to dismantle Franklin Roosevelt's legacy received equally appreciative responses.[36] These reactions indicated the arrival of a new American audience, one that steered the direction of Cold War comedy, which insisted on hip, sophisticated, and worldly commentary, yet often bowed uncritically toward male prerogatives and the baubles of affluence.

It is no mere coincidence that both Sahl and *Playboy* magazine debuted in December 1953. Both were products of a time that offered a sense of intellectual sophistication that was tied to the titillation of broken taboos, the objectification of women, and brazen public expressions that mirrored patrons' hidden desires—all wrapped in a stubbornly patriotic package that declared itself to be fundamentally American. Sahl later recounted that *Playboy* publisher Hugh Hefner recognized that they rolled along parallel tracks, suggesting that the "magazine has got to do what you do. You make the people feel hip." In his memoir, radical cartoonist Jules Feiffer, whose *Village Voice* sketches were appropriately titled "Sick, Sick, Sick," notes the combined effect of these two new social forces that tackled "the undiscussable subjects: politics, the FBI, the Cold War, and sex."[37] Although *Playboy* ultimately had a deeper impact on national culture, in the late 1950s Sahl ran neck and neck with the magazine's popularity. His albums under the jazz label of Verve Records—*The Future Lies Ahead*

(1958), *1960 or Look Forward in Anger* (1959), and *At the hungry i* (1960)—each sold in the hundreds of thousands. Sahl also began to appear on Broadway, in feature films, and on national TV. The pair's tracks even occasionally crossed, as Sahl hosted *Playboy's* first Chicago Jazz Festival in 1959 and appeared on Hefner's *Playboy's Penthouse* and *After Dark* television shows through the 1960s.[38]

The overlaps ended there, however. Hefner's empire was founded firmly in the realm of mass media, always on a trajectory of undifferentiated expansion, even as it offered the illusion of hip exclusivity, consciously linking sex and status.[39] Sahl, on the other hand, remained primarily a boutique commodity. The attraction of his humor was its immediacy, that of an artisan hand-crafting each improvised performance for audiences who were enough in the know to make their way into subterranean cabarets. Feiffer's comments underscore this aspect of Sahl's significance, as well as the feeling that Rebel Café patrons participated in a kind of resistance movement: "Mort Sahl opened the discussion. If you were in his audience, you felt that this stuff was dangerous, truly underground humor. One might be arrested for listening."[40] Sahl sated the desires of audiences thirsty for commodities that proclaimed their emerging class status and worldly sophistication: in other words, cultural literacy as conspicuous consumption. Yet audience desires were inflamed by the notion that they were not simply consumers, but active producers of the "conversation" in the hungry i's showroom.

Sahl's orbit first extended outside San Francisco in the fall of 1954, when he traveled to New York City for a short run at the upscale Blue Angel. Owner Max Gordon must have seen the potential Sahl had for Gordon's more-bohemian Village Vanguard, however. In early 1955, the rising comic returned to New York for a Vanguard stint—another thread in the bicoastal bohemian tapestry.[41] Paul Desmond's connections in the jazz club circuit also led to shows in Boston and Chicago. Throughout the late 1950s, Sahl's friends in the jazz world, particularly Dave Brubeck, connected him with management, as well as with bookings at hip Rebel Café venues.[42]

Sahl's appearances at the Village Vanguard fit organically within the oppositional atmosphere created by Max and Lorraine Gordon. Sahl later asserted that in the mid-1950s, Max was "a disappointed freethinker" who mourned that "people don't come out, and they don't want to change the world."[43] Despite this pessimism, the Gordons continued to provide a public forum for the expression of provocative ideas. For over a decade, Sahl remained a staple in the Village, where satirical humor reverberated through an active and engaged community. For Village scribbler Dan Wakefield, visits to neighborhood jazz clubs were part of daily existence, and his walk to and from home regularly included a look "to see if there was any musician or group I wanted to catch," or a late night visit to hear "some stand-up comedians" such as "Mort Sahl, Jackie Mason, Redd Foxx." Ronald Sukenick also noted the comic's effect on himself and "a number of novelists" who were inspired by his satire "to break away from established styles." Even those in the neighborhood's gay community recalled Sahl's humor as part of the "crosscurrents flowing beneath the prevailing calm of the fifties."[44]

For Sahl, challenging the norm was an expression of nationalism. He saw himself in a tradition of dissent-as-patriotism, always in defense of the country. Although he was uncomfortable with comparisons to the Beats, the notion that dissent was a fundamental part of the American experiment, perhaps central to the belief in its perfectibility, was something Sahl shared with aesthetic radicals like Kenneth Rexroth and Allen Ginsberg. Many of the same themes in the poetry of City Lights' Lawrence Ferlinghetti—from the New Deal through the Second World War, transnational consciousness, patriotism, dissent, and the New Saloon—were also present in Sahl's satire.[45] Noting the liberatory potential of nightspots, in 1963 Sahl proclaimed that he had "constructed a network of theaters where people can speak—they happen to be saloons, and people said it could not be done—in complete freedom." On the flip side of the discursive coin, Sahl touted himself as a lodestar of public opinion. "I found out, I guess, what teachers feel like. You know, . . . [a school is] not a democracy, [it's] a school," he noted, "and if you owe anything to the students, it's to uplift them, to make knowledge attractive. If you leave it to them, they're going to say, 'On a democratic basis, we prefer recess and chocolate milk.'" More succinctly, and pessimistically, Sahl suggested that the American public was easily misled and insisted that his function was to wake people up, or even act as the nation's conscience.[46]

Sahl projected himself as a public spokesman for fundamental American principles that were in danger of erosion from without and within. Many of his signature routines unfavorably juxtaposed American and Soviet leadership, wringing laughs from the harsh truth that hypocrisy and misuses of power did not fester solely behind the Iron Curtain. Sahl was staunchly anti-Soviet and frequently referred to their leader, Nikita Khrushchev, as a "thug." But he also took the unpopular stance of supporting Fidel Castro's revolution after its 1959 takeover of the Cuban government—a clear demonstration of his antiauthoritarian populism. Sahl credited nightclub audiences with being ready for such controversy, asserting that this nightclub rapport underpinned a more authentic form of satire, allowing him to express "what I really cared about instead of an act."[47]

Sahl's style ultimately undercuts the idea that he was only educating and entertaining passive patrons. In a 1958 *New York Times* editorial, Sahl declared that his audiences were allies, insisting that "the scarcity of satire on the American scene" was because the average comic lacked the courage to be critical and "projects his inadequacies onto the audience." Enjoying Sahl's routines demanded a level of fluency in world affairs—or, perhaps more to the point, an awareness of *commentary* on them. "To keep up with Mr. Sahl," said one perspicuous critic, "you have to be not only equally quick but also equally familiar with what is going on, and with what Mr. Sahl has said about what people are saying about what is going on in his creation of himself as one of the conspicuous figures." Sahl later recalled those years, somewhat wistfully, as a period when "I was playing back the sounds of my time."[48] Even as followers congratulated themselves on their superior taste, a persistent democratic ethos ran through Sahl's popular appeal.

Left-coast liberal: Mort Sahl. Grey Villet / Getty Images, TLPE 50405533

Sahl's inability to translate nightclub intimacy into larger venues only highlighted his act's populist, even therapeutic, aspects. After Sahl premiered a Broadway show in 1958, one critic wrote that his motor-mouth delivery left theater audiences "feeling a certain defensive edginess." Yet, the critic concluded, Sahl's iconoclastic humor was a welcome change "after too many muddy and fearful years," adding that "it's nice to know that improper things can once more be said in public."[49] As such, Sahl became a touchstone: a symbol of incoherent rebellion for some, and a redeemer of a humorless age for others. Some saw his assaults on authority as "a symptom of the 20th century's own sickness," portending the nation's decline. "It's like the last days of Rome," asserted *Time* magazine's feature on the New Comedians in 1959. "They joked about father and Freud, about mother and masochism, about sister and sadism." In conjunction with Sahl's reputation in the press as a "saloon talker," these connotations suggested a social parallel with psychoanalysis. To raise underlying issues to the level of public discussion, Sahl said, plainly, "I discovered I had to *talk*." In so doing, he contributed to a vein of critique that managed to "see the worm in the golden apple" of postwar prosperity, furthering mainstream public debate about the nature of American society.[50] As scholars like economist John Kenneth Galbraith, as well as Michael Harrington and C. Wright Mills questioned the beneficence of corporate liberalism, Sahl offered a similar message to audiences who might not have cracked open a copy of Galbraith's *Affluent Society* (1959).

When Sahl ended a performance with the exhortation to "break off into buzz groups and discuss the real meaning of the material," he was only half joking. As noted by sociologists and the popular press, talk between nightclub patrons following a performance was common.[51] Supporters asserted that Sahl "brought to the stage a type of talent heretofore unknown in this country," which "finds its antecedents in the 17th and 18th century French and English aristocratic salons." As the *New York Times* opined—invoking European literary authority—audiences followed Sahl's lead as "a sort of bistro Voltaire." His youngish, professorial crowds recognized that he "demands a great deal from his audiences" and hoped that his political, psychological, and literary perspectives would rub off, elevating their late night talk.[52] While the historical record of audience conversations after his shows is obviously thin, ABC television's 1962 special report on political comedy offers some insight. News cameras captured patrons after Sahl's performance at Mr. Kelly's, a Chicago nightclub, as groups of young men milled on the sidewalk. The reporter, however, interviewed mostly white, middle-class couples. While one self-identified Bostonian registered his displeasure at Sahl's satire of President Kennedy, a woman in pearls and furs firmly asserted that "it's healthy" to embrace criticism of US policy: "As Americans it brings a serious problem into focus." Another man applauded the ability of satire to help the public see the government objectively.[53] At least in front of the cameras, political discussion continued beyond the doors of the nightclub, suggesting the sorts of exchanges that took place on the sidewalks of San Francisco and New York.

Sahl therefore played two roles in the public sphere. First, he interpreted the news of the day for his audiences, encouraging discussions within the nightclub and, by extension, wherever his record albums were played and listened to in group settings. Second, Sahl's critiques, which were explored—and deplored—in the press, further contributed to a broad social dialogue. Throughout, he was always quick to note the centrality of the hungry i's milieu to this process. "I went to the cover of *Time* magazine without ever leaving the city of San Francisco," he boasted in characteristically hyperbolic fashion, "and I did it by having a one-club platform. If you have a place to stand, you can move the world. Consider what a television audience is by numbers then figure what it means to have only 265 people in a club. Yet everybody knew the hungry i, and everybody knew that its connotation was Mort Sahl."[54]

Despite his Rebel Café origins, however, Sahl held traditionalist views of women and African Americans that ultimately contributed to his irrelevance in the 1960s. Sahl's memoir is peppered with disdainful comments about civil rights leaders, betraying a deep-seated antipathy to black equality that occasionally broke through even during his most egalitarian period, in the 1950s. In one incident, Sahl was booked to open for the Duke Ellington Orchestra at Hollywood's Crescendo Club, but, in a flight of hubris, he refused to take second billing to the legendary jazz artist, revealed his underlying, prejudiced assumptions. The press justifiably railed against the Canadian-born comic for failing to recognize Ellington's status as America's foremost composer—the very embodiment of erudite sophistication in African American arts.[55] While such coverage certainly ignored the many times Sahl had previously been an opening act for African American headliners, it is nonetheless telling that Sahl was willing to aim his newfound show-business firepower at Ellington, even when doing so had deeply insulting racial implications.

Although Sahl occasionally took shots at southern segregation, he never supported the civil rights movement. He adopted a paternalistic attitude toward black liberation, a common stance among postwar liberals, and often suggested that while overt racist oppression should be condemned, African Americans were not ready for complete inclusion in the body politic. In an interview in the summer of 1963, Sahl simultaneously demanded recognition for his outspokenness against segregation and asserted that African Americans were not fully equipped to vote. Condemning the upcoming March on Washington, Sahl unleashed a condescending tirade, inflected with both racism and sexism:

> You *can't* march on Washington. . . . Demonstrations are fine to let the Congress know that they're not insulated. . . . But I want to know how you can control that. I like hostility at times, when it's justified by the situation, but if hostility can't be controlled it then becomes an instrument of terror, even to the person who possesses it. . . .
>
> It may end in a lot of blood, because . . . if somebody gets out of line, you will have to call in the law, because the Negroes will represent outlaws in that situation. . . . I don't think that's getting anything accomplished.
>
> You can't *sit in* on Congress. It's *against the law*. . . . And I'm talking about getting something *done*, not expressing the individual neuroses of those Jewish girls who belong to the NAACP. Let 'em take it out on their husbands, like they used to.[56]

Sahl ended by suggesting that women's liberation—while offering the potential for women to become "human beings, like men are now"—would, in the short term, create misery for those who "don't have skills" to compete in a masculine world.[57]

Sahl's derailment was completed by the assassination of President John F. Kennedy, for whom he had written jokes during the 1960 election period. Convinced that the assassination was hatched from within the US government, Sahl became mired in conspiracy theories and an acerbic brand of social conservatism. He had lost sight of the Rebel Café by not keeping pace with cultural change and then taking a wrong turn entirely. Other New Comedians had already stepped in, however, continuing the march toward controversial cultural horizons.

Lenny Bruce: Holy Fool and Tragic Shaman

Lenny Bruce is more widely remembered today than Mort Sahl—Lenny the Martyr, who was hounded to death by the puritan police and fig leaf–applying district attorneys in America's most cosmopolitan cities. As a free speech proponent and cultural gadfly, his story is well known. He developed a national reputation as an irreverent "sick" comic in 1958, selling hundreds of thousands of live comedy albums for Fantasy Records, appearing on Steve Allen's television show, and packing nightclubs across the country. Bruce's downfall started in 1961, when he was arrested on drug charges in Philadelphia. The case was dismissed amid implications of police corruption, but it was followed by more than a dozen busts in other cities for "obscene" nightclubs performances, from San Francisco's Jazz Workshop and Los Angeles's Troubadour to Chicago's Gate of Horn and New York's Café au Go-Go. Bruce was acquitted in San Francisco in 1962, signaling that city's political sensibilities. His trials in New York and Chicago over the next two years, however, had the opposite outcome, and he became the victim of a de facto blacklist when club owners feared prosecution and refused to hire him. Bruce made his case to audiences in his few remaining venues, and a stream of high-profile supporters—from Norman Mailer, James Baldwin, and Susan Sontag to liberal theologian Reinhold Niebuhr—rallied to his defense, but to no avail. The controversial comic died, penniless, of a heroin overdose in 1966. He was posthumously vindicated two years later, when his New York case was overturned on appeal.[58]

Bruce's status as a countercultural icon was cemented in 1974, both with Albert Goldman's sensationalistic biography, *Ladies and Gentlemen—Lenny Bruce!!*, and the Hollywood film *Lenny*, starring Dustin Hoffman. This movie, a more sympathetic but equally problematic portrayal, followed Goldman's formula of sex, drugs, and dirty jokes. Subsequent popular texts and documentaries apotheosized Bruce as a cultural martyr who saved America from the repression of the 1950s and almost single-handedly freed what he referred to as "the word" from puritanical restraint. More recently, scholars have fleshed out these one-dimensional views. Stephen Kercher, for instance, places Bruce in a historical context through comparisons with the Beats and the sexually liberated *Playboy* lifestyle. Tracing the comedian's Jewish working-class roots and identity in relation to audience expectations of authenticity and social justice, Kercher also compares Bruce's work with critics' concerns in the 1950s about "momism," conformity, and mass society. In addition to his jazzy inflections and lingo, Bruce was an example of a hipster holy fool, who racially cross-dressed in a mantle of African American culture and translated subterranean language as part of the Rebel Café's socially Freudian, shamanistic, and Rabelaisian psychosexual catharsis.[59]

While Goldman's biography had the merit of expansiveness, tracing many of Bruce's social connections in North Beach and Greenwich Village, he artificially separated the comic from this milieu—a failing that has hobbled subsequent accounts. Lenny Bruce was directly engaged with the Beats and other overlapping Rebel Café circles. Similarly, he embraced their views of reinvention and authenticity, questioning powerful institutions and popular orthodoxies and speaking out instead in favor of a liberated personal moralism. Controversy over his satire was also rooted in a Cold War consciousness, with debates springing up over individual, sexual, and racial liberation versus fears of national decline and Soviet dominance. Placing Bruce within this context sheds light on his public role as a subterranean critic of American culture and politics.

Bruce's comedy was the next logical step for the Rebel Café: its move into the realm of satirical entertainment. Only familiar aspects of a society or a culture are subject to humor, while unfamiliarity with a punch line simply leaves audiences feeling perplexed. Bruce's material not only absorbed the ethos of North Beach and Greenwich Village night people, but it also reflected their milieu back to them—as well as broadcast it to hip mainstream patrons who wanted to show that they were in on the joke. His routines were peppered with references to the Black Hawk's Helen Noga, Chicago's nightclub mafiosi, New York's Blue Angel, the modernism of Gertrude Stein, the Scottsboro Nine's Popular Front civil rights case, the Beats, jazz poetry, drug addiction, gays and lesbians, interracial marriage, and Freud. This was his task as a modern shaman: to delve, intoxicated, into the underworld and into the past, bringing back a new perspective on current events. This outsider vision allowed him to skewer the politics of the day, from segregationist Governor Faubus to the Cold War, while intermixing them with nightclub culture, such as comparing Sahl with South Korea's first president, Syngman Rhee. Bruce was no intellectual; his insights were mostly prosaic. But they were effective, allowing audiences to look directly at troubling issues, and themselves. In the process, he legitimated the underground as worthy of satirical scrutiny. "I was not born in a vacuum," Bruce told one San Francisco audience, acknowledging his transmissive and transgressive function. "Every thought I have belongs to somebody else. . . . So I am not placating you by making the following statement. I want to help you if you have a dirty-word problem."[60]

Bruce's confrontation with taboos—what Freud defined as sacred, unclean, or forbidden aspects of life denoted as *unapproachable*—placed him squarely in the underground's mental geography. The most important precedent for Bruce's style was the vaudevillian turned hipster Lord Buckley, whose "white Negro" mystique emanated from his theatrically regal persona, which was infused with hip-jive jargon. Henry Miller had once praised Buckley with invocations of both Roman sewers and a Christ-like secular sacrifice, stating, "It seems to me that your Lordship opened a new vein, leading from the medulla oblongata (hold on to this one!) and the Cloaca Maxima." Miller than added, "I say it as a writer who knows the power of language, the miracles it can work."[61]

Such a characterization was equally suited to Bruce's oeuvre, with his Freudian "toilet" jokes and satires of religious hypocrisy, such as "Religions, Inc." and the notorious "St. Paul giving up fucking." A juxtaposition of the scatological, the sacred, and the profane was Bruce's stock in trade—to the extent that he recited sections of Henry Miller's banned 1934 novel, *Tropic of Cancer*, onstage. Bruce confronted the social construction of language itself, exploding the notion that the word itself is equivalent to the object it represents. But underlying this semantic commentary was the fundamental question of what constituted *public* propriety. For instance, Bruce routinely critiqued the orthodox Christian notion that nakedness is inherently sinful, stating that "if God created the body, and the body is dirty, then the fault lies with the manufacturer." And he was well known early in his career for appearing on stage naked—a parallel with Allen Ginsberg's insistence on "nakedness" (in its various forms) as a sign of honesty.[62] Bruce, who was Jewish and bisexual, shared a common identity with many in the bohemian underground. While he was not publicly open about his sexuality and, equally, shied away from obvious left-wing alliances, his personal queer bohemian hipsterism influenced the content of his comedy and its transgressive political potential. Bruce's tribute to Henry Miller was a prime demonstration of his immersion in Rebel Café culture. Its literary past and its street language—the humor of which rarely comes through on the written page—laid a foundation for his avant-garde style.[63]

Lenny Bruce, born Alfred Leonard Schneider in 1925 to a lower-middle-class family living on Long Island, changed his name when he followed his mother into show business after World War II. Like Jack Kerouac, he had served in the navy and was dismissed for erratic behavior—in the comic's case, for cross-dressing. Unlike Kerouac, Bruce saw action during the war (and also had his first homosexual experience then), but he did not seek a psychiatric discharge until 1946, well after the guns at Anzio had stopped blazing. After a stint in the merchant marine, Bruce segued into comedy, working in Catskill resorts in New York State and at seedy burlesque joints in Los Angeles, with one brief television appearance on the *Arthur Godfrey Talent Show*, doing rather poor impressions of Hollywood gangster movies. He slowly developed his hip style, blending the blue humor of the spritz spewed by comics as they hung out after hours in New York's all-night cafeterias with the jive of jazz musicians who backed up burlesque-house strippers. He finally made a splash in 1958, at Ann's 440 in San Francisco.[64]

His "radical" innovation was to bring underground talk into the spotlight, turning what was formerly private into public speech. As one compatriot recalled, in the nightclubs of North Beach Bruce openly presented "things you only talked about to friends." Like the Beats, this revelatory style was driven by postwar disillusionment, paralleling their apocalyptic consciousness. Given the history of the United States' brutal conquest and genocide against Latin American and Native American foes, Bruce insisted that the fight against the Nazis' racist aggression bore more than a hint of hypocrisy. "War spells out my philosophy of 'No right or wrong'—just 'Your right, my wrong,'" he wrote. "Everything is subjective."[65]

Bruce's hip style both directly and indirectly reflected a rapidly swirling milieu of mutual influences. His earliest breakthroughs were clearly modeled on Mort Sahl's act, complete with a newspaper prop. But Bruce moved on into edgier territory, as saxophonist Pony Poindexter recalled about the night when the comic was arrested in Philadelphia in 1961. For Poindexter, Bruce represented the true oppositional sensibility of the jazz/bohemian underground: "The opening night was packed. Lenny had the big crowd cracking up—and me too. I was sitting on a chair close to the entrance to the dressing room. I was laughing my ass off, along with everyone else." Poindexter, always politically and racially conscious, continued:

> Then Lenny told the story of the black dude that had got busted in New York for dealing cocaine, and when his buddy went to a lawyer, the lawyer asked, "Yes, but does he have any money?" His buddy said, "Aw, man, he's got more money than Billy Graham!"
>
> At that point, I fell off my chair on the floor and completely lost my decorum, bent over, kicking my feet in the air. I had to be helped into the dressing room. . . . Here was Lenny Bruce, a white comic, closer to the black dude playing jazz than any other white cat out there. And here also was white officialdom's reaction to all this. A staged raid!—with all the resultant publicity.

North Beach guitarist Eddie Duran remembered simply: "Lenny Bruce was part of the jazz scene, too. I used to run into him at the clubs all the time. Once he came into the 'hungry i' while I was playing there . . . and he did an impromptu show, just got up on the stage and started talking."[66]

Such connections were at the heart of Bruce's career. He first came to Fantasy Records' notice through Paul Desmond and Mort Sahl. The latter featured Bruce as an opening act when performing at the Crescendo Club in Los Angeles. And the public sometimes literally conflated Bruce with the Beats. In 1958 at the hungry i, after Bruce left a record-release party for *The Sick Humor of Lenny Bruce* in a huff, he described his chagrin to a reporter: "Seven people asked *me* who Lenny Bruce was. Finally, somebody asked me if *that* was Lenny Bruce and pointed over in a corner to a guy with long hair, dirty sweatshirt, blue jeans, Pernod and Peter Orlovsky—it was Allen Ginsberg!"[67]

This circle soon extended to New York, as Harry Belafonte's former manager, Jack Rollins, brought Bruce to the Village Vanguard. Max Gordon then booked him into the Blue Angel, where Bruce alternately entertained and offended what he called the club's "literate, erudite audience." The *Village Voice*'s John Wilcock recalled Bruce's debut at the Vanguard, where the comic characteristically turned his satirical barbs toward his own milieu. Wilcock asserted that "the very first thing . . . he came in and he looked around this little tiny room with about four hundred people crammed in, and he said, 'I don't know how Max Gordon can afford to pay me a grand a week to work a place this size. . . . I've come to the conclusion he must be a crook.'" Such cracks might explain Gordon's ambivalence toward Bruce, although he always saw the comic as "money in the bank." Gordon also recognized a generational divide, describing his nephew—the club's manager and a student at the New School—as a friend and fan of Bruce, alongside the "college kids, hookers, fags, the jet set,

Harlem society, [and] the Broadway and Hollywood crowd" who "jammed the place every night." During Bruce's New York obscenity trial in 1964, left-wing cartoonist Jules Feiffer underscored this view, testifying that Bruce's career was a reaction to "the Eisenhower administration . . . when political and social commentary were not encouraged, but were permitted in night clubs." He insisted that Bruce presented a "personal kind of theater," arguing that "he's going to the very core of what the American experience is today, in terms of my generation."[68]

Just as the abstract expressionists emphasized free movement in painting, and jazzmen and Beats celebrated spontaneity and authenticity, Bruce extended improvisation, social critique, and overtones of masculine sexuality into the realm of comedy, doing so even more stridently than Sahl had. In the liner notes for *Sick Humor*, music critic Ralph Gleason laid out a striking, if overstated, case for the social import of Bruce's underground satire of America:

> Bruce's comedy is a dissent from a world gone mad. To him nothing is sacred except the ultimate truths of love and beauty and moral goodness—all equating honesty. . . . It is strong stuff—like jazz, and it is akin to the point of view of Nelson Algren and Lawrence Ferlinghetti as well as to Charlie Parker and Lester Young . . . [which is] why his comedy of dissent has flourished in the jazz clubs. . . . The jazz musician is a rebel with humor, if with a cause, and there is no more effective putdown of the political speeches, the incongruities in the news, the fatuous posing of the tent show religious carnivals than that which goes on in the conversation of the jazz musician and the humor of Lenny Bruce.

"The jazzman may be anti-verbal, as Kenneth Rexroth says," Gleason concluded, but "if so, he has Lenny Bruce to speak for him with power."[69]

The evolution of Bruce's material was telling. He went from jazzy comedy to satirical public confessions during the pivotal years when the Beat generation came to widespread acclaim. *The Carnegie Hall Concert*, recorded in 1961 but unreleased for a decade, captured Bruce at his popular and satirical peak. The performance was almost entirely socially critical and confessional, with few prepared routines. Bruce was clearly concerned with authenticity and couched most of his criticisms in personal terms—even if thinly veiled. In "Dykes and Faggots," Bruce offered a Kinsey-like redefinition of homosexuality as "anybody that's ever been involved in any homosexual act . . . 'cause I assume that you're all faggots, then—the old cliché that there's no such thing as being a little pregnant . . . we are sometimes homosexuals, all of us." He also recognized that his popularity was generational, insisting that anyone over forty-five failed to understand his humor, due to their lack of "exposure," instead getting hung up on his jive jargon and Yiddish words. Always self-critical, Bruce revealed the process of the subterraneans' translation into the mainstream, acknowledging what he called his own prejudice against small-town "Gray Line tour people," who just wanted to learn the lingo so they could be in on the joke. Consciously or

The tragic shaman on stage: Lenny Bruce. Copyright © Dennis Stock /
Magnum Photos, STD1959013W00003/05

not, Bruce paralleled New Bohemia's contradictory claims to authenticity, hip community, and personal liberation.

While it appears as though Bruce never overtly acknowledged Beat influences on his work, an early version of an excerpt from his autobiography is revealing, bearing a striking resemblance to Ginsberg's "America" and its satirical denouncement of "them bad Russians. / Them Russians them Russians and them Chinamen. And them Russians." Writing in 1960 of a friend's World War II experience, Bruce declaimed, in sardonic, atomic-apocalyptic terms, that it was

> a chance to kill . . . those poor dirty Japs, those poor pregnant women that stood in the silent Army . . . unconcerned with politics and their only association with economics is that thirty-nine cents a pound for chop meat is ridiculous, those dirty

Japs . . . that in the near future would sell us cameras . . . because now there are no more dirty Japs, there are dirty Commies and when we run out of them they'll just be dirty, dirty and then a few hippies who discovered that the earth is dirty and the whole world will just bomb the shit out of the earth and there will be no more dirty, dirty.[70]

Unlike Ginsberg, Kerouac expressly disliked Bruce's apparent nihilism and his stabs at the Catholic Church. Yet Kerouac's distaste for Bruce perhaps reflected an unconscious fear that he himself was being mocked, as they shared an eerie similarity in the cadences and rhythms of their spoken-word performances. Both were fans of Lord Buckley, and each used a singsong phrasing, inflected with the rounded consonants of a New York City accent and punctuated by quick jabs of hip jargon. Kerouac's friend David Amram could not help but compare him to Bruce—a parallel that was most notable in the Beat writer's narration for the 1959 film, *Pull My Daisy*. Similarly, Beat poet Philip Whalen noted with some aplomb, after the *San Francisco Chronicle* covered a reading by him in 1964, that "Gleason reviewed the scene favorably . . . except he thought I can't read very well & my writing 'owes much to Lenny Bruce.'"[71]

Beat disagreements over Bruce illustrate the Rebel Café's vitality in the public sphere, not as a monolithic lock-step movement, but as pluralistic one, full of contention and debate. This extended to Bruce's admittedly peripheral engagement with politics. When his New York legal troubles heated up in 1964, Ginsberg, Beat poet Diane di Prima, and bohemian author Helen Weaver quickly organized a defense committee in the Village. (Apropos of his dislike for Bruce, Kerouac refused to sign Ginsberg's petition.)[72]

Bruce's own activism, however, was limited to the stage. "There are words that offend me," he asserted on the *Steve Allen Show* in 1959, adding that "Governor Faubus, segregation offend me." His recognition of desegregation's importance was appropriate, given his concerns about free speech and access to public space being fundamental to American citizenship. But most often, he focused purely on the relationship between language, consciousness, and racism. Power, he insisted, was invested in the word. "By the way, are there any niggers here tonight?" he asked one stunned-silent audience before launching into a rapid, auction-block list of racial epithets, from "kikes" to "funky hunkies" and "micks." "The point," he concluded, was that "if President Kennedy got on television every day and said 'I would like to introduce all the niggers in my cabinet,' and all the niggers called each other niggers . . . in front of the ofays . . . in the second month 'nigger' wouldn't mean as much as 'goodnight' or 'God bless you' when you sneeze or perhaps as much as 'I promise to tell the truth, the whole truth, so help me God.'" With this stab at the heart of a linguistic taboo, he declared, "nigger would lose its impact and never make any four-year-old nigger cry when he came home from school. *Zug gornischt* [say nothing] gives it the power, Jim."[73]

This approach was problematic, missing the larger structures of power that guide cultural meaning. But Bruce put his money where his mouth was, donating to Bayard Rustin's Committee to Defend Martin Luther King Jr. in 1960. Rustin responded, spotlighting the controversy over Bruce's humor among blacks, and speculating "on where you'd be without the Negro race." "Well, to reverse the situation," Rustin then concluded, "I know a couple of Negro students in Montgomery who might still be in a cozy Dixie jail if it were not for your $500."[74] Further, Bruce felt that his immersion in jazz culture and his close friendships with African Americans like guitarist Eric Miller gave him grounds to criticize the hypocrisy of liberals who threw money at the civil rights movement but remained silent about northern redlining. At least with the Ku Klux Klan, Bruce reasoned, you knew where you stood: "It's very easy to criticize the South with their obvious Anti-Christ: '*Shlepp* them away from the lunch counters and don't let them use the toilet.' Now I know that Philly is worse than Little Rock and New York is more twisted than Atlanta will ever be." Yet Bruce's self-interest limited his activism. He refused to cancel shows and sacrifice himself either financially or physically to join protests on the front line—a position that, when pressed, he readily admitted. ("I'm a hustler. As long as they give, I'll grab.")[75] When it came to martyrdom, Bruce was a solo act.

Ultimately, Bruce's standpoint sat best with his left-leaning liberal proponents in the press, such as jazz critics Ralph Gleason and Nat Hentoff. Both were staunch supporters of civil rights and became key interlocutors, writing about controversial issues that then became fodder for the comic's increasingly radical nightclub act. As Hentoff noted in Rustin's *Liberation* magazine in early 1963, Bruce "provides a galvanic antidote to the currently prevalent image of 'success' personalized in the dehumanized pragmatism of the Kennedys." Aligning Bruce with the democratic-anarchist wing of the civil rights movement and exploiting that link in equal parts, Hentoff concluded, "Bruce is more likely to feel in context with the absolutist resisters . . . and radically uncompromising workers for integration in the Student Nonviolent Coordinating Committee in the South, and perhaps with Jimmy Hoffa. ('I'd nominate him as the Christian of the year. He hires ex-convicts.')"[76] If Christ were to come back to New York, Bruce mused, and watched powerful Cardinal Francis Spellman from the back of St. Peter's Cathedral, "Christ would be confused, because their route took them through Spanish Harlem, and he would wonder what forty Puerto Ricans were doing living in one room and this guy was wearing a ring worth eight grand." Bruce refused to openly embrace the Left, however. He denounced the execution of Julius and Ethel Rosenberg, for instance, not from a base of ideology, but as an act of "communal savagery," a betrayal of the human instinct for sympathy. As he wrote to his friend Alvah Bessie, the Hollywood Ten screenwriter who was the sound man at the hungry i, "I am doing some lovely anarchistic material." But Bruce asked that their collaboration on a screenplay avoid any "unsafe social commentary," concluding, "It's bad enough I'm a drug addict without being a Communist."[77]

Perhaps, as critic Kenneth Tynan once said, Bruce could have used a solid "reading of Marx," but his role as a hipster holy fool made him suitable for countercultural magazines like Wallace Berman's *Semina*, as well as the pages of *Liberation*.[78] Both would have agreed, however, that urban nightclubs were his true venue. As the *New York Times* wrote, "Mr. Bruce regards the nightclub stage as 'the last frontier' of uninhibited entertainment." Hentoff also placed Bruce's affective power squarely within the nightclub, asserting that his direct connection with audiences underpinned his politically transformative potential. Fans of other New Comedians, he proposed, were "expectant, but pleasurably so. After all, they are about to be invited to witness to their own superior sophistication by laughing at the anti-Establishment impieties of the performers." Bruce, on the other hand, was confrontational, Hentoff declared:

> The expectancy of the night club is laced with anxiety. . . . Bruce, in sum, continually puts his audience on trial; and there is never a final passing grade. . . . Being entertained by those satirists across the chasm from Bruce is like walking through a gallery of fun house mirrors. Your reflection goes through a succession of grotesqueries, but you know perfectly well that once you're outside, you'll be your comfortable, familiar, rather stale self. After an encounter with Bruce on one of his more demonic nights, however, you may look at the mirror with gnawing doubt that you indeed know who you are, or rather, what you really feel. About sex. About justice.

"Do you people think yourselves better," Bruce whispered at the Gate of Horn in 1962, taking on the accent of recently executed Nazi war criminal Adolf Eichmann, "because you burned your enemies at long distance with missiles without ever seeing what you had done to them? Hiroshima *auf Wiedersehen*."[79]

Hentoff presciently concluded that "Bruce is a distillation of the unfocused rebelliousness among more and more of the young," and that his critical subterranean spirit would soon engulf the next generation who "protest segregation and testing and the hollowness of their parents" but "cannot yet say what they are for, what new society they desire." As a satirist, Bruce reflected the Rebel Café back on itself, completing a circular form of public discourse, even as he revealed the process of its popularization to a wider public. Jeering at the arrival of North Beach tourism, he quipped to an audience at the Jazz Workshop in 1961 that the hungry i "took all the bricks out and put in Saran wrap. That's it. And Ferlinghetti is going to the Fairmont." Moreover, the task of transformation was not for patrons alone. Bruce took his shamanistic role to heart, alongside an unhealthy dose of creative self-destruction. As Hentoff proclaimed, "because of the persistent tensions endemic to his nightly act of self-exposure, Bruce is coming closer and closer to the possibility of quite literally destroying himself." Whether or not it was Bruce's true intention, such self-sacrifice sparked larger conversations about the notion of social justice in America. As the Reverend Howard Moody wrote in a 1965 article that ran in both the *Village Voice* and *Christianity and Crisis*, denouncing Birmingham's fiercest segregationist, "The dirtiest word in the English language is not 'fuck' or 'shit' in the mouth of a tragic shaman, but the word 'NIGGER' from the sneering lips of a Bull Connor."[80]

Of Cops and Cocksuckers: The Trials of Cold War Comedy's Sick White Negro

It's entirely fitting that Lenny Bruce's first arrest for obscenity, and the only jury acquittal he received during his lifetime, both occurred in San Francisco, the city that legitimated Ginsberg's "Howl" as a defensible use of profanity and sexual content. Many of the same actors were at work in both cases, and the same underground social networks helped bring these controversies into the public eye. Some parallels were simply the result of the area's general bohemianism. Paralleling Ginsberg, who had arrived seeking the literary circles of Rexroth and The Place, Bruce worked the fertile ground that Sahl had broken at the hungry i. Journalist Ralph Gleason championed both Lawrence Ferlinghetti's sale of Ginsberg's book *Howl* and the Jazz Workshop's presentation of Bruce. Al Bendich served as the chief attorney in both cases and later became an executive at Fantasy Records, which released Bruce's catalog of albums and the first audio recording of "Howl," as well as readings by Ferlinghetti and Rexroth. In a city known for pushing the boundaries, conservative forces were bound to push back. But in the instance of Baghdad by the Bay, as opposed to comparable prosecutions in New York or Chicago, pressure did not radiate downward from city hall, but instead boiled up at street level. Absent political pressures, the police took it upon themselves to maintain moral rectitude, singling out troublemakers in the hopes of quieting the more boisterous bohemians.[81]

Bendich's defense of Bruce was no coincidence. When performing in San Francisco, Bruce stayed in North Beach and was a regular at City Lights Books. Ferlinghetti recommended Bendich to Bruce and also carried copies of the comic's self-published 1962 pamphlet, *Stamp Help Out*, a pastiche of photos, press clippings, letters, and routines that reflected bohemia's subterranean humor. In 1963, Bruce sent Ferlinghetti a pair of telegrams, noting his "farewell tour of the courts" and telling him to "destroy any and all books titled 'Stamp Help Out' I left with you on consignment," insisting that "they will hang me if they catch any body selling that book."[82] Given Bruce's verbal bebop dissonance, it is not very surprising that he was the only nonmusical performer ever featured at Art Auerbach's Jazz Workshop. But Bruce was also intertwined with the aura of New Bohemia, his satire a fully formed expression of the Rebel Café, featuring precisely the kind of personal disclosures that conservative critics found objectionable. As Ernest van den Haag (who later testified against Bruce in New York) said of Kerouac, he "cultivates his hysteria in public."[83] This makes Bruce's first arrest for obscenity, in the heart of North Beach, worthy of close examination.

The routine that caused Bruce's arrest portrayed his appearance at Ann's 440, primarily a lesbian bar, but one that also enjoyed some gay and bohemian patronage. Bruce began by facetiously imitating his agent's description of the booking:

LENNY: What kindava show is it, man?

AGENT: Well, ya know.

LENNY: Well, no, I don't know, man. . . .

AGENT: Well, it's not a show. They're a bunch of cocksuckers, that's all. A damned fag show.

LENNY: Oh. Well, that is a pretty bizarre show. I don't know what I can do in that kind of show.

AGENT: Well, no. It's . . . we want you to change all that.

LENNY: Well—I don't—that's a big gig. I can just tell them to stop doing it.[84]

Several elements of this routine are notable in the context of the nightclub underground. The first and most obvious is Bruce's use of the word "cocksucker." Clearly a source of amusing titillation for less streetwise patrons, such lingo was an affirmation for local bohemians, a recognition of their legitimacy through the rejection of bourgeois language. Second, this comedic bit is a commentary on nightclub culture itself. The agent is a stand-in for "straight" businessmen, the necessary organizers of the nocturnal world populated by creative, and decidedly disorganized, folks like Bruce. From this perspective, Bruce's sympathy with the marginalized gay community was clear (despite his careless conflation of gays and lesbians). The straight character's suggestion that Bruce could change all that is met with the dismissive response—couched in jazzman jargon—that such an undertaking would indeed be a big gig. Notably, the audio recording of the Jazz Workshop performance reveals one of the biggest laughs following this line. In other words, the audience shared Bruce's assessment that the agent's request to change the character of a North Beach gay club and its patrons represented a ridiculous task.

Bruce's bust at the Jazz Workshop fit snugly within previous patterns of police intimidation in the area, including frequent arrests at gay bars like the Black Cat and harassment of interracial couples at The Place and the Coexistence Bagel Shop. For nightspot owners, kickbacks to cops were also a regular part of doing business.[85] Given these tensions, the exchange between Bruce and the arresting officers following his Jazz Workshop performance is revealing:

"We've tried to elevate this street," Sergeant James Solden complained. "I can't see any right, any way you can break this word down, our society is not geared to it."

Bruce rejoined, "You break it down by talking about it. How about a word like 'clap'?"

"Well, 'clap' is a better word than 'cocksucker.'"

"Not if you get the clap from a cocksucker."[86]

Beyond showing that Bruce's improvisational wit was razor-sharp, even offstage, this exchange highlighted the issue at stake for the San Francisco police: the use of street language in a performance, a formalized reflection of the bohemian underground, threatened the status quo. And the police took it upon themselves to be the arbiters of community standards.

Bruce's San Francisco obscenity trial differed fundamentally from the later ones in Chicago or New York by remaining almost entirely focused on *local* issues. As Bruce's lawyer, Martin Garbus, suggested, "once you become a somewhat notorious defendant" in one city, police elsewhere had to arrest you or else public officials looked soft. Particularly in New York, Bruce's 1964 trial was used for public grandstanding by District Attorney (DA) Frank Hogan, Assistant DA Richard Kuh, and even Judge John Murtagh, who knew that the case would garner national coverage. All three used it to climb the political ladder.[87] In San Francisco, both the arrest and subsequent trial bore the hallmarks of issues that had been swirling around North Beach from 1958 through 1960: questions of sexuality, gender, race, and public space. Bruce was astute when he described nightclubs as the "last frontier." Indeed, urban areas such as North Beach were battlegrounds over the boundaries of public propriety. While not addressed directly in the Bruce case, the general atmosphere of the Cold War and the civil rights movement hung in the air, hinted at in fleeting comments about national decline or social justice.

Prosecuting attorney Albert Wollenberg's opening statement clearly indicated that Bruce's use of the word "cocksucker" in a public place, the Jazz Workshop, was the source of the obscenity charge, claiming that "Section 311 of our code . . . states that every person who knowingly sings or speaks any obscene song, ballad, or other words in any public place is guilty." The definition of "obscene," he specified, was "whether it went to prurient interest . . . a shameful or morbid interest, in nudity, sex, or excretion . . . beyond the limits of candor . . . [and] without redeeming social importance."[88]

Al Bendich's successful defense echoed that of the *Howl* trial—a reprise all the more familiar, as Judge Clayton Horn was the one who ruled on both cases—focusing on the question of social importance. Bendich trotted out a series of journalists and literary scholars, including high school teacher Kenneth Brown, who had attended the Jazz Workshop show and testified that Bruce's satire was in the tradition of Rabelais and Jonathan Swift. These authors, Brown argued, were "generally available to the public," despite their graphic sexual themes—particularly Rabelais, for whom, as one scholar put it, "the penis is almost . . . a leading character." Bendich convinced the jury that Bruce's effect was not "to deprave or corrupt the average adult by tending to create a clear and present danger of anti-social behavior." He asserted that the "law may not require the author to put refined language into the mouths of primitive people" and that the "speech of the performer must be considered in relation to its setting and the theme or themes of his production." In other words, the audience of the Jazz Workshop—around 150 patrons, which Ralph Gleason noted were older and better-dressed than the jazz crowd, each paying a $2.50 cover charge—sufficiently constituted a "public" worthy of judging the value of Bruce's routines. At the center of this argument was the nightclub itself, what Gleason called, in holy fool terms, Bruce's "unorthodox pulpit." As another of Bruce's lawyers unsuccessfully argued to an offended judge, "you get a different impression hearing the word in court than you would have at the club."[89]

Just beneath the surface of the obscenity question, however, simmered concerns about homosexuality and gender—particularly women's claims on public space and sexual expression. In a neighborhood where prosecutions against gay bars had been common, despite state supreme court protections, the prosecutor's legal logic was guided by precedents, which declared that gay *identity* was acceptable, while homosexual *behavior* was prohibited. Wollenberg, who referred to gays and lesbians during the trial as "deviates," made it clear that discussions of cocksuckers at Ann's 440 or elsewhere were excluded from acceptable social codes. Rhetorically querying the jury about whether Bruce knowingly violated public propriety, he answered: "Well, this is manifested by the way in which he did it; what he said to Officer Solden when Solden asked him, 'Do you think this is right to talk this way in public?' And what does he say? The world is full of those kind of people, using that descriptive term of his. What is said by stevedores down on the wharf loading a ship, this isn't in the same classification, and the stevedores . . . aren't saying it in a place crowded with people."[90] This tacit dismissal of "those kind of people" from public visibility stood in sharp contrast to the acceptance of male heterosexuality in the testimony of Sergeant Solden's partner, Officer James Ryan, about the character of North Beach. In Broadway's nightclub culture, Ryan said, burlesque houses and housewives in "amateur night" stripper contests at sites like the President Follies Theater and the Moulin Rouge were commonplace. Even more striking was the open acceptance of Finocchio's drag shows.[91] Once again, within San Francisco's social codes, transgressive appearances were one thing, but sexual acts—even if only speech acts—were another.

Yet the defense proved to be successful, marshaling the *Howl* precedent ("I'm very familiar with it," Judge Horn quipped at one point), as well as using the renown of gay poets to legitimate public discussions of homosexuality. Moreover, Gleason's testimony pointed to the comic's translational function, bringing street language into mainstream vernacular: "The word was used as many similar words are used in slang and discussing homosexuals, and the nightclub . . . and he used the word 'cocksucker' as you might use the word 'faggot' or as you might use the word 'fairy,' and it is common in the language of these people to use it in that context."[92]

The logic of acts versus appearances extended significantly, if more subtly, to women. The only other Bruce routine that Wollenberg had in his sights was "To Come Is a Verb," in which Bruce chanted, as he tapped lightly on the club's drum kit, "Did ya come good, did ya come good? Don't come in me, don't come in me!" As Kenneth Brown testified, this bit highlighted "the sexual fears in our society and the inability of people to respond"—especially women's "common fear of becoming pregnant."[93] Tellingly, in Wollenberg's closing argument, he pointed to Molly Bloom's soliloquy in James Joyce's 1922 novel *Ulysses* (which focuses mostly on female sexuality) as his single example of literary obscenity. The prosecutor asserted that "there are other redeeming features in the book that make it literature of some value—not Molly Bloom's portion of it, certainly."[94]

The underlying double standard of this statement was more obvious when Mary Brown, Kenneth's spouse, took the stand. Describing her occupation as a "housewife, mother," she admitted that she was not particularly "entertained" by Bruce, despite seeing some value in his satire. But Mary Brown's testimony came to a head when Bendich asked, as he had of her husband and other defense witnesses, whether she was "sexually stimulated" by the performance. Judge Horn upheld an objection by the prosecutor that the question was "irrelevant," despite Bendich's complaint that it had previously been allowed. Judge Horn erroneously declared that the question had taken "a different form," finally leading Bendich to rephrase it acceptably, as "Mrs. Brown, did the performance arouse your prurient interest?" Her response, "No."[95] Given the trial's frank discussions of burlesque-house strippers, male genitalia, and sexual arousal—underscored by Officer Ryan's admission that "cocksucker" was considered acceptable language in the masculine environs of the police stationhouse, despite it being a public place—Judge Horn revealed the gendered assumptions underlying the Jazz Workshop obscenity case.[96] Open discussion of a middle-class housewife's sexuality was strictly verboten.

The issue of race was even more submerged, yet still present. Witnesses like Ralph Gleason relied on Bruce's association with both jazz and civil rights to add legitimacy and moral weight to his defense. Others, like Kenneth Brown, expressed admiration for his concern with "our attitudes toward each other in a society, our attitudes toward races." And articles by Arthur Gelb in the *New York Times* and Nat Hentoff in the *Reporter*, which cited Bruce's antiracism and satire of the "first plateau liberal" who "preaches but cannot practice genuine integration," were read into the evidence.[97] Not only did this bring the public sphere full circle, with the press itself being used to support Bruce's value as a social critic, but it also spotlighted his racial cross-dressing as another aspect of his prosecution. By 1959, journalists had commonly associated Bruce with "the 'beatnik' set" and noted his use of jazz "jargon." As the British comedian and Shakespearean director Jonathan Miller wrote admiringly in the *Partisan Review* in 1963, combining Norman Mailer's notion of the hipster with the period's Freudian parlance, Bruce was the ultimate "sick white Negro." Bruce, Miller glowingly declared, evoked "the thousand sordid images of the urban American imagination."[98] These jazz/hipster/beatnik connotations were enough to raise red flags for San Francisco's conservative forces, who were concerned about interracial sex. In effect, they painted Bruce symbolically black.

In the wider American context during the Cold War era, Bruce's San Francisco acquittal was almost meaningless. Just as Sergeant Solden's effort to "elevate this street" expressed a fear of decline, public discussions of "sick" comics bore concerns about national decay, signified by "all this horror and mayhem in humor." Anti-obscenity groups explicitly linked their efforts with the need to uphold the global power of the United States. "So great is the concern of the Soviet Union for the physical and mental fitness of its youth that no salacious magazines are permitted," proclaimed Operation Yorkville, an anti-smut league that urged Bruce's prosecution in New York. "*Will Soviet youth grow strong as American youth becomes weak and perverted?*" The glaring irony of using Soviet totalitarian censorship as a model to protect American "democracy and freedom" seems to have escaped them. Yet the Operation Yorkville group expressed understandable dismay at the loss of their local voice in the face of US Supreme Court obscenity decisions, such as *Jacobellis v. Ohio*, which cleared Henry Miller's *Tropic of Cancer* of obscenity charges in 1964. The organization's plea for "the forgotten people—the community" highlights the tensions between local and national concerns.[99] Nightclub culture and Lenny Bruce played a significant public role in this dialectic, as evidenced by his stances on race, religion, and sexuality, which made him a visible target for Gotham's prosecutors.

While Bruce's 1964 New York trial featured several national figures as witnesses—including journalists from *Newsweek* and *Ebony*, and syndicated gossip columnist and game show star Dorothy Kilgallen—the list also included Rebel Café denizens, such as Nat Hentoff and Art D'Lugoff. In addition, tufts of grassroots encouragement arose among a new generation of bohemians. During the Jazz Workshop trial, a City College of New York student had distributed pamphlets titled "Welcome to the Farce!," which asserted that Bruce was "playing an unwilling part as a straight man in a social comedy put on by the City and County of San Francisco." Over the next three years, Bruce became a staple of the countercultural press, featured in civil rights and antiwar journals such as *Soulbook* and *Open City Press*.[100] But a letter to Mayor Robert Wagner from one supporter equally reveals Bruce's social role. "I am not a 'beatnik,' 'pinko,' or 'left-wing atheistic communist,' just an ordinary 33 year old happily married suburbanite who occasionally sees a good show in New York," he began. After describing the performance he saw at the Café au Go Go, he insisted, "Neither I, my wife, nor the two other couples who were with us (all of whom are fairly normal and fairly well adjusted people) could understand why Mr. Bruce has been subjected to harassment by New York City Officials. . . . He uses four letter words as emphasis, and his interpretations of social conditions are done in a humorous vein." Albert Goldman is on target in stating that an aspect of Bruce's performances was to provide "the vicarious thrill of being a really bad boy" for the middle class.[101] But to reduce Bruce's public function only to this was a gross oversimplification.

Cultural critic Andrew Ross has argued that Bruce's free-speech crusade, supported by America's intelligentsia, was an elitist turn away from popular tastes—what Assistant DA Richard Kuh termed "reverse McCarthyism"—as liberal literati were compelled to support the comic's "filth" or be labeled philistines.[102] Ross is correct to assert that the largest gap in Bruce's following was in the working class.

Bruce's fan base was largest among hip artistic elites and the middle class, who aspired to upwardly mobile sophistication and feared "self-condemnation as squares."[103] The upper working class, with their postwar unionist gains and flight to the suburbs, rejected Bruce, in line with the cultural conservatism that can accompany hard-won but fragile social status, which led many of them into the ranks of the Reagan Democrats by 1980.

Yet Ross misses a key group in this analysis: the underclass of American cities. Urban "night people"—sex workers, bartenders, musicians, taxi drivers, and greasy-spoon food servers—flocked to Bruce's shows (when they could afford it or had the social connections to bypass cover charges).[104] The presence of this specific section of the working class attested to Bruce's use of *their* language. He spoke to them, and, as his routines became entrenched in the larger public sphere, he spoke *for* them, transforming urban bar talk into a form palatable to the mainstream, which otherwise would have been threatened by its unfamiliarity and dangerous indifference to middle-class norms. In return, Bruce praised his fans, such as jazz musicians, for their "heavy intellect . . . unlike these other first plateau *Time, New Yorker*, pseudo-intellect jack-offs who quote esoteric passages from James Joyce and Flaubert." As an autodidact whose formal education never went past the fifth grade, Bruce unconsciously strove to become the kind of intellectual whose social critiques would spring from life experience, rather than the academy.[105] Instead of making police censors the plebeian butt of his jokes, Bruce saw them as the "foot soldiers" whose dirty job it was to carry out the will of elite authorities—prosecutors and politicians who openly feared his popularity as a sign of social decay. In fact, he *shared* law enforcement's humor. Part of the Bruce legend grew from the outbursts of laughter that erupted during court proceedings, as gallery audiences, bailiffs, and attorneys alike were unable to contain their amusement. Remarkably, one North Beach resident recalled overhearing stationhouse cops uproariously listening to tapes of Bruce's Jazz Workshop show, even as they prepared for his arrest. Bruce's rejection of *this* kind of hypocrisy, his impassioned denunciations of the social lie, begat his image as America's "evangelist of the new morality."[106]

At the same time, Bruce rejected moral absolutes, instead embracing the post-modern sensibilities of cultural pastiche and camp, as seen in his parodies of Hollywood B-movies. For every onstage boast about his "erudite, pedantic" vocabulary, Bruce just as quickly undercut his status as being socially structured and relativistic. It is "how much *exposure* you've had" to "hip idiom, Yiddish idiom" that will "make you hip or square," he told one audience. "I am part of everything I indict." Yet this introspection was always backed by a modernist faith in the perfectibility of society. Bruce's declaration that "the world is sick and . . . I'm a surgeon with a scalpel for false values" relied on the idea that there was a cure. Like Sahl, Bruce's self-critique tacitly recognized the nightclub's social purpose: not simply to move toward consensus, but to spark debate as part of the public sphere's democratic function. "I'm not a comedian," he insisted. "I don't have an act. I just talk. I'm just Lenny Bruce."[107]

While Bruce was disingenuous in separating entertainment from social commentary, the controversies over New Comedy's content did highlight the cultural role of satirical performances, in which humor served as an acceptable, benign way of exploring the otherworldly nature of bohemianism. The trials of Lenny Bruce—his first in San Francisco, and his last in New York—in many ways perfectly bookended the nightclub underground's hipster/holy fool function. Moreover, Bruce and Sahl were each part of the changing public image of Jewish Americans, claiming secular space as intellectuals and social critics. As Stephen Kercher has argued, this was particularly true for Bruce, whose Yiddish phrases "afforded him the vantage point of the marginal, the alienated, and the hip." This stance also drew from a tradition in which humor was intertwined with claims on morality and rights. "I am a Jew," Bruce riposted to Assistant DA Richard Kuh's request for immediate imprisonment, due to the comic's "lack of remorse" at his sentencing. "I come before the court not for mercy but for justice."[108]

The limits of Bruce's dedication to the broader concept of social justice were also clear, however, as highlighted by a bizarre incident in 1960: a practical joke in which he humiliatingly sprayed singer Pearl Bailey with a fire extinguisher onstage in Las Vegas. Afterward, he left a note: "I couldn't take your act. All the Uncle Tom bits you did like a lazy Negro."[109] Bruce's stunt exposed the ugly underbelly of hipster demands for racial authenticity. Yet his call for public honesty had a parallel in the political realm. The civil rights movement demanded the removal of pretense and a recognition of blacks' humanity and citizenship that dismantled stereotypes by establishing African American identity as authentic. Culturally, this approach was well established by the end of the 1950s in music, ranging from bebop to blues, and in Hollywood, where Harry Belafonte and Sidney Poitier had entrenched a new image of the black leading man as both urbane and tenacious. Even on national television (despite the objections of the stations' southern affiliates), interracial performances were more frequent than is commonly recalled. More telling was the lack of interracial nightclub comedy, with white audiences entertained almost exclusively by white comics, while black comedians remained on the "chitlin' circuit" of African American clubs. Euro-American audiences were just not willing to have their foibles publicly satirized by black comics.[110] In 1961, as the civil rights movement began to peak, that suddenly changed.

The Unmasked Man: Dick Gregory and the Comedy of Civil Rights

On May 11, 1964, several hundred African Americans took to the streets of the small Eastern Shore community of Cambridge, Maryland, to protest a planned speech by Alabama's segregationist governor George Wallace. Demonstrations, rent strikes, and clashes with National Guard units, fueled by anger over unemployment and unfair housing practices, continued off and on for two weeks. Amid the unrest, after a failed attempt by Maryland officials to calm both law enforcement personnel and protest-

ers by bringing in Billy Graham, civil rights activists contacted comedian Dick Gregory. What might seem like an odd choice in retrospect actually made perfect sense
at the time. Over the previous three years, Gregory had risen to national fame, as both
an insightful satirist and a dedicated activist. He had the trusting ear of both the protesters and the Kennedy White House, who soon reached an agreement for improved conditions in Cambridge.[111]

In fundamental ways, Gregory was the Rebel Café's living legacy. Just as the Beats,
Lenny Bruce, and Mort Sahl pricked the pretensions of the postwar mainstream,
Gregory marshaled the notion of authenticity to become the first black standup
comedian to find widespread success with white audiences, performing in clubs
such as the Blue Angel and the hungry i. With the expansion of the black freedom
struggle, Gregory's satire became an important cultural symbol: a window into the
African American community for Euro-Americans who sought greater awareness,
and a performer with an entertaining yet trenchant form of critique that helped
propel the civil rights movement forward. Moreover, Gregory personally bridged
the nightclub underground's oppositional culture and full political participation
with his activism in the civil rights movement and the New Left throughout the late
1960s.

Gregory's humor marked a decided break from previous African American comedy. The dissemblance and misdirection of the trickster, and the pathos and primitivism deeply embedded in minstrelsy, had been the norm well into the twentieth
century, as black comedians were forced to hide signs of discontent behind bumbling
Sambo characters. Even respected comics such as Bert Williams donned the burnt
cork of blackface, a mask that confirmed white expectations of shuffling "darkies"—
an attitude underscored by the violent reaction to his sans-blackface appearance in
the 1914 film *Darktown Jubilee*, when white audiences nearly began a race riot. These
performative elements continued through characters such as Stepin' Fetchit and Amos
'n' Andy into the 1950s, even as more-sophisticated comedians such as Moms Mabley and Redd Foxx turned to the raunchy blue material of black nightclubs and party
records, which white audiences stereotypically associated with hypersexuality.[112]

As African American humor scholar Mel Watkins has argued, Gregory was the
comic who finally removed the mask, refusing to play either the clown or the blue
humorist. Standing before Euro-American audiences simply as himself, Gregory used
comedy to address the issues that were meaningful to him and, by extension, to the
black community. In so doing, he publicly revealed his full humanity, an inherent
goal of the civil rights movement. As Gregory told *Playboy* interviewer Paul Krassner just after the Cambridge protests: "I've been able to help all organizations—the
NAACP, CORE, SNCC, the Urban League—because when I come in to help, I
don't come in associated with any one group. All they associate me with is Dick
Gregory."[113]

Gregory's breakthrough was the culmination of New Comedy, which, in addition
to Sahl's and Bruce's advance guard, saw other significant developments in the late

1950s and early 1960s. The duo of Mike Nichols and Elaine May, who started at the Blue Angel and broke into the big time in 1958, were a prime example. Their style of improvisational humor grew out of Chicago's Compass Theater—which had its roots in community theater and the leftist theories of Bertolt Brecht—and the pair's brand of topical satire became increasingly popular, later peaking with television's *Saturday Night Live* in the 1970s. Nichols went on to spread the Rebel Café sensibility to Hollywood as he directed films such as *Who's Afraid of Virginia Woolf* (1966). Woody Allen, who began his career at the Bitter End and the hungry i, did likewise. Bill Cosby would later have the same effect in television. Equally important was Phyllis Diller, who started at San Francisco's Purple Onion. Following edgy pioneers like Moms Mabley, Belle Barth, and Rusty Warren, Diller legitimated standup comedy as a woman's pursuit: her reversals of standard jokes about stale marriages supported a long and successful television career.[114] But Gregory did more than simply capitalize on and disseminate the nightclubs' underground sensibility. He was a more significant pathbreaker, because his career blended the Rebel Café with a major political movement, making him its most vital, if overlooked, exemplar. Along with Lenny Bruce, broad acceptance of his brand of humor signaled a key moment: when the Rebel Café was no longer underground, but became indistinguishable from American culture as a whole.

Richard Claxton Gregory was born in 1932 and grew up in an economically disadvantaged family in St. Louis, raised by a single mother who remained an object of his affection and admiration throughout his career. He attended Southern Illinois University on a track scholarship, but his comedic talents first bloomed while in the army, where he won a talent contest. In the late 1950s, he began to perform in small working-class black clubs, like the Esquire Show Lounge in Chicago, and for six months in 1959 he ran his own joint, the Apex. With shades of the New Saloon ethos, Gregory remembered that the Apex "had been something like a home" for him and his staff, but financial pressures forced him to close it down. By the new year, Gregory had clawed his way into Roberts Show Club in Chicago, known as the largest black nightclub in the country, where he was filmed for a documentary in the television series *Bell and Howell Close Up!*, performing a satirical bit on segregation for an interracial audience. Between Roberts Show Club and other gigs, including a "beatnik coffeehouse off Rush Street, the Fickle Pickle," Gregory developed a reputation in Chicago as a solid comic.[115]

The place that "opened the door to the top" for Dick Gregory, however, was Hugh Hefner's Playboy Club. On January 13, 1961, the club's manager called Gregory's agent with the news that comic Irwin Corey was sick, and they wanted Gregory as a substitute. When he arrived, the manager nearly sent him home, having not realized that the club had been booked by a convention of southern frozen food executives. Gregory, "cold and mad and . . . broke," insisted that the show go on. Despite the "dirty, little insulting statements" by the resistant patrons, Gregory's routines soon won them over. "Good evening ladies and gentlemen," he began, "I understand there are a good many Southerners in the room tonight. I know the South very well. I spent twenty years there one night." Gregory continued with deceptively self-deprecating quips that actually cut to the heart of structural racism in America, such as: "You see, when I drink, I think I'm Polish. One night I got so drunk I moved out of my own neighborhood." By the time he finished, "that room broke and the storm was over."[116]

Gregory later recalled: "Before Hugh Hefner brought Dick Gregory into the Playboy Club, a black comic was not permitted to work white night clubs in America. You could sing, you could dance. But you couldn't stand flat footed and talk to white folks." Yet this moment meant more than just breaking the comedy color line. Hefner's Playboy Club was a conscious attempt to bring an underground aura to the surface, signaling the point when the Rebel Café milieu was mainstream enough to be commodified by a corporation more interested in profits than politics. While the venue was recognized by subterraneans as merely an "ersatz" nightclub, Hefner nonetheless concocted a balanced mix of the urban demimonde's masculine, transgressive sexuality and hints of oppositional liberalism—bolstered by his vocal support of Lenny Bruce and civil rights. This particular blend of nightclub sophistication traded on subterranean cultural currency, giving Hefner the social space to break previous taboos, as well as providing a high-profile stage for Gregory's talents.[117]

Gregory was conscious of his relationship with the nightclub underground. "If I've done anything to upset you," he quipped, "maybe that's what I'm here for. Lenny Bruce shakes up the Puritans; Mort Sahl, the conservatives; and me—almost everybody."[118] Yet his humor was not produced by the Rebel Café milieu. Instead, it was an heir to its progressive legacy. While owing some debt to Sahl, Gregory's routines were often conventional, with hipper versions of vaudeville jokes ("Say, who was that crazy chick I saw you with yesterday?" "Man, that was no chick, that was my brother—he's just got a problem") or old-school zingers ("My wife can't cook. How do you burn Kool-Aid?"). But Gregory mostly reflected the folk humor that was, as Mel Watkins notes, "common currency in black communities" during his youth— often used as a defense mechanism in a hostile world ("A redneck walks up to a black man about to eat a chicken dinner and says, 'Boy, whatever you do to that chicken, I'm gonna do to you.' The black man picks up the chicken and kisses its ass").[119]

Nonetheless, the Rebel Café *was* fundamental to Gregory's success, offering a ready-made institution to legitimate his rise. A deluge of press coverage praised Gregory's performances at clubs like the Village Gate, the Blue Angel, and the hungry i (although fellow black comics, such as Nipsey Russell and Slappy White, complained that the young upstart was pilfering their material). Throughout, Gregory subtly steered expectations toward his own objectives. "They call me the Negro Mort Sahl," he quipped to audiences. "In the Congo they call Sahl the white Dick Gregory."[120] This Rebel Café legitimation was underscored by Gregory's second album, *East & West*, in 1961, which prominently proclaimed that it was recorded live "at the Blue Angel" and "at the hungry i." At the Blue Angel, Gregory joked about New York politics and smoothly linked the city's atmosphere to both Cold War concerns and civil rights. "How about them East German Freedom Riders, aren't they weird?" he asked. "Just goes to show you we're not the *only* ones! Yeah, you've been reading about the East German Freedom Riders, jump in the truck, put the gas pedal all the way down to the floor, look neither left or right, crash through everything. In New York we call them cab drivers."[121]

At the hungry i, Gregory's direct connection with the nightclub's audience was even more apparent. Coming onstage after Enrico Banducci's introduction, Gregory immediately addressed an audience member in the front row: "You didn't clap. That's right, you must clap when I come out. I don't mind you not clapping when I go off, because if you don't clap then, that means you didn't dig me, you know. But when I come on and you don't clap, that makes me think you resent me. This is different." He then proclaimed, "If there's any resentment in the house, get up, burn your cross and leave!" When the laughter and applause died down, Gregory began to talk with the crowd, asking patrons where they were from and what they thought of the hungry i. When one man answered boldly that he was from New Orleans, an unsettled hum went through the audience. "Louisiana's alright," Gregory quickly quipped. "Hell, you people could go to South Africa and be considered liberals." A New Yorker, asked by Gregory whether he had ever seen a club like the hungry i before, insisted that he had. "No, there's no place in the world like this crummy joint," the comic rejoined. "This is a basement! Three dollars a head they charge you. . . . I bet you don't go in your own basement [even though it's] free." Noting North Beach's tourist trade, Gregory quipped that the hungry i was "sort of like a nice place to visit but you wouldn't want [it] in your own neighborhood."[122]

Cementing the civil rights implications of this line, Gregory queried a couple from Chicago's North Side, "You ever go back? You're in for a hell of a surprise, my brother just moved in there a couple of weeks ago." He then continued: "And you heard what Bobby Kennedy said, that thirty years from this year a Negro could become president. . . . If I was president . . . I think I'd grab Satchmo and make him Secretary of State. Dizzy Gillespie would be my Vice-President. And I'd give you a job, just so they won't say I'm prejudiced. That's what I would do my first day in office. My second day I'd take Georgia, North Carolina, Mississippi, Louisiana, Alabama and make it an H-bomb testing area." Yet Gregory offered more than a simple dismissal of the backward south lagging behind the enlightened north. "It happens all over," he said. "But up north we're more clever with it. . . . When the Negroes move into one large area and it looks like they might control the votes, they don't say anything to us—they have a slum clearance. You do the same thing out here on the West Coast, but you call it freeways."[123] Within the intimacy of the nightclub, Gregory's audience rapport and quick wit led white audiences to face the complexities of black life in America—a rare perspective in a media environment that kept a keen eye trained on southern Jim Crow policies, while remaining largely blind to redlining in northern cities.

Equally importantly, as Gregory became active in civil rights protests, politically conscious club owners like Enrico Banducci and Art D'Lugoff accepted his frequent last-minute cancellations and continued to supply him with a steady income. In May 1963, when civil rights leader Medgar Evers called for his participation in Jackson, Mississippi, demonstrations during Gregory's run at the hungry i, the comic approached Banducci and "told him I wanted to leave, that my people needed me. A white man, and he had waited all year for my engagement, but he never batted an eye."[124] D'Lugoff both offered Gregory this flexibility at the Village Gate and participated, along with press agent Ivan Black, in organizing and promoting Gregory's causes. This included his 1964 "Xmas for Mississippi" program, which airlifted 25,000 frozen turkeys to poor families after that state cut off their food assistance in retaliation against demonstrations and voter registration drives. D'Lugoff, in turn, traded on Gregory's aura of authenticity, simultaneously promoting him as a "satirist of the general fraud" who was "virtually the house comedian at the Gate," as well as a "national institution in the fight for civil rights of all Americans." In this way, both Gregory and the Village Gate established their bona fides in a tradition of socially conscious entertainment that stretched back to the Popular Front.[125]

Gregory underscored this mutual authenticity when he determinedly returned to the hungry i following Evers's murder in June 1963. When asked by a friend how he could possibly go on stage and be funny, he replied that "when a man sells his talents he's a prostitute, and when you're a prostitute you lay like the customer wants you to lay." By the summer of 1964, Gregory estimated that he had personally donated around $100,000 to the civil rights movement, while forfeiting upward of $250,000 in bookings. He later remembered the Village Gate as being both a financial supporter and a hub in social networks that actively advanced the civil rights cause. In a mid-1960s interview following one show at the Gate, Gregory insisted that the necessity of educating audiences about "social problems and social conditions" made New Comedy a necessary force. He was adamant that "we need good comedians just as much as we need good leaders."[126]

Gregory appeared at a time when liberal white America was looking for black spokespeople, seeking clues to penetrate the apparent opaqueness of black culture (which even extended to political demands, as seen in Gregory's mediation between the White House and Maryland's Cambridge protesters.) What is often called the modern civil rights movement—from Rosa Parks's bus boycott in 1955 through the 1965 voting rights protests—was only new for *Euro*-Americans. *African* Americans had been demanding their rights since Reconstruction. The *Plessy v. Ferguson* case in 1896, for example, was an attempt to *challenge* emerging Jim Crow laws—a call to uphold the Fourteenth Amendment—which fell on deaf ears in the US Supreme Court. Now, in the 1960s, white America was finally beginning to hear what black America had been saying all along.

In a 1961 article titled "Dick Gregory: Desegregated Comic," African American writer John Williams described this translational dynamic. Characterizing the comic as a jazz fan, but not a hipster, he noted that Gregory used hints of black dialect to put white audiences at ease. At the Blue Angel, he cracked up the "99 per cent white"

The man behind the mask: Dick Gregory live at the hungry i. Courtesy of Bob Fitch Photography Archive, Department of Special Collections, Stanford University Libraries

audience with topical jokes about race. These included jabs at owners Max Gordon and Herbert Jacoby for trying to make him feel at home with black olives in his martini, and a lampoon of then–vice president Lyndon Johnson's Texas roots, saying that President Kennedy "wanted to build a great cross on the lawn of the White House, but he was afraid the Vice President would burn it." These jokes, Williams asserted, revealed the "innermost thoughts of Negroes under oppression," even as they partly assuaged the guilt of the club's hip white patrons. Amid economic pressures and racial unrest, Gregory acted as a "timely safety valve, draining off that tension," while his persona transcended minstrelsy's trappings and whittled away at stereotypes.[127]

Gregory's ability to walk this fine sociocultural line earned him even wider fame, with television spots on Ed Sullivan's and Jack Paar's popular shows. As his activism heated up, however, his television appearances dried up in equal measure. His cultural role remained inherently tied to nightclubs, where his impact was in the very immediacy of the sensory and artistic experience. This experiential mix was highlighted in Gregory's accounts of performances for white audiences, such as his debut at the Playboy Club. While it would certainly tax the imagination to think that those southern businessmen returned home as converts, preaching desegregation as a result of Gregory's influence, it is just as certain that his material was not the kind previously seen or heard on television or radio. Moreover, the southerners had *experienced* this fresh perspective in a "tactile" way. The resulting effect stemmed not simply from the authenticity of a firsthand performance, but from their immersion within the club's fully human social space. This was seen in Gregory's interactions with hungry i patrons, for example, and his comments on the club itself as he tailored his material for white patrons. He pointed out that, for white comics, a female patron leaving her table for the restroom was an opportunity for a humorous, if crass, remark. But both Gregory's and audience's awareness of interracial taboos made such moments tense, as comedic expectations clashed with racial and gender norms. Yet this subtle interjection, which called attention to sensitive cultural codes, only heightened the impact of Gregory's challenges to other taboos, such as when he noted the absurdity of social distinctions based on skin color. "Wouldn't it be a hell of a thing if all this was burnt cork," he quipped, "and you people were being tolerant for nothing?"[128]

Yet this way of lifting the mask had its limits. Demonstrating what W. E. B. Du Bois termed "double consciousness," Gregory was well aware that he had to simultaneously tailor his material and address undercurrents of racial tension. Not only did he go "digging into musty old books on humor" in order to "figure out what Whitey was laughing at" (including "mother-in-law jokes and Khrushchev"), but he also addressed racist language head on. Gregory, reflecting the individualist, liberatory postwar ethos, insisted that this allowed him to be a "colored funny man, not a funny colored man," to stand onstage as "an individual first, a Negro second." Linguistically, he sometimes handled racist hecklers with evasion, such as adapting Moms Mabley's line: "You hear what that guy just called me? Roy Rogers' horse. He just called me Trigger." More often, Gregory was direct, as in the title of his 1964 autobiography, *Nigger*. His strategy here turned racism against itself, as revealed in the memoir's dedication: "Dear Momma—Wherever you are, if you ever hear the word 'nigger' again, remember they are advertising my book." To nightclub audiences, he simply announced: "You know, my contract reads that every time I hear that word, I get fifty dollars more a night. . . . Will everybody in the room please stand up and yell nigger?"[129]

Unlike Bruce, however, Gregory matched his challenge to the word with satires of structural racism. As he said in one of his most pointed routines: "The President is willing to give Lockheed $250 million. . . . When it comes to giving welfare layouts to black folks, so many legislators say, 'They ought to learn to pull themselves up by their own bootstraps.' So I sent the president of Lockheed Aircraft a telegram. . . .

'Why don't you learn to pick yourself up by your own landing gear?' I just can't understand Lockheed asking for all that welfare money and they don't even have any illegitimate planes!" In the conclusion of his autobiography, Gregory wove together threads of liberationism and structural criticism, calling for white Americans to "learn to love and hate us as individuals," even as he called for a revolution against "a system where a white man can destroy a black man with a single word." Moreover, he connected this with both a recognition of race as a social construct—a product of consciousness—and the notion of America's global mission. "Every white man in America knows we are Americans. . . . So when he calls us a nigger, he's calling us something we are not, something that exists only in his mind," Gregory declared to his fellow black activists. "[If] I have called [an object] something it is not . . . I'm the sick one, right?" He continued, "Something important happened in 1963, and . . . for some reason God has put in your hands the salvation of not just America . . . but the salvation of the whole world."[130]

In the coming years, Gregory maintained this ambitious vision of change. Throughout, he remained steadfast in his determination to be more than merely a celebrity cheering from the sidelines; he got into the game. He expanded his focus from civil rights into the broader New Left, participating in the antiwar protests at the Democratic National Convention in 1968 and then declaring his own, only partly satirical presidential candidacy. More dramatically, during the Watts uprising in Los Angeles in 1965, Gregory had taken a bullet in his leg while trying to help calm the crowds—a clear sign that his activism was no joke.[131]

In comparison, Mort Sahl and Lenny Bruce had failed to live up to their sociopolitical potential. Bruce, in particular, fell into the trap of creative self-destruction that crashed many fellow subterranean aviators. The difference was that Bruce's travails had sparked massive press coverage, thereby raising his resistance to the level of a crusade. "There is still no more accurate voice of social satire in America," a young reporter suggested in 1965, opining that Bruce's critiques were "much like preaching, a very vivid description of the hell fires we live with each day."[132] The gasoline smell of napalm in Southeast Asia and the flames rising from tattered buildings in Watts would soon confirm the poignancy of his remark. Meanwhile, the New Comedians had taken Rebel Café humor to its limit and left it with nowhere to go. Its social satire became institutionalized in mainstream comedy clubs and, eventually, television. The experiences of Rebel Café comedy and its challenges to previous orthodoxies sparked changes—some small, some transformative—in the worldviews of nightclub patrons, which incrementally changed the nation's wider culture.

the new cabaret

*Performance, Personal Politics,
and the End of the Rebel Café*

Aesthetic values may function in life for cultural adornment and
elevation or as private hobbies, but to *live* with these values is the
privilege of geniuses or the mark of decadent Bohemians.
Herbert Marcuse, 1955

Poetry is a response to the daily necessity of getting the world right.
Denise Levertov, 1962

From 1958 through 1961, a bumper crop of New Bohemian nightclubs flourished, from the Coffee Gallery, the Cellar, and Turk Murphy's Easy Street in San Francisco to the Café au Go Go, the Gaslight, Gerde's Folk City, the Bitter End, and Café Wha? in New York. These clubs were points of connection between the mainstream and "the machinery of night," where the Rebel Café's molten subterranean culture began to burst through to the surface. Later, they became launching pads for 1960s music icons, from Bob Dylan and Joan Baez to the Fugs, Janis Joplin, and Jimi Hendrix.[1] But first, these small venues played a fundamental sociocultural role for bohemia, bringing together modern jazz, poetry, and the folk revival, carrying elements of the European cabaret tradition, and even serving as bases for political activism. By 1963, as bohemia's brand of rebellion became commonplace in American cities and on college campuses, the Rebel Café began to lose its distinctive function. Subterranean culture was, by then, simply a growing part of mainstream American culture.

Dylan arrived in Greenwich Village in 1961, seeking the nightclub underground— an event that Michael Harrington suggested marked "the beginnings of [its] end," when the singer "showed up at the Horse in a floppy hat." Dylan absorbed and then transmitted Rebel Café sensibility into the national culture, such as he did three years later in the cryptic liner notes for his *The Times They Are A-Changin'* album. Channeling a field of phenomena into a single identifiable point, Dylan presented a verbal collage that invoked Woody Guthrie, the music and talk of Eighth Avenue bars and 1930s union halls, economic struggles in Harlem, the Red Scare's hysteria, and the artistic visions of William Blake, Marlene Dietrich, Allen Ginsberg, Pete Seeger, and Miles Davis. More succinctly, in "Ballad of a Thin Man," Dylan sang to the everyman, "Mr. Jones," whose confusion grew more deranged as he failed to get on board with the changing times: "There's something happening here, but you don't know what it is."[2]

More and more, the Joneses of America *did* want to know. Live performances were a kind of modern ecstatic ritual of discovery, no less true for mainstream audiences than for underground bohemians. Nightclubs welcomed crowds of college students, suburban seekers, and tourists who all came to soak in the otherworldly entertainment, particularly the quintessential beatnik style of poetry and jazz. These nocturnal excursions, exemplified by the Gray Line bus company's North Beach tours—which were seen as intrusions by bohemian regulars and as necessities by club owners stitching together always-tenuous profits—had a significant function for suburbanites, offering potential ways to make sense of a society that had so recently become unmoored from traditional community and familial structures. In both a metaphorical and an anthropological sense, the role of performers as shamans paralleled the rise of mass-media evangelicals like Billy Graham, whose charismatic revivals served much the same purpose, albeit on a larger scale. They brought a certain kind of knowledge from the otherworld and translated it into the language of material existence.

During the Rebel Café's peak, nightclubs' transmission of subterranean sensibilities into the mainstream was a partial return to the role of Cafe Society and the Village Vanguard in the Popular Front. Most notably, new ideas about sophistication applied social pressure to accept a more assertive public presence for both middle-class and Beat women, as well as bolstered support for the civil rights movement as a sign of hip politics. Ironically, this emphasis on sophisticated performative pretense— including the winking "campy" style prevalent in gay venues—was interwoven with a longing for authenticity. For many, the nightclub was a place to let go of society's expectations and be themselves.

Nightclub rebels were emblematic of the changes in American society since the end of World War II. The public invisibility of women, African Americans, gays, and lesbians had always been an illusion, a lie of omission, and in the 1960s these entities refused to be contained by other people's perceptions. The Rebel Café had played its part in the growth of what is now called identity politics, offering spaces where a sense of self could be nurtured into public visibility and self-determination. Squeezing into tiny cracks in the Cold War's traditionalist facade, bohemian women and queer public figures planted seeds that eventually widened openings for full-fledged feminism and gay liberation, while black cultural producers smashed the stereotypes that had shaped their oppression. The various cultural tactics and strategies of these groups should not be conflated. They used whatever means necessary to bring about their own liberation and often took different, even opposite, paths. But they also shared a desire to reverse the old order, and the Rebel Café was one base of operations.

Throughout the underground, oppositional figures pushed against the dominant boundaries of sexuality, masculinity, race, and Cold War militarism. These elements came together in a series of conflicts over urban space that pitted Rebel Café owners and patrons against municipal authorities and mainstream social forces.

Protests known as the Battle of the Beatniks and the Battle of the Black Hawk in San Francisco, and as the Village Coffeehouse Crisis in New York City, bloomed from the seeds of previous oppositional generations as they vitalized the broader movements of the 1960s, a genealogy of twentieth-century American activism.

This renewal of leftist politics also demonstrated the continued function of nightspots within the urban fabric. Yet, at the same time, it marked the beginning of the end of the Rebel Café. Rather than attrition brought about by municipal moralists or citizen calls for traditional notions of decency, bohemian nightspots in San Francisco and Greenwich Village were victims of their own success. Nightclubs, especially for suburbanites, were spaces for an exploration of urban culture and sensual experiences that sometimes had important effects on social awareness. But the personal and political consciousness the Rebel Café helped spawn soon made its role obsolete.

Revenge of the Words: From Jazz Poetry to the New Left Literati

In December 1957, Jack Kerouac appeared at the Village Vanguard, reading poetry and excerpts from *On the Road* to a jazz accompaniment. The readings marked a turning point in both the Beat generation and nightclub culture, as Kerouac was thrust into the spotlight and the Vanguard firmly solidified itself as a jazz venue. Earlier that year, Max Gordon had ended the Vanguard's sojourn in the early 1950s as a supper club by featuring Miles Davis's modern jazz and Lenny Bruce's edgy comedy. Kerouac's Vanguard stint symbolized the advent of Beat sensibilities into mainstream entertainment, although it was panned by critics as an artistic failure and a betrayal of bohemian authenticity. Reporting for the *Nation*, Dan Wakefield described one performance, with Kerouac under the stage lights reading a poem about the Cellar in North Beach, obviously drunk and disheveled in "a gold-thread open-neck sportshirt that glistened in the dark and hung out over his belt." Kerouac then continued with one of Allen Ginsberg's poems, sparking Wakefield's sneer that it was "only yesterday that Ginsberg dedicated his almost-banned book of poems, *Howl*, to Jack Kerouac, 'the new Buddha of American prose' whose eleven books were published in heaven. . . . And now one is published by the Viking Press and the others are being read at the Village Vanguard." Wakefield concluded by stating that the "glow-in-the-dark, gold-thread shirt worn by the Buddha seems to be the principal symbol of his 'protest' still remaining."[3]

Wakefield was not alone in disparaging the Vanguard readings. Even the generally supportive Joyce Johnson was hard pressed to defend them as anything more than an enormous fiasco. This was a transitional moment, caught in a bind between authenticity and social transformation, and Kerouac's holy fool was reduced to acting like a drunken clown.[4] His own ambivalence was clear in a letter to Kenneth Rexroth in early 1958, as he alternately put down the performances and propped up his subterranean bona fides:

I raced to the Village Vanguard . . . and blew my heart out but lots of drunks talked on tho some people did hush. Generally I did well, because the musicians (Lee Konitz, etc) said they could hear the music, the jazz. I didn't want music behind me because that's really hearts & flowers Victorian poetry. . . . But the boss made the house pianist make chords behind me anyway. . . . Steve [Allen] is rather good at it. . . . He sat in the opening night. It was a mad night. Madison avenue was there, as well as guys with rucksacks who got thrown out (I was in the back, oblivious, drinking pernod, listening to colored musicians tell me wild stories.)[5]

With the Vanguard's beers at $1.25 a pop and a $4 minimum per person, few genuinely Beat characters could afford to attend, leading to accusations that Kerouac was selling out. "He smiles and goes to sit among the wheels and agents," declared the *Village Voice*. "He is prince of the hips, being accepted in the court of the rich kings. . . . He must have hated himself in the morning—not for the drinks he had, but because he ate it all up the way he really never wanted to."[6] Yet this view denied the performativity of bohemianism itself, with its long history of pretension, posturing, and exclusivity. Kerouac's latest readings exposed them, revealing an uncomfortable truth: bohemian notions of spontaneous authenticity were a myth. If his Vanguard shows failed, it was because he believed in the myth too deeply for his own good, showing up drunk and unrehearsed.

Yet Kerouac's performance was also an example of the nightclub's translational role. By associating with the Beat generation, the Vanguard rejoined the Rebel Café dialogue between live experience and media that drove literature in new directions. It was no coincidence that Gilbert Millstein had arranged the Vanguard readings. He was the *New York Times* critic who first brought attention to *On the Road*, as well as being a longtime supporter of the Vanguard, even as he bewailed its move to a jazz policy as a betrayal of the club's original intent to harbor "intellectuals looking for a refuge from bourgeois life." Like Kerouac's editor at Viking Press, Malcolm Cowley, Millstein subtly translated Popular Front sensibilities into 1950s terms by supporting New Bohemia's socially charged art forms.[7] As Ronald Sukenick has cogently written about Kerouac's readings at the Village Vanguard:

> Many subterraneans want to violate the taboos of the middle class, while simultaneously needing its indulgence, as if you could bite the hand of oppression and then expect it to feed you. . . . Cowley's career is exemplary. Cowlies are indispensible to the underground. . . . It is the cowlies who always sooner or later discover the commercial value of the underground and figure out how to vend it to the middle class, either diluted by time, or in denatured imitations, or filtered through de facto censorship. . . . There's a difference between selling and selling out. . . . [But now] the artists themselves . . . sell themselves to the middle class. . . . And when you start selling yourself, you may stop selling your art and wind up selling your lifestyle.[8]

The mistake of those who failed to recognize this dialectic, who thought that the inevitable next step for bohemian opposition was straight into the bop apocalypse, missed the fact that *On the Road*, for all its spontaneous iconoclasm, was the product of five years of edits, rewrites, and promotion by a corporate publishing house. Equally importantly, however, critics like Sukenick have missed the subtle ways in which past programs like the Popular Front threaded their way through the culture industry's large corporations, carried forward by those such as Cowley and Millstein. Nightclub performances were simply the most tactile way the underground made contact with the mainstream.

Jazz clubs connected poets and patrons alike with underworld figures, as well as with an evolving form of left-wing politics. For example, the Cellar's owner and pianist, Bill Weisjahn, provided both musical accompaniment and a supply of illicit intoxicants for Beats seeking to expand their poetic expressions and their consciousness. Painter Wally Hedrick later noted that the Cellar was a space that bridged the New Saloon, the underground drug and jazz scenes, the Beat generation, and the counterculture that followed it in the coming years: "The Place was all verbal. . . . But around the corner on Union was another place called The Cellar which was really subterranean. . . . The beatniks had their drug scene which was the equivalent of what goes on now but it was deeper, darker and sort of mysterious. . . . The center of that was sort of The Cellar . . . the place with the connection between [the Beats and] avant-garde jazz."[9] Poet David Meltzer had seen the basement club's key form of expression—performances combining poetry and jazz—as a symbol of left-wing bohemian rebellion. In the "good old bad old days" of 1958, when Meltzer earned only $20 a night, one night a week, for his performances, jazz poetry was inseparable from apocalyptic politics: "My workingclass immigrant Brooklyn popularfront coming of age propelled both by Old World and New World energies: *shtetl* orthodox Judaism and CP/USA storefront; Euro classical music and . . . Duke Ellington, Bebop, hipster culture, comicbooks, radio, movies, and sanctuary in Public Libraries, pushed me out into a new world that ultimately couldn't renew itself, fixed as it was in irreconcilable oppositions made more acute in 1945 in the faces of the Holocaust, Hiroshima and Nagasaki." Meltzer then traced the development of jazz poetry and bebop through free jazz and the Black Arts Movement in the 1960s, which "worked to unite factions and redefine the cultural perimeters in the same ways the Beat movement worked," eventually finding its full expression in hip-hop.[10]

Meltzer rightly noted that the Beats hogged the spotlight, too often leaving black innovators in the shadows. But his demand for authenticity and spontaneity also led him to dismiss the importance of the nightclub's translational role for those on Gray Line bus tours, the "suburban wannabes" who "donned black tights, berets, shades, goatees," came to the Cellar, and declared "it's the looks [i.e., the style, or surface], not the books" that counted.[11] This adoption of sartorial style symbolized the broader cultural embrace of bohemianism as the underground moved from the basement to street level. Although the Cellar closed in 1963, by that time its tradition of cutting-edge performances had already carved out a significant space in San Francisco's culture.

Questioning the importance of the underground's spontaneity has its caveats, too. As Judy Holliday once quipped about the terror of nightclub performances, in contrast to the protection of the theater's formality, you were "out there playing yourself, where they can get at you." This lower bar of pretense meant that there was a certain amount of unity between performers and audiences—reflecting a larger postwar process that eroded distinctions between high and low culture. In a 1958 essay, Lawrence Ferlinghetti noted that the poetry of urban clubs used street language, that is, the argot of the jazz musician, the hipster, and others left down and out by having fallen through the cracks of the affluent society: "Some of it has been read with jazz, much of it has not. A new 'ashcan' school? Rock and roll? Who cares what name it's called. . . . In some larger sense, it all adds up to the beginning of a very inevitable thing—the *resocialization* of poetry. But not like in the Thirties." In 1960, Ferlinghetti described Beat poetry as being both public and integrated with the everyday, asserting: "That's why we are getting an audience. *We're seeing the world again.* Our poems make you say, 'I never saw the world like that before.'"[12] This emphasis on expanded consciousness, rather than class consciousness, underpinned Ferlinghetti's brand of Marxism, which differed from Depression-era radicalism, as well as from the precepts of the nascent New Left. While the messy work of formal politics still lay ahead, Beat poetics helped pave the way by suggesting that psychic well-being was just as important as material gain.

In response to the Beats' rising visibility, in 1958 Rexroth published "San Francisco's Mature Bohemians" in the *Nation*, championing the new poetic movement and tracing it back to the city's proletarian, anarchist-libertarian, and conscientious objector roots in the 1930s and 1940s. Calling it the "potent social leaven in their community," Rexroth laid out his (somewhat vague) view of the poet's place in San Francisco: "The role of poetry out here has been compared to that of jazz in Chicago of the twenties, or to the heroic age of bop in New York. . . . Poetry out here, more than anywhere else, has a direct, patent measurable, social effect, immediately grasped by both poet and audience." But he soon excoriated the Beats in "Some Thoughts on Jazz as Music, as Revolt, as Mystique," critiques he apparently continued at his poetry readings, as well. According to Philip Whalen, Rexroth denounced his former protégés as "professional debauchers of women, who call themselves Zen Buddhists" and who "don't know anything about Negros &/or jazz, ain't socially responsible, ain't real San Francisco."[13]

This conflict illuminates a generational shift that became more visible by the late 1950s, as the Beats resisted comparisons with the Old Left made by those like Kenneth Rexroth and Lawrence Lipton. "This is getting kind of tenuous but your criticism is relatively tenuous," Ginsberg retorted to Rexroth in 1959. "Who's stealing your San Francisco? There is nothing to be 'stolen,' this is all madness. . . . For you must remember, re[garding] my work and Kerouac's—the whole conception of it as social protest fitting into westcoast-wobbly-political-responsible-etc context is your interpretation. With which I have differed, actually (particularly in seeing my poetry as an outgrowth of proletarian 30's)." For Ginsberg and Kerouac, the 1930s meant doctrinaire adherence to the Communist Party line, reflecting the Scylla-and-Charybdis fear of both Left and Right totalitarianism in the period after World War II. Kerouac wrote to Rexroth in 1958 that "on publication of *On the Road* last fall I disassociated myself from your sphere of influence, and that was because I knew you were too political, past, present, or future, to join with my own sphere of 'beatitude' religious beatness and lush. I've never, never will, join even a rotary club." Instead, Kerouac's notion of liberation was to avoid the crushing power of an oppressive state, to withdraw from politics, and to drain power relations from the very system itself. "All I want is stars, wine, friends, talk, mebbe guitar music," Kerouac concluded. Ginsberg extended this to Rexroth's racial criticism, asserting that cross-racial interaction at ground level—in daily life at New Saloons and poetry readings—was an effective source of antiracism.[14] For the Beats, however disingenuous their disavowal of the 1930s might have been, jazz poetry was part of a project to transform the nature of American life.

As the beatniks gained national press, they offered the kind of incendiary poetry that helped to spark a larger conflagration. "Their characteristic literary theme is the decline and fall of practically everybody," a journalist for *Time* magazine reported from the Cellar in late 1957. "At the GHQ of the San Francisco poets, a tiny joint on Grant Avenue known simply as The Place, the non-squares were invited to gather on Sunday afternoons to 'snarl at the cosmos, praise the unsung, defy the order.'" The article quoted Rexroth's ode to Dylan Thomas, "Thou Shalt Not Kill":

"Who killed him?
Who killed the bright-headed bird?
You did . . .
You drowned him in your cocktail brain . . .
You killed him! You killed him.
In your God damned Brooks Brothers suit,
You son of a bitch."

As Rexroth told the reporter: "Poetry is a dying art in modern civilization. Poetry and jazz together return the poet to his audience." The *Time* article sneered (somewhat justifiably) that the "poetry was usually poor and the jazz was worse," yet a crowd of 500 flocked to the tiny Cellar, lining up to hear Rexroth and Ferlinghetti declare their oppositional verse.[15]

Rexroth subsequently undertook a jazz poetry tour of Rebel Café nightclubs that included the Jay Landesman's Crystal Palace in St. Louis and the Five Spot in New York City (with Ivan Black as emcee). Meanwhile, Langston Hughes and Kenneth Patchen read their works, with Charles Mingus's musical accompaniment, in other

Gotham venues, such as the Vanguard and the Living Theatre.[16] Rexroth noted that these performances offered much-needed income for struggling poets, as well as socio-cultural edification for nightclub crowds. "If jazz is music of revolt, it is a revolt towards more natural, wholesome, normal human relationships," he wrote in 1958, temporarily adopting the Beat position on aesthetic politics. "After all, a revolution in basic human relationships is a very important revolution indeed. Just incidentally, nothing shows better the way in which the arts play a social role—secretly, behind the scenes, seldom understood by the official critics of art and literature, and, eventually, totally subversive." The Beats' new poetry directly invoked this language, "the natural rhythms of American speech" that were "from one point of view, 'social,' but it makes the past generation of proletarian poets look like ignorant bumblers."[17]

Amiri Baraka used even stronger terms for this intersection of social commentary and art, stating that all poetry is political. Yet he insisted that it must be backed by effective activism. "The words of an incendiary poet are finally less frightening than a political organizer," he wrote. "The one can be used merely to titillate, the other assumes a functional presence in the world that can intimidate." Norman Mailer agreed, suggesting that the Beat movement offered only rebellion, not revolution, asserting that it "has no center to its rage, and so is sentimental enough to assume that the world can be saved with words."[18]

North Beach poet Bob Kaufman in many ways exemplified these views, embodying the cultural front's legacy in jazz poetry, while his activism bridged time periods, art, and politics. Kaufman, a talented and irascible poet, was a legendary figure who concocted an autobiography of stories that portrayed a romantic, cosmopolitan, and radical bohemian past. He claimed that he was born to a German Jewish father (a New Orleans nightclub owner) and a black mother from the island of Martinique (a schoolteacher). He supposedly left the oppressive south for Mexico at age fifteen, taking up with a twenty-eight-year-old prostitute, and then working as a merchant marine, circling the globe nine times and suffering multiple shipwrecks, before heading into communist activism. Kaufman also spoke of his grandmother's arrival in the Americas on a slave ship directly from Africa, and his mother's grounding in Catholic/voodoo culture, all of which added to his mystique and betokened pride in his African roots. These stories circulated widely in North Beach and in the press, well past his death in January 1986. They were also largely fictitious. Kaufman's performative persona was, in itself, a form of artistic expression.[19]

The facts were simultaneously more mundane and far more significant. Robert G. Kaufman was born on April 18, 1925, in New Orleans, but neither of his parents was foreign born. Instead, both were African Americans from Louisiana. His father worked at various hospitality jobs, including as a Pullman porter and a waiter at a Storyville nightclub. His mother, married at age twenty, was a homemaker and former schoolteacher who raised thirteen children, instilling them all with a love of literature.[20] Far from undermining Kaufman's complex understanding of race, his actual background reflected New Orleans's intricate and shifting racial hierarchy, as his family line straddled distinctions between black and white. And his claim of Martiniquan origins symbolically placed him in the radical heritage of that French colonial island's poet-politician, Aimé Césaire. Kaufman did have a very real history of leftist activism, however. He eventually joined the merchant marine (although not at the tender age of fifteen), was politically active with the NMU, helped "smuggle Jewish refugees from Europe into Palestine," and was reportedly once severely beaten by southern policemen for working as a communist organizer.[21]

Personally, he was involved with nightclub singers and prostitutes as he worked up and down both coasts, and in the early 1950s, he was part of the Village jazz/bohemian scene. One North Beach poet recalled meeting Kaufman from the days when he hung around the Village in New York, where the two went to the same bars. Radical poet and activist Jack Micheline remembered Kaufman as a "well-read human being" and a "street poet" who counted jazz musicians such as Charlie Parker, Billie Holiday, and Cecil Taylor among his close friends, declaring that "Mingus loved him." Kaufman apparently tired of his itinerancy. Stumbling into North Beach while venturing ashore in the mid-1950s, he settled down, marrying journalist Eileen Kohl in 1958 and focusing on writing.[22] Settled down is a relative term when describing Kaufman, however. He cultivated friendships with local radicals like Richard "Specs" Simmons—a self-proclaimed "rough Boston sheet metal worker Communist" (who later opened his own bar at the site of the old 12 Adler in 1968). Kaufman also developed a reputation as the "black American Rimbaud" for his outrageous and often drunken behavior, as well as his sexual escapades with women and men.[23]

Kaufman crafted a public persona within North Beach boîtes such as The Place, the Coffee Gallery, and the Coexistence Bagel Shop, where he "would speak spontaneously on any subject, quote great poetry by Lorca, T.S. Eliot, e.e. cummings, or himself," boisterously spouting verses from atop tables and upright pianos. Kaufman was virtually the personification of the beatnik as a social phenomenon, carving out a living that was supported by tourists and by fellow scenesters who enjoyed basking in his ecstatic monologues. Eileen recalled that devotees were "delighted to buy a pitcher of beer, bottle of champagne, or anything we wanted—just to be a part of the Life emanating from our table." Nonetheless, Kaufman was no saint. He regularly conned unwitting tourists and "college girls" out of money and underscored his howling reputation by breaking windows at his favorite haunts.[24]

Kaufman's performances were part of a frequently necessary African American tactic, living up to Euro-American expectations as a way of making do. As fellow beatnik Russell FitzGerald wrote of Kaufman in 1957: "He's a negro. . . . Alive as only negroes are. Spiteful to those he cons. . . . There are times when he has a fire about him that seems to come from a knowledge of life's ugliness and a passionate commitment to human dignity." As historian Clinton Starr has argued, this dynamic was apparent in Kaufman's interactions with middle-class slummers, as "racial exoticism intersected with countercultural tourism." Despite Jack Micheline's insistence that Kaufman "totally transcended color," race was an ever-present vexation. The Place's

Leo Krikorian later suggested that Kaufman was "pissed off at society, I think because people didn't accept him as being Jewish instead of black. . . . He used to talk about it. It really fucked him up."[25]

Kaufman's rambunctious, rambling life means that he left little in the way of personal correspondence for the historical record. Instead, his poetry is the best way to gain insight into his rebellious cultural perspective. "Shadow people, projected on coffee shop walls," Kaufman wrote in "The Bagel Shop Jazz," "where time is told with a beat . . . / The ancestral cross, the Othello laid curse, / Talking of Bird, Diz, and Miles / The secret, terrible hurts / Wrapped in cool hipster smiles."[26] While his approach hinted at the mystical, Kaufman's radical leftism and elements of social protest continuously threaded through his work. "Of life, of love, of self, of man expressed / In self determined compliance, or willful revolt," he wrote, expounding the dialectic of solidarity and individual autonomy that characterized the postwar Left. "Secured in this avowed truth, that no man is our master, / Nor can any ever be." Specs Simmons placed Kaufman's work directly within a genealogy of social justice activism, asserting that "back in the 40s he had been involved in the civil rights movement in New Orleans and New York City." But Kaufman also exhibited a satirical streak and counted the hipster comedian Lord Buckley among his influences. One jazz drummer who met Kaufman at the Coexistence Bagel Shop in 1957 recalled the poet's sense of humor, declaring that "he was concerned with current events, just like Lenny Bruce." African American poet Tony Seymour also noted Kaufman's wry humor. On first meeting Seymour at City Lights Bookstore, Kaufman immediately satirized the era's racial codes, remarking, "What would you do if your daughter married a black man?"[27]

These various threads were woven together most vividly in Kaufman's "Abomunist Manifesto." The poem, a parody of Marx's *Communist Manifesto*, was published in 1959 under the pseudonym "Bomkauf," a sly nod to Cold War–era atomic politics. It also captured the Rebel Café's oppositional sensibility, including a list of definitions from the "Lexicon Abomunon":

> *Abommunity*: n. Grant Avenue & other frinky places. . . .
> *Abomunasium*: n. Place in which abomunastics occur, such as bars, coffee shops,
>   USO's, juvenile homes, pads, etc. . . .
> *Abomunicate*: v. To dig. (Slang: to frink). . . .
> *Frink*: v. To (censored). n. (censored) and (censored).

Kaufman closed with a series of political demands ("low-cost housing for homosexuals," "statehood for North Beach," "universal frinkage") and satirical news briefs, such as "Both sides in Cold War stockpiling atomic missiles to preserve peace, end of mankind seen if peace is declared, UN sees encouraging sign in small war policy, works quietly for wider participation among backward nations. . . . End of news." Intertwining his poetic protest with the Beats' concern for authenticity, in 1960 Kaufman declared: "The United States has failed to produce real people. It has produced everything else—but not real people. We intend, above all else, to be real people."[28]

Poetic justice. *Top*, Bob Kaufman reading at the Coffee Gallery. Kenneth Rexroth (*bottom left*) and Lawrence Ferlinghetti (*bottom right*) in the Cellar. *Top*, courtesy of C.R. Snyder; *bottom left and right*, *Look* Magazine Photograph Collection, Library of Congress, Prints & Photographs Division, (*bottom left*) L9-58-78425-FR-19, job 58-7842-HHH, contact sheet image #24 and (*bottom right*) job 58-7842-GGG, contact sheet image #15

With his rejection of the "bourgeois wasteland," Kaufman's identity politics and demands for a new consciousness—all drenched in the acid of satirical absurdity— stood in for the Old Left's programmatic proletarian politics.

Kaufman's existential claims often took the form of outspokenness in the Coffee Gallery or the Coexistence Bagel Shop—particularly in his resistance to police brutality and harassment. One officer in particular, William Bigarani, made a one-man crusade out of "cleaning up" North Beach, arresting beatniks for wearing sandals and especially focusing on interracial couples like Bob and Eileen. Bigarani violently arrested Kaufman multiple times (once on the poet's birthday) and bohemians frequently complained that Kaufman was assaulted by police while in custody—complaints that were summarily ignored. In response, Kaufman penned a pair of poems in protest, placing them in the window of the Bagel Shop. "One day Adolph Hitler had nothing to do," Kaufman wrote. "All the Jews were burned, artists all destroyed, / So he moved to San Francisco, became an ordinary / Policeman, devoting himself to stamping / out Beatniks." Bigarani responded by arresting the poet, sparking a wave of protest that resulted in the policeman's transfer to another precinct. This case—which drew criticism from *Howl* lawyer Al Bendich as a "violation of freedom of speech"—epitomized Kaufman's career, illustrating both the role of literary bars in conflicts over what constitutes "material offensive to the public" and the role of the poet as a voice of social critique.[29]

Although the poetry and jazz of the late 1950s failed to represent the best of either—even its most adventurous explorations fell short of the aural avant-gardism of Mingus's 1956 *Pithecanthropus Erectus* album, nor could it match the raw impact of Ginsberg's poem "Howl"—it nonetheless played a major part, albeit briefly, in national culture. Jazz poetry's popularity waned by the end of the decade, so its significance is easily forgotten. Yet its elements were absorbed into the massively popular folk and rock & roll of the 1960s. Dylan Thomas had set the tone for poetry's prominence through the 1950s. He drew thousands to his readings and was accorded the kind of celebrity we now associate with pop stars. It is perhaps the most prescient move in popular culture that Bob Dylan (né Robert Zimmerman) took Thomas as his namesake. Both of them skirted the line between poet and popular performer, and the folksinger's public fanfare mimicked the poet's to an eerie degree. Moreover, the political slant of Bob Dylan's breakthrough albums bore more than a hint of the Rebel Café's leftist literary style—an influence that took hold as the young folksinger hung out with left-wing bohemians Dave Van Ronk and Suze Rotolo at the Gaslight and Gerde's Folk City.[30]

A similar concoction of Rebel Café nightlife and politics also connected bohemianism with a network of radical literati and activists, from Norman Mailer in New York; through the War Resister's League and *Liberation* magazine's Bayard Rustin, David McReynolds, and Paul Goodman; to poets Tram Combs in the US Virgin Islands and Kenneth Rexroth in San Francisco.[31] Yet their own work as writers and editors for publications such as the *Village Voice* and the *Nation* undermined the Rebel Café's social function, even as it grew in political significance.

Michael Harrington was a prime example. Beginning as a Catholic Worker activist, he left the organization in 1953 when he embraced atheism. He continued to collaborate with Dorothy Day, however, through the period of his leadership in the Young Socialist League (YSL) and, ultimately, in the League for Industrial Democracy, the educational branch of the Left (founded in 1905 by Jack London, Upton Sinclair, and Florence Kelley) that spawned Students for a Democratic Society (SDS) in the early 1960s. The White Horse was central throughout Harrington's social and intellectual development, as he began translating his bohemianism into political action. "We had our tabs, our phone messages, even our mail," he recalled. "So the Horse fulfilled a classic Bohemian function: it was, to borrow from a French writer, 'a kind of organization of disorganization.'" Harrington asserted that this was where the American Left and bohemianism came together: "When the Beats first came around we had friendly relations with them; they thought we were much too square and organizational, and worrying about things like the labor movement. But a guy like Allen Ginsberg had been . . . around the SYL [Socialist Youth League] though his homosexuality would have kept him from being related to the CP. Sometimes after YSL meetings we'd go over and sit in the back room of the White Horse. The thing that kept it from being completely Bohemian was that we were involved in organizing civil rights marches; we were involved in anti-Franco picket lines."

Harrington's backroom bar talk with Allen Ginsberg, Norman Mailer, or Daniel Patrick Moynihan; his White Horse debates with local conservatives from Young Americans for Freedom; his flirtations with "pretty girls"; and his sing-alongs with Dylan cohorts like the Clancy Brothers were all woven into his oppositional lifestyle, in order to help process his ideas. After reenergizing from these nights by sleeping until noon, he recalled: "I worked for twelve hours after I got up, reading, writing, or doing socialist organizing. The late night was a gregarious, potentially erotic release from a disciplined existence. The world of nine-to-five was a routine; of twelve-to-twelve a choice."[32]

"A transcript of a barroom chat with Michael Harrington would read like the first draft of a slightly discursive *New Republic* essay," wrote one admiring scribbler. But many of his nocturnal interlocutors were surprised by the product of his daytime labor, *The Other America*, not realizing that their discussions were helping to distill an important work of social criticism. Published in 1960, this study of poverty in the affluent society was groundbreaking, and it helped to spawn Lyndon Johnson's Great Society legislation. The book solidified Harrington's position as "a virtual folk hero of the Left," wrote the *Village Voice* in 1962. Now, commentators noted, instead of being "confined to one faction of the Young People's Socialist League and the back room of the White Horse Tavern," Harrington was "knighted by Arthur Schlesinger Jr. as 'the only responsible radical in America.'" Although he fell out with the SDS over the "Port Huron Statement" in 1962, Harrington was nonetheless a key link from the Rebel Café's underground to the broad New Left initiatives of the 1960s, maintaining ties with civil rights groups and the antiwar movement. Meanwhile, the milieu that had helped to nurture this new opposition succumbed to its own success. As its underground sensibilities became absorbed into the mainstream and the 1960s counterculture, Harrington proclaimed, "America lost that faith in its own philistine righteousness and Bohemia began to die."[33]

Print culture played a continual role in this widening of the underground public sphere. Jane Warwick, a Rebel Café regular and assistant editor at *Mademoiselle*, agreed that, although Harrington was "not a friend of mine because of politics" but instead was "socially and a bar friend," it was "no accident" that a 1961 article by the SDS's Tom Hayden, praising Harrington and proclaiming the start of student activism, found its way into the magazine. The magazine's editors, Warwick asserted, worked to stay "politically . . . on the ball."[34] While this still included connections to the nightclub underground, it increasingly meant linking New Left leadership with national issues in the public eye.

Further, in 1961, activist Jane Jacobs published *The Death and Life of Great American Cities*, which argued that mixed-use development and mutual support were key factors for urban renewal. Rather than large-scale slum clearances, with open green spaces punctuated by high-rise housing, Jacobs called for attention to the human scale of sidewalks and street life, which meant fostering a mix of housing, bars, shops, and restaurants. Jacobs used the bars of her own Greenwich Village neighborhood as examples. "Strangers become an enormous asset on the street on which I live," she wrote. "On a cold winter's night, as you pass the White Horse, and the doors open, a solid wave of conversation and animation surges out and hits you; very warming. The comings and goings from this bar do much to keep our street reasonably populated until three in the morning, and it is a street always safe to come home to." Rejecting "puritanical and utopian conceptions" of urban planning, such as Robert Moses's freeway-focused New York dreamscapes, Jacobs recognized the saloon's role within the city's vibrant bustle, arguing that "the White Horse bar and the church-sponsored youth center, different as they undoubtedly are, perform much the same public street civilizing service." During a later battle to save Washington Square from a new thruway, Jacobs put this theory into practice, helping to form the Committee to Save the West Village and using the White Horse and the Lion's Head coffeehouse for campaigning and organizing meetings. An alliance with Art D'Lugoff later paid off directly. After she was arrested for disrupting a city council meeting in 1968, the Village Gate held a benefit to augment her legal defense fund.[35]

Admittedly, Jacobs's depiction of urban life was limited by middle-class aesthetics and norms—as well as a too-sanguine view that elided the messier side of the bar business, such as drunken fisticuffs or payoffs to both the police and organized crime. As Harrington later noted, she also ignored the continued racial tensions in the area, illustrated by a Village bar called the Ideal, which was "nicknamed The Ordeal by the White Horse regulars," as it was the "scene of tense confrontations between Bohemia and square America."[36] Nonetheless, Jacobs's study was a compelling plea for a renewed, humanistic urbanism. At the same time, like Harrington's rise to national prominence, it symbolized one of the last gasps of the Rebel Café's outsider status. Both beatnik poetry and the Village's left-wing literati had contributed to the new, increasingly mainstream, political language of the 1960s.

A Certain Feeling of Degeneracy: Sophistication, Camp, and the Erotics of Art

While bohemia may have been relatively exclusive in the 1950s, it always existed in dialogue with the larger society, since the press publicized its quasi-utopian model of sexual experimentation and aesthetically oriented lifeways. The simultaneous labeling of oppositional culture as sick, however, indicated the era's notions of homosexuality, and even feminism, as deviant. As a result, such identities often remained performative and were limited to particular public spaces, as seen in the sometimes outrageous aesthetics of "camp." Even as jazz poetry faded from the scene, new styles of campy continental decor became one of the Rebel Café's most enduring cultural expressions.

Older Greenwich Villagers, like Larry Rivers, had long cultivated the romanticism of the nightclub scene's European style and cabaret sensibilities. While in Paris in 1950, Rivers had attended one of Dadaism pioneer Tristan Tzara's "happenings" and "understood the role played by Parisian nightclubs in bringing the public new ideas in theater, music, and the visual arts." Depression-era bohemians, such as Lawrence Lipton, also recognized this continuity with cabaret and sought to make their own jazz and poetry in the leftist café idiom, declaring the influence of the "café-Berlin-Left-Underground between-the-wars" spirit of Marc Blitzstein and Kurt Weill's *Threepenny Opera*.[37]

New arrivals in the Village had similar notions. Dylan later recalled that he joined the scene as his "consciousness was beginning to change," declaring that "if you want to leave America, go to Greenwich Village." He found the Vanguard, the Kettle of Fish, Café Wha?, and the White Horse to be carnivalesque, filled with "literary types with black beards, grim-faced intellectuals—eclectic girls, non-homemaker types."[38] Suze Rotolo, who became a cultural icon when she appeared arm-in-arm with Dylan on the cover of his 1963 album, *Freewheelin'*, later portrayed Greenwich Village as America's answer to Montmartre, noting the dingy flair of the Gaslight Club and D'Lugoff's Village Gate. As tourism made clubs financially viable, they were ultimately undermined by corporate scouts, who spirited the performers away to Hollywood and concert halls. But for a generation of young radicals like Rotolo, raised as "red-diaper babies" in the pre-McCarthy milieu of the communist Camp Kinderland and Pete Seeger's People's Songs, the Village "was the public square of the twentieth century for the outsiders, the mad ones, and the misfits . . . and New York replaced Paris as the destination for the creative crowd."[39] Rotolo's sense of continuity evinced the Rebel Café's long legacy, in which continental styles met American sociopolitical realities.

While relishing a similar sensibility, middle-class patrons used nightclubs to construct identity differently than bohemians, as seen in publicity for Max Gordon's Blue Angel. That venue's "high sophistication," noted one early 1960s guidebook, was part and parcel with the "luminaries of entertainment" who graced its stage. The club was a stateside manifestation of the continental cabaret for New York's upper echelons.[40] In such "sophisticated" nightclubs, jazz served a Janus-faced function as both a high-minded taboo breaker—with its sexual connotations and rebellion against the workaday world—and a buffer against overt transgression. Sociologist Sherri Cavan, in a study of 1960s nightclubs, noted that patrons wanted to enjoy public entertainment while also limiting their contact with each other. By giving "deference to the show," audiences seated at tables moved less freely through the club's spaces and interacted mostly with acquaintances. Within this stricter social dynamic, a performance acted as a bonding agent, drawing the attention of isolated groups into a common sphere of awareness, while still allowing some separation.[41] This mental matrix also kept more distance between the performers and audiences than in less formal settings, such as the Cellar or bohemian bars, furthering a *feeling* of engagement with the "real" world, a substitute sense of community, while maintaining a characteristic level of postwar American individualism.

This simultaneous display of economic status and exploration of the demimonde reflected another aspect of sophistication that ran through public discourses about nightclub culture. In important ways, Beat sensibilities corresponded with mainstream nightclub audiences' notions of their own class consciousness. Patrons claimed sophistication by treating their own affluence with casual disdain—a backhanded form of conspicuous consumption. Whether they were young intellectuals whose "psychiatrists had psychiatrists," "Dun and Bradstreet types" charging drinks to their expense accounts, or "out-of-towners" (defined as "anyone who lives west of Hoboken"), audiences came to spend a tidy sum in order to soak up a "certain feeling of degeneracy" in New York's cabarets.[42]

Meanwhile, performers, patrons, and critics in San Francisco blithely assumed that the city's politically oriented cabarets would draw high-minded crowds. Even their disdain for the philistine audiences of tourists reveals the expectation that nightclubs were sites of "casual atmosphere and modern, sophisticated entertainment."[43] The hungry i, Purple Onion, Jazz Workshop, and the Cellar invoked cabaret sensibilities as their patrons basked in exotic nocturnal culture. The Paris Louvre restaurant featured murals with "authentic scenes from Paris" and at 12 Adler, the "cramped, smoky confines" featured Turkish music and belly dancing that was "provocative, primitive and passionate." As journalist Herb Caen observed, "On a corner in North Beach, where it always looks like summer, a beautiful girl ran her fingers through her hair and said in wonderment, 'It's just like Europe'—and so it seemed."[44] On both coasts, American nightclub culture remained a multifarious mix of exoticism and transnational imagination, all easily purchased with the price of admission.

The nightclub formula of performance, talk, and identity exploration also challenged norms of gender and sexuality. Unsurprisingly, nightclubs played a contradictory role. As sociologist Wini Breines argues, Euro-American women countered the Cold War–era "containment" of their sexuality by embracing rock & roll, working-class culture, jazz, and the Beats. Though these women usually lacked a deep under-standing of black culture, it represented an escape from domesticity. But because women's subversive strategies required extra levels of dissemblance, they often remained hidden in bohemian enclaves, away from the watchful eyes of authorities. Meanwhile, the sophisticated nightclub structure of physical separation and psycho-logical cohesion made them more-respectable public spaces for women.[45]

Changes in nightclub culture's gender norms were visible in the policies of differ-ent venues. Max Gordon, for instance, explicitly discouraged the Blue Angel from becoming a "pick-up scene." Although the club was a site for single gay men to meet, Lorraine Gordon later asserted, "Max didn't allow women alone at the bar." San Fran-cisco's legal restrictions against B-girls and female bartenders similarly pressured clubs to monitor women. For many middle-class women, nightclubbing raised the specter of social stigma. Despite being an insider at the Black Hawk and the Jazz Workshop, one scenester reported that she always attended with her husband, to avoid nightlife's associations with prostitution.[46] Younger bohemians who frequented North Beach and Greenwich Village venues like the Coffee Gallery and Gerde's Folk City, however, were less concerned with such perceptions. Even Gordon's Village Vanguard welcomed single women (to the extent that prostitutes were counted among its patrons). And the Village Gate's Art D'Lugoff actively fought New York's municipal policy that prohibited female performers from interacting with customers, arguing that it was "anti-female" and a "very sleazy law."[47]

Given the impact of suburbanization and massive sociocultural shifts, it is not surprising that intentionally sophisticated clubs, such as the Blue Angel, began to ex-perience a serious decline by the mid-1960s. The more liberated spirit of Greenwich Village and North Beach presaged the future of America's nightclub culture, which no longer required such pristine notions of propriety. These changes, however, could also be problematic when paired with lingering, male-dominated norms. "'Beat Gen-eration' sold books . . . sold a way of life that seemed like dangerous fun," Joyce Johnson recalled. "Suburban couples could have beatnik parties on Saturday nights and drink too much and fondle each other's wives."[48] But, despite the misogynistic aspects of Beat writing, its popularity solidified New York City's and San Francisco's reputations as places of possibility, worlds apart from Middle America.

Many women did find liberation from the containment of the 1950s by fleeing to the Village and North Beach, enacting a personal form of politics that demanded public visibility. A new generation of women came to claim their own place on the terrain where those like Joyce Johnson, Eileen Kaufman, Diane di Prima, and Het-tie Jones had cleared a path. Janis Joplin famously went on the road to North Beach's nightclubs after reading Kerouac, and many other less renowned women followed suit. As one North Beach bohemian told a local journalist, "I live here because I've found a reasonable degree of happiness here. . . . I could have settled for a home on the peninsula somewhere with an educated ape for a husband. But you know what? One night this idiot would kick off his shoes and start babbling about how he was high point man at the Amalgamated Toilet Bowl Company, and I'd mix him a cyanide martini." Similarly, in 1961, the *Village Voice* profiled a "new girl in town." She had arrived from Scranton, Pennsylvania, against the objections of her parents and claimed that her experiences had already made her more "broad-minded" after only two weeks in bohemia. The *Voice* reported the sights that raised the new girl's consciousness: "Such things as Negro-white couples, . . . girls kissing each other as they walked along, and a pomaded youth dressed all in pink ('He had a lovely figure; I nearly asked him how he kept so thin')." She concluded by asserting that her "determination to stay in the Village is equaled only by her disinclination to return to Scranton, and she feels optimistically that an apartment, a job, and a whole new life are just around the corner."[49]

Nonetheless, contradictory elements continued within this tentative and contested feminism as notions of fulfillment remained tied to domesticity. Even within bohemia, women had to force open social and artistic spaces wherever they could find cracks in a largely masculine culture. Poet Dora Dull remembered that in North Beach circles, it was difficult to gain respect as a literary equal. "I was Harold [Dull]'s woman," she said. "It was sort of like—There wasn't room for me to write, too." She found openings through solidarity with gay poets in Jack Spicer's circle, who were less threatened by her talents: "For me, coming to San Francisco and meeting gay men was a wonderful experience, because I had just been through that season in my life where you're seen as a sex object . . . and then when I met gay men in San Francisco, and realized, 'They're interested in my ideas,' I was just overjoyed! . . . The world of ideas and poetry and politics that gay friends would talk to me about, that's where I felt at home."[50]

Unconventional women who claimed a public voice within the Rebel Café were part of a broad public discussion in which the media interacted with subterranean bar talk, resulting in a conversation that helped to transform American gender norms. Although identity politics did not reach fruition until the feminist and gay rights movements of the late 1960s and the 1970s, early stirrings were visible in the Rebel Café. In 1959, novelist Ann Bannon published *I Am a Woman*, which expressed many of the nightclub underground's sentiments, sensibilities, and settings. Bannon's protagonist, Laura, leaves her father to go to New York City, seeking a job and "a few friends." She soon finds her way to the Village, stumbling into a gay bar called the "Cellar," where the patrons looked like "students," with women in cotton pants and men in open-collar shirts. During Laura's introduction to lesbianism, she revels in the Village patrons' "sophisticated sarcasm." After a series of conflicts with lovers and weeks of soul searching, she ultimately finds a happy ending in the Cellar. As Laura kisses her partner, Bannon wrote in classic (if melodramatic) Rebel Café style, the reunited couple "turned and walked into the night toward Cordelia Street."[51]

As Bannon's novel suggests, the Rebel Café translated the subterranean ethos for unfamiliar audiences and transmitted these underground ideas into the mainstream—much like Marlene Dietrich's *The Blue Angel* had done in the 1930s. As critical theorist Susan Sontag argues in her groundbreaking 1964 essay, "Notes on Camp," Dietrich was not only a public model of powerful femininity, but she was also associated with the "outrageous aestheticism" celebrated by urbane gay men. Nan Boyd has convincingly argued that this camp sensibility contained the potential for political resistance, as seen in the activism of Black Cat drag queen José Sarria, whose campaign for the post of San Francisco city supervisor in 1961 energized the Bay Area's gay rights movement.[52] In particular, the performative aesthetics of camp bolstered the visibility of gays and lesbians in the public sphere. Yet the lines between sexual and gender transgression should not be drawn too sharply. Bohemian women also embraced camp's flamboyant and satirical style, making it part of early feminism's personal politics.

Perhaps the most significant—and subsequently overlooked—nightclub within this mix was San Francisco's Tin Angel. Formal entertainment was largely secondary to the Tin Angel's appeal. Rather, the club's owner, local wit and raconteur Peggy Tolk-Watkins, was the main attraction, and the club was an extension of her bohemian performativity. She was born in New York City in 1922 to Jewish parents. Her mother was a seamstress, and her father, a low-level gangster. Peggy Tolk studied photography under Arnold Eagle in Franklin Roosevelt's National Youth Administration (NYA) and was a social worker on the Lower East Side in the early 1940s. In 1945, she came to San Francisco, again doing social work, as well as teaching art to children and participating in a mural project on the Oakland side of the bay, in the Richmond area. She soon gravitated toward the Black Cat's bohemian crowd, where she probably first met Kenneth Rexroth. The following year she bounced back east, teaching children's art classes at the Negro Baptist Church in Asheville, North Carolina, and studying English literature at Black Mountain College. There she met bohemian writer Harriet Sohmers Zwerling, who became her lover, and Ragland "Rags" Watkins, who became her spouse. Succumbing to Tolk-Watkins's "seduction by music," which included Billie Holiday and Marlene Dietrich records—as well as her literary tastes that ranged from Djuna Barnes's *Nightwood* to Proust and Faulkner—both followed her back to the Bay Area in 1948. The trio became a fixture on the jazz/queer/bohemian scene.[53]

The Tin Angel, which first opened the next year, was more an extension of the Tolk-Watkins persona than a definitive site. Its first location was across the bay from San Francisco, in Sausalito, and it featured eye-popping colors, including a bright yellow piano, courtesy of Black Mountain College friends and local artist Jean Varda. Locals invoked Montmartre and Greenwich Village to describe its flavor, redolent of jazz bands and abstract art exhibitions.[54] The Sausalito Tin Angel closed in 1951 and two subsequent locations followed, each in San Francisco's Embarcadero neighborhood. Throughout, Tolk-Watkins's razor-sharp conversations and whimsical sense of decor heightened the club's allure. Jazz critic Ralph Gleason remembered that while she was "not always diplomatic in her relations with her staff and entertainers," she consistently enlisted seasoned musicians, such as Turk Murphy, as part of the club's "carnival atmosphere." "Peggy Tolk-Watkins had flair," Gleason gleefully recalled, contending that she, along with the Black Hawk's Helen Noga, stood as "important figures in the entertainment world." A self-avowed socialist, she also was part of the city's anarchist-libertarian circle, bringing together elements of jazz/bohemianism and the city's gay and lesbian community.[55]

Tolk-Watkins's influence as a pivotal subterranean force radiated into the mainstream, far beyond her individual renown. She was a prime example of the traditional holy fool—an eccentric aesthete who modeled transformative possibilities for those who met her. Harriet Zwerling, whose first significant sexual experiences were with Tolk-Watkins, remembered her as central to Zwerling's own free-spirited identity. "My time at Black Mountain had radically altered the roadmap of my life," she recalled. "Early in our relationship, Peggy had told me, 'You're not a lesbian. You're just in love with *me*.' Several other women and many years showed me that she had been right. . . . In so many ways, Peggy was my creator. From her, I had learned to be fearless, extravagant, a wanderer, an explorer. She had taught me about pain and obsession, betrayal and ambivalence, risk and reward."[56] Tolk-Watkins was always ready with a clever quip and, as Gleason put it, had "the knack, as had some of the most successful night club entrepreneurs in New York and Paris, of getting interesting people to come to the club regardless of the entertainment." A letter to friends Bill and Joan Roth in 1960 contained some of what must have greeted patrons at the Tin Angel. Opening with the salutation, "Sunday 8 A.M. Happy Easter. . . . (If J. C. could get up early so can I)," Tolk-Watkins concluded her missive by relating an act that reflected her irreverence, along with a symbolic rejection of the postwar media and materialism: "Actually this rebirth began very few days after an evening that WITH NO AUDIENCE AND DEAD SOBER I KICKED THE TELEVISION SET DOWN THE STAIRS AND RIGHT OUT THE DOOR AND OUT OF THE HOUSE . . . FOR REAL."[57]

Tolk-Watkins's reputation was backed by a "spider-web deviousness and humor," as in the poetry of her whimsical book, *Pigs Ate My Roses*. Through her friendship with Fantasy Records' Max Weiss (who became part owner of the Tin Angel in 1956), *Pigs Ate My Roses* and its author, along with her partner Irmine Droeger and Weiss himself, were featured on the cover of Lenny Bruce's first album, *Interviews of Our Times*, in 1958. Ralph Gleason wrote that, like Bruce, Tolk-Watkins was a "genuine character with a brilliant, erratic mind."[58] Gleason's insistence that she "practically invented camp as interior decoration" further underscored her bleeding-edge tastes. The San Francisco Tin Angel's atmosphere—which was featured in the 1955 film *Cinerama Holiday*—was "part Greenwich Village, part Paris." Blending experimental art, cabaret, and queer culture, Tolk-Watkins decorated the club with Buckminster Fuller–style globe lights, Renaissance paintings, vintage circus posters, a carnivalesque stage set, and the club's trademark—a silhouetted tin angel, salvaged from a condemned Manhattan church—spotlighted atop the roof.[59]

For many, the Tin Angel's Embarcadero milieu—on the waterfront, less than a mile from North Beach—evoked the New Saloon. While the Tin Angel was recog-

The essence of camp. *Top*, Peggy Tolk-Watkins (*center*) and unidentified patrons at the Fallen Angel. *Bottom*, the interior of the Tin Angel. Courtesy of Ragland Tolk Watkins

nized nationally as the club that spawned Odetta's folk-singing career and served as a base for Rexroth's jazz poetry revival, it was also embedded in the local bohemia. When *Time* magazine covered the jazz poetry phenomenon, it unconsciously captured the close connections that ran from Rexroth's poetic performances to The Place, harkening back to Tolk-Watkins as part of the 1940s Iron Pot crowd and her

Black Mountain College friendship with Leo Krikorian. This history also reflected her penchant for bars, which she frequented "for the conversation and the drinks," as well as friendships with jazzmen whose social circles overlapped with the Beats. Moreover, Tolk-Watkins's partner, Irmine Droeger—a Women's Army Corps veteran, journalist, and Berkeley alumnus—was part of the Bay Area literary bohemian scene.[60]

In 1955, Tolk-Watkins further expanded that scene, opening the Fallen Angel near the original Black Cat's old cabaret district. The building's legendary history as madam Sally Stanford's former brothel further enhanced the club's allure. Columnist Herb Caen noted that the guests included "Mme. Stanford herself, looking around nostalgically at the scene of past glories (there was enough necking in dark corners to make her feel at home)." The Fallen Angel allowed middle-class patrons to display their sophistication within a safely performative public space—perhaps best illustrated by the fountain in the club's atrium, which spouted sparkling burgundy and was scheduled to feature stripper Tempest Storm in a "milk bath."[61] Tolk-Watkins's queer feminist persona and sartorial style complemented the club's sensibility. She preferred Brooks Brother's shirts and corduroys, topped off with a pixie-crop hairstyle that was both reminiscent of the Jazz Age and—as she often declared— Prince Valiant. Tolk-Watkins completed her cross-dressing persona with a series of aliases, from "Bubbles Rabinowitz" to "Snowhite Goldstein," which, with Beat-like word playfulness, simultaneously satirized her own Jewish heritage and the aliases of San Francisco madams such as Stanford.[62]

This intertwining of lesbian and sex-worker overtones made Tolk-Watkins's image emblematic of Cold War–era transgression. As historians Nan Boyd and Donna Penn have argued, "The very essence of the lesbian, like the prostitute, was an expression of uncontained female sexuality." This was seen concretely in underground North Beach bars such as Tommy's, where lesbian owner Tommy Vasu welcomed sex workers as patrons in the early 1950s. Conversely, however, with the statistical reality of increased middle-class female sexual activity since the 1920s, prostitution diminished, making it a small-scale street business, since lavish bordellos like Stanford's became unviable after World War II.[63] The Tin and Fallen Angels, therefore, were spaces in which new notions of sexuality could be publicly explored, with Tolk-Watkins as a sort of sociosexual scout, guiding initiates through unfamiliar territory and translating the transgressions of places like Tommy's into legible terms for middle-class patrons.

In addition to the Tin Angel's publicly performative role, the club served as a locale for private mutual-aid functions, much like The Place did for local bohemians. Its hatcheck girl, for example, was Tolk-Watkins's mother Sadye, who lived in a nearby low-rent hotel and was a motherly mentor to neighborhood prostitutes. Legends abound concerning Tolk-Watkins's largesse with Tin Angel employees, ranging from freely sharing money from the till for medical bills to giving a Jaguar to a waitress when the car didn't meet Tolk-Watkins's expectations. Such generosity (or, as her son

Ragland says, "Generous or a show-off—I've never been able to determine") was dampened by nightclub economics, with its higher operating costs than those for bohemian bistros, as well as Peggy's mercurial nature. Many of Tolk-Watkins's financial problems were self-generated, as alcohol abuse complicated an already unpredictable business—another tale of creative self-destruction paralleling those of Jack Kerouac and Lenny Bruce. Moreover, San Francisco's complex sexual politics tempered the Tin Angel's liberatory potential. Perhaps fearing a shutdown by authorities if the club developed a reputation as a queer venue, Tolk-Watkins sometimes refused admittance to overtly gay or lesbian patrons.[64]

Although the Fallen Angel closed within a year and Tolk-Watkins sold the Tin Angel building to jazzman Kid Ory in August 1958, she was not afraid to come out swinging once again, immediately opening a third Tin Angel on Vallejo Street, which lasted through 1960. Meanwhile, an incident in a Sausalito nightspot demonstrated Tolk-Watkins's determination to claim social space on her own terms. As she was drinking at the bohemian Bridgeport Inn, a young man reportedly approached Tolk-Watkins's "girlfriend," with the result that the Tin Angel owner "splintered a glass over [his] head." The conflict continued next door at Leo Krikorian's café, the Kettle, where, "before it was over, three (3) other free spirits . . . went through two (2) plate glass windows. No one was hurt." In a follow-up report in the *San Francisco Chronicle*, Tolk-Watkins insisted: "I didn't hit him with a glass, I whacked him with my fist. If I'd hit him with a glass, he wouldn't have been able to walk."[65] While perhaps fueled by alcohol, this incident both paralleled Tolk-Watkins's assertiveness in the largely masculine world of nightspot owners and was a forceful defense of her queer identity.

Even after the Tin Angel closed for good in 1960, she demonstrated an anarchist bohemian spirit that skirted feminism and queer culture, maintaining a presence in Sausalito's saloons, such as Krikorian's Kettle. Artist and writer Brio Burgess remembers Tolk-Watkins as a mentor, from the time she met Peggy in 1963 until the nightclub owner's death from cancer in 1973. Throughout, she steered Burgess through her development as a nonconformist in between moments of outrageousness, including Tolk-Watkins's "drug- and alcohol-inspired performances" as a "folk musicologist" who sang songs "when she was 'in her cups', quite often around 4 a.m." Burgess recalls Tolk-Watkins as being a key influence, a model of possibility for a new generation of outsider women. As Burgess states: "Peggy was a poet and a painter, a mother and a nightclub owner, an entrepreneur, an operator, a godmother and a comedian, a tragic clown. She was rough, she was tough, and had been built to last . . . she's lasted in my mind for over thirty years."[66]

Tolk-Watkins's brand of personal politics, combining queer culture and unrepentantly individualist feminism, planted campy aesthetics into Bay Area bohemia and beyond. But the Tin Angel's influence radiated in another way, as well. The club was an important site for the multitalented intellectual Susan Sontag during her formative years at Berkeley. It offered psychosexual liberality that deeply affected her work, particularly her essay "Notes on Camp," which helped raise the public visibility and legitimacy of homosexuality in the 1960s. Sontag and Tolk-Watkins, whose paths briefly intersected in 1949, were exemplars of an oppositional queer feminist dynamic. Both flouted the gender norms of the 1950s with unconventional styles, working in male-dominated fields while demanding sexual and socioeconomic autonomy. Their protofeminism demonstrated one of the most important aspects of the vaunted sexual revolution in the 1960s: women's control and public expression of their own sexuality. At the same time, Tolk-Watkins's Tin Angel and Sontag's cultural criticism were part of a newly visible queer culture.

Many of the same broad sociocultural forces that were inherent in the Tin Angel's performative sensibility later came through in Sontag's criticism. Her experiences in Sausalito and North Beach helped to direct a life journey that took her through the bicoastal bohemia to her position as a public intellectual. Born in 1933, the precocious Sontag began undergraduate studies at the University of California, Berkeley, at age fifteen. In January 1949, soon after her sixteenth birthday, Sontag met a group of literary bohemians in Berkeley's coffeehouse scene, including Harriet Sohmers Zwerling, who worked at the campus bookstore. Zwerling encouraged her to attend a Saturday-afternoon class on Samuel Johnson, after which they mingled with San Francisco's queer bohemian set at the Black Cat and at lesbian hangouts such as Mona's, where Sontag first met and Peggy and "Rags" Watkins. Zwerling then took her to the original Tin Angel in Sausalito.[67]

Sontag recorded the process of her intellectual and sexual awakenings in a series of notebooks, which traced, in her words, a "juvenile" exploration of aesthetics and the self through to the full flowering of her ideas in the early 1960s. Her entries in May 1949, after she met Zwerling, were particularly significant. They reveal the unfolding of a new consciousness, an inchoate intellectualism on the cusp of sophistication. "I am not living up to the whole of myself," she wrote. The notion of life itself as aesthetic became particularly important in Sontag's thinking. Amid philosophical musings on "meaning" and "causality," Sontag played with the conventions of writing, testing plot ideas such as "*the* life, life as *the aesthetic phenomenon*."[68]

Sontag's experiences with North Beach nightlife, the Tin Angel, Tolk-Watkins, and—most significantly—Zwerling were crucial catalysts for her ideas about the inseparability of aesthetics, performativity, sexuality, and identity. This transformation revolved around a pivotal moment, the weekend of May 21, 1949, when Zwerling first took Sontag to North Beach and Sausalito. On the train from Berkeley to San Francisco, Zwerling already began to crack Sontag's "sardonic-intellectual-snob pose," arguing that fellow students who denounced her liberated notions of sexuality were "narrow and insensitive and not alive." "I felt Harriet to be right," Sontag noted, "that I was not horrible. . . . And I need so to be rid of that consciousness of being sinful." The pair first went dancing with Rags and Peggy, then to 12 Adler (where "Henri, the owner, wears a beret") and the Paper Doll for beer and bar talk with local bohemians, before driving to Sausalito in Tolk-Watkins's orange-and-pink

Model A Ford. "The ride to Sausalito is over the Golden Gate Bridge," Sontag gushed, "and while Peggy and Harriet were sitting next to me and necking, I watched the bay and felt warm and alive. . . . I had never truly comprehended that it *was* possible to live through your body and not make any of these hideous *dichotomies* after all!"[69]

Sontag recorded that on their arrival, this sense of possibility bloomed into the realm of experience, all within the walls of the nightclub: "Peggy's place was . . . a tiny joint. . . . When we walked back I discovered two more girls plus Peggy's baby son. . . . The idea of Peggy's harem seemed very ridiculous—I especially wondered how Rags took it . . . but it became obvious that they all loved Peggy that much—(who, as Harriett told me, has an enormous need for sexual infidelity) and, of course, a lover does not love on the conditions that his love will not cause him pain or be unfaithful." "The three of them went to sleep in the other bed," she concluded, "and Harriett and I went in to sleep on a narrow cot in the back of the Tin Angel."[70] Much as Tolk-Watkins had done for Zwerling at Black Mountain College, Zwerling now awakened Sontag to a wider spectrum of sexuality. "Perhaps I was drunk, after all, because it was so beautiful when Harriet began making love to me," Sontag confided. "The first time Harriet kissed me, I was still stiff, but this time it was just because I didn't know how, not that I didn't like it (as with Jim). . . . We talked some more, and just when I became fully conscious that I desired her, she knew it, too."[71] Over the next few days, Sontag recorded her postsexual transformation: "This weekend has been a beautifully patterned summation and, I think, a partial resolution of my greatest unhappiness: the agonized dichotomy between the body and the mind that has had me on the rack for the past two years. . . . My concept of sexuality is so altered—Thank god!—bisexuality as the expression of fullness of an individual. . . . I know now a little of my capacity. . . . I shall involve myself wholly . . . *everything matters*! The only thing I resign is the power to resign, to retreat: the acceptance of sameness and the intellect. I am alive. . . . I am beautiful." Acknowledging the "wonderful widening of my world which I owe to Harriet," Sontag wrote that "everything begins from now—*I am reborn*."[72]

The affair lasted only a few more weeks, until Zwerling moved to New York. During this time with her lover, Sontag witnessed the riotous behavior of Bay Area bohemia, including a night at the Tin Angel when "Rags and Peggy got very drunk, naturally, and broke one of the windows." Like many in the Rebel Café's bohemian milieu, Sontag made sense of her experiences through the lens of the literary past, even though nightspots were the places of present experimentation and intellectual development. In particular, Djuna Barnes, the subject of Sontag's thesis for her bachelor's degree, was a touchstone. Describing a night in the Paper Doll, Sontag noted that "we realized what a parody of *Nightwood* this all was." Meanwhile, she had received a scholarship to the University of Chicago, where she moved that fall. Sontag periodically met with Zwerling back in San Francisco, including once at a party where she "almost went to bed with Peggy's husband, Rags, but finally—not to disgrace my sex!—slept with Harriet," whom she found "even more magnificent than I remembered her." But the two gradually grew apart. In Chicago Sontag was briefly married to sociologist Philip Rieff, although she and Zwerling occasionally rekindled their romance in New York and Paris as the decade wore on.[73]

Throughout the 1950s, the Rebel Café continued to play a role—albeit one of diminishing importance—as Sontag sharpened her ideas and cultivated her career as a critic. Although most of her journals from 1950 to 1957 are lost, the entries that bookended this period make it safe to suppose that, much like the Beats, bohemian café culture was a continual aspect in her life. In August 1949, for instance, next to lists of subcultural gay slang (including "straight (east)," "jam (west)," and "*Jonny*—Dietrich . . . *Short Haired Woman*"), Sontag made a list of parallel San Francisco and New York nightspots, such as the Black Cat and the San Remo. She began to move back and forth between New York and Paris, all the while reading Joyce, Kafka, Marx, Rabelais, and Baudelaire. She mused about city life, American politics, psychology as an expression of the Enlightenment, Paul Goodman's anarchism, and the relation of sexuality to intellectualism. In 1956, planting the seed of her sociocultural stance in the 1960s, she noted the two "attitudes I can't tolerate . . . 1. anti-intellectualism among intellectuals [and] 2. Misogyny."[74]

Sontag found café life in Paris and New York to be comparable. In both cities, she interacted with fellow left-wing literary figures, including Allen Ginsberg, Gregory Corso, and Simone de Beauvoir, in sites like the Deux Magots and the Cedar Tavern. "The city as labyrinth," she wrote in Paris, noting its urban psychogeography in Joycean terms. "This, among other things, attracts me." Returning to New York in early 1959, Sontag remarked on the city's "ugliness" but continued: "I do like it here. . . . In NY sensuality completely turns into sexuality—no objects for the senses to respond to, no beautiful river, houses, people. . . . Nothing except eating, if that, and the frenzy of the bed." Critiquing her chosen milieu, Sontag noted in 1957 that the "essence of Bohemianism is envy—must be a solid intelligentsia to which it is peripheral—can only exist in certain communities—e.g., S.F., N.Y., . . . Black Mountain, etc." Yet Village bars like the San Remo and the Cedar were a regular part of her social and intellectual exploration, as captured in her concept of "X"—"when you feel yourself an object, not a subject"—a state defined by a performative persona of "boasting & name-dropping" or "being very cool." Indiscretion, she wrote in 1960, "is a classic symptom of X. Alfred [Kazin] pointed this out at the White Horse the other night." Looking cynically at her own role in Rebel Café circles, she concluded: "How many times have I told people that Pearl Kazin was a major girlfriend of Dylan Thomas? That Norman Mailer has orgies? That [F. O.] Matthiessen was queer? All public knowledge to be sure, but who the hell am I to go advertising other peoples sexual habits?"[75] Like many other patrons, Sontag publicly displayed her ideas and identity in the nightclub underground, even as she used it as a laboratory to experiment with both.

While Sontag's breakthrough essays in *Against Interpretation* (1966) cannot be re-duced to her experiences at the Tin Angel and other nightspots, her book nonethe-less bears the clear stamp of the Rebel Café. It was the first major published work on camp, reflecting the sensibility among "small urban cliques" of "seeing the world as an aesthetic phenomenon." The opening epigraph is by Oscar Wilde: "It is only shallow people who do not judge by appearances. The mystery of the world is the visible." Sontag argued against a false division between form and content. Critical interpreta-tion, she asserted, "makes art into an article for use, for arrangement into a mental scheme of categories." Conversely, art should be integrated into life. "The aim of all commentary on art now should be to make works of art—and, by analogy, our own experience—more, rather than less, real to us," Sontag wrote. Camp, therefore, "in-troduces a new standard: artifice as an ideal," a "comic vision of the world" that laughs away the pretense of surface appearance in order to discover its affective qual-ity. Recognizing art as an unmasking tactic, Sontag demanded an aesthetics of sen-sual experience, a means toward achieving authenticity through "experiencing the luminousness of the thing in itself."[76]

Sontag correctly noted that camp's new, largely gay sensibility was "disengaged, depoliticized—or at least apolitical." Yet the social forces that produced its postmodern aesthetic were part of the rise of identity politics, in which the ostensibly biological categories of gender and sexuality gained sociopolitical valence. While Sontag never fully engaged as a queer activist, her characterization of camp helped legitimate gay life as being worthy of intellectual exploration. She entreated critics to embrace camp's capacity to neutralize "moral indignation" as it "sponsors playfulness." Sontag concluded with a sentence that clearly echoed the Tin Angel's performative-sexual aesthetic, asserting the preeminence of subjective identity over objectivity—a unity of Eros and culture—stating, "In place of a hermeneutics we need an erotics of art."[77]

The Battles of the Beatniks and the Black Hawk

Paralleling Sontag's Tin Angel experiences of sexualized art/life unity—which nur-tured ideas about the self that later infused identity politics—the beatnik rebellion presaged the youthful political engagement and social transformations of the 1960s. As cultural critic Greil Marcus has suggested about Parisian radicals, it appeared to many bohemian anarchists that "the future of humanity was decided in the cafés," with spiritual salvation radiating from the culture of the street.[78] Activism reemerged out of the bohemian milieu of withdrawal as Rebel Café denizens connected their politics of place to wider currents—first within local struggles, and then in expand-ing circles.

Art D'Lugoff was a case in point, uniting artistic expression with formal protest. By focusing on the avant-garde and folk music, the Village Gate helped to build the folk revival that redefined Greenwich Village in the early 1960s. In addition, D'Lugoff hosted protests against an April 1961 ban on folk music performances in Washington Square, which was later lifted in response to a popular outcry in the Village.[79] Throughout the 1960s, he continued to organize community-action groups and to act as a spokesman to the press. As chairman of the Committee for a Vital Village, an organization of nightclub and coffeehouse owners, D'Lugoff advocated restrictions on a slum clearance that would have diminished the architectural character of the historic neighborhood and forced out longtime residents. During this coffeehouse crisis, D'Lugoff noted the role of folk venues in maintaining a sense of community, stating that "if the coffeehouses were shut down," Villagers would "lose out entirely because the tenements would be replaced by luxury apartments," unaffordable for either ethnic residents or bohemians. This Village folk culture underpinned later protests against Mayors Robert F. Wagner's and John Lindsay's rezoning and gentrification efforts, which Norman Mailer described as "highways and housing projects gutting the city of its last purchase on beauty."[80]

On the other hand, this kind of urban neopastoralism was no guarantor of social harmony. Village residents often complained about the noise made by late-night revelers.[81] As North Beach became established as an alternative community in the mid-1950s, conflicts within that city's neighboring areas flared, fueled by sociocultural differences. At the height of The Place's popularity, members of the queer bohemian community lamented that there was "a gang from the Mission District which hangs around North Beach beating people up and one of them has an uncle in the Police dept. They seem on the most part to catch poor innocents, rather than the queers they think they are beating up." In 1958, bomb threats against Jay Hoppe's Coexistence Bagel Shop were followed by a pair of small explosions. The first blew up the plumbing in the club's restroom, the second—a US Army practice charge dismissed by police as "no worse than a big firecracker"—was thrown onto the sidewalk from a speeding sports car.[82]

Meanwhile, a sign on the Bagel Shop's storefront warned "no more Coexistence, Pressniks go home, this is a tourist trap." Tourists did indeed disrupt the venue's feeling of community, but what became of more concern were beatnik exposés in the *San Francisco Examiner* and the *San Francisco Chronicle* that brought unwanted police attention. The day after the *Examiner* article appeared, an officer walked into the Coexistence Bagel Shop holding a copy of the Hearst rag and told Hoppe, "Now that you made the papers, you're going to get in trouble." Soon afterward, the *Chronicle* reported, "two cops stalked into the Bagel Shop" and "announced to the assembled beatniks: 'Awright, we're gonna vag [i.e., charge with vagrancy] anybody who can't prove employment.' This was greeted with such a roar of laughter that the cops wavered, fell back, broke ranks, [and] fled in vagrant confusion." For weeks, officers were posted for "sentry duty" outside the front door as regular vagrancy rousts continued. More damaging was Hoppe's arrest on a drunk-and-disorderly charge after he was "beaten up by a customer while sober."[83]

Hoppe sued, but the unusually strict police attention continued, particularly targeting blacks, interracial groups, and gays. Questionable arrests and cases of brutality against African Americans included those of an artist, a physician, and an interracial clique swept up in drug stings at nightspots, including the Coffee Gallery. The press evinced these last suspects' "beatnik" bona fides by their "wisecracking and hip talk" at the police station. The arrestees included a writer, a "TV technician and reported Judo expert," several musicians, and a "nude model at a North Beach figure studio" who "kept her face buried in a paperback James Joyce novel."[84] Police also burdened The Place with a capacity restriction and the Black Cat with renewed charges of public indecency. Local bohemians were abuzz about the controversy, a sign of the queer bohemian public sphere's vitality. Artist Robert LaVigne reported to Allen Ginsberg that The Place's "balcony [was] condemned and capacity of customers was limited to 24 persons." LaVigne planned to use the resultant publicity to sell paintings, however, turning police attention to his advantage: "I will leak the word secret and the fuzz will come down on things, preferably about the time of my opening at Lion on Polk Street. . . . Anyway, the PD is [plaguing] the Beach and I may as well get even with them." John Allen Ryan similarly wrote to Ginsberg in sardonic terms, mentioning the Black Cat's legal struggles over openly gay customers and relating that owner Sol Stoumen insisted to the liquor board, "QUOTE my patrons are merely members of the bohemian intelligentsia who gather at the Black Pussy to discuss art and semantics UNQUOTE."[85]

Organized responses soon materialized when police harassment, combined with the tourist influx, disrupted North Beach's sense of community. The first, in August 1958, was one part protest and one part performance piece. An interracial group of 100 beatniks, "equipped with bongo drums and bagels and booze," boarded Gray Line buses at the Coexistence Bagel Shop for a "tourist-tour-in-reverse." The so-called tour took them marching through the sophisticated and un-Beat St. Francis Hotel and other swanky spots, chanting "Hello, friendly neighbors" and exchanging bagels with an "anti-beatnik" delicatessen. Appropriately, Bob Kaufman led the march, maintaining a playful yet sincere claim on public space that combined his leftist political past and his performative persona. He closed the event with a recitation at The Place, titled "Things We Have Seen in the Bourgeois Wasteland."[86]

Kaufman helped revive political protests in San Francisco—a Battle of the Beatniks—including demonstrations against censorship and HUAC, all of which put his organizing experience to work, along with that of fellow North Beachers. In early 1959, Pierre Delattre, pastor of the local Bread and Wine Mission—a bohemian institution that offered both cheap meals and poetry readings—organized the North Beach Citizens Committee, which advised locals on nonviolent resistance and tactics to avoid false arrest. This was followed on January 30, 1960, by a rally of 300 beatniks in San Francisco's Washington Square Park, decrying police harassment. Speakers called for fellow beatniks to stop "performing" for tourists, but also to "fight back in every legal way" if "roughed up" or "falsely arrested." Just months later, in a show of bicoastal bohemian solidarity, North Beach's Coffee Gallery held a poetry reading to protest the recent shutdown of coffeehouses in Greenwich Village. Tellingly, a local paper reported that "much of what was said attempted to draw analogies between coffeehouses of both cities and the necessity for maintaining an atmosphere of free exchange of ideas within them."[87]

Such activism was not without precedent—and, in the civil rights era, not without significance. In 1952, the NAACP had successfully targeted city officials for discrimination in North Beach public housing, an outgrowth of the Italian residents' resistance to desegregation. Concern over interracial spaces, in fact, was directly stated by some as the cause for the suppression of New Saloons, as older residents conflated (not without some grounds) bohemianism, communism, homosexuality, and the fight for civil rights. One owner reported that a San Francisco police officer made this issue explicit: "Why do you allow so many Commies . . . and jigs to patronize this place? After all, if you give 'em an inch, they'll take a mile." At the Washington Square rally, artist Jerry Kamstra chided the policemen, especially Kaufman's nemesis, Officer Bigarani, for their flagrant civil rights violations. In a declaration of interracial solidarity, Kamstra proclaimed, "I admit that if Officer Bigarani is whacking a 'nigger' over the head, he isn't whacking me—but that 'nigger's' head is much akin to mine." Calling into question a recent raid on a private apartment, he asserted that police "found some authoritative texts on communism, called the occupants filthy communists, and tore the books apart" before they "handcuffed the owner." Within months, Kamstra was leading a sit-in protest against HUAC investigations in San Francisco—the start of a career in activism that spanned into the 1970s and included issues such as prison reform and Native American land rights.[88]

The final significant skirmish between the Rebel Café and municipal authorities came in January 1961. The previous year, San Francisco's Black Hawk (now co-owned by Max Weiss, of Fantasy Records) had begun a policy of allowing underage listeners to sit in a special section behind the stage, separated from the bar by chicken wire, which enabled them to hear the music without having access to alcohol. In response, Mayor George Christopher led an effort to shut down the club, asserting that "the book should be thrown" at the Black Hawk, "whether they're breaking the law or not." He ended by proclaiming: "I wouldn't want kids in a place like that. They are at an age when they're formulating opinions and their minds [are] beginning to jell. A lot of things can happen."[89] What became known as the Battle of the Black Hawk resulted in vocal protestations from Bay Area residents against what they saw as a misguided attempt to "clean up" the city. Ralph Gleason led the charge in the *San Francisco Chronicle*, including a call for poems in support of the club. The *Chronicle* was flooded with letters decrying Christopher's campaign, and outside the club, the mayor was hanged in effigy by a pair of college students. Supporters pointed to other public facilities, from opera houses to baseball stadiums, where minors were in even closer proximity to alcohol. A vocal defense of jazz as a legitimate art form was a major theme throughout, demonstrating the genre's growing social cachet.[90] Ultimately, the Alcoholic Beverage Control Board (ABC) determined that the Black Hawk had adequately separated minors from the bar, and on February 24, a judge dismissed the case.[91]

Much like the Battle of the Beatniks in North Beach, issues of race and gender underlay the mayor's attack. In a revealing statement, Christopher asserted: "One day a girl will be raped in a parking lot next door. And you know who'll be blamed—me and the chief of police." One incensed letter to the editor confronted the mayor's stance, asking, "Is he against rape in the parking lot, or is he just against being blamed for it?" Meanwhile, saxophonist Pony Poindexter wrote to the *Chronicle*, arguing that the "alcohol excuse is merely a camouflage for the real issue which is racial integration," since, as a rule, "jazz audiences are integrated." Poindexter then linked the issue with the legitimation of jazz itself, arguing that "Mayor Christopher apparently would rather see San Franciscan teen-agers out hot-rodding and drinking than focusing their attention on good jazz and integration." Gleason spotlighted this theme—poignant in the era of sit-ins and freedom rides—describing the Black Hawk's teen section as "separate but equal facilities."[92]

Although racial mixing and women's full access to public spaces were certainly paramount, a more subtle yet equally significant issue was also at stake. Gleason's article, "Defense of the Lowly Saloon," during the Black Hawk case rested in part on the notion of nightspots as community spaces—a role the club had played throughout the 1950s. Mayor Christopher, however, at some level recognized a social shift that Gleason missed. In a decade when teenage autonomy had increased, with access to cars and some independent income, which was combined with suburbanization and massive mobility in general, the saloon was losing its status as a *community* institution and instead was becoming a purely *public* one. Black Hawk supporters had unwittingly illustrated this point, arguing that closing the underage section would merely lead teens to "forge ID cards"—a pointless move in a face-to-face community.[93] Whether minors per se should be in proximity with alcohol was ultimately not the most important question in the Battle of the Black Hawk (which, in any event, was settled by the ABC). Mayor Christopher's failed effort was far more significant as a cultural marker, signaling the beginning of the end of Rebel Café nightlife in San Francisco.

This shift had been palpable at San Francisco's Washington Square rally in 1960, when one young woman presciently declared to the crowd the start of "a great American general strike." While the alliance she envisioned between radical bohemians and "workingmen who have no democracy" never fully emerged, these protests were indeed early salvos in the social justice movements of the 1960s, practice runs for middle-class Euro-Americans who soon joined the civil rights and antiwar demonstrations. By then, New Bohemia was no longer a marginal culture contained purely in areas like North Beach, Greenwich Village, Venice Beach, or Chicago's Hyde Park. As Michael Harrington later said, stressing "one of the crucial differences" between

Bohemian battlefields. *Top*, beatniks marching through San Francisco's "bourgeois wasteland," crossing from Union Square to I. Magnin's, in 1958. *Bottom*, the Black Hawk's underage section, circa 1960. *Top*, courtesy of the Bancroft Library, University of California, Berkeley, *San Francisco News-Call Bulletin* photograph archive, BANC PIC 1959.010—NEG, part 3, box 127, beatnik tour of San Francisco; *bottom*, courtesy of the San Francisco History Center, San Francisco Public Library, photo ID AAZ-0415 bohemia and the 1960s counterculture, "the Village . . . was small and organized on a human scale."[94] Increasingly, rebelling against the status quo no longer needed small basement sites like the White Horse. Slowly, it began to emerge from the underground Rebel Café into broad daylight.

. . . And into the Streets

The sights and sounds of the Rebel Café entered the mainstream in the 1960s. In particular, Max Roach's *We Insist!: Freedom Now Suite*, with Abbey Lincoln's a cappella wails and screams alternating with eerie sotto voce passages, echoed back and forth across Atlantic Ocean and southern routes. Musicians under its influence included contemporaries such as Juan Esquivel ("Mexico's Duke Ellington") and, later, British-invasion bands like Led Zeppelin and Pink Floyd, whose exploitation of black styles laid the foundation for their psychedelic blues—the soundtrack of rebellion for post-1968 bohemians. This was part of the larger shift in American society and politics that was first signaled by John Kennedy's 1960 defeat of Richard Nixon, who, as Dwight Eisenhower's vice president, had perhaps embodied the Cold War 1950s more than Ike himself. Little did it matter that Kennedy's policy positions were only separated from Nixon's by a razor's width (as was his electoral majority). His election marked a transition from the black-and-white politics of the 1950s to the living-color flamboyance of the social revolutions in the 1960s. After all, as Norman Mailer famously pronounced, Kennedy was the nation's first "hipster" president.[95]

Nor that anticommunism had come to an end. The Bay of Pigs invasion and the Vietnam War were proof enough of that. But the days when Americans would be trotted out before paranoiacs like Senator Joseph McCarthy, with the full support of the public, were gone—for the time being, at least.[96] In 1953, the majority of Americans accepted McCarthyism's trampling of civil liberties and sat by as the US government, using electric chairs, orphaned the children of communist spies Julius and Ethyl Rosenberg.[97] By the time blacklisted actress Judy Holliday died in 1965, the main controversy surrounding her was whether her marriage to a jazz saxophonist was a bit unseemly for an Academy Award winner. In other words, those who argued for the significance of culture and identity over party and class politics had gained major ground.

In retrospect, Dick Gregory's appearance at the Playboy Club had marked the end of the Rebel Café as a postwar sociocultural phenomenon. His subsequent shows at the hungry i or the Village Gate were merely residual—an extension of their long-held ethos. Nonetheless, Gregory's assertion that no previous black comic could "stand flat footed and talk to white folks" was largely true. Black comedian Godfrey Cambridge's Village Vanguard performances in the 1950s have gone unnoticed by scholars, because they were an infinitesimally small blip on the national cultural radar. They were also unremarkable within the nightclub underground's long history of challenging racial norms. Cambridge hardly seemed out of place in a nightclub culture that had regularly welcomed Dizzy Gillespie's interracial jams and spoken-word performers like Canada Lee. The difference was that Gregory's Playboy Club appearance was anything but underground.

The examples of the Tin Angel, Susan Sontag, the Battle of the Beatniks, and Dick Gregory encapsulated much of the Rebel Café's transformative role, as well as its conclusion. If the Kennedy years were a period of transition from the sheltered 1950s to the tumultuous 1960s, late 1963 was the moment of explosion, a time of triumph and tragic violence. The March on Washington in August marked the high point, followed all too quickly by the Birmingham church bombing and Kennedy's assassination. These events were graphic symbols of the sweeping changes in American society and politics.

For some, the world seemed to turn upside down, and in a way they were right. The Rebel Café underground had surfaced. The notion of it as separate from the broader culture had always been an illusion, as the very spatial logic of the metaphor demands: "underground" has no meaning without reference to street level. But as the Beats' loyal opposition and the subterraneans moved out of the cellars and into the streets, the illusion no longer served its social function. Cultural developments, such as Sontag's intellectual criticism and Gregory's rise to fame, merely lifted the veil. Without the hocus-pocus, rebel culture simply became American culture. And so, as its ethos slowly faded like a whiff of smoke from the open door of a bar, the Rebel Café disappeared.

playboys and partisans

*American Culture, the New Left,
and the Legacy of the Rebel Café*

> To John Dillinger and hope he is still alive.
> Thanksgiving Day, November 28, 1986
> Thanks for the wild turkey and the passenger pigeons, destined to
> be shat out through wholesome American guts. . . . Thanks for "Kill
> a Queer for Christ" stickers. . . . Thanks for Prohibition and the war
> against drugs. . . . Thanks for a nation of finks. Yes, thanks for all the
> memories—all right let's see your arms! You always were a headache
> and you always were a bore.
> Thanks for the last and greatest betrayal of the last and greatest of
> human dreams.
> **William Burroughs, "A Thanksgiving Prayer"**

"Love-fuck," began Charles E. Artman, addressing the student union audience during a Berkeley free speech movement (FSM) rally in 1965. "It means a great deal to me. . . . Sexual fucking, as I understand, was a part of the way of living of . . . [the] early Christian community. . . . Well, I think it is about time . . . that we change them back to what they were originally meant to be." Such public use of controversial and confrontational language was one of the legacies of the Rebel Café—in particular of Lenny Bruce, whose obscenity trials made him a model for young radicals seeking to express their outrage during the height of the black freedom struggle and the US invasion of Vietnam. Throughout the Berkeley protests, Bruce was invoked, sometimes in name, and often in spirit.[1] The new consciousness of the Beats also found audible expression in Artman's call for a resexualized Christian community. Along with the musical soundtrack that accompanied the New Left and the counterculture, these allusions made it clear that the Rebel Café was no longer underground. Threads of earlier bohemianism and cabaret culture wove through the following decades. The spirit of Dadaism and the transgressive allure of Dietrich's *The Blue Angel* were still apparent in American culture, as well as in the theatrical politics of the 1960s. What had previously been rebel culture became the mainstream—sometimes watered down, sometimes commodified, but always out in the open. Yet this openness also exposed the limitations of Rebel Café liberationism. Like Bruce's focus on freedom of the word and sexuality, personal politics often nudged out attention to structural inequality and systems of power. Artman's language may have been intended to shock, but it did so only on the dominant society's terms.

By the start of the free speech movement in the fall of 1964, the role of beatnik culture was firmly planted in both the public mind and the sensibilities of its participants. Connecting the Beats and the FSM, Lawrence Ferlinghetti noted in a postcard to Allen Ginsberg: "Berkeley Free Speech Movement great scene here. Everybody in town getting into act, [Ralph] Gleason quoting from my Routine 'Servants of the People' with Graduate Student's speeches." News reports across the country alternated from expressing support to horror, but both ends of this spectrum cited the student uprising as a Battle of the Beatniks or the product of outside agitators from the bohemian "colonies" of North Beach.[2] FSM participant Jeff Lustig, however, saw the Beat influence as fundamental, infused within world-historical changes, from the black freedom struggle to the Cuban revolution: "SNCC writer Julius Lester wrote that in the late fifties . . . 'While Fidel liberated the Sierra Maestra, the beat generation created a liberated zone . . . in San Francisco.' What linked Castro and the beatniks despite the vast differences in their personal and historical importance was that both had taken up residence outside the American dream. Both established liberated zones outside the presumably inevitable Brave New World."[3]

As the 1960s progressed, however, the nightclub culture of North Beach and Greenwich Village lost much of its subversive allure. The Rebel Café had aided a level of cultural synthesis, but its lack of attention to economics left its politics atomized and effective only at the margins, without significant cross-class alliances. While the gains made by focusing on personal issues around feminism and gay rights were certainly crucial, the New Left only slowly infused liberation politics into a mainstream that otherwise began a sharp rightward turn after 1968.[4] In some ways, the post-1964 splits among the Beats—who fell victim to their own revolution as change came in unanticipated forms and identity politics led them down different individual paths—personified the dissipation of underground politics. Some, like Ferlinghetti and Ginsberg, embraced the consciousness-raising and environmentalism of the counterculture. Others followed Kenneth Rexroth in decrying the loss of tradition (both Marxist and literary) that had driven the San Francisco Renaissance. Kerouac and, to a certain extent, Gregory Corso retreated toward the reactionary Right, while still resisting party politics. A third group moved the other way, from cultural resistance into activism. LeRoi Jones, as a Black Nationalist renamed Amiri Baraka, helped Kenneth Gibson become elected as the first African American mayor of Newark, New Jersey, in 1970. Poet Tram Combs used his Mattachine Society membership to support his successful campaign against bans on public homosexuality in the US Virgin Islands.[5] Ginsberg, as always a bridge between cultural and political radicalism, organized protests, first in support of Lenny Bruce and Cuba, and then as a leading figure in the massive opposition to the Vietnam War—appropriate extensions of the urban underground that had spawned the New Comedy and bohemia's pacifism and multicultural activism.

Ironically, and hardly recognized at the time, North Beach had already shifted away from bohemianism by 1964. Bar and club owners courted the increased tourist trade with performances that caricatured Beat culture, or that exploited relaxed social norms to introduce topless entertainment aimed at businessman crowds. The *Howl* trial's infamy and the influx of a new generation of hopeful outcasts drawn by *On the Road*'s notoriety had changed the character of the area for good. In 1960, Leo Krikorian shut down The Place. The Cellar and the Jazz Workshop closed their doors in 1962 and 1971 respectively, signaling, along with the end of the hungry i and the Coffee Gallery during that same period, the shift in North Beach away from both the counterculture and jazz.[6] Perhaps the most symbolic alteration in North Beach was the demolition of the Montgomery "Monkey" Block to make way for the towering Transamerica Building that now dominates the San Francisco skyline.

These changes meant little to those who arrived in the wake of the 1950s San Francisco Renaissance. Hopeful bohemians, such as Janis Joplin and Peter Coyote, continued to pour into the city throughout the early 1960s, adding to the hippie movement or to the street theatrics of radicals like the Diggers. This growing population was matched by a mushrooming number of little magazines, which continued the symbiotic relationship through which the nightclub underground supported these small presses with advertising dollars, in return gaining visibility among a new generation of nonconformists. Unbeknownst to most mainstream news commentators, however, the San Francisco counterculture had already moved to the more affordable and interracial Haight-Ashbury neighborhood. As Beat poet Gary Snyder observed in 1966: "Rock & Roll and LSD have taken over. It's fun. The clothing and behavior *all over* town is deliciously outrageous. Everybody's on acid—I mean like dentists and lawyers. Haight Ashbury is really the center—N. Beach has gone back to topless, cops, wops and City Lights."[7]

Vesuvio is now the last of the Rebel Cafés in North Beach, and it survives by trading on the Beat generation as a kind of countercultural tourist trap—or, perhaps, national monument—in conjunction with City Lights Bookstore, across what is now Jack Kerouac Alley. Much the same can be said of Greenwich Village, which has remained a nightlife and countercultural neighborhood, due in part to the stability of its nightspots. Although the Five Spot, the San Remo, and the Cedar Tavern all closed in the 1960s, the Village Gate remained open until the 1990s, while the White Horse Tavern and the Village Vanguard are still standing, subsisting largely on the aura of their literary and jazz pasts.

North Beach still wrestles with an uneasy legacy of bohemianism, alongside the area's less-cerebral hedonistic pursuits. Its reputation for sexual allure made it a prime location for businesses that traded in bared female flesh. A topless nightclub called the Cellar opened there in 1965, as did a San Francisco franchise of the Playboy Club, and, as of this writing, a club called the hungry i remains in operation as a strip club. Yet even this development was fraught with contradictions. The city's Playboy Club became an oppositional rallying point, both for feminists and for those who saw it as an assault on the area's bohemianism. After several protests, it closed in 1976. Hefner's clubs in general became a national target, especially following Gloria Steinem's 1963 exposé articles and a series of strikes by its wait-staff Bunnies in the mid-1960s.[8] Further complicating this picture were the feminist elements *within* the topless clubs in North Beach. While primarily aimed at turning a profit for male club owners, they were also expressions of the sexual revolution, with women sometimes performing topless as a recognition of their sexual liberation. The North Beach milieu fostered the feminist activist Margo St. James, for example, whose organization, COYOTE (Call Off Your Old Tired Ethics), has advocated for women sex workers' civil rights and health care since the 1970s. These threads of social change were further tangled by *Playboy* magazine's occasional alliances with feminists. This contrasted sharply with the nearly unanimous opposition to Hefner's nightclubs among progressives, an emblem of the growing separation between nightlife entertainment and political advocacy.[9]

Such divisions had yet to become clear during the mid-1960s, however, as American nightlife intertwined with full-fledged political movements, ranging from feminism and black power to gay rights. Maybe most dramatically, the Village Vanguard's Lorraine Gordon became a key New York organizer and spokesperson for Women's Strike for Peace (WSP), a group that was among the first to organize opposition to the Vietnam War. Gordon used the relationships she developed with Soviet officials through her protest work to arrange a visit to Moscow in 1965. From there, she traveled to North Vietnam, becoming the first American peace activist to witness the devastation wreaked by US bombs around Hanoi. While subsequent news reports about her visit largely ignored the civilian toll of "controlled" B-52 missions, which ostensibly were aimed only at military targets, Gordon's harrowing stories energized WSP protests. Moreover, her Hanoi trip laid the groundwork for later activist visits and a scrutiny of US policy in Southeast Asia.[10] Max Gordon, meanwhile, maintained the Vanguard's tradition of public discussion with a series of "Speak Outs": panels on the club's stage featuring countercultural luminaries—such as Timothy Leary, LeRoi Jones, and Paul Krassner—crossing swords with conservative New York politicians. At the hungry i, Enrico Banducci tried to hire FSM spokesman Mario Savio as a monologist, seeing him as the next Mort Sahl. And Art D'Lugoff featured a symposium at the Village Gate on race in the jazz world, which included a blowup between African American musicians and white club owners, whom the performers charged with exploitation.[11]

The black freedom struggle was also a frequent subject in mimeographed magazines that circulated through the free speech movement's ranks, such as *Rag Baby* and *Soulbook*. *Rag Baby* included mentions of a revived "Blabbermouth Night" at the Coffee Gallery and an antiwar benefit held by The Committee, a satirical troupe. *Soulbook*, which counted contributions by soon-to-be Black Panther Bobby Seale, featured Rebel Café subjects scrutinized through the lens of black power. This radical magazine criticized Langston Hughes for rejecting LeRoi Jones's plays (while defending

Lenny Bruce), decried whites' appropriation of rock & roll, and printed poetry inspired by socially conscious jazzmen, such as Mingus saxophonist Eric Dolphy.[12]

Dick Gregory even more fully mixed remnants of the Rebel Café with New Left
activism. Putting his performance skills to work for the cause of peace, Gregory participated in the founding of the Youth International Party (YIP, or the Yippies) with
Abbie Hoffman and Paul Krassner. This included testifying at the conspiracy trial
of the Chicago Eight—along with Norman Mailer and Ed Sanders, the radical poet
and member of The Fugs, a satirical rock group—when New Left leaders were
charged with inciting the riots outside the Democratic National Convention in 1968.
Later that year, Gregory ran for US president, receiving 1.5 million votes. His campaign had kicked off with a press conference at the Village Gate. Art D'Lugoff
remained a key supporter, promoting Gregory as a "week-end wit, weekday warrior"
who was not merely a "satirist of the general fraud," but a "Freedom Fighter." Further
cementing this mix of performance and politics, Gregory shared the Village Gate
stage with Krassner and LSD guru Timothy Leary. As one New York reporter sardonically wrote, Gregory continued to influence the politics of fresh audiences, performing for young women with "wide-eyed, unguarded glances" and young men with
"extra long hair." Although Gregory began to repudiate comedy as a "narcotic" in the
face of serious political struggles, the Village Gate's patrons remained attracted to his
authenticity, which he confirmed by discussing his gunshot wound from the Watts
uprising in Los Angeles and hunger strikes in support of Native American land
rights.[13]

Even mainstream politicians got in on the act. For instance, Eugene McCarthy's
1968 presidential primary campaign held a nightclub benefit at New York's countercultural Cheetah Club, which was attended by radicals such as Michael Harrington
and Allen Ginsberg. But the Rebel Café's political legacy was perhaps most visible
during Norman Mailer's 1969 run for New York City's mayor. Campaigning on a
platform advocating the city's independence from Albany (the state capital) and, thus,
the creation of the fifty-first state, Mailer garnered enough signatures to be placed on
the ballot for the Democratic primary election. In celebration, and in an attempt to
energize supporters and spawn media coverage, on May 7, Mailer and his campaign
manager Joe Flaherty organized a rally at the Village Gate. A diverse audience of
countercultural volunteers and conservative "straights" who were exploring the Mailer
camp packed the club amid the pulsing music and lights of an acid-rock band.
D'Lugoff supplied not only his safe to protect the precious petitions, but bread bas-
kets, which were passed around for donations. Around 1:00 a.m., overcome with an
exuberance fueled in equal measure by the crowd's exhortations and whiskey, Mailer
mounted the stage and—taking a page from the Lenny Bruce playbook—embarked
on a speech that the *New York Times* said "alternately entertained and harangued"
the raucous audience. Much of his profanity-laden display was in response to a group
of heckling feminists. Mailer's saucy responses and the ensuing press reports undermined whatever legitimacy he had established, effectively ending his chances—

however slim—for an electoral victory. Goaded by the vocal exchanges in an urban space noted for its alternative community, the Village Gate fundraiser "proved to be an unshakable hangover" for Mailer's campaign.[14]

The Village Gate rally's vocal interactions between Mailer and the feminist contingent there dramatized the shifts in nightclub culture since the 1950s. The days of the nightclub as a structured space enforcing traditionally gendered notions of propriety were all but gone. "Sophisticated" nightclubs became relics in New York. Only the famous Copacabana survived the 1960s, and even it closed in 1973, only to reopen three years later as a disco.[15] The rise of rock & roll among the college-age crowd had changed the direction of nightclubs, as desires to sit attentively at tables or engage in close, cheek-to-cheek dancing to the strains of jazz standards gave way to the Twist, the Frug, and the Fall. The result was a proliferation of discothèques (including one at the former site of Cafe Society), modeled on European venues that saved money by playing records rather than live music, and that opened most of the available space for dancing. The decentered nature of this dancing obliterated gendered space within the nightclub. One report from a New York club in 1964 noted that "the crowd was so thick one night that a girl managed to hold hands with two boys at once, without either being aware of the conditional nature of her affections." This new freedom for women was also reflected in newly fashionable, higher skirt lines. While sexual objectification certainly accompanied miniskirts, author Helen Weaver nonetheless notes that changes in music and dance were key to a woman's feeling of liberation, when suddenly "she could dance with herself . . . with the whole room."[16]

As the influence of thinkers such as Paul Goodman and Marshall McLuhan led to an emphasis on authentic experiences, nightclubs also became the sites of "be-ins," where the entire space was utilized for multimedia performance. College-age audiences flocked in to become part of the show. "Dancing has become an open war on self-consciousness and inhibition," asserted a self-proclaimed Village bohemian tract, "a confrontation with LIFE, which is 'out there.'" Some venues were quick to accommodate a new generation of night people. Even as the Blue Angel went out of business in 1965, the Village Vanguard began to feature a disco format between jazz sets and after hours. Earlier that year, Art D'Lugoff had decided to open a new club: the Disc-au-Gate. "It's going to be a disease, just like the folk clubs," he noted jovially of the new craze. "You have to go with a winner, let's face it."[17]

The most popular rock group in these early dance clubs was undoubtedly the Beatles, who, in many ways, embodied the era's sociocultural changes. Their very name invoked Ginsberg and Kerouac's transatlantic movement. Their music evoked the earthiness of England's working-class Liverpool and African American R&B—although polished around the edges. In addition, their whiteness made them safe for popular Euro-American consumption. The Beats themselves quickly embraced their musical namesake. In 1965, Ginsberg made it a point to visit Liverpool's rock clubs, which he compared with those in San Francisco, and declared the Beatles (along with Bob Dylan) to be an expression of 1960s oppositional consciousness. In the midst of conservative Barry Goldwater's presidential run in 1964, poet Philip Whalen similarly intermixed music and politics in a letter to painter Robert LaVigne, briefing his friend on the latest West Coast developments: "Everybody has registered to vote, all of us are campaigning against Goldwater & the anti-Negro housing Proposition 14. We all love the Beatles."[18]

As the band's sound developed, however, British (and, increasingly, psychedelic) inflections overtook their bluesy roots—a cultural parallel to the channeling of identity politics during which whites withdrew from the black freedom struggle and women led second-wave feminism beyond the earlier issue of gender equality. Musically, this was most notable on the album *Sgt. Pepper's Lonely Hearts Club Band* (1967). But the cover artwork was also a tribute to the Rebel Café, featuring the four Beatles surrounded by a collage of life-sized photos, ranging from Edgar Allan Poe, Karl Marx, Dylan Thomas, and Marlene Dietrich to Bob Dylan and Lenny Bruce. The Beatles' massive popularity grew at least in part from their ability (like Dylan's) to collapse widely dispersed sociocultural phenomena into a single identifiable point, with elements of postmodernism's erasure of time, space, and high/low art divisions. At the same time, they exemplified cultural canalization into increasingly narrow channels.

These trends were visible in literature, too. Following Norman Mailer and New Journalism were the grotesqueries of Hunter S. Thompson's gonzo journalism. The ground broken by James Baldwin nurtured the bold fiction of Toni Morrison and John Rechy. Kerouac's ecstatic American road gave way to Don DeLillo's darker, more sophisticated vision of the national underground. Thomas Pynchon probably best represented the Rebel Café sensibility, particularly in his first novel, *V.* (1963). Pynchon's sweeping tale of a man in search of a mysteriously powerful woman known only as "V." distinctly echoed Dashiell Hammett's cultural front detective fiction. But Pynchon's novel was also an early postmodernist tour-de-force that marshaled the twentieth century's previous six decades of history into an intricate web of connections. Like Joseph Heller's *Catch 22* (1961), Pynchon's biting satire reflected both the dark humor of "sick" comics and the Rebel Café's oppositional consciousness. Themes of identity, usable pasts, Freudianism, and left-wing bohemianism suffused *V.*, as its protagonists wandered though underworld bars and cafés spanning across Africa in the early 1900s (where a femme fatale had "plucked [her] eyebrows to look like Dietrich's"), war-torn Europe, and New York City in the 1950s. At the center of the story was the "Whole Sick Crew," a permutation of Kerouac's subterraneans, who gathered at the Village's "V-Note Café" jazz club and the "Rusty Spoon" bar, declaring their signature "Catatonic Expressionist" phrase, "Wha?"[19]

The Rebel Café's dark embrace of bar talk also ricocheted through Hollywood. In 1960, Kerouac's *The Subterraneans* was adapted into a film (a flop), followed a year later by Truman Capote's own portrayal of New York City's cocktail set and café society, *Breakfast at Tiffany's* (a hit).[20] Comedian Mike Nichols followed in the verbal tradition of Tennessee Williams when he made the jump to directing with *Who's*

Afraid of Virginia Woolf? (1966) and *The Graduate* (1967)—a stylistic and career trajectory paralleled by hungry i and Village Vanguard comic Woody Allen. Dustin Hoffman, the star of *The Graduate*, had been a waiter at the Village Gate and portrayed Lenny Bruce onscreen a few years later. The director of *Lenny* (1974), Bob Fosse, had previously directed the most forthright homage to the Rebel Café's roots, *Cabaret*, in 1972.[21] In 1971, *Village Voice* cartoonist Jules Feiffer brought ample verbosity to the script for Nichols's *Carnal Knowledge* (which starred singer Art Garfunkel, who, along with musical partner Paul Simon, had dedicated their 1966 album *Parsley, Sage, Rosemary, and Thyme* to Bruce, featuring an eerie version of "Silent Night" overdubbed with the sound of a news report that included an announcement of the comic's death). But this trend truly culminated with Robert Altman's overlapping dialogue in *M*A*S*H** (1970), the antiwar black comedy scripted by Hollywood Ten writer Ring Lardner Jr., which mimicked the kind of cacophony produced by loquacious nightspot patrons.

While most former leftists like Lardner tempered their political views in the wake of the Red Scare, Kenneth Rexroth remained staunch in his Marxism. Yet he was also willing to blend this with the liberatory potential of rock & roll. He was a fan of the Fugs, for instance, and declared that the most effective weapon in the band's push for an alternative society was their use of humor. Rexroth quipped that while Ed Sanders's and Tuli Kupferberg's "free-verse doggerel full of dirty words" resembled "an occupational-therapy project in a very permissive asylum," this "only cripples, but it does not invalidate, their posture of social responsibility" and opposition to "the evils of society—war, sexual conflict and racial persecution." In 1969, Rexroth dismissed the desirability of political programs, arguing that rock-music consciousness was more effective over the long term, because formal movements—however radical— can be co-opted by power structures or by the state:

> The techniques of massive paramilitary confrontations are, in my opinion, absurd. . . . The "Sunflower Sutra" [by Ginsberg] has more effect than a Columbia University takeover . . . [because] the counterculture as a culture, as a way of life . . . [is] in the bloodstream of society. You can't pin it down. Its effect is continuously corrosive. . . . This is true of the whole protest-rock and protest-folk bit. Young people are wise to the fact that Donovan is more revolutionary than Dylan. . . . Leonard Cohen is more subversive than Country Joe and the Fish. . . . Leonard Cohen . . . doesn't give a fuck whether he sings or not. I mean . . . he's in direct communication with people.[22]

Rexroth spent a large part of his final years understandably railing against being forgotten as a trailblazer, since his radical bona fides were tarnished by his criticisms of black power and feminism. He failed to see the contradiction in his demand that others follow *his* prescriptions for *their own* liberation. While his oppositional edges smoothed enough to take a university teaching post in the 1970s, he nonetheless pushed for the kind of participatory pedagogy that was groundbreaking at that time, although it has since become a part of humanities education, bringing Rebel Café principles into classroom discussions. "Creative education, development, liberation, occurs more often in coffee shops off campus than on the campus," he insisted. "If you really want to do something about creative people, move the coffee shop into the curriculum."[23]

Changing how universities taught was just one outgrowth of the New Left's demand for authentic ideas and language "that can make luminous the inner self that burns for understanding," since political radicals, such as those in the SDS, also espoused the Beat notion of living artistically. By the early 1970s, studious introspection became a facet of American culture. As Lou Reed said in his 1972 album *Transformer*, which featured gender-bending imagery and the hit single "Wild Side," his songs were explorations of an *inner* frontier, in the tradition of the New York City experience, with Allen Ginsberg and William Burroughs as forebears. (Hints of the Rebel Café even appeared more directly, as the album was dedicated to White Horse Tavern poet Delmore Schwartz.) But while these claims for authenticity and unfettered sexuality had their roots in the 1950s and Herbert Marcuse—who hearkened back to Freud—they had almost exclusively assumed the liberation of male sexuality. One of the significant gains of feminism was to overturn these views and make an equal claim for women's full personal and political expressions. Feminist consciousness raising fundamentally changed the relationship between culture and politics, seeking not just to bring cultural meaning to social struggles, but to also declare that issues of the self were *inherently* political. The conflicts between "radical" and "cultural" feminists quickly made it clear that this did little to end the debate about the precedence of social structures versus consciousness. But feminism did solidify and fully entrench questions of authenticity, sexuality, and the self as aspects of American politics. Fundamental to the process of consciousness raising were the talk sessions carried out in the living rooms of radicals, which, like the New Left's rap sessions, were highly reminiscent of the Rebel Café's bohemian bar talk.[24]

If there is a single lesson to be learned from the Rebel Café, it is that the political/cultural dichotomy is a false one. They are always in a dialectic relationship, continually in tension, each breaking down and reconstituting the other. This was illustrated most vividly in the Stonewall Inn uprising in June 1969, in many ways a culmination of the postwar nightclub underground. The police raid on this Greenwich Village bar brought thousands of protesters into the streets, clashing with police for two days, but it did not start the gay rights struggle. Instead, the liberation movement that emerged after the uprising relied on long-established organizations and networks. Nor was the event unique. Similar clashes had already occurred in San Francisco and, notably, at a Los Angeles bar called the Black Cat Tavern in 1967. But Stonewall was a unifying, symbolic moment, an eruption that made the movement clearly visible, both to broader society and to the queer community itself. The Villagers resisted authorities—throwing bottles and rocks amid trashcan fires and graffiti calling for "Gay Power!"—a stance that was echoed by young voices releasing their anger and

frustration. As historian John D'Emilio has noted, the previous generation of activists responded vocally to the event. Ginsberg arrived on the second night and
proclaimed: "You know, the guys were so beautiful. They've lost that wounded look that
fags all had ten years ago." The Mattachine Society printed a special-edition newsletter, infused with camp humor, declaring it, "the hairpin drop heard round the
world."[25] Stonewall encapsulated much of the Rebel Café's ethos and legacy, as political mobilization grew from the communal strength gathered within the nocturnal
underground—which itself drew from a usable past that intertwined politics and culture. Even if only semiconsciously, the Stonewall rebels recognized that while the
cabaret tradition could open doors to a new consciousness, that alone was not enough
to confront systems of power.

Bohemia's black denizens similarly leveled criticisms of the Rebel Café's shortcomings. Integration is not the same as racial justice, and the necessity of creating African
American institutions was apparent, lest these citizens become an integrated minority
devoid of power. But the Rebel Café did serve a purpose, giving black artists such as
Amiri Baraka and the Umbra group a platform from which to launch independent
cultural and political campaigns. The beatniks were undoubtedly naive and premature in proclaiming the end of racism in their ranks, and the continued racism and
inequality that plague the United States today make both political correctness and
the declaration that "black lives matter" a necessary part of our national discourse.[26] The relevance of bohemia in the 1950s was its willingness to relinquish at
least some privileges of race and class, and to think outside the lines about what the
shape of the nation *should* be. The bohemians of North Beach and Greenwich
Village recognized this and attempted, however fumblingly, to devise a new kind of
community in response. This tentative relinquishing of white privilege was Kerouac's
connection to the 1960s, which he failed to see as he grew increasingly conservative,
disillusioned with fame and dissipated by drink. At the same time, the New Left absorbed the Beat tendency to see the African American struggle as their *own* path to
redemption, which helps to explain why it was such a shock when Stokely Carmichael
declared in 1966 that blacks could take care of things themselves, thank you very
much.

Truman Capote once famously rejected Kerouac's prose as mere "typing," but
Capote nonetheless followed with his own novel about what it meant to be on the
road in the middle of America. Kerouac, however, had made the road itself invisible
by its ubiquity. As much as the automobile was an individualistic symbol of social
mobility in America, the federal highway system was the product of collectivism, a
project made possible through the pooling of resources and labor (even if ultimately
driven by the auto industry, to the detriment of public transportation). Kerouac would
have been better served to recognize the full symbolism of the road, not simply as a
stream that carried his effusive version of the American dream westward, but as
a fractal circuit, the dream as dialectic, which destroys itself by its own uses, yet
whose destruction once again opens up space for dreaming. While Capote's *In Cold*

Blood (1966) was certainly superior in craft to *On the Road*, Kerouac's *The Subter-raneans* equally bested *Breakfast at Tiffany's* representation of New York City scenesters. The accessibility of Capote's novel was another sign marking the Rebel Café's end and the expansion of America's culture of rebellion. What would have been provocative a decade earlier—the alcohol-soaked story of an independent urban woman, with its themes of homosexuality, drug use, organized crime, and interracial sex—was, by the time of its film adaptation in 1961, as banal as a trip to a department store.

The notion of culture as a dialectic, however, is too simplistic to capture the complexity of such sociocultural change. Rather than picturing polar opposites and a mediating synthesis, a better metaphor is that of various forms of culture as waves that crash onto the beach of society. Just as there are multiple and massive forces driving every wave, each is equally shaped by its landfall. No two waves are ever the same. And with every incoming crash, the beach itself is also reshaped, transformed at a granular level that only becomes recognizable when the shoreline changes enough to have to redraw the maps. The nocturnal underground was one such wave. By the end of the 1960s, it washed onto an American beach with an altogether new geography—one with shifting sands that could no longer support the Rebel Café's foundation, leaving its walls and halls unsteady and mostly abandoned.

From the 1960s through the 1990s, the boards and mortar of the Rebel Café were dismantled and repurposed—here as a plank in the New Left, there as the brick wall of a comedy club. Echoes of the Cabaret Voltaire rang through the proto-punk of the Velvet Underground and the Stooges, the Ramones and (echoing back across the Atlantic) Siouxsie and the Banshees; grunge-rock clubs; edgy urban galleries and loft parties that boom with hip-hop and techno rhythms; the satire of *The Rocky Horror Picture Show* (1975) and the long-running *Saturday Night Live* television program. The show found much of its first cast through former Harry Belafonte manager and Village Vanguard ally Jack Rollins.[27] The mainstream that they countered more easily absorbed them, however, a peril that came with postmodernism. Even the political Right adopted elements of the Left's satirical strategy. While Rush Limbaugh long ago started taking himself seriously, it is important to remember that he started out as a comic. History's lessons come in all shapes and sizes.

The 1976 film *Next Stop, Greenwich Village* in many ways best captured the ethos of Cold War bohemia as a liberatory, if contradictory, usable past. Told from the perspective of the film's director, Village Vanguard comedian Paul Mazursky, *Next Stop* was an inside representation of the Village in 1953, replete with discussions about the Rosenberg executions and trips to Mexico in fictionalized versions of the Minetta Tavern and Café Reggio.[28] A key character in the bohemian circle of Mazursky's alter ego, Larry Lapinsky, is "Bernstein"—a gay African American clearly modeled on James Baldwin. Bernstein represented the two central themes of *Next Stop*: the search for social and sexual identity, and the establishment of self-authenticity over a performative posture. In a pivotal scene, Bernstein, scorned by a lover and emotionally crushed, retreats from the underground community, insisting that his persona of suave sophistication was "all fiction," and that "only the gay is real." Yet he confirms his blackness as well, hinting at his difficult childhood in the south, where both his body and spirit were brutalized. The Village, therefore, was the place not only where he could claim his own personal sovereignty—defining himself, even if just in a false persona—but also where the mask could be removed when the revelry of bohemia's continual costume ball became too much. Bernstein captured the central contradiction of the Rebel Café. It was rooted in performativity, the conscious reshaping of self, but it was also in search of authentic community—and even love.

The film's inability to reconcile the two illustrates that, even by the 1970s, the denizens of the urban underground could not see their own false dichotomy. The performative and the authentic are continually intertwined, each recreating the other—as well as the Other—and reproducing reality through the material/ideological process of communication. Bernstein characterized this process: a gay black man as the living representation of the tension between performativity and authenticity, with sexuality trapped in the middle. "I think I'm in love," Bernstein announces at a rent party in Lapinsky's apartment. His new partner embodies the elusiveness of bohemia's possibilities: a sailor, who is beautiful, but who is shipping out to Marseilles and thus is unattainable. Nonetheless, the attraction itself is affective, a ghost of meaning in Bernstein's dislocated existence, an idea just as powerful as a physical presence. And a nightspot was the point of connection. "I met him in a bar this morning," Bernstein declares. "He's incredible! Tall, blonde—sort of a butch Marlene Dietrich."

Introduction. Can You Show Me the Way to the Rebel Café?

Epigraph. Edward Sanders, *Hymn to the Rebel Cafe* (Santa Rosa, CA: Black Sparrow Press, 1993). Reprinted by permission of David E. Godine, Publisher, Inc., copyright © 1993 by Edward Sanders.

1. Margaret Parton, "Cellar World Conference: Youth, with Lofty Aims, Rivals the Big Show," *San Francisco Herald Tribune*, June 6, 1945, unpaginated clipping, vol. 1, Henri Lenoir Papers, BANC MSS 92/842c, Bancroft Library, University of California, Berkeley [hereafter UC Berkeley].

2. Sanders, *Hymn to the Rebel Cafe.*

3. Irving Howe and Lewis Coser, *The American Communist Party: A Critical History* (New York: Praeger, rev. ed. 1962; first published 1957), 518–19.

4. C. Wright Mills, *The New Men of Power* (New York: Harcourt Brace, 1948), 251–52.

5. Mari Jo Buhle, Paul Buhle, and Dan Georgakas, eds., *The Encyclopedia of the American Left* (Urbana: University of Illinois Press, 1992), 36–38, 146–58, 593, 672–74; Howe and Coser, *American Communist Party*, 337–64; Robin D. G. Kelley, *Hammer and Hoe: Alabama Communists during the Great Depression* (Chapel Hill: University of North Carolina Press, 1990); Martha Biondi, *To Stand and Fight: The Struggle for Civil Rights in Postwar New York City* (Cambridge, MA: Harvard University Press, 2003), especially 4–9.

6. Herbart Gans, in his sociological study of the 1960s suburbs, notes that suburbanites desired to create an independent family space that broke away from urban multigenerational housing and close quarters with neighbors. Men reported that distance from their parents improved their marriages at three times the rate claimed by women, 50% to 14%. Meanwhile, Gans suggests, organizations like the Veterans of Foreign Wars became "a suburban substitute for the city's neighborhood tavern." Herbert Gans, *The Levittowners: Ways of Life and Politics in a New Suburban Community* (New York: Vintage Books, 1967), 26, 36–37, 260. See also James Gilbert, *Men in the Middle: Searching for Masculinity in the 1950s* (Chicago: University of Chicago Press, 2005); Alan Petigny, *The Permissive Society: America, 1941–1965* (New York: Cambridge University Press, 2009).

7. Arnold Green, "Why Americans Are Insecure," in *The Scene Before You: A New Approach to American Culture*, ed. Chandler Brossard (New York: Rinehart, 1955), 161–79. Green notes that, from 1920 to 1934, 46 million Americans moved between rural and urban areas, and that during World War II alone, 30 million people changed addresses. Even more staggering was the shift in labor trends. In 1820, 90% of Americans worked in agriculture, which both encouraged the family as an economic unit and placed its financial gains or losses literally in its own hands. By 1940, that number was 10%.

8. W. T. Lhamon Jr., *Deliberate Speed: The Origins of a Cultural Style in the American 1950s* (Washington, DC: Smithsonian Institution Press, 1990), xii, 3, 67–72, 89, 98–112; Leerom Medovoi, *Rebels: Youth and the Cold War Origins of Identity* (Durham, NC: Duke University Press, 2005), 1–2, 30–31; Joel Foreman, ed., *The Other Fifties: Interrogating Midcentury Icons* (Urbana: University of Illinois Press, 1997); Peter J. Kuznick and James Gilbert, eds., *Rethinking Cold War Culture* (Washington, DC: Smithsonian Institution Press, 2001).

9. See Henri Lefebvre, *The Production of Space*, trans. Donald Nicholson-Smith (Cambridge, MA: Blackwell, 1991; originally published in French 1974).

10. Tyler T. Schmidt, *Desegregating Desire: Race and Sexuality in Cold War American Literature* (Jackson: University Press of Mississippi, 2013), 3, 13.

11. According to Jürgen Habermas, the public sphere's appearance in the eighteenth century accompanied the arrival of civil society, in which private commercial concerns were separated from government and followed abstract law, which was based on the Enlightenment principle of reason. Public exchanges in the world of letters, adhering to universally recognized rules, confirmed equality and individual subjectivities as the basis for politics (later solidified into notions of liberty), while debate was carried out in public spaces, such as the coffeehouses of Paris or London. Jürgen Habermas, *The Structural Transformation of the Public Sphere: An Inquiry into a Category of Bourgeois Society* (Cambridge, MA: MIT Press, first paperback ed. 1991; first published 1962). For a collection of critiques, see Craig Calhoun, ed., *Habermas and the Public Sphere* (Cambridge, MA: MIT Press, 1992).

12. My notion of creative self-destruction is adapted from Joseph Schumpeter's characterization of capitalism, in which material advances rely on the creative destruction of old forms. Like Schumpeter, I recognize that this process has its limits and ultimately results in mere destruction, without the ability to overcome the weight of its own internal contradictions. Joseph Schumpeter, *Capitalism, Socialism and Democracy* (New York: Harper, first Harper Colophon ed. 1975; first published 1942), 82–85.

13. Scott Lettieri, "Peering in at Specs," *North Beach News* (Summer 2004), unpaginated clipping, Specs file, Biography Collection, San Francisco History Center, San Francisco Public Library [hereafter SFPL].

14. As shorthand evidence for this, one of the most consistent predictors of a gentrifying urban neighborhood is the presence of a Starbucks coffeehouse.

15. David A. Hollinger, *Cosmopolitanism and Solidarity: Studies in Ethnoracial, Religious, and Professional Affiliation in the United States* (Madison: University of Wisconsin Press, 2006), xviii, xi.

Chapter 1. Blue Angels, Black Cats, and Reds

1. Christine Sismondo, *America Walks into a Bar: A Spirited History of Taverns and Saloons, Speakeasies and Grogshops* (Oxford: Oxford University Press, 2011), xv; James Scott, quoted in Mark Lawrence Schrad, *Vodka Politics: Alcohol, Autocracy, and the Secret History of the Russian State* (New York: Oxford University Press, 2014), 17.

2. Robert Darnton, *The Great Cat Massacre and Other Episodes in French Cultural History* (New York: Basic Books, 1984), 89–96. The priest-parodying youth groups of the abbeys of misrule periodically enacted raucous rituals intended to legitimize adolescent males on the cusp of adulthood—as well as to shame older men who failed to live up the expectations of masculine behavior—through charivari, or shivarees, such as delivering spankings and riding through town backward on an ass.

3. Peter Jelavich, *Berlin Cabaret* (Cambridge, MA: Harvard University Press, 1993), 24–29; Hollister Noble, "Montmartre Mourns Its Poet Laureate: Bruant Is Dead, but the Paris Underworld He Loved and Knew Still Sings His Songs," *New York Times*, March 29, 1925, SM-10.

4. Jelavich, *Berlin Cabaret*, 119–22.

5. Ibid., 33–35; Sigmund Freud, *The Joke and Its Relation to the Unconscious*, trans. Joyce Crick (New York: Penguin Classics, 2003; originally published in German 1905), 7, 114.

6. Alan Lareau, *The Wild Stage: Literary Cabarets of the Weimar Republic* (Columbia, SC: Camden House, 1995), 17–24.

7. Greil Marcus, *Lipstick Traces: A Secret History of the Twentieth Century* (Cambridge, MA: Harvard University Press, 1989), 241–42; Barry Wallenstein, "The Jazz-Poetry Connection," *Performing Arts Journal*, vol. 4, no. 3 (1980), 122–34. Wallenstein notes that the influence of Dadaism in jazz came through a member of the Beat generation, LeRoi Jones.

8. Jelavich, *Berlin Cabaret*, 191–92; Lisa Appignanesi, *The Cabaret* (New York: Universe Books, 1976), 9–12, 26, 82.

9. Jelavich, *Berlin Cabaret*, 187, 75; Richard A. Reuss and JoAnne C. Reuss, *American Folk Music and Left-Wing Politics, 1927–1957* (Lanham, MD: Scarecrow Press, 2000), 233–35, 248–53; Lareau, *Wild Stage*, 116 n32. Lareau notes that Brecht performed at Wild Stage for only six days.

10. Lareau, *Wild Stage*, 1–17, 35, 49, 76, 84–85, 92. Lareau argues that while most histories focus on the political aspects of cabaret, to do so is to mistake form for method. Cabaret, he suggests, was an attempt to find an audience while also asserting artistic styles, particularly *Kleinkunst* (chamber art). Intellectual efforts to differentiate between *Kabarett* (literary cabaret) and the lewd pub styles that were most prevalent included theatrical elements and small doses of political satire. *The Blue Angel*'s main setting, for instance, was an example of a *tingeltangel* (roughly, honky-tonk), a provincial working-class nightspot that was a precursor (along with vaudeville) to cabaret but distinct from it, due to a lack of aesthetic polish or social satire.

11. Ibid., 104, 185–88; Jelavich, *Berlin Cabaret*, 33–35, 191–92; Shane Vogel, "Where Are We Now?: Queer World Making and Cabaret Performance," *GLQ: A Journal of Lesbian and Gay Studies*, vol. 6, no. 1 (2000), 29–60. Vogel discusses cabaret as a social space that transcends performance and "lends itself to . . . 'queer world making.'" Vogel, however, is primarily concerned with European cabaret as imagined in the United States, rather than its historical reality. German censorship was institutional, enforced by local police departments, and, before 1918, cabaret scripts required prior authorization. The police made few objections, largely because the authorities feared negative publicity around such censorship (a lesson that seemed to elude US censors), and racy nocturnal performances did test the boundaries of social acceptability. For instance, struggling against censorship was viewed as a demand for individual freedom, as reflected in Heinrich Mann's *Professor Unrat* (whose titular character was the model for *The Blue Angel*'s pedantic protagonist). Post-1933 critiques of the Nazis became veiled, and the cabaret's antifascism, often celebrated in postwar American culture, was perhaps exaggerated, as little evidence has survived to support such a portrayal.

12. Lareau, *Wild Stage*, 16–24.

13. "The Founder of the Famous Black Cat Cafe Is Dead," *San Francisco Chronicle*, March 23, 1897, 4; Leonard Lyons, "The Post's New Yorker," *Washington Post*, June 8, 1938, X-11; "Black Cat Cafe Will Celebrate Anniversary," *San Francisco Chronicle*, November 8, 1913, 14.

14. Djuna Barnes, *New York*, ed. Alyce Barry (Los Angeles: Sun & Moon Press, 1989), 225–31, 240–44, 252.

15. Emily Epstein Landau, *Spectacular Wickedness: Sex, Race, and Memory in Storyville, New Orleans* (Baton Rouge: Louisiana State University Press, 2013), 16–31; Lewis A. Erenberg, *Steppin' Out: New York Nightlife and the Transformation of American Culture, 1890–1930* (Chicago: University of Chicago Press, 1981), xi, 113–42, 177, 206–27, 234–59; Chad Heap,

Slumming: Sexual and Racial Encounters in American Nightlife, 1885–1940 (Chicago: University of Chicago Press, 2009), 25–96.

16. Roy Rosenzweig, *Eight Hours for What We Will: Workers and Leisure in an Industrial City, 1870–1920* (Cambridge: Cambridge University Press, 1983), 9–27, 35–64.

17. Warren Unna, *The Coppa Murals: A Pageant of Bohemian Life in San Francisco at the Turn of the Century* (n.p.: Book Club of California, 1952); Idwal Jones, *Ark of Empire: San Francisco's Montgomery Block* (New York: Doubleday, 1951); Oscar Lewis, *Bay Window Bohemia: An Account of the Brilliant Artistic World of Gaslit San Francisco* (New York: Doubleday, 1956).

18. Nan Alamilla Boyd, *Wide Open Town: A History of Queer San Francisco to 1965* (Berkeley: University of California Press, 2003), 56; Black Cat display ad, "Opening Night: Nov. 9th," *San Francisco Call*, November 9, 1911, 2; display ad, "You Are Cordially Invited to Attend the Fourth Anniversary of the Black Cat Cafe," November 11, 1915, 8, display ad 8, July 17, 1913, 18, display ad 29, November 27, 1913, 8, "Black Cat Cafe Offers Great Show," September 14, 1913, 36, display ad 1, October 15, 1913, 2, and display ad 24, September 18, 1913, 7, all in *San Francisco Chronicle*. For evidence of the cabaret craze, see, in particular, display ad 34, *San Francisco Chronicle*, January 15, 1919, 53. Boyd mistakenly states that the Black Cat opened in 1906 and that Charles Ridley, the cabaret's conductor, was the manager after 1911. City directories list both Cohn and Crowley as liquor suppliers and bartenders before 1911 but do not include the Black Cat until the following year. Their original partners were Johnny Grosso and H. Adreozzi.

19. US Bureau of the Census, "San Francisco, Enumeration District no. 174," *Thirteenth Census of the United States: 1910*, 8-B, roll T624-97, National Archives, Washington, DC; US Bureau of the Census, "San Francisco, Enumeration District no. 356," *Fourteenth Census of the United States: 1920*, 11-A, roll T625-133, National Archives, Washington, DC; *Crocker-Langley San Francisco City Directory, 1915* (San Francisco: H. S. Crocker, 1915), 477; *Crocker-Langley San Francisco City Directory, 1920* (San Francisco: H. S. Crocker, 1920), 551.

20. Boyd, *Wide Open Town*, 56; "Cafe Wants to Run as a 'Soft' Drink Cabaret: Is One of Those Affected by Police Order; Labor Council Pleads for Black Cat," February 6, 1917, 9, "Old Folk too Made Happy on Christmas Day," December 26, 1920, D-6, and classified ad 11, January 16, 1914, 13, all in *San Francisco Chronicle*.

21. "Woman Robbed by Bandit in Taxicab," January 6, 1914, 55, and "Fischler Is in Santa Cruz Jail," June 12, 1914, 1, both in *San Francisco Chronicle*; Heap, *Slumming*, 101–88; Christine Stansell, *American Moderns: Bohemian New York and the Creation of a New Century* (New York: Metropolitan Books, 2000), 56–57, 227–51.

22. Display ad 25, December 15, 1913, 7, and "Purcell's Cafe," January 19, 1921, A-68, both in *San Francisco Chronicle*. See also Eric Lott, *Love and Theft* (New York: Oxford University Press, 1993); Ronald Radano, *Lying Up a Nation: Race and Black Music* (Chicago: University of Chicago Press, 2003), 19–29; Boyd, *Wide Open Town*, 29. Radano notes that black performers adopted forms of minstrelsy, due to an economic necessity to please white audiences, yet found tactics to subvert its more degrading aspects through subtle satire that was recognizable mainly to fellow African Americans. Further, Nan Boyd has noted cross-dressing as an aspect of minstrelsy that became part of the performative heritage of San Francisco's twentieth-century gay culture.

23. See Jeffrey H. Jackson, *Making Jazz French: Music and Modern Life in Interwar Paris* (Durham, NC: Duke University Press, 2003); Micol Seigel, *Uneven Encounters: Making Race and Nation in Brazil and the United States* (Durham, NC: Duke University Press, 2009). Seigel notes that this process included the exoticism of Latin American styles.

24. In addition to accusations that the club had hired "disreputable" women (hinting at prostitution), police noted that some performers had "mingled with the guests, singing to them, sometimes eating and drinking at their tables, and usually dancing with them." "Police Commission Stops Cafe Dances," April 26, 1921, 16, and display ad 50, May 5, 1921, 7, both in *San Francisco Chronicle*; Boyd, *Wide Open Town*, 56; "Old Madrid Cafe Owners Arrested," *San Francisco Chronicle*, December 27, 1921, 3; "Golden State News of Interest to All," *Gridley (KS) Herald*, October 27, 1923, 2.

25. "Police Asked to Ban Costumes of Cafe Singers," November 7, 1921, 11, "Dance License for Down Town Cafe Rejected," November 15, 1921, 13, "Vote Seekers Present When Raid Is Made," July 2, 1922, G-3, and "Banker Held for Carrying One 'on Hip,'" February 6, 1920, 1, all in *San Francisco Chronicle*. An organization called the West of Powell Street Association found common cause with the Police Commission, the Women's Vigilant Committee, the Hygiene Board, the YMCA, and the Federation of Women's Clubs as financial incentives blended with concerns for public morals, resulting in a campaign to expunge unsavory characters who might impede business development. Prohibition left an uneven legacy in San Francisco, however. Many local politicians flaunted the law, openly imbibing while on the stump. But prominent residents were also arrested for Volstead Act violations, and many of the city's niteries were closed down during the 1920s, shifting the center of nightlife northward, away from the shopping and financial districts.

26. Leonard Lyons, "The Post's New Yorker," *Washington Post*, June 8, 1938, X-11; "New York's Real Bohemia Is Dead and Gone," *New York Times*, July 24, 1910, SM-11.

27. "Dry Agents Sweep City in Big Raid: 100 Are Arrested," *New York Times*, February 27, 1921, 1; classified ad 7, *New York Tribune*, January 1, 1922, 12; display ad 15, *New York Times*, April 20, 1934, 16; "Harlemites Guests at Village Black Cat Cafe," *New York Amsterdam News*, June 24, 1939, 16.

28. James Gilbert, *Writers and Partisans* (New York: Wiley, 1968), 49–51.

29. Heap, *Slumming*, 189–230; Lorraine Gordon, as told to Barry Singer, *Alive at the Village Vanguard: My Life In and Out of Jazz Time* (Milwaukee: Hal Leonard, 2006), 106; Robert A. Holland, *Chicago in Maps: 1612–2002* (New York: Rizzoli, 2005), 164–67; Dominica A. Pacyga, *Chicago: A Biography* (Chicago: University of Chicago Press, 2009), 219–48; Boyd, *Wide Open Town*, 42–52. See also Christopher Breu, *Hard-Boiled Masculinities* (Minneapolis: University of Minnesota Press, 2005).

30. Erenberg, *Steppin' Out*, 234–59; Heap, *Slumming*, 229; Lewis A. Erenberg, "From New York to Middletown: Repeal and the Legitimization of Nightlife in the Great Depression," *American Quarterly*, vol. 38, no. 5 (Winter 1986), 761–78. See also John D'Emilio and Estelle B. Freedman, *Intimate Matters: A History of Sexuality in America* (Chicago: University of Chicago Press, 2nd ed., 1997; first published 1988), illustrations following page 274, #45–46, for examples of this culture's spread into the nation's hinterlands.

31. H. I. Brock, "Now Our Night Life Glows Anew: In the Two Months Following Repeal, New York Has Taken On the Color of a European Capital, Found Its Old Gayety and a New Decorum in Drinking," February 11, 1934, SM-10, classified ads, February 2, 1934, 20, and February 7, 1934, 16, "Cabarets Banned in Home Sections," September 1, 1934, 15, B. C., "Night Club Notes," October 6, 1934, 20, "Topics of the Times," October 25, 1934, 22, "Court Holds Two in Weylin Bar Raid," September 17, 1934, 38, and "Police Open Drive on 'Gyp' Resorts," September 5, 1934, 23, all in *New York Times*; "Nightlife Problem," August 20, 1938, 6, and "Harlem Boycott Seen When Whispering War Is Begun," March 25, 1939, 11, both in *New York Amsterdam News*. See also Burton W. Peretti, *Nightclub City: Politics and Amusement*

in Manhattan (Philadelphia: University of Pennsylvania Press, 2007), 99–169, 220. Peretti notes that the LaGuardia administration regularly enacted cleanups of the city's nightclubs in response to municipal pressures, most notably during preparations for the 1939 World's Fair.

32. New York and California differed in the structure of their liquor regulations, with New York being regulated statewide, while California was more reliant on local control. "San Francisco Heralds 1934 amid Wild Repeal Whoopee," January 1, 1934, 4, display ads, October 4, 1934, 13, and October 11, 1934, 13, "Gorgeous Girls, Scintillating Shows, Moving Music at S.F. Night Clubs," November 22, 1934, 30, "Alfred Dupont, Artist, Trims Walls of Club," December 26, 1934, 28, "Hard Drinks Sale Banned in Drug Stores," January 9, 1935, 1, "S.F. Grand Jury Launches Probe of Girl Traffic in Liquor Taverns," January 9, 1935, 3, "Police Open Drastic War on Beer Halls," January 10, 1935, 1–3, "Beer Parlor Girls Prey of White Slavers," January 11, 1935, 1–4, "Proprietor, Seven Patrons Seized in Drive on Drink Taverns," January 12, 1935, 1, "Liquor Dealers Approve *Chronicle*'s Demand for Cleanup," January 13, 1935, 1, display ad, "San Francisco, a City Famed 'Round the World for Its Cafes and Clubs," February 11, 1935, 22, and "Bright Night Spots Lure Crowds to Dine and Dance," March 15, 1935, 18, all in *San Francisco Chronicle*.

33. *Polk's Crocker-Langley San Francisco City Directory* (San Francisco, R. L. Polk), for the years 1936–1939; US Bureau of the Census, "Supervisor's District no. 4, Enumeration District no. 38-26, San Francisco, CA," *Sixteenth Census of the United States: 1940*, 82-B, roll T627-299, National Archives, Washington, DC.

34. *Polk's Crocker-Langley San Francisco City Directory* (San Francisco: R. L. Polk), for the years 1935 and 1938–1944; US Bureau of the Census "Enumeration District no. 38-26," and "Enumeration District no. 38-24," *Sixteenth Census*, 82-A, 1-A; Jennifer Shaifer, "Metal Rising: The Forming of the Metal Arts Guild, San Francisco (1929–1964)," MA thesis, Smithsonian Associates and Corcoran College of Art & Design (2011), 27–31; Linda Gordon, *Dorothea Lange: A Life beyond Limits* (London: W. W. Norton, 2009), 75–87, 91–131. Carl "Charlie" Haberkern first lived at 645 Clay Street and then moved with Letizio Bonetti to 36 Columbus Avenue. Other artists included José Ramis and Harry Dixon. Lange and Dixon's circle at Coppa's included Ansel Adams, the poet Elsa Gidlow, and, later, their Monkey Block compatriots, including Kenneth Rexroth and Shirley Staschen Triest. Gordon's account also indicates the limits of interwar liberalism, noting Dixon's prejudice against Jews and African Americans.

35. John Bruce, "The Block," *San Francisco Call Bulletin*, June 14, 1933, 11.

36. Isadore "Izzy" Gomez was legendary within the city's bohemian tradition, a "magnificent mug" who opened his venue before the great 1906 earthquake and openly defied Prohibition—reputedly continuing to wine and dine his supporters from behind bars. Jack Lord and Jenn Shaw, *Where to Sin in San Francisco* (San Francisco: Richard F. Guggenheim, 1939), 35, 55; Herb Caen, *Only in San Francisco* (New York: Doubleday, 1960), 16–17.

37. Ruth Taylor, "Bohemian Spot's Gayety Liked—and How!," February 7, 1938, 28, "North Beach Night," February 18, 1938, 4, "Vice Raids Catch 10; Ousted B-Girls Helped," February 5, 1938, 1, B. W. Horne, "Men, Women, Liquor Don't Mix," February 10, 1938, 3, and *Angel* display ad, February 3, 1938, 12, "Gertrude Atherton on Fascism," February 11, 1938, 20, all in *San Francisco News*.

38. Jack Lord, Lloyd Hoff, and Beniamino Bufano, *Where to Sin in San Francisco* (San Francisco: Richard F. Guggenheim, midcentury ed., 1953; first published 1939), 113.

39. Caen, *Only in San Francisco*, 262, 233; Richard Donovan, "The Black Cat: A Drama in Four Acts," *San Francisco Examiner*, February 14, 1942, unpaginated clipping, Black Cat envelope, café files, *Examiner* morgue, San Francisco History Center, SFPL.

40. Donovan, "Black Cat"; Henri Lenoir, "A Brief Account of the Black Cat Cafe and of the Painting by Cornelius Sampson, depicting the 'Regulars' in the Depression Year 1938," undated press release, vol. 1, Henri Lenoir Papers, BANC MSS 92/842c, Bancroft Library, UC Berkeley; Shirley Staschen Triest, "A Life on the First Waves of Radical Bohemianism in San Francisco," 120, interviews in 1995 and 1996, conducted by Victoria Morris Byerly, Regional Oral History Office, Bancroft Library, UC Berkeley, 1997.

41. The New York Libertarian League offers some insight into the (admittedly idealistic) principles of libertarian anarchism. They propose that "the only salvation for a world satiated with exploitation and war . . . lies in a new, free, classless social order yet to be created," resting on "the goodness of people and in the possibility of Humanity saving itself and emerging on a higher plane of social consciousness." This would rely on mutual aid, collective effort, the end of statism and racism, and the maintenance of individual freedom. See Kenneth Rexroth to Weldon Kees, December 11, 1939, box 23, folder 15, Kenneth Rexroth to Louis Brigante, December 16, 1950, box 23, folder 14, and the Libertarian League, "Provisional Statement of Principles," undated, box 14, folder 4, all in Kenneth Rexroth Papers, collection 175, Department of Special Collections, Charles E. Young Research Library, University of California, Los Angeles [hereafter UCLA]; Kenneth Rexroth, *Excerpts from a Life*, ed. Ekbert Faas (Santa Barbara, CA: Conjunctions Books, 1981), 61.

42. Rexroth, *Excerpts from a Life*, 14; Kenneth Rexroth to Franklin Folsom, May 12, 1941, box 23, folder 14, Rexroth Papers.

43. Morgan Gibson, *Revolutionary Rexroth: Poet of East–West Wisdom* (Guilford, CT: Archon Books, 1986), 1–23; Linda Hamalian, *A Life of Kenneth Rexroth* (New York: W. W. Norton, 1991), 10–21, 33–34, 378 n7; Kenneth Rexroth, *An Autobiographical Novel* (Santa Barbara, CA: Ross-Erikson, 1964), 162–67.

44. Rexroth, *Autobiographical Novel*, 341–42. There is, as far as I have found, no independent confirmation of Rexroth's meeting with Tzara. It is entirely possible that he manufactured this episode for the sake of lending himself authority as the elder statesman of the Beat movement. Whether or not the meeting actually took place, his advocacy of Dadaism at various times in his career was a significant point of connection between the Cabaret Voltaire and the Rebel Café.

45. Hamalian, *Life of Kenneth Rexroth*, 44–48, 67; Rexroth, *Autobiographical Novel*, 365; US Bureau of the Census, "San Francisco, Supervisor's District no. 6, Enumeration District no. 38-397," *Fifteenth Census of the United States: 1930*, 19-A, roll T626-209, National Archives, Washington, DC.

46. The Labor School is best characterized as a progressive institution, despite its being closed in 1957 amid charges that it was communist dominated. Shaifer, "Metal Rising," 27–31, 65–67; Hamalian, *Life of Kenneth Rexroth*, 160; Mari Jo Buhle, Paul Buhle, and Dan Georgakas, eds., *The Encyclopedia of the American Left* (Urbana: University of Illinois Press, 1992), 122–23; Kenneth Rexroth to Lawrence Lipton, January 15, 1953, box 2, folder 5, Lawrence Lipton Papers, collection 819, Department of Special Collections, Charles E. Young Research Library, UCLA; Alan Wald, "A Minority within a Minority: Cannonite Bohemians after World War II," *Against the Current* (July/August 2012), 25–35; Stephen Schwartz, "Cultivating the Fine Art of Printing," *San Francisco Chronicle*, May 11, 1997.

47. Michael Denning, *The Cultural Front: The Laboring of American Culture in the Twentieth Century* (London: Verso, 1997), 44–45, 77–81; A. Joan Saab, *For the Millions: American Art and Culture between the Wars* (Philadelphia: University of Pennsylvania Press, 2004).

48. *San Francisco: The Bay and its Cities; Originally compiled by the Federal Writers' Project of the Works Progress Administration for Northern California*, ed. Gladys Hansen (New York: Hastings House, new rev. ed., 1973; 2nd ed. rev., 1947; first published 1939), v; Ellen Schrecker, *Many Are the Crimes: McCarthyism in America* (Boston: Little, Brown, 1998), 90–91; Irving Howe and Lewis Coser, *The American Communist Party: A Critical History* (New York: Praeger, rev. ed., 1962; first published 1957), 365; Victoria Grieve, *The Federal Art Project and the Creation of Middlebrow Culture* (Urbana: University of Illinois Press, 2009); Lawrence Lipton interview, 770, 830, conducted by Donald Schippers, Oral History Department, UCLA, 1962. Right-wing ideologues of the 1930s, such as Representative Martin Dies—who led the special House Un-American Activities Committee in 1938—as well as liberal critics of the 1950s, such as Irving Howe, denounced the WPA cultural program as a communist-infiltrated boondoggle. Revisionist historians, on the other hand, have decried its middlebrow style and lack of radicalism. In reality, elements of both were true, although the latter ultimately proves to be a more satisfying characterization.

49. The regulars were later identified and numbered in a key provided by Cornelius Sampson, Henri Lenoir, and four other 1930s habitués. Of the twenty-three regulars for whom reliable information is extant, thirteen were WPA artists. A number of others had left-wing bohemian ties. An online search reveals most of their WPA links, but see also Donald J. Hagerty, *Desert Dreams: The Art and Life of Maynard Dixon* (Layton, UT: Gibbs Smith, 1993); E. Breck Parkman, "Missiles of Peace," *California History*, vol. 84, no. 3 (2007), 43–63; interviews with Theodore C. Polos, January 31, 1965, Dong Kingman, January 12, 1965, Max McCarthy, October 15, 1964, Richard Ayer, September 26, 1964, Shirley Staschen Triest, April 12-April 23, 1964, and Hebe Daum Stackpole and Jack Moxom, January 9, 1965, Archives of American Art, Smithsonian Institution. The name of another mural figure, Bae Zaleel, suggests a wry nickname. Bezaleel was a Biblical character, called by God to be the architect heading work on the tabernacle and the artist who made the Ark of the Covenant.

50. Anne Loftis, *Witnesses to the Struggle: Imaging the 1930s California Labor Movement* (Reno: University of Nevada Press, 1998), 57; Rick Wartzman, *Obscene in the Extreme: The Burning and Banning of John Steinbeck's* The Grapes of Wrath (New York: Public Affairs, 2008), 76, 122; "Kenneth Rexroth (1969)," interview, in *San Francisco Beat: Talking with the Poets*, ed. David Meltzer (San Francisco: City Lights Books, 2001), 231; "McKiddy at the Iron Pot," photograph by Henri Lenoir, undated, vol. 1, Lenoir Papers. Rexroth later also claimed to have taken Steinbeck to a cotton-workers' strike in Bakersfield, California, in conjunction with his work for the Agricultural Workers' Industrial Union. Nan Boyd, in *Wide Open Town*, refers to Steinbeck's patronage of the Black Cat, but she relies on Michael R. Gorman, *The Empress Is a Man: Stories from the Life of José Sarria* (New York: Harrington Park Press, 1998), as her source. Gorman's book is an impressionistic collection of North Beach oral histories and offers no contemporaneous textual support for the claim of Steinbeck's presence there.

51. "Kenneth Rexroth (1969)," in *San Francisco Beat*, 241.

52. That this intellectual talk leaned leftward is unmistakable. In a letter to Rexroth from his friend and publisher at New Directions Books, James Laughlin, Laughlin congratulates the poet on a recent rave review in the *San Francisco Chronicle* before jokingly asking the notoriously anticommunist anarchist, "Or was that a crypto-Stalinist reverse English plot to ruin you in The Black Cat?" Bill Morgan, *The Beat Generation in San Francisco: A Literary*

Tour (San Francisco: City Lights Books, 2003), 34; Triest, "Life on the First Waves," 86; James Laughlin to Kenneth Rexroth, "Wed." [ca. 1951], box 13, folder 7, Rexroth Papers.

53. "Dong Kingman," *New Yorker*, October 10, 1942, 10–11; "Items of Peculiar Interest," *Montgomery Street Skylight*, December 24, 1945, unpaginated clipping, and unidentified clipping, both in vol. 1, Lenoir Papers.

54. Elsa Gidlow, *Elsa, I Come with My Songs: The Autobiography of Elsa Gidlow* (San Francisco: Booklegger Press, 1986), 77–78, 224–28, 296; unpaginated clipping, *San Francisco Examiner*, May 7, 1948, Black Cat envelope, *Examiner* morgue, SFPL.

55. Boyd, *Wide Open Town*, 61–62, 159–93.

56. Knute Stiles interview, 69–70, May 30, 1982, conducted by Lewis Ellingham, at the East–West House, 733 Baker Street, San Francisco, box 4, folder 7, Lewis Ellingham's *Poet Be Like God* research materials, MSS 126, Special Collections and Archives, University of California, San Diego [hereafter UC San Diego], courtesy of the Poetry Collection of the University Libraries, University at Buffalo, State University of New York [hereafter SUNY].

57. Peter Macchiarini's injury was reported by an Iron Pot habitué, journalist Mike Quin, in his 1949 book, *The Big Strike*, which is an account of the demonstrations. It is unclear whether Macchiarini was himself a member of the CP, but he was accompanied at the waterfront protest by communist activist Louis Goldblatt. "Louis Goldblatt: Working Class Leader in the ILWU, 1935–1977," 100, interviews in 1978 and 1979, conducted by Estolv Ethan Ward, Oral History Office, UC Berkeley; Mike Quin, "The Big Strike: A Journalist Describes the 1934 San Francisco Strike," [1949], *History Matters*, US Survey Course on the Web, George Mason University, http://historymatters.gmu.edu/d/124/; "Mike Quin in the Iron Pot," undated [ca. 1945] photograph by Henri Lenoir, vol. 1, Lenoir Papers.

58. Another Black Cat regular, Ralph Stackpole, had been instrumental in bringing communist Mexican muralist Diego Rivera to the United States. The Coit Tower strike was a show of support for muralists whose work was under attack for containing Marxist imagery. Stackpole also helped to establish a group of studios with café regular Timothy Wulff at 716–720 Montgomery Street, which (along with the Montgomery Block building) solidified the Black Cat as a bohemian site. Hebe Daum Stackpole and Jack Moxom interview, January 9, 1965, and Shirley Staschen Triest interview, April 12–April 23, 1964, Archives of American Art, Smithsonian Institution; Harvey Smith, "The Monkey Block: The Art Culture of the New Deal in the San Francisco Bay Area," January 6, 2013, FoundSF, www.foundsf.org; Triest, "Life on the First Waves," 75–78; Hamalian, *Life of Kenneth Rexroth*, 82; Raymond L. Wilson, "The Northern Scene," in *American Scene Painting: California 1930s and 1940s*, ed. Ruth Westphal and Janet Blake Dominik (Irvine, CA: Westphal, 1991), reprised in Traditional Fine Arts Organization, www.tfaoi.com/aa/3aa/3aa52.htm; "Canessa Building," Canessa Gallery Artists Resource, http://canessagallery.wordpress.com/history/.

59. Triest, "Life on the First Waves," 80–86, 101; Caen, *Only in San Francisco*, 16–17. The Black Cat's networks also extended interpersonally. Triest met her husband at the café through Rexroth, who had previously brought Frank into the San Francisco branch of the John Reed Club during the time when they shared lodgings at the Montgomery Block.

60. Schwartz, "Fine Art of Printing."

61. The WPA's Richard Ayer, who worked with Shirley Staschen Triest, got his position through Kenneth Rexroth, while artist John Sacco met leading New York muralist Arshile Gorky through friends at the Black Cat. Triest, "Life on the First Waves," 152; Richard Ayer interview, September 26, 1964, and John Saccaro interview, June 18, 1964, Archives of American Art, Smithsonian Institution.

62. Kenneth Rexroth to Peirro Seghers, undated [ca. 1953], box 23, folder 17, and Shirley Triest [unsigned] to Kenneth Rexroth, August 22, 1936, box 30, folder 12, both in Rexroth Papers.

63. Cafe Society soon did reopen under new management, but it closed again in 1952. Barney Josephson, with Terry Trilling-Josephson, *Cafe Society: The Wrong Place for the Right People* (Urbana: University of Illinois Press, 2009), 255, 358–59 n.1.

64. Max Gordon, *Live at the Village Vanguard* (New York: St. Martin's Press, 1980), 24; Robert Sylvester, *Notes of a Guilty Bystander* (Englewood Cliffs, NJ: Prentice-Hall, 1970), 61–62.

65. "Kenneth Rexroth (1969)," in *San Francisco Beat*, 242; Lawrence Lipton to Kenneth Rexroth, April 9, 1954, box 14, folder 7, and Kenneth Rexroth to Lawrence Lipton, January 15, 1953, box 2, folder 5, both in Lipton Papers. Max Gordon and Rexroth both counted countercultural poet Maxwell Bodenheim as a close friend—Rexroth from his days in Chicago, where Bodenheim was part of the 1920s literary renaissance, and Gordon from the Village scene in the 1930s.

66. Lorraine Gordon notes that the Vanguard's early clientele was political and that several of Max Gordon's friends fought in the Spanish Civil War. M. Gordon, *Live at the Village Vanguard*, 16, 19, 22; L. Gordon, *Alive at the Village Vanguard*, 97.

67. Whitney Balliett, *Barney, Bradley, and Max: Sixteen Portraits in Jazz* (New York: Oxford University Press, 1989), 16–18; M. Gordon, *Live at the Village Vanguard*, 7–8, 11–12; US Bureau of the Census, "Enumeration District no. 31-252," *Fifteenth Census*, 3-A, roll T626-1558, National Archives, Washington, DC.

68. Balliett, *Barney, Bradley, and Max*, 18–19; M. Gordon, *Live at the Village Vanguard*, 16–18.

69. Gordon's memoir is a semifictionalized account, filled with composite characters and dialogues that he termed "life fiction." Yet his reminiscences were notably accurate. Having checked relevant passages from both his memoir and the interview that makes up most of Balliett's chapter on the Vanguard against independent sources, I found only one minor factual error. This suggests that Gordon both possessed a sharp memory and utilized the historical record to aid him. Balliett, *Barney, Bradley, and Max*, 21–22, 35; M. Gordon, *Live at the Village Vanguard*, 14–16.

70. Lisa W. Foderaro, "Upstairs/Downstairs," *New York Times*, November 15, 1987, SM-A-8.

71. Malcolm Cowley, "The Greenwich Village Idea," in *On Bohemia: The Code of the Self-Exiled*, ed. Cesar Grana and Marigay Grana (New Brunswick, NJ: Transaction, 1990), 130–38. See also Heap, *Slumming*, 57–70, 82–97; Kathy Lee Peiss, *Hope in a Jar: The Making of America's Beauty Culture* (New York: Metropolitan Books, 1998); Gary S. Cross, *An All-Consuming Century: Why Commercialism Won in Modern America* (New York: Columbia University Press, 2000).

72. Max Gordon should not be confused with the Communist Party organizer of the same name. It is telling that while we were discussing Max's activism, Lorraine also alluded to his friendship with Mark Rothko and the fact that they sold newspapers together in Portland, which suggested to me that these were communist publications. Max mentioned this detail in both his memoir and his 1971 interview with Balliett, with his invocation of Rothko subtly hinting about his political leanings. Lorraine herself was immersed in leftist circles, although she insisted that "I was not in the party" because "it became too dogmatic." Lorraine was friends with the activist David Kimmelman, who hosted gatherings at his Village apart-

ment that included Alger Hiss and CP head Gus Hall. She also maintains a sense of humor about her supposedly subversive leanings. "Well, you meet a lot of people at the Vanguard," she said during our interview, laughing. "Alger Hiss was a friend—too handsome to be a spy!" J. Dosbriora Irwin, "Village Portraits," *Greenwich Village Weekly News*, no. 33 (May 1933), 3; author's interview with Lorraine Gordon, April 22, 2011, at the Village Vanguard, New York City; Balliett, *Barney, Bradley, and Max*, 17; M. Gordon, *Live at the Village Vanguard*, 7; Michael Kimmelman, "Seeing Red: My Communist Childhood in Greenwich Village," *New York Times*, September 10, 2006. E-34.

73. Eli Siegel tied the Vanguard to a circle of poets, including William Carlos Williams and Kenneth Rexroth, who later hailed Siegel as the "un-laureled laureate of below 23rd Street." Rexroth also hinted at his connection to the 1930s Vanguard, declaring, "Most of us who were there remember Eli Siegel as almost the sole survivor of the Golden Age of Greenwich Village." Holly Farrington has argued that Siegel is also linked to the Beats as an early performer of jazz poetry, citing Maxwell Bodenheim's description of Siegel reciting at the Troubadour Tavern. Bodenheim critiqued the primitivism of Siegel's rendition of the Vachel Lindsay poem, "The Congo," during which he "rolled his eyes, twitched his face, foamed at the mouth, banged on the table" and then "emitted unearthly, Paleozoic shrieks." But this description suggests that it scarcely resembled jazz. If anything, Siegel's performance demonstrates that Villagers still equated African American forms with a kind of exoticism that was only marginally less demeaning than minstrelsy—a notion that would change drastically over the course of the 1930s. "Music Notes," November 1, 1934, 24, "Village Bohemian Now Its Laureate," July 11, 1935, 23, Jon Pareles, "In Music and Memories, a Tribute to Max Gordon," May 22, 1989, D-11, Kenneth Rexroth, "From the Past, Two Familiar Voices," July 28, 1957, 178, and Kenneth Rexroth, "Hail, American Development: By Eli Siegel," March 23, 1969, BR-37, all in *New York Times*; Holly Farrington, "'I Improvised behind Him . . . Ahead of Time': Charles Mingus, Kenneth Patchen and Jazz-Poetry Fusion Art," *Journal of American Studies* (Cambridge), vol. 41, no. 2 (August 2007), 365–75; Maxwell Bodenheim, *My Life and Loves in Greenwich Village* (New York: Bridgehead Books, 1954), 199–200; Sascha Feinstein, *Jazz Poetry: From the 1920s to the Present* (Westport, CT: Greenwood Press, 1997), 16–21.

74. In addition to radicals, such as the "National Maritime Union poet" Jack Sellers, appearances by expatriates who had returned from Parisian sojourns confirmed the Vanguard's place in cosmopolitan New York, which Malcolm Cowley, in the 1930s, declared to be an international city. Cowley himself sometimes attended readings that included Dadaist poetry or Eli Siegel's Yiddish antifascist quips, such as *A fa-SHIST Passt NISHT* (A fascist is unbecoming, an embarrassment). Cowley furthered these ties by hiring Vanguard poet Joe Gould to write book reviews or poems, such as "Communism Is Twentieth Century Americanism" (which Gould later retracted after the Hitler-Stalin pact in 1939) for the progressive *New Republic*. The latter also printed a letter from Rexroth denouncing the magazine's pro-war stance. M. Gordon, *Live at the Village Vanguard*, 24–26; Gilbert, *Writers and Partisans*, 195; "Books in Brief," vol. 79, no. 1026 (August 1, 1934), 327, vol. 96, no. 1240 (September 7, 1938), 132, vol. 81, no. 1045 (December 12, 1934), 144–45, and vol. 87, no. 1120 (May 20, 1936), 52–53, all in *New Republic*; Gordon, *Live at the Village Vanguard*, 28; "The Bandwagon," May 13, 1936, 19, and "Correspondence," October 4, 1939, 246, both in *New Republic*.

75. Bodenheim, *My Life and Loves*, 202, 199; M. Gordon, *Live at the Village Vanguard*, 32, 22.

76. M. Gordon, *Live at the Village Vanguard*, 43–50; "Josh White Featured in New Movie Short," December 13, 1941, 21, and Dan Burley, "Back Door Stuff: There's a Man Going

Around, Jack, Taking Names," December 20, 1941, 14, both in *New York Amsterdam Star-News*.

77. Josephson, *Cafe Society*, 8–9, 12–17.

78. Denning, *Cultural Front*, 325–26; Theodore Strauss, "Notes on Night Clubs: The Center's Rainbow Room Gets a New Show—also the Onyx Club," *New York Times*, March 12, 1939, 151; James Gavin, *Intimate Nights: The Golden Age of New York Cabaret* (New York: Grove Weidenfeld, 1991), 25–29; Balliett, *Barney, Bradley, and Max*, 24; Leo Shull to Barney Josephson, May 27, 1944, box 7, folder 2, Ivan Black Papers, JPB 06-20, Music Division, New York Public Library for the Performing Arts [hereafter NYPL]; Dan Burley, "Back Door Stuff: Portrait of a Columnist Columning," *New York Amsterdam News*, October 30, 1943, B-8; Reuss and Reuss, *American Folk Music*, 32–36.

79. Denning, *Cultural Front*, 323–61; Josephson, *Cafe Society*, 8–12, 39–40, 86–87; David Stowe, "The Politics of Cafe Society," *Journal of American History*, vol. 84, no. 4 (March 1998), 1384–1406; Lewis Erenberg, "Greenwich Village Nightlife, 1910–1950," in *Greenwich Village*, ed. Rick Beard and Leslie Cohen Berlowitz (New Brunswick, NJ: Rutgers University Press, 1993), 357–70.

80. Denning, *Cultural Front*, 324; Howe and Coser, *American Communist Party*, 366.

81. The historical record is unfortunately mute about the Vanguard's transition from poetry to political cabaret. Max Gordon apparently neglected advertising or seriously courting the press until 1939. Gordon's memoir (in one of its few factual errors) states that the Popular Front group called the Almanac Singers, which featured left-wing populist musicians Woody Guthrie and Pete Seeger, began to make regular appearances sometime before 1939. The group, which indeed would perform at the Vanguard in the coming years, was not formed until 1941, although Almanac members may have been solo acts there prior to the 1940s. M. Gordon, *Live at the Village Vanguard*, 33; Reuss and Reuss, *American Folk Music*, 148–49.

82. M. Gordon, *Live at the Village Vanguard*, 33; Theodore Strauss, "Notes on Nightclubs," March 26, 1939, 134, and June 18, 1939, 114. John Martin, "The Dance: Pas de Deux; Some Thoughts on Patricia Bowman and Paul Haakon—Coming Events," July 30, 1939, X-8, and "News of Night Clubs: A New Bill at the Lofty Rainbow Room—the Russian Kretchma Reopens," September 17, 1939, 136, all in *New York Times*; M. Gordon, *Live at the Village Vanguard*, 34–36. Strauss stated that the troupe had been performing at the Vanguard in the previous months, making their debut almost simultaneously with that of Cafe Society.

83. "News of Night Clubs: Notes on One or Two Spots Locally as well as on the Near-By Road," *New York Times*, September 10, 1939, X-2. For details on Judy Holliday's left-wing ties and Red Scare experiences, see Stephen R. Duncan, "Not Just *Born Yesterday*: Judy Holliday, the Red Scare, and the (Miss-)Uses of Hollywood's Dumb Blonde Image," in *Smart Chicks on Screen: Representing Women's Intellect in Film and Television*, ed. Laura Mattoon D'Amore (Lanham, MD: Rowman & Littlefield, 2014), 9–28.

84. M. Gordon, *Live at the Village Vanguard*, 33; Theodore Strauss, "Late Events in the Night Clubs: The Maestro of Swing, Mr. Goodman Himself, Enters the Waldorf—Miss Francine and the Coq Rouge," October 15, 1939, 140, and "News of the Stage: Jack Haley Changes His Mind and Decides to Cast His Lot with Wiman," December 23, 1939, 8, both in *New York Times*; Denning, *Cultural Front*, 115, 228.

85. Irwin Corey's routines were similar to those of blacklisted Cafe Society comedian Zero Mostel, who satirized prominent figures with characters such as Professor Remorse (modeled on the Nazi-appeasing Neville Chamberlain) and the segregationist senator Polltax Pellagra ("they call me by my first disease"). Louis Calta, "News of Night Clubs," *New York Times*,

October 25, 1942, X-5; Buhle, Buhle, and Georgakas, *Encyclopedia of the American Left*, 344; Reuss and Reuss, *American Folk Music*, 124; Louis Calta, "News of Night Clubs: Two Events Are Scheduled for This Week," *New York Times*, December 20, 1942, X-5; Josephson, *Cafe Society*, 353.

86. Stowe, "Cafe Society"; Josephson, *Cafe Society*, 7–9.

87. "Mary Lou Williams," in *Reading Jazz: A Gathering of Autobiography, Reportage, and Criticism from 1919 to Now*, ed. Robert Gottlieb (New York: Pantheon Books, 1996), 115; Josephson, *Cafe Society*, 150; "'Misunderstanding' Is Blamed for Billie Holliday Walkout," *Chicago Defender*, August 26, 1939, 20.

88. Another troubling report indicated that Cafe Society once refused to serve a black female customer, which, if nothing else, counters Josephson's claim that he always put African American patrons ahead of white ones, instructing his maitre d' to "give them the best tables." It is also suggestive, although wholly circumstantial, that the photographs of Cafe Society in Josephson's memoir feature almost no black audience members. By contrast, both Max and Lorraine Gordon's memoirs, which make no particular point of their club's integration, contain numerous photos of interracial crowds. David Stowe's work notes Cafe Society's racial tensions but does little to balance Josephson's paternalism against statements by performers, such as Lena Horne, that it was foundational in the development of their social consciousness. Max Gordon was probably no less guilty of such racial objectification but was less outspoken, making the evidence sketchier. Certainly he was vulnerable to accusations that he used black performers to benefit himself financially—a criticism that would be leveled by race-conscious Black Nationalists in the 1960s. Billie Holiday, *Lady Sings the Blues* (New York: Doubleday, 1956), 84; "Holiday at Cafe Society: Boogie-Woogie Pianists Back in Village; Ida Cox Arrival Delayed; Hazel Featured," *New York Amsterdam News*, November 18, 1939, 20; Simone de Beauvoir, *America Day by Day* (New York: Grove Press, 1953), 71; Josephson, *Cafe Society*, 60, 72; Stowe, "Cafe Society," 1392–93; Ingrid Monson, *Freedom Sounds: Civil Rights Call Out to Jazz and Africa* (New York: Oxford University Press, 2007); Lena Horne, in honor of Barney Josephson at the National Urban League Guild's Beaux Arts Ball, New York, February 26, 1982, quoted in Josephson, *Cafe Society*, 131.

89. Denning, *Cultural Front*, 339–40; Eduardo Bonilla-Silva, "Rethinking Racism: Toward a Structural Interpretation," *American Sociological Review*, vol. 62, no. 3 (June 1997), 465–80.

90. The African American press was quick to praise the club's racially integrated band and policies, stating that it was the only joint outside of Harlem where "a colored couple is as welcome as anybody else" and calling Josephson a "crusader for racial equality." Ivan Black's press releases are also revealing, as he commended the club, with references to its refined interracial entertainment and satirical murals. Bandleader Joe Sullivan, Black crowed, "was first taught to play the piano by a nun" and remained "a true Christian, utterly free of race or religious prejudice, and as a result is not only willing to be the white leader of a Negro band but proud to be." While this statement evaded the question of whether he would have been equally willing to play under an African American bandleader, Sullivan's stance was nonetheless groundbreaking in the era of segregation. Black was careful to include leftist publications in his press lists. Ivan Black to Frank Farrell [*New York World-Telegram* reporter], October 4, 1940, and Ivan Black to Charles Payne, July 4, 1940, both in folder 1, Ivan Black, "Man Bites Dog—Cafe Society Downtown to Have Complete New Show on October 1st Including Sister Tharpe and Art Tatum," undated [1940], folder 3, and Ivan Black, "Children's Night at Cafe Society Uptown," May 23, 1942, folder 5, all in box 7, Black Papers,

NYPL; "Cafe Society Swings High," *New York Amsterdam News*, January 7, 1939, 16; "Billie Holiday Clicks in Village," *Chicago Defender*, January 14, 1939, 18; "Mixed Band at 'Cafe Society': Joe Sullivan Organizes 1st Name Negro-White Orchestra," *New York Amsterdam News*, November 25, 1939, 1; Major Robinson, "Mixed Band at Cafe Society Proves a Hit: Patrons Pleased With Set-Up and Musicians Like It," *Chicago Defender*, December 30, 1939, 17; "Hope Day Nursery Cocktail Party at Cafe Society Will Be Super!" *New York Amsterdam News*, February 1, 1947, 6.

91. John Martin, "The Dance: A Document; Autobiography of Ruth St. Denis as a Source Book—Coming Events," September 24, 1939, 136, and Meyer Berger, "About New York," March 11, 1940, 10, both in *New York Times*; Dan Burley, "Back Door Stuff: Which Back Door Digs the World?," *New York Amsterdam News*, December 7, 1940, 20.

92. The *New York Amsterdam News* singled out the Vanguard for its participation in one such event, alongside Small's Paradise and Cafe Society, congratulating these venues for organizing talent and funds to "help to make some deserving folks happy" during that year's Christmas season. "Honor Zutty, Drum King," December 28, 1940, 17; St. Clair Bourne, "Top-Ranking Stars Slated for Program: Choicest Tickets Now On Sale for Best Show," December 7, 1940, 1, and "Cabaret Fete for Art Sake: E. Simms Campbell There with Other Socialites," June 22, 1940, 14, all in *New York Amsterdam News*; "Pittsburgh Honors Maxine: She Flies Home for Frog Week Party," *Chicago Defender*, August 17, 1946, 10; "Camera Highlights: Prizes in Camera Contest!" *New York Amsterdam News*, January 15, 1949, 5; photo standalone 5, no title, *Chicago Defender*, May 21, 1949, 5; "Cafe Photography," *New York Times*, February 12, 1950, 102.

93. M. Gordon, *Live at the Village Vanguard*, 84–85; Patrick Burke, *Come in and Hear the Truth: Jazz and Race on 52nd Street* (Chicago: University of Chicago Press, 2008).

94. Ralph Ellison, "Minton's," in *Reading Jazz*, 550; Sidney Finkelstein, *Jazz: A People's Music* (New York: International, International Publisher's ed., 1988; first published 1948), 4.

95. Finkelstein, *Jazz*, 5–6, 139, 145–53; Eric Hobsbawm, *The Jazz Scene* (New York: Pantheon Books, 1993), 229–37; Eric Hobsbawm, *Uncommon People: Resistance, Rebellion, and Jazz* (New York: New Press, 1998), 242, 263; LeRoi Jones, *Blues People: Negro Music in White America* (New York: William Morrow, 1963), 82–86, 145, 176–93, 200–202; Ingrid Monson, "The Problem with White Hipness: Race, Gender, and Cultural Conceptions in Jazz Historical Discourse," in "Music Anthropologies and Music Histories," special issue, *Journal of the American Musicological Society*, vol. 48, no. 3 (Autumn 1995), 396–422. Jones further argues that the arrival of modern jazz rejected the pretensions found at Cafe Society and signaled a separation between black folk culture and assimilationism. Bebop claimed the blues tradition of authentic blackness, but it also had to contend with its role as art, due to whites' acceptance of jazz. Bebop's stance, therefore, served the dual social function of both black self-determination and white rebellion. Monson has critiqued this view, mentioning the gender and racial assumptions in a notion of black authenticity that was coded as male and antibourgeois.

96. Ellison, "Minton's," in *Reading Jazz*, 549–54; Gilbert S. McKean, "The Diz and the Bebop," *Esquire*, October 1947, in Ralph Gleason, ed., *Jam Session: An Anthology of Jazz* (London: Jazz Book Club, 1961), 122.

97. Dizzy Gillespie, with Al Fraser, *To Be, or Not . . . to Bop* (New York: Doubleday, 1979), 142, 144–8; Linda Dahl, *Stormy Weather: The Music and Lives of a Century of Jazzwomen* (New York: Pantheon Books, 1984), 262.

98. Lucien Carr interview, 16, March 9, 1986, box 23, folder 6, Barry Miles Papers, Rare Book and Manuscript Library, Columbia University; John Clellon Holmes, *Go* (Mamaroneck, NY: Paul P. Appel, reprint, 1977; first published 1952), 136–41.

99. L. Gordon, *Alive at the Village Vanguard*, 96; Robin D. G. Kelley, *Thelonious Monk: The Life and Times of an American Original* (New York: Free Press, 2009), 144, 493 n10; Lillian Scott, "Along Celebrity Row: Our Own Bird Book," *Chicago Defender*, September 5, 1948, 16. There is some debate about the exact date of Monk's Village Vanguard debut. In her memoir, Lorraine Gordon reports the date as September 14, 1948, but Robin D. G. Kelley's exhaustively researched biography of Monk asserts that it was October 14. Kelley bases this on Monk's thirty-day jail sentence for his drug arrest, handed down on August 31, and musician Billy Taylor's recollection that he shared the bill with Monk sometime after his own booking, which began on October 1. Kelley does not document Monk's release date from jail, however, and the *Chicago Defender* reported on September 25 that Monk had appeared on the Vanguard's kickoff fall show, implying a prior date. Further, despite a lack of documentation for Monk's marriage, Kelley suggests that it was in September 1948, which would also preclude the full thirty-day sentence having been carried out. Therefore, it seems likely that Monk secured an early release and that Gordon's date of September 14 is correct.

100. Kelley, *Thelonious Monk*, 82, 139–42; Orrin Keepnews, *The View from Within: Jazz Writings, 1948–1987* (New York: Oxford University Press, 1988), 123; Nat Hentoff, *The Jazz Life* (New York: Dial Press, 1961), 181–86. Bebop's anticommercialism was always more myth than reality. Dizzy Gillespie and Charlie Parker openly sought mass audiences, each appearing in Hollywood films and making records with big band or string arrangements. Yet they always maintained the core bebop sound, insisting that the mainstream would have to meet them more than halfway. Monk also sought commercial success but conceded even less to popular tastes.

101. Folksinger Richard Dyer-Bennet was best man at the Gordons' wedding. Lorraine Gordon's brother was the ardent leftist artist Philip Stein, who painted under the name "Estaño" and studied with the communist muralist David Alfaro Siqueiros, a political ally of Diego Rivera, with whom Stein also worked. In 1958, Stein painted a social-realist mural on the back wall of the Village Vanguard. L. Gordon, *Alive at the Village Vanguard*, 96–103; Earl Wilson, "It Happened Last Night," *Sandusky (OH) Register-Star-News*, June 16, 1950, 10; William Grimes, "Philip Stein, Muralist Who Adorned Village Vanguard Jazz Club, Dies at 90," *New York Times*, May 18, 2009, www.nytimes.com/2009/05/18/arts/design/18stein.html; Mark Vallen, "An Interview with American Artist, Philip Stein—aka Estaño," February 2004, Estaño, www.mexicanmuralschool.com/interview/interview.htm.

102. Maxwell T. Cohen, *The Police Card Discord* (Metuchen: Scarecrow Press and Institute of Jazz Studies, Rutgers–The State University of New Jersey, 1993), 19–20; Paul Chevigny, *Gigs: Jazz and the Cabaret Laws in New York City* (New York: Routledge, 2nd ed., 2005; first published 1991), 59.

103. Kelley, *Thelonious Monk*, 145.

104. Ben Sidran, *Black Talk* (New York: Holt, Rinehart & Winston, 1971), 114–15; Jack Kerouac, *On the Road* (New York: Viking Press, fourteenth printing, 1971; first published 1957), 14; Norwood "Pony" Poindexter, *The Pony Express: Memoirs of a Jazz Musician* (Frankfurt, Germany: JAS, 1985), 48–49.

105. Kelley, *Thelonious Monk*, 118; Keepnews, *View from Within*, 187.

106. Langston Hughes, "Greenwich Village Negroes," *Chicago Defender*, October 19, 1946, 14; "Better Protection Promised in Village," *(Baltimore) Afro-American*, November 2, 1946, 14; Dan Burley, "Back Door Stuff: Long Skirts to Thin Out Wolfpacks!," *New York Amsterdam News*, September 20, 1947, 21.

107. Holmes, *Go*, 161.

108. For a thorough overview of how intimidation, innuendo, and blacklisting underpinned the Red Scare, see Schrecker, *Many Are the Crimes*.

109. The African American reaction to the case was tellingly mixed. Adam Clayton Powell Jr. was one of only two congressmen to vote against Leon Josephson's conviction. Some in the black press supported HUAC, however, arguing that the CP was exploitative and that Cafe Society had "won Negro 'artists' to the party line by giving them employment." Others supported Leon's insistence that HUAC was unconstitutional, echoing a statement by the Civil Rights Congress that HUAC violated the rights of labor and free speech. The mainstream white press uniformly condemned Josephson, proclaiming that CP alliances with African Americans sought the "overthrow of the United States" and the establishment of a "Negro republic in the South." "'No. 2 Red' Gets One Year in Jail for Contempt: Fined $1,000; He Defied House Group," *Chicago Daily Tribune*, October 16, 1947, 9; "Josephson Gets Year, $1000 Fine," *Washington Post*, October 16, 1947, 7; Stowe, "Cafe Society," 1396–97; Josephson, *Cafe Society*, 229–31, 249–51, 355–56 n.5; George S. Schuyler, "Views and Reviews," May 10, 1947, 7, and "Civil Rights Congress Defending All-Comers," May 31, 1947, 4, both in *Pittsburgh Courier*; "Ex-Red Tells of Subversive Talk by Eisler," *Washington Post*, July 19, 1947, B-2.

110. Stowe, "Cafe Society," 140–44; Josephson, *Cafe Society*, 238, 241, 255.

111. "Obituaries: Judy Holliday Dies; Played Dumb; IQ 172," *Boston Globe*, June 8, 1965, 35; "Weavers to Sing Their Final Song: Folk-Music Quartet Plans to Disband at End of Year," *New York Times*, November 9, 1963, 14; "No Direction Home: Bob Dylan," directed by Martin Scorsese, American Masters Series, PBS, aired September 27, 2005.

112. Duncan, "Not Just *Born Yesterday*"; "Zero Mostel," IMDb, www.imdb.com/name /nm0609216/?ref_=fn_al_nm_1/.

113. Denning, *Cultural Front*, 361.

114. In his memoir, Barney Josephson's recounting of Hazel Scott's testimony suggests that he was not only damaged professionally but also hurt personally: "After seven and a half years at Cafe Society she could give such testimony. That's the way she washed herself. Put it on my back. When she gave this testimony, that was the end of Hazel Scott with me." Chilton, *Hazel Scott*, 144–45; "No Red Stain on Me: Hazel Scott," *Chicago Defender*, September 23, 1950, 21; Louis Lautier, "Artist Asks to Testify before House Committee: Hazel Scott Is Latest Star to Deny 'Red' Connections," *New Journal and Guide* (Norfolk, VA), September 23, 1950, 1; "Josh White," IMDb, www.imdb.com/name/nm0925024/?ref_=fn_al_nm_2/; "Hazel Scott," IMDb, www.imdb.com/name/nm0779220/?ref_=fn_al_nm_1/; Josephson, *Cafe Society*, 260–61.

115. "Comedian Zero Mostel Balks at Red Question: Invokes Fifth Amendment, Denies He Is Communist at Present Hearing Here," *Los Angeles Times*, October 15, 1955, 1; Willard Edwards, "Reds Invade TV Industry, Probe Reveals: Quiz to Open," *Chicago Daily Tribune*, August 11, 1955, 6; "6 More Witnesses Balk at Red Probe Questions," *Washington Post and Times Herald*, August 19, 1955, 21. Ivan Black's mispronunciation of Representative Sherer's name might have been a sly insult. In Yiddish slang, a *schnorrer* is a beggar or freeloader.

116. M. Oakley Stafford, "Informing You," *Hartford (CT) Courant*, March 1, 1952, 7; Hazel Garland, "3-D Films May Revolutionize Movie Industry—Ivan Black," *Pittsburgh Courier*,

January 10, 1953, 14; Walter Winchell, "Of New York: TWA Sleeper to N.Y.," *Washington Post*, May 20, 1953, 39; "Biographical Note," Ivan Black Papers finding aid, NYPL.

Chapter 2. Subterranean Aviators

1. Jack Lord and Lloyd Hoff, *Where to Sin in San Francisco* (San Francisco: Richard F. Guggenheim, 1953), 77; "Notice to Tourists," Iron Pot menu, 1943, vol. 1, Henri Lenoir Papers, BANC MSS 92/842c, Bancroft Library, UC Berkeley.

2. J. R. Goddard, "The Wonderful World of the White Horse," *Village Voice*, June 22, 1961, in *The Village Voice Anthology (1956–1980): Twenty-Five Years of Writing from the* Village Voice, ed. Geoffrey Stokes (New York: William Morrow, 1982), 92.

3. Ross Wetzsteon, *Republic of Dreams: Greenwich Village, the American Bohemia, 1910–1960* (New York: Simon & Schuster, 2002), 12.

4. Many works on the Beats quote this phrase, and even the most cursory list of titles demonstrates this ubiquity. See, for example, David Sterritt, *Mad to be Saved: The Beats, the '50s, and Film* (Carbondale: Southern Illinois University Press, 1998); Blake Bailey, "Mad to Talk," *New York Times*, August 6, 2010, www.nytimes.com/2010/08/08/books/review/Bailey -t.html.

5. George Rawick telephone interview, August 17, 1984, box 1, folder 71, Maurice Isserman research files for *The Other American: The Life of Michael Harrington*, TAM.239, Tamiment Library / Robert F. Wagner Labor Archives, Elmer Holmes Bobst Library, New York University.

6. John Gruen, *The Party's Over Now: Reminiscences of the Fifties—New York's Artists, Writers, and Their Friends* (New York: Viking Press, 1972), 128; Michael Harrington, *Fragments of the Century* (New York: Saturday Review Press / E. P. Dutton, 1973), 42. Harrington later recalled gaining his first invitation to one of Norman Mailer's famous parties through Barbara Bank, whom he met at the San Remo.

7. Lord and Hoff, *Where to Sin*, 77.

8. Knute Stiles interview, 19, 23–24, 85, May 30, 1982, conducted by Lewis Ellingham, at the East–West House, 733 Baker Street, San Francisco, box 4, folder 7, Lewis Ellingham's *Poet Be Like God* research materials, MSS 126, Special Collections and Archives, UC San Diego, courtesy of the Poetry Collection of the University Libraries, University at Buffalo, SUNY.

9. "Philip Lamantia (1998)," interview, in *San Francisco Beat: Talking with the Poets*, ed. David Meltzer (San Francisco: City Lights Books, 2001), 136; James Brook, Chris Carlsson, and Nancy J. Peters, eds., *Reclaiming San Francisco: History, Politics, Culture* (San Francisco: City Lights Books, 1998), 203.

10. Henri Lenoir to Kenneth Rexroth, undated [ca. 1964], box 13, folder 11, Kenneth Rexroth Papers, collection 175, Department of Special Collections, Charles E. Young Research Library, UCLA; *Census of England and Wales, 1911* (London: His Majesty's Stationery Office, 1911), schedule no. 355; Mel Fowler, "Henri Lenoir—a Sketch," *Comprehension*, vol. 1, no. 3 (Winter 1950/51), 20; Henri Lenoir, "The Painting by Cornelius Sampson of the Habitués of the Black Cat Cafe in 1938" [undated press release], "A Comparison of the Daily Bar Receipts before and after I Handled the Promotion Starting July 24, '41," and "Agreement between Johnny Romero and Henri Lenoir, July 20, '41," all in vol. 1, Lenoir Papers; Knute Stiles interview, 14, Ellingham research materials; US Department of Labor, "List or Manifest of Alien Passengers, SS *Carmania*, Sailing from Liverpool, September 5, 1925," vol. 1, Lenoir Papers. At one point Lenoir took the name Henry Black and identified himself as an antique dealer from Liverpool.

11. Iron Pot menu, 1943, vol. 1, Lenoir Papers.

12. "Black Cat, Bohemian Bar, Raided after Brawl: Six Jailed," September 4, 1947, "Three of Six Seized in Raid on Black Cat Cafe Released," September 5, 1947, and "Tavern Ban Lifted by Court's Order," October 25, 1949, all unpaginated, all in *San Francisco Examiner*, Black Cat envelope, and untitled clipping, *San Francisco Examiner*, April 20, 1948, unpaginated, Iron Pot envelope, all in café files, *Examiner* morgue, San Francisco History Center, SFPL; "Iron Pot," undated clipping, unpaginated, vol. 1, Lenoir Papers.

13. After the war, Lenoir supplemented Rexroth's tenuous income by hawking the latter's poems at the Iron Pot. In 1949, Marie Rexroth casually wrote to her husband that their friend from the WPA days, painter Richard Ayer, was doing well—healthy and (temporarily) sober—and "has two pictures hanging in the Iron Pot." Linda Hamalian, *A Life of Kenneth Rexroth* (New York: W. W. Norton, 1991), 142–33; Marie Rexroth to Kenneth Rexroth, "Monday Night," undated, box 24, folder 5, Rexroth Papers.

14. Tommy Lott, "Sargent Johnson: The 'New Negro' Artist," December 28, 2008, FoundSF, www.foundsf.org; Richard Ayer interview, September 26, 1964, Archives of American Art, Smithsonian Institution.

15. Jennifer Stone, "At the Black Cat, the Iron Pot and the Jackpot," *Mother Jones* (August 1976), 38.

16. Brian J. Godfrey, *Neighborhoods in Transition: The Making of San Francisco's Ethnic and Nonconformist Communities* (Berkeley: University of California Press, 1988), 8–17, 22–53, 94–127.

17. Untitled clipping, *San Francisco Examiner*, May 4, 1948, unpaginated, Iron Pot envelope, *Examiner* morgue, SFPL; Fowler, "Henri Lenoir—a Sketch"; untitled clipping, August 26, 1949, unpaginated, photograph of Vesuvio at the time of its purchase, and account sheet, all in vol. 1, Lenoir Papers; Charles Modecke interview in *The Beach*, directed by Mary Kerr (San Francisco: CA Palm, 1995), DVD.

18. Herb Caen, "Talk of the Town," September 9, 1949, unpaginated clipping, and "Name Contest Entry Blank," March 28, 1950, both in vol. 1, Lenoir Papers; Charles Modecke interview in *The Beach*.

19. Charles Modecke interview in *The Beach*.

20. Henri Lenoir to Kenneth Rexroth, undated [ca. 1964], box 13, folder 11, Rexroth Papers.

21. Robert Celli, "Vesuvio Café," July 16, 2013, FoundSF, www:foundsf.org.

22. Photograph, undated, in vol. 1, Lenoir Papers; "These Foolish Things," *San Francisco Examiner*, September 22, 1950, unpaginated, Vesuvio envelope, *Examiner* morgue, SFPL.

23. "Don't Be Surprised," *San Francisco Examiner*, September 5, 1950, unpaginated, Vesuvio envelope, *Examiner* morgue, SFPL; untitled clipping, *San Francisco News*, May 8, 1950, unpaginated, vol. 1, Lenoir Papers; Knute Stiles interview, 65–66, Ellingham research materials; "Vesuvio Cafe," *Inside San Francisco*, vol. 1, no. 2 (March 1958), 13.

24. J. G. Hillard, "The Iron Pot," condensed from "Western Restaurant," *Pacific Coast Record*, undated clipping, unpaginated, vol. 1, Lenoir Papers; Don McClure, "A Speakeasy Remembered: Back Through Izzy's Door," February 20, 1959, unpaginated clipping, and "An Agreement between Belfast Beverages, Inc. of San Francisco, California, and Mr. Henri Lenoir, Owner of Vesuvio Café, 255 Columbus Avenue, San Francisco, California," February 9, 1959, both in vol. 2, Lenoir Papers.

25. Charles Modecke interview in *The Beach*.

26. Knute Stiles interview, Ellingham research materials; Larry Pitt interview in *The Beach*.

27. Lewis Ellingham and Kevin Killian, *Poet Be Like God: Jack Spicer and the San Francisco Renaissance* (Hanover, NH: University of New England Press, 1998), 41–42; Charles Modecke and Leo Krikorian interviews in *The Beach*.

28. Ann Charters, *Kerouac: A Biography* (San Francisco: Straight Arrow Books, 1973), 60; Joyce Johnson, *Minor Characters* (Boston: Houghton Mifflin, 1983), 3, 8–9.

29. Charters, *Kerouac*, 44–46, 64, 73–74.

30. Alex Haley and Malcolm X, *The Autobiography of Malcolm X* (New York: Random House, Ballantine Books ed., 1999; first published 1964), 76–99.

31. San Francisco artist Robert McChesney recalled that Rueben Kadish was part owner of the Cedar. Whitney Pastorek, "My New York Haunt," *New York Times*, December 3, 2006, CY-17; Goddard, "Wonderful World," 92–96; Ernest Wohlleben draft registration card, Local Board Division 164, June 5, 1917; US Bureau of the Census, "New York, Enumeration District 726," *Fourteenth Census of the United States: 1920*, 17-B, roll T625 1203, Records of the Bureau of the Census, Record Group 29, National Archives, Washington, DC; *New York City Directory, for 1933* (New York: Doggett & Rode, 1933); Bill Morgan, *The Beat Generation in New York: A Walking Tour of Jack Kerouac's City* (San Francisco: City Lights Books, 1997), 88–89; "Business Leases Dominate Trading," *New York Times*, July 27, 1933, 32; Hebe Daum Stackpole and Jack Moxom interview, January 9, 1965, Archives of American Art, Smithsonian Institution.

32. WPA artist Harold Rosenberg, who was also part of the Artist Club that included de Kooning and Kline, and who counted poets like Max Bodenheim and Eli Siegel as friends, remembered the group coalescing in 1943. They often went to local cafeterias to talk, but Pollock preferred the Cedar, because he did not like "doing stuff with coffee." John Wilcock, *The Village Square* (New York: Lyle Stuart, 1961), 170–71; Gruen, *Party's Over*, 128, 174–82.

33. Milton Klonsky, "Greenwich Village: Decline and Fall," in *The Scene before You: A New Approach to American Culture*, ed. Chandler Brossard (New York: Rinehart, 1955), 22; Harold Norse, *Memoirs of a Bastard Angel* (New York: William Morrow, 1989), 108–11; David Leeming, *James Baldwin: A Biography* (New York: Alfred A. Knopf, 1994), 49–50. Charlie Hershkowitz was yet another tie between bohemia and anarchist networks. An acolyte of Henry Miller, Hershkowitz was also in touch with George Leite, who printed Rexroth's Libertarian group's journal, *Circle*. See Phil Nurenberg's interview with Bern Porter, August 25–27, 1980, in Belfast, Maine, *Vagabond White Paper Number 5*, www.panmodern.com/bern_nurenberg .html.

34. Mimi Sheraton, "In the Village, 50-Year Affair for a Walker Still in Love," *New York Times*, January 10, 1997, C-1; Harrington, *Fragments of the Century*, 39–40.

35. Mary V. Dearborn, *Mailer: A Biography* (New York: Houghton Mifflin, 1999), 88–89; Wetzsteon, *Republic of Dreams*, 552.

36. Harold Norse to Paul Carroll, November 30, 1959, box 2, folder 22, Paul D. Carroll Papers, Special Collections Research Center, University of Chicago Library; Norse, *Memoirs*, 108–12; Lucien Carr interview, March 9, 1986, folder 6, and Allen Ginsberg interview, 1983, folder 7, both in box 23, *Ginsberg: A Biography* materials, Barry Miles Papers, Rare Book and Manuscript Library, Columbia University.

37. Barry Miles, "The Beat Generation in the Village," in *Greenwich Village: Culture and Counterculture*, ed. Rick Beard and Leslie Cohen Berlowitz (New Brunswick, NJ: Rutgers

University Press, 1993), 165–67; Lucien Carr interview, Miles Papers; Allen Ginsberg, journal (typescript), 15, 25, box 3, folder 6, series 2, Allen Ginsberg Papers, M0733, Department of Special Collections, Stanford University Libraries.

38. Harold Norse to Paul Carroll, November 30, 1959, Carroll Papers. The name of the fascist was John Kasper.

39. Noting the significance of Billie Holiday's "Strange Fruit" to his social awakening, Norse also stated, "Jazz and blues provided the expression of these feelings." Norse, *Memoirs*, 78–85, 95, 101–2, 166–67.

40. Anatole Broyard, *Kafka Was the Rage: A Greenwich Village Memoir* (New York: Carol Southern Books, 1993), 19, 83–85; Bill Morgan, *I Celebrate Myself: The Somewhat Private Life of Allen Ginsberg* (New York: Penguin Books, 2006), 101–2, 138–39; Harrington, *Fragments of the Century*, 40–45; Paul Goodman to Paul Carroll, January 9, 1961, box 1, folder 48, Carroll Papers.

41. Harrington, *Fragments of the Century*, 22–23; John Clellon Holmes, *Go* (Mamaroneck, NY: Paul P. Appel, reprint, 1977; first published 1952), 32; Broyard, *Kafka Was the Rage*, 80, 30.

42. Harrington, *Fragments of the Century*, 46, 52; Michael Harrington notebook, "Me: Boheme," box 3, folder 1, Michael Harrington Papers, TAM.209, Tamiment Library / Robert F. Wagner Labor Archives, Elmer Holmes Bobst Library, New York University.

43. Charters, *Kerouac*, 39, 52; Harold Norse biographical statement, box 2, folder 22, Carroll Papers; Norse, *Memoirs*, 95; Morgan, *I Celebrate Myself*, 47–48, 67–71; Kingsley Widmer, *Paul Goodman* (Boston: Twayne, 1980), 14, 38.

44. Jack Kerouac to Allen Ginsberg, September 18, 1948, folder 15, and August 17, 1945, folder 14, both in box 11, Allen Ginsberg Papers, Rare Book and Manuscript Library, Columbia University; Allen Ginsberg, journal, 110, box 4, folder 5, Ginsberg Papers, Stanford; Norse, *Memoirs*, 155–56, 177–84; *Paul Goodman Changed My Life*, directed by Jonathan Lee (New York: JSL Films, 2011), streaming on Netflix; Ronald Sukenick, *Down and In: Life in the Underground* (New York: Beech Tree Books, 1987), 23.

45. Widmer, *Paul Goodman*, 92–99; Judith Malina, *The Diaries of Judith Malina* (New York: Grove Press, 1984), 211.

46. Anaïs Nin, *The Diary of Anaïs Nin, 1947–1955* (New York: Harcourt Brace Jovanovich, 1974), 211–14, 215; Hamalian, *Life of Kenneth Rexroth*, 134, 153.

47. Simone de Beauvoir, *America Day by Day* (New York: Grove Press, 1953), 15–20, 70–75, 130–43. Dwight Macdonald recommended that she contact Rexroth, an "eccentric and genial poet" whose group of "anarchist bohemians" represented the leading West Coast intellectuals, "if only by default." She apparently rejected the idea, thus missing the opportunity to travel full circle through America's left-wing bohemia. In a letter to George Woodcock, the founder and editor of the antiwar paper *Now*, Macdonald further revealed both the ties and the divisions between bicoastal intellectuals in the 1930s, characterizing Rexroth as "a brilliant crackpot" with "imagination, wit, and a sense of the heart of the matter." Macdonald then added, "But he's also a kind of comic-strip anarchist in his wilder moments, and that kind of thing does no good, in print, either to him or to the ideals all three of us share." Dwight Macdonald, *A Moral Temper: The Letters of Dwight Macdonald*, ed. Michael Wreszin (Chicago: Ivan R. Dee, 2001), 136–39.

48. Judith Malina, "The Voyage," *Neurotica*, vol. 3 (Autumn 1948), 51–52; Malina, *Diaries*, 159, 211, 214, 234–35; Alice Denham, *Sleeping with Bad Boys: A Juicy Tell-All of Literary New York in the Fifties and Sixties* (New York: Book Republic Press, 2006), 9.

49. Allen Ginsberg, journal, 11–12, box 3, folder 10, and journal, 81, box 4, folder 8, both in Ginsberg Papers, Stanford; Jack Kerouac to Allen Ginsberg, September 23, 1945, folder 14, and September 18, 1948, folder 15, both in box 11, Ginsberg Papers, Columbia.

50. Jack Kerouac to Allen Ginsberg, undated postcard and letter [December 1948], box 11, folder 15, Ginsberg Papers, Columbia; Widmer, *Paul Goodman*, 97.

51. Norse, *Memoirs*, 155–56; Gruen, *Party's Over*, 218, 220; Mark Stevens and Annalyn Swan, *De Kooning: An American Master* (New York: Alfred A. Knopf, 2004), 364–65; Widmer, *Paul Goodman*, 97; Michael Hrebeniak, *Action Writing: Jack Kerouac's Wild Form* (Carbondale: Southern Illinois University Press, 2006), 1–6, 14, 130–46.

52. Holmes, *Go*, 310; Dan Wakefield, *New York in the Fifties* (New York: St. Martin's Griffin, 1992), 130–31.

53. Allen Ginsberg to Louis Ginsberg, undated [ca. 1948], box 7, folder 14, Ginsberg Papers, Columbia; Wetzsteon, *Republic of Dreams*, 472. Unfortunately, the text of Ginsberg's novel is not extant. See Morgan, *I Celebrate Myself*, 74.

54. Wakefield, *New York in the Fifties*, 80–88; Wetzsteon, *Republic of Dreams*, 472.

55. Jack Kerouac to Allen Ginsberg, note and clipping, undated [1950], box 11, folder 17, Ginsberg Papers, Columbia; Ellen Schrecker, *Many Are the Crimes: McCarthyism in America* (Boston: Little, Brown, 1998), 96–131, 211–20, 298, 317–40, 359–415; Steven Casey, "The Campaign to Sell a Harsh Peace for Germany to the American Public, 1944–1948," *History*, vol. 90, no. 297 (2005), 62–92; Westbrook Pegler, "Van Doren's Background," *Post-Standard* (Syracuse, NY), October 31, 1950, section 2, 11.

56. Irving Howe and Lewis Coser, *The American Communist Party: A Critical History* (New York: Praeger, rev. ed., 1962; first published 1957), 437–99; Michael Denning, *The Cultural Front: The Laboring of American Culture in the Twentieth Century* (London: Verso, 1997), 80, 462.

57. Kenneth Rexroth to Lawrence Lipton, January 15, 1953, Lawrence Lipton Papers, collection 819, Department of Special Collections, Charles E. Young Research Library, UCLA; Lawrence Lipton interview, 770–71, 803–11, 830, conducted by Donald Schippers, Oral History Department, UCLA, 1962. See also Shirley Triest to Kenneth Rexroth, February 5, 1937, box 30, folder 12, Kenneth Rexroth to Weldon Kees, undated [1939], undated [ca. 1940], January 12, 1940, and June 1941, box 23, folder 15, Audrey Goodfriend to Kenneth Rexroth, March 13, 1946, box 8, folder 3, Philip Lamantia to Kenneth Rexroth, August 3, 1948, box 12, folder 15, James T. Farrell to Kenneth Rexroth, February 14, 1948, July 7, 1948, and August 20, 1948, box 6, folder 11, Henry Miller to Kenneth Rexroth, January 16, 1945, box 16, folder 6, Marie Rexroth to Kenneth Rexroth, August 17, 1948, box 24, folder 5, all in Rexroth Papers. For Rexroth's correspondence with James Laughlin, 1937–1948, in which the two frequently mention interactions with a wide variety of leftist and cultural figures—from William Saroyan, Hilaire Belloc, and Tennessee Williams to Dwight Macdonald and his circle of Trotskyists—see box 13, folder 6, Rexroth Papers.

58. Frank Triest to Kenneth Rexroth, November 11, 1945, and May 18, 1946, both in box 30, folder 12, Rexroth Papers; Paul Goodman to Jackson Mac Low, February 7, 1943, box 17, folder 15, Jackson Mac Low Papers, MSS 0180, Mandeville Special Collections Library, UC San Diego; Widmer, *Paul Goodman*, 37–42; Hamalian, *Life of Kenneth Rexroth*, 99–129; Richard Cándida Smith, *Utopia and Dissent: Art, Poetry, and Politics in California* (Berkeley: University of California Press, 1995), 51–56.

59. Ellen Tallman, "My Stories with Robert Duncan," in *Robert Duncan and Denise Levertov: The Poetry of Politics, the Politics of Poetry*, ed. Albert Gelpi and Robert J. Bertholf (Stanford, CA:

Stanford University Press, 2006), 63; Kenneth Rexroth to Franklin Folsom [Writers Congress], May 12, 1941, Kenneth Rexroth to "Dear Jacobsen," July 12, 1946, and Kenneth Rexroth to Louis Brigante, July 16, 1950, all in box 23, folder 14, Rexroth Papers; Howe and Coser, *American Communist Party*, 99, 111, 311, 421.

60. Robert Duncan to "Dear Jack" [Jack Spicer], undated [1947], box 1, Robert Duncan Papers, BANC FILM 2053, Bancroft Library, UC Berkeley; Kenneth Rexroth, *Excerpts from a Life*, ed. Ekbert Faas (Santa Barbara, CA: Conjunctions Books, 1981), 58–61.

61. Paul Goodman to Kenneth Rexroth, undated letters [ca. 1948], box 8, folder 3, and Lawrence Lipton to Kenneth Rexroth, January 28, 1953, February 28, 1953, April 5 and 17, 1953, May 3 and 27, 1953, June 27, 1953, and October 15, 1953, box 14, folder 6, all in Rexroth Papers; Jackson Mac Low journal, January 9–February 15, 1948, folder 1, and September 9, 1949, folder 2, both in box 1, and Jackson Mac Low to Paul Goodman, February 5, 1943, box 17, folder 15, all in Mac Low Papers.

62. Robert Duncan to Jack Spicer, February 26, 1947, and undated [ca. 1947], box 1, and notebooks, box 2, all in Duncan Papers; Robert Duncan to Kenneth Rexroth, undated [1946], box 5, folder 18, Rexroth Papers; Allan Ginsberg to Lionel Trilling, August 17, 1945, and Louis Ginsberg to Allen Ginsberg, November 1, 1945, box 9, folder 13, both in Ginsberg Papers, Columbia; Lawrence Lipton interview, 187–224, 770, UCLA; Knute Stiles to Tram Combs, December 10, 1952, and May 1, 1952, box 3, folder 3, both in Tram Combs Papers, Mandeville Special Collections Library, UC San Diego.

63. Knute Stiles to Tram Combs, April 24, 1951, Combs Papers; Robert Duncan to Kenneth Rexroth, undated [ca. 1946], box 5, folder 18, Rexroth Papers.

64. Quoted in Gelpi and Bertholf, *Robert Duncan and Denise Levertov*, 11; Robert Duncan to Kenneth Rexroth, undated [1946], box 5, folder 18, Rexroth Papers.

65. Kenneth Rexroth to Robert Duncan, undated [1956], box 5, folder 18, Rexroth Papers.

66. Michael Harrington deftly characterized Ginsberg's blend of bohemianism and political consciousness: "He traces himself back, of course, to Walt Whitman and he has obvious affinities with the Bohemia of personal exploration typified by Henry Miller. But his penchant for organization and detail . . . was part of his radical political background. So in one aspect Ginsberg is a literary-political rebel on the model of the pre–World War I Villager. . . . The young who turned him into a guru tended to ignore his traditionalism and critical standards." Harrington, *Fragments of the Century*, 52. For examples of Ginsberg's left-wing political roots and activism, see Michael Harrington interview, November 19, 1982, folder 35, and George Rawick telephone interview, both in box 1, Isserman research files; Morgan, *I Celebrate Myself*, 5–6, 21, 31–32.

67. James Laughlin to Kenneth Rexroth, August 9, 1945, box 13, folder 5, Rexroth Papers; Paul Goodman to Paul Carroll, January 9, 1961, box 1, folder 48, Carroll Papers.

68. Paul Goodman, "Casper's Birthday," in *The Galley to Mytilene: Stories, 1949–1960*, ed. Taylor Stoehr (Santa Barbara, CA: Black Sparrow Press, 1980), 99–109. Goodman's anarchist ideal, to "increase intrinsic functioning and diminish extrinsic power," was a utopian call for life on a human scale, in which aesthetics and community took precedence over the dominant American consumerist-consumption notion of a high standard of living. As critic Kingsley Widmer notes, this ideal overshadowed broader themes of justice, freedom, and equality yet it did offer ambitious alternatives to capitalism and state power. In this sense, the San Remo scene was a synecdoche for the dialectic Goodman endorsed, where "depowering and liberating are not devices and dogmas but a philosophy." Widmer, *Paul Goodman*, 42–50. For a critique of the psychological embrace of community and identity as

a political stance, see Richard Sennett, *The Fall of Public Man* (New York: Alfred A. Knopf, 1977), 251–61.

69. Allen Ginsberg journal, 118, box 4, folder 5, and 67, folder 8, both in Ginsberg Papers, Stanford.

70. Morgan, *I Celebrate Myself*, 86; Allen Ginsberg journal, 69–70, 122, box 4, folder 5, Ginsberg Papers, Stanford.

71. Holmes, *Go*, 309–11.

72. Ibid., 35; Jack Kerouac to Allen Ginsberg, "December" [1948], box 11, folder 15, Ginsberg Papers, Columbia; John Malcolm Brinnin, *Dylan Thomas in America: An Intimate Journal* (Boston: Little, Brown, 1955), 13; Gruen, *Party's Over*, 219.

73. *Life* magazine made a habit of such flippant, inflammatory language, referring to recent arrivals in Washington Square as "art-struck invaders from surrounding Greenwich Village"—despite the square's longtime status as *part* of the Village, and the article's exultation of the neighborhood's literary claims to Mark Twain and Theodore Dreiser—and recalling Washington Square's associations with communism in the 1930s. Jackson Mac Low notebooks, 1949, folder 2, Mac Low Papers; Winthrop Sargeant, "Bernard Maybeck: He Is a Sage, a Dreamer, and Eccentric and California's Greatest Architect," May 17, 1948, 148, "Washington Square: Its North Side Homes Linger On, an Outpost of Patrician New York," August 14, 1950, 67–68, and Ruth Fischer, "Conspiracy Inside Communism," May 8, 1950, 103, all in *Life*.

74. Jack Kerouac to Allen Ginsberg, September 6, 1945, box 11, folder 14, Ginsberg Papers, Columbia.

75. Wetzsteon, *Republic of Dreams*, 430; Michael Hayward, "The Absorption of the Avant-Garde," chapter 4.0.0, *Unspeakable Visions: The Beat Generation and the Bohemian Dialectic*, August 1991, Simon Fraser University, www.sfu.ca/~hayward/UnspeakableVisions/Absorption .html.

76. While there was an increase in the number of nightspots in Greenwich Village in the 1950s, a shrinking percentage of their patrons actually lived in the Village. Its population of fifteen- to thirty-four-year-olds decreased between 1940 and 1960, due to rising rents. This stood in contrast to North Beach, which remained affordable throughout the 1950s and thus was maintained as a cohesive neighborhood and community. R. David Corwin, Jerome Krase, and Paula Hudis, *Greenwich Village: Statistical Trends and Observations* (New York: Department of Sociology, New York University, 1969), 3–5.

77. Henri Lenoir, "The Painting by Cornelius Sampson of the Habitués of the Black Cat Cafe in 1938," undated press release, vol. 1, Henri Lenoir Papers; San Francisco death certificate for Carl Haberkern, July 26, 1949, State of California, *California Death Index, 1940–1997* (Sacramento, CA: State of California Department of Health Services, Center for Health Statistics, n.d.).

78. Hamalian, *Life of Kenneth Rexroth*, 163, 213.

79. In 1940, Sol Stoumen married Gay Van Natta, who was among those listed on Cornelius Sampson's painting of Black Cat regulars. This is strong evidence for his familiarity with the WPA circles of which she was a part. "Black Cat Cafe Wins Right to Open, Pending a Hearing," October 25, 1949, "Black Cat Owner Sued," October 10, 1953, and "Black Cat Bar Litigation," March 20, 1954, all unpaginated *San Francisco Examiner* clippings, *Examiner* morgue, SFPL; US Bureau of the Census, "Supervisor's District no. 4, Enumeration District no. 38-26, San Francisco, CA," *Sixteenth Census of the United States: 1940*, 69-A, roll T627-317, National Archives, Washington, DC.

80. "Its Last Life," *San Francisco Chronicle*, October 25, 1963, unpaginated; Mildred Harcourt, "A Gallery with a Colorful Past," August 14, 1979, and "Black Cat Owner Defends Bohemians," January 29, 1957, both unpaginated *San Francisco Examiner* clippings, *Examiner* morgue, SFPL; "S.F. Lawyer Heads Jewish Congress," *Oakland Tribune*, December 7, 1958, 64; "Homosexuality Discussion Set," *Daily Review* (Hayward, CA), December 25, 1958, 23; "Pornography Bill Defeated by Assembly Committee, 7–5," *Bakersfield Californian*, May 2, 1961, 2; "Assessor Audit Suit Opposed," *Oakland Tribune*, March 2, 1966, 6-E; Morris Lowenthal to Milton Chernin, March 30, 1951, loyalty oath, carton 21, folder 47, BANC MSS 78/18, Bancroft Library, UC Berkeley; "Bride Not to Desert Career," *Oakland Tribune*, May 2, 1935, 22-B; Boyd, *Wide Open Town*, 170; Daniel Hurewitz, *Bohemian Los Angeles and the Making of Modern Politics* (Berkeley: University of California Press, 2007). Morris Lowenthal's spouse Juliet, the first woman to become a lawyer in Richmond, California, actively supported lesbian rights through the Daughters of Bilitis. Together, the Lowenthals also signed an amicus curiae brief to aid in the defense of a prosecuted lesbian bar, Mary's First and Last Chance, in the mid-1950s. Hurewitz similarly notes the intertwined histories of bohemianism, the Left, gay rights, and identity politics in midcentury Los Angeles.

81. Charters, *Kerouac*, 81–83, 110–12; Holmes, *Go*, 35, 182; Allen Ginsberg to John Clellon Holmes, "July" [1949], and John Clellon Holmes to Allen Ginsberg, June 14, 1949, box 1, folder 32, both in Ginsberg Papers, Stanford.

82. Jack Kerouac, *On the Road* (New York: Viking Press, 1957), 146–47.

83. Gerd Stern, "From Beat Scene Poet to Psychedelic Multimedia Artist in San Francisco and Beyond, 1948–1978," 16, 20, interview in 1996, conducted by Victoria Morris Byerly, Regional Oral History Office, Bancroft Library, UC Berkeley, 2001; Allen Ginsberg, *Journals: Early Fifties, Early Sixties*, ed. Gordon Ball (New York: Grove Press, 1977), 18; "Philip Lamantia (1998)," interview, in *San Francisco Beat*, 134–39.

84. "Philip Lamantia (1998)," 134.

85. "Lawrence Ferlinghetti (1969)," interview, in *San Francisco Beat*, 91, 93; Knute Stiles interview, 33–35, Ellingham research materials; Morgan, *Beat Generation in San Francisco*, 1.

86. Gruen, *Party's Over*, 43–49; *Obscene: A Portrait of Barney Rosset and Grove Press*, directed by Neil Ortenberg and Daniel O'Connor (New York: Double O Film Productions, 2007), streaming on Netflix; *Neurotica* (St. Louis), vol. 3 (Autumn 1948), vol. 5 (Autumn 1949), vol. 6 (Spring 1950), and vol. 7 (autumn, 1950); Michael Harrington notebook, "Me I: Village," box 3, folder 2, Harrington Papers; Jay Landesman, *Rebel without Applause* (New York: Paragon House, 1987), 43–70.

87. "Philip Lamantia (1998)," interview, in *San Francisco Beat*, 139; Morgan, *Beat Generation in New York*, 77–78; Jackson Mac Low to Bayard Rustin, "Statement on Civil Defense Drill Protest of June 15, 1955," box 32, folder 4, Mac Low Papers; Tram Combs to Bayard Rustin, August 2, 1957, Bayard Rustin to Tram Combs, August 13, 1957, and David McReynolds [*Liberation*] to Tram Combs, August 19, 1957, all in box 2, folder 10, Combs Papers; Herb Boyd, *Baldwin's Harlem: A Biography of James Baldwin* (New York: Atria Books, 2008), 80–81; James Laughlin to Marie Rexroth, undated [ca. 1944], folder 6, and James Laughlin to Kenneth Rexroth, "April 8" [ca. 1950], folder 7, both in box 13, Rexroth Papers; Hamalian, *Life of Kenneth Rexroth*, 156; Michael Kazin, *American Dreamers: How the Left Changed a Nation* (New York: Alfred A. Knopf, 2011), 180, 218. Even America's first listener-supported radio station, San Francisco's KPFA, had roots in this milieu, having grown, in part, out of Rexroth's Libertarian Circle. Moreover, Rustin himself got his start within the early Rebel Café, as a backup singer for Popular Front folksinger Josh White.

88. Marie Rexroth to Kenneth Rexroth, March 5, 1948, "Thursday" [ca. 1948], and August 17, 1948, all in box 24, folder 5, Rexroth Papers; Eileen Fantino Diaz interview, March 16, 1995, folder 15, and Mary Perot Nichols interview, March 16, 1995, folder 65, both in box 1, Isserman research files.

89. Dylan Foley, "Elizabeth Pollett, Novelist, Rest in Peace," June 23, 2012, *The Last Bohemians*, http://lastbohemians.blogspot.com/2012/06/elizabeth-pollet-novelist-rest-in-peace .html.

90. James Baldwin, *Notes of a Native Son* (Boston: Beacon Press, reprint, 1984; first published 1955), xv; James Baldwin, "Here Be Dragons," in *The Price of the Ticket: Collected Nonfiction, 1948–1985* (New York: St. Martin's / Marek, 1985), 686–87; Jennifer Guglielmo, *Living the Revolution: Italian Women's Resistance and Radicalism in New York City, 1880–1945* (Chapel Hill: University of North Carolina Press, 2010).

91. Anatole Broyard, "Reading and Writing: Perennial Bloom," *New York Times*, October 18, 1981, BR-13; Broyard, *Kafka Was the Rage*, 110–18.

92. James Laughlin to Kenneth Rexroth, "Thursday—NYC" [ca. 1945], box 13, folder 6, and Kenneth Rexroth to Carey McWilliams, July 28, 1955, box 17, folder 2, both in Rexroth Papers; Kenneth Rexroth to Lawrence Lipton, January 15, 1953, box 2, folder 5, Lipton Papers.

93. Walter Lowenfels to Kenneth Rexroth, March 17, 1937, box 14, folder 11, Rexroth Papers.

94. Allen Ginsberg journal, box 4, folder 8, series 2, Ginsberg Papers, Stanford; Brinnin, *Dylan Thomas in America*, 271–72; Norse, *Memoirs*, 185–94; Wetzsteon, *Republic of Dreams*, 471–84.

95. Allen Ginsberg to Paul Carroll, September 27, 1959, box 1, folder 44, Carroll Papers; Jack Kerouac to Allen Ginsberg, "March or April" [1952], box 11, folder 19, Ginsberg Papers, Columbia.

96. Maya Angelou, *The Collected Autobiographies of Maya Angelou* (New York: Modern Library, 2004), 163–64.

Chapter 3. Bop Apocalypse, Freedom Now!

1. Allan McMillan, "Allan's Alley: Notes of a Dawn Patroler," *New York Amsterdam News*, February 17, 1951, 22; Jeffrey H. Jackson, *Making Jazz French: Music and Modern Life in Interwar Paris* (Durham, NC: Duke University Press, 2003); Martha Biondi, *To Stand and Fight: The Struggle for Civil Rights in Postwar New York City* (Cambridge, MA: Harvard University Press, 2003), 188.

2. Biondi, *To Stand and Fight*, 186–90; Allan McMillan, "Allan's Alley: Cafe Society Intelligence," *New York Amsterdam News*, June 24, 1950, 30. Josephine Baker also successfully brought criminal charges against a belligerent patron in Los Angeles when he verbally assaulted her in a hotel lounge, again demonstrating her dedication to claiming black dignity in public spaces.

3. Allison Graham, *Framing the South: Hollywood, Television, and Race during the Civil Rights Struggle* (Baltimore: Johns Hopkins University Press, 2001); Court Carney, *Cuttin' Up: How Jazz Got America's Ear* (Lawrence: University Press of Kansas, 2009), 31–56.

4. Kenneth Rexroth to Eli Jacobsen [*sic*], December 12, 1946, box 23, folder 14, Kenneth Rexroth Papers, collection 175, Department of Special Collections, Charles E. Young Research Library, UCLA.

5. Grace Elizabeth Hale, *A Nation of Outsiders: How the Middle Class Fell in Love with Rebellion in Postwar America* (Oxford: Oxford University Press, 2011), 9–10, 118.

6. Barney Josephson, with Terry Trilling-Josephson, *Cafe Society: The Wrong Place for the Right People* (Urbana: University of Illinois Press, 2009), 242–43; Robert W. Cherny, William Issel, and Kieran Walsh Taylor, *American Labor and the Cold War: Grassroots Politics and Postwar Political Culture* (New Brunswick, NJ: Rutgers University Press, 2004), 207.

7. C. H. Garrigues, "A Decade of Jazz at the Blackhawk," *San Francisco Examiner*, March 1, 1959, unpaginated, *Examiner* morgue, San Francisco History Center, SFPL.

8. Black Hawk display ad, July 1, 1950, 6, and Hy Porter, "Acapulco Offering Draws 'Bay White Way,'" July 8, 1950, 16, both in *San Francisco News*.

9. Josephson, *Cafe Society*, 8–12, 39–40, 54–55.

10. Robin D. G. Kelley, *Thelonious Monk: The Life and Times of an American Original* (New York: Free Press, 2009), 226–27; Robert Shelton, "Jazz Man Is Changing His Beat: Charlie Mingus at Work on Story of His Hard Times," *New York Times*, August 27, 1962, 17.

11. Lorraine Gordon noted that her husband Max "began reinventing the Village Vanguard as a jazz club exclusively, more out of necessity than anything else. Max was finding it increasingly difficult to book the comics and nightclub performers who had carried the Vanguard." Yet the club continued its cabaret tradition, featuring satirists like Irwin Corey and Lenny Bruce. *Time* magazine stated: "The music rooms have taken away the nightclub audience, but nobody is exactly sure why. The 20% federal cabaret tax plainly had something to do with it (instrumental music only, without dancing or floor show, is not considered entertainment under the law, hence is tax-free)." Jesse H. Walker, "Theatricals," January 3, 1959, 11, and "Village Vanguard Newest Jazz Club," June 1, 1957, 15, both in *New York Amsterdam News*; "Rise of the Music Rooms," *Time*, May 27, 1957, 44–45; Lorraine Gordon, as told to Barry Singer, *Alive at the Village Vanguard: My Life In and Out of Jazz Time* (Milwaukee: Hal Leonard, 2006), 201.

12. Kelley, *Thelonious Monk*, 229; John S. Wilson, "'Village' Becomes Focal Center for Modern Jazz: Five Spot Cafe and the Half Note Spur Move Downtown," *New York Times*, October 27, 1960, 43; Chris DeVito, ed., *Coltrane on Coltrane: The John Coltrane Interviews* (Chicago: Chicago Review Press, 2010), 18–19; Amiri Baraka [LeRoi Jones], *The Autobiography of LeRoi Jones* (Chicago: Lawrence Hill Books, 1984), 235–36.

13. David Amram, *Offbeat: Collaborating with Jack Kerouac* (New York: Thunder's Mouth Press, 2002), 5; Kelley, *Thelonious Monk*, 227–28; Jesse H. Walker, "Theatricals," *New York Amsterdam News*, May 25, 1957, 16.

14. Ann Waldman, "Lineages and Legacies," in *Beat Down to Your Soul: What Was the Beat Generation?*, ed. Ann Charters (New York: Penguin Books, 2001), 593–96.

15. Allen Ginsberg, "4 AM, March 18, 1957," in *Journals: Mid-Fifties, 1954–1958*, ed. Gordon Ball (New York: HarperCollins, 1995), 84–85; Alice Denham, *Sleeping with Bad Boys: A Juicy Tell-All of Literary New York in the Fifties and Sixties* (New York: Book Republic Press, 2006), 103.

16. Hettie Jones, *How I Became Hettie Jones* (New York: E. P. Dutton, 1990), 34–36, 115.

17. Ibid., 233.

18. Charles Mingus to Langston Hughes, July 31, 1956, box 57, folder 19, Charles Mingus Collection, ML31.M56, Music Division, Library of Congress; Kelley, *Thelonious Monk*, 233–35.

19. Nat Hentoff, *The Jazz Life* (New York: Dial Press, 1961), 15, 21–22.

20. Earl Warren, *The Memoirs of Earl Warren* (Garden City, NY: Doubleday, 1977), 291.

21. Billie Holiday, with William Dufty, *Lady Sings the Blues* (New York: Penguin Books, 1984; first published 1956), 50–51, 94; Dizzy Gillespie, with Al Fraser, *To Be, or Not . . . to Bop*

(New York: Doubleday, 1979), 164; Robert George Reisner, *Bird: The Legend of Charlie Parker* (New York: Bonanza Books, 1962), 62.

22. Joyce Johnson, *Minor Characters* (Boston: Houghton Mifflin, 1983), 213–16; Baraka, *Autobiography of LeRoi Jones*, xxiii–xxiv, 279–80.

23. Hettie Jones to "Aunt Lee," "Weds. night" [ca. 1961], box 11, folder 12, and Hettie Jones to "Mother," undated [ca. 1959], box 54, folder 3, both in Hettie Jones Papers, Rare Book and Manuscript Library, Columbia University Library.

24. Charters, *Beat*, 279–80, 321, 619.

25. "Hot Five Jazz Club Faces New Charges," August 27, 1952, "Reopening of Notorious S.F. Bar Fought," October 8, 1954, and "'Red' Ferrari Must Close Bar Today," July 14, 1956, unpaginated clippings, all in *San Francisco Examiner*, Examiner morgue, SFPL. The Say When closed in June 1954 and Ciro's, in July 1956, both amid charges of mob ties, drug trafficking, stolen property, and violation of gun laws.

26. Don Steele, "Going Places," *Oakland Tribune*, November 7, 1956, 2-E; Eileen Kaufman, "Introduction," Beatitude Poetry, www.beatitudepoetry.com/introd.htm.

27. "Art Wanted It That Way," *Oakland Tribune*, June 2, 1966, 18-E; "Jazzmen Mourn Arthur Auerbach," June 2, 1966, Richard Hadlock, "How the Jazz Workshop Manages to Stay Alive," and Phillip Elwood, "Jazz Workshop Sold to Lou Ganapoler," October 27, 1963, all unpaginated clippings in *San Francisco Examiner*, Examiner morgue, SFPL. After Auerbach's untimely death from a heart attack in 1966, the club was sold to Lou Ganapoler, a former booking agent for the Village Vanguard and a friend of Max Gordon.

28. Bill Morgan, *The Beat Generation in San Francisco: A Literary Tour* (San Francisco: City Lights Books, 2003), 55–56; "Reviews in Brief," July 20, 1958, C-9, Russ Wilson, "World of Jazz," March 3, 1957, 6-B, and Russ Wilson, "Death Knell Sounds for Jazz Poetry," June 19, 1960, 18-B, all in *Oakland Tribune*.

29. Johnson, *Minor Characters*, 155; *The Beat Generation: An American Dream*, directed by Janet Forman (New York: Renaissance Motion Pictures, 1987), VHS.

30. Calvin Hernton, "Umbra: A Personal Recounting," 579–84, and Lorenzo Thomas, "Alea's Children: The Avant-Garde on the Lower East Side, 1960–1970," 573–78, both in *African American Review*, vol. 27, no. 4 (Winter 1993).

31. Baraka, *Autobiography of LeRoi Jones*, 219, 280; *Charles Mingus: Triumph of the Underdog*, directed by Don McGlyn (Newton, NJ: Shanachie Entertainment, 1998), DVD; Peter Orlovsky to Allen Ginsberg, undated [ca. 1958/59], box 4, folder 41, Allen Ginsberg Papers, M0733, Department of Special Collections, Stanford University Libraries.

32. Art D'Lugoff interview, 5–22, December 24, 1993, conducted by Trudy Balch, box 215, no. 3, **P, Oral Histories, NYPL; "The Reminiscences of Art D'Lugoff," 1–8, interviews on September 20 and November 6, 1996, conducted by Christiane Bird, Oral History Research Office, Columbia University, 1999.

33. Samuel Haynes, "Robeson Had 'Whole World in His Hands,'" *Baltimore Afro-American*, May 17, 1958, 1. D'Lugoff also worked as Robeson's personal manager for a time.

34. The hard work of remodeling the club, D'Lugoff later recalled, was how "I . . . developed my beard," referring to his renowned beatnik appearance. Tom Robbins, "Art D'Lugoff, Village Royalty, Gone Too Soon at 85," November 5, 2009, *Village Voice*, https://www.villagevoice.com/2009/11/05/art-dlugoff-village-royalty-gone-too-soon-at-85/; John Wilcock, *The Village Square* (New York: Lyle Stuart, 1961), 133; Art D'Lugoff oral history, 22–45, NYPL; "Reminiscences of Art D'Lugoff," 8–10, 18–19.

35. Liam Clancy, *The Mountain of the Women: Memoirs of an Irish Troubadour* (New York: Doubleday, 2002), 108, 199, 256–59; Nina Simone, with Stephen Cleary, *I Put a Spell on You: The Autobiography of Nina Simone* (New York: Da Capo Press, 1991), 67–70; "Reminiscences of Art D'Lugoff," 48–49; Robert Nemiroff, "The 101 'Final' Performances of *Sidney Brustein*," in Lorraine Hansberry, *"A Raisin in the Sun" and "The Sign in Sidney Brustein's Window"* (New York: 1st Vintage Books ed., 1995; first published 1966), 175, 207. D'Lugoff's brother Bert was one of the producers of Hansberry's play, as well as her personal physician.

36. Nina Simone, "Mississippi Goddam," *In Concert*, Phillips PHS 600-135, 1964. See also Ruth Feldstein, "'I Don't Trust You Anymore': Nina Simone, Culture, and Black Activism in the 1960s," *Journal of American History*, vol. 91, no. 4 (March 2005), 1349–79.

37. Simone, *I Put a Spell*, 95, 71, 101; Marc Myers, "Interview: Art D'Lugoff," October 13, 2008, *JazzWax*, www.jazzwax.com/2008/10/interview-art-d.html; "Nina Simone," in LaShonda Barnett, ed., *I Got Thunder: Black Women Songwriters on Their Craft* (Philadelphia: Thunder's Mouth Press, 2007), 152–53.

38. James Baldwin, *Another Country* (London: Corgi Books, 1962), 197.

39. Dizzy Gillespie both expressed his weariness with nightclubs as mere "places where they serve whiskey" and recognized that clubs like New York's Jazz Gallery could be transformed into miniature concert halls, where patrons "could hear good jazz in a different kind of format." Harold H. Hart, *Hart's Guide to New York City* (New York: Hart, 1964), 877, 918–19; Gillespie, *To Be, or Not*, 448.

40. Del J. Boubel, "Jazz Knight," July 15, 1961, and August 15, 1961, both unpaginated clippings in *S.F. Territorial News*, Periodicals Collection, San Francisco History Center, SFPL; Martin Williams, "A Night at the Five Spot (1964)," in Robert Gottlieb, ed., *Reading Jazz: A Gathering of Autobiography, Reportage, and Criticism from 1919 to Now* (New York: Pantheon Books, 1996), 683.

41. Ralph J. Gleason, "A New Jazz Experience at the Cellar—Three One-Acts," *San Francisco Chronicle*, January 15, 1961, 16; Williams, "Night at the Five Spot," 680–83; John S. Wilson, "'Village Becomes Focal Center for Modern Jazz: Five Spot Café and the Half Note Spur Move Downtown," *New York Times*, October 27, 1960, 43.

42. Williams, "Night at the Five Spot," 684; Jones, *How I Became Hettie*, 34.

43. Jerry Kamstra, "San Francisco Jazz in the Old Days," *San Francisco Bay Guardian*, November 1, 1972, 7, 9.

44. Baraka, *Autobiography of LeRoi Jones*, 77–78, 83, 270.

45. Ralph J. Gleason, ed., *Jam Session: An Anthology of Jazz* (London: Jazz Book Club, 1961), 229; LeRoi Jones, *Blues People: Negro Music in White America* (New York: William Morrow, 1963), 82–86, 145–51.

46. One fan, who was studying for the priesthood, was active in this campaign, sending black-market jazz recordings to a pen pal in East Germany, who sought them as symbols of freedom and individuality. The fan requested an autographed photo for his friend behind the Iron Curtain, which Brubeck sent. Dorothy Radulski to Dave Brubeck, July 14, 1958, box 1, 1958: P–S, Wally Pyip Jr. to Dave Brubeck, January 24, 1960, box 2, 1960: L–R, and Richard J. Shmaruk to Dave Brubeck, April 18, 1960, box 2, 1960: S–Z, all in series 1.C, Dave Brubeck Papers, University of the Pacific, Stockton, California.

47. Clipping fragment, March 13, 1960, Black Hawk envelope, café file, *Examiner* morgue, SFPL.

48. Eric Porter, *What's This Thing Called Jazz?: African American Musicians as Artists, Critics, and Activists* (Berkeley: University of California Press, 2002), 102.

49. Although the book was unpublished until 1971, it was largely written between 1954 and 1962, in collaboration with Louis Lomax, and therefore significantly reflects Mingus's pre-1960s views. Brian Priestley, *Mingus: A Critical Biography* (New York: Da Capo Press, 1983), 1–3, 18, 50; Charles Mingus, *Beneath the Underdog: His World as Composed by Mingus*, ed. Nel King (New York: Alfred A. Knopf, 1971), 52, 298; Janet Coleman and Al Young, *Mingus/Mingus: Two Memoirs* (Berkeley: Creative Arts, 1989), 4; Shelton, "Jazz Man."

50. Mingus's stage patter also revealed his performativity, as seen in one San Francisco show, where he berated a white band member for having caused trouble on a nonexistent southern tour. When corrected, Mingus responded, "Don't mess with my act!" Priestley, *Mingus*, 64–65, 78, 41–42, 86–87; Porter, *What's This Thing*, 128; Nat Hentoff, "Charles Mingus," *Down Beat*, January 11, 1956, 8.

51. Mingus, *Beneath the Underdog*, 191; Shelton, "Jazz Man."

52. Mingus, *Beneath the Underdog*, 348; Priestley, *Mingus*, 43, 83, 88–94; Jesse H. Walker, "Theatricals," *New York Amsterdam News*, May 25, 1957, 16; L. Gordon, *Alive at the Village Vanguard*, 223–24. Lorraine Gordon emphasized Mingus's larger-than-life appetites by describing him eating a package of raw hamburger in the Vanguard's kitchen one night, suggesting that it may have had something to do with his death from Lou Gehrig's disease. (It did not.) Whether this story is true is less important than her choice to include it in her memoir, which shows the continued power of black jazzmen as mythical figures.

53. Janet Coleman remembered Mingus as a complicated but caring friend who both offered (facetiously) to "put me out" as her pimp and scolded comedian Lenny Bruce for using the word "cunt" while the three were in a Village bar. Despite Mingus's four failed marriages, Coleman insisted that Mingus maintained a utopian view of romantic relationships, which she found to be "old-fashioned, macho, idealistic and reassuring." Celia and Charles Mingus to Ralph Gleason, September 26, 1956, and June 29, 1956, Ralph Gleason to Charles and Celia Mingus, September 14, 1955, and August 14, 1956, all in box 57, folder 19, Mingus Collection, Library of Congress; Priestley, *Mingus*, 43–46; Mingus, *Beneath the Underdog*, 294–95; Coleman and Young, *Mingus/Mingus*, 29–30.

54. Mingus, *Beneath the Underdog*, 4–5, 176–78; Coleman and Young, *Mingus/Mingus*, 4, 26.

55. Scott Saul, "Outrageous Freedom: Charles Mingus and the Invention of the Jazz Workshop," *American Quarterly*, vol. 53, no. 3 (September 2001), 387–419; Diane Dorr-Dorynek, "Mingus," in *The Jazz Word*, ed. Dom Cerulli, Burt Korall, and Mort Nasatir (New York: Da Capo Press, paperback ed., 1987; first published 1960), 14–15.

56. This interpretation relies heavily on Saul, "Outrageous Freedom." See also "Writings by CM, with *Beneath the Underdog*," 845, box 45, folder 10, Mingus Collection.

57. Laura Mulvey, *Visual and Other Pleasures* (Bloomington: Indiana University Press, 1989), 14–26.

58. Jack Kerouac, *On the Road* (New York: Viking Press, 14th printing, 1971; first published 1957), 180–81, 194–203.

59. Other examples of Kerouac's vision metaphor include a scene in the bohemian Black Mask bar, where the "leader of the subterraneans" sat with "head thrown back thin dark eyes watching everybody as if in sudden slow astonishment." Even the main protagonist's name, Leo Percepied, is an elaborate pun on "perception" and "pie-eyed," a common 1950s term meaning drunk. Jon Panish, *The Color of Jazz: Race and Representation in Postwar American Culture* (Jackson: University Press of Mississippi, 1997), 20, 59, 140; Jack Kerouac, *The Subterraneans* (New York: Grove Press, 1958), 4, 14, 84, 96.

60. Jack Lind, "When Jazz Was King," *North Beach Magazine*, vol. 1, no. 2 (Fall 1985), 10; Morgan, *Beat Generation*, 134; Amram, *Offbeat*, 73. David Amram asserts that Dizzy Gillespie thought Kerouac was "one of the first to understand what Bird and I were doing." See also Jack Kerouac, "Origins of the Beat Generation," in *On Bohemia: The Code of the Self-Exiled*, ed. Cesar Grana and Marigay Grana (New Brunswick, NJ: Transaction, 1990), 198.

61. Kerouac, *On the Road*, 204–6.

62. Live jazz improvisation fits into the dialectic's basic schema of thesis/antithesis/synthesis as follows. The musicians propose a theme (*thesis*), understood by them as an expression of self, that is subsequently understood by listeners as their own subjective experience (*antithesis*). Performers and audiences finally become aware of this tension and seek to transcend it through their interaction (*synthesis*), an unstable state that is continually renewed with each new improvisatory theme.

63. Eric Lott, *Love and Theft: Blackface Minstrelsy and the American Working Class* (New York: Oxford University Press, 1993), 93–95; Ronald Radano, *Lying Up a Nation: Race and Black Music* (Chicago: University of Chicago Press, 2003), 19–44; Paul Gilroy, *The Black Atlantic: Modernity and Double Consciousness* (Cambridge, MA: Harvard University Press, 1993), 1–5, 19.

64. Mingus, *Beneath the Underdog*, 158–59; Gillespie, *To Be or Not*, 242–49; "Miles Davis," from Miles Davis, *Miles: The Autobiography*, reprinted in Gottlieb, *Reading Jazz*, 256–58; Eric Hobsbawm, *The Jazz Scene* (New York: Pantheon Books, 1993), 140–62, 170–93.

65. While jazz was "an exploration in public," as saxophonist Jackie Kelso insisted, "if you're really attending to your business, you are not at all concerned with whether or not your offering is being consumed by those people out there." From the audience "you get the energy" but not the content. Jackie Kelso interview, 109–10, in 1993, conducted by Steven L. Isoardi, Oral History Program, UCLA; Kenneth Rexroth, "Some Thoughts on Jazz as Music, as Revolt, as Mystique," *Bird in the Bush* (New York: New Directions, 1959), 40; Porter, *What's This Thing*, 240–86.

66. Pony Poindexter epitomized this trend when he leveled the most heinous insult he could muster against Richard Nixon, pegging him as a racist "faggot." Norwood "Pony" Poindexter, *The Pony Express: Memoirs of a Jazz Musician* (Frankfurt, Germany: JAS, 1985), 77.

67. Reisner, *Bird*, 51. Art Blakey's comments notwithstanding, there is substantial evidence that Charles Parker enjoyed a racially diverse audience. See James Baldwin, "Sonny's Blues," in Herbert Gold, ed., *Fiction of the Fifties: A Decade of American Writing* (New York: Doubleday, 1959), 31–64; John Williams, *Night Song* (Chatham, NJ: Chatham Bookseller, 1961); Dan Burley, "Back Door Stuff: Introducing Bleep, the Blop," *New York Amsterdam News*, March 8, 1947, 19; Meredith Johns, "Parker's 'Mood Music' Is Out of This World," October 14, 1950, 20, and "Death Of 'Yardbird' Parker May Affect Bebop's Fight to 'Live': New York (Special)," March 26, 1955, 6, both in *Chicago Defender*.

68. Poindexter, *Pony Express*, 44–45, 56, 71–72; Louise Davis Stone, "Theater Wing," *Chicago Defender*, August 8, 1964, 10; Orrin Keepnews, *The View from Within: Jazz Writings, 1948–1987* (New York: Oxford University Press, 1988), 123.

69. Kenneth Rexroth to Lawrence Lipton, November 18, 1957, box 2, folder 6, Lawrence Lipton Papers, collection 819, Department of Special Collections, Charles E. Young Research Library, UCLA; "Writings by CM," 747, box 45, folder 10, and 570, folder 8, and Charles Mingus to Max L. Arons (AFM), undated [ca. 1961], box 45, folder 3, all in Mingus Collection.

70. See Penny Von Eschen, *Satchmo Blows Up the World: Jazz Ambassadors Play the Cold War* (Cambridge, MA: Harvard University Press, 2004); Mary L. Dudziak, *Cold War Civil*

Rights: Race and the Image of American Democracy (Princeton, NJ: Princeton University Press, 2000); John Tomlinson, *Cultural Imperialism: A Critical Introduction* (Baltimore: Johns Hopkins University Press, 1991).

71. Poindexter, *Pony Express*, 70, 163–68.

72. One journalist compared the debates over John Coltrane's music to "some of the truculent, hysterical aspects of political arguments in neighborhood bars." Poindexter, *Pony Express*, 147; Lind, "When Jazz Was King," 10; DeVito, *Coltrane on Coltrane*, 229.

73. DeVito, *Coltrane on Coltrane*, 9, 30, 175–82, 201, 221, 263, 283–84; George J. Bennett, "Integration through Jazz," *Baltimore Afro-American*, September 6, 1955, 7. Coltrane's friend was August Blume, who founded the Interracial Jazz Society as a successful response to a 1955 Baltimore law segregating nightclubs.

74. This cultural phenomenon paralleled the political sphere, as seen in the association of the civil rights movement with male leaders like Martin Luther King Jr., while grassroots activists such as Ella Baker and Fannie Lou Hamer were largely ignored. See Chana Kai Lee, *For Freedom's Sake: The Life of Fannie Lou Hamer* (Urbana: University of Illinois Press, 1999); Charles Payne, *I've Got the Light of Freedom: The Organizing Tradition and the Mississippi Freedom Struggle* (Berkeley: University of California Press, 1995).

75. "Odetta ([born] December 31, 1930)," in Barnett, *I Got Thunder*, 177; "Folk Singer Odetta Back to Ash Grove," *Los Angeles Sentinel*, February 18, 1960, C-1; Dean Gitter, "Odetta Biography," liner notes for *Sings Ballads and Blues*, Tradition TLP 1010, 1956, LP; Michael Denning, *The Cultural Front: The Laboring of American Culture in the Twentieth Century* (London: Verso, 1997), 360; Maya Angelou, *The Collected Autobiographies of Maya Angelou* (New York: Modern Library, 2004), 452–60; "'Mambo King' Stars at Downbeat Club," *San Francisco News*, March 13, 1954, 4; James Gavin, *Intimate Nights: The Golden Age of New York Cabaret* (New York: Grove Weidenfeld, 1991), 120; "Biography," Maya Angelou, http://mayaangelou.com/bio/; Henry Louis Gates Jr., *Thirteen Ways of Looking at a Black Man* (New York: Random House, 1997), 159–61; Max Gordon, *Live at the Village Vanguard* (New York: St. Martin's Press, 1980), 89; "Belafonte's Second Try," *Oakland Tribune*, June 16, 1957, 2-B; Maurice Zolotow, "Belafonte," *American Weekly*, May 10, 1959, 11–13; Sally Vincent, "What Makes Harry Wild," *Guardian*, November 16, 1996, B-13.

76. Nat Hentoff, *Free Speech for Me—but Not for Thee: How the American Left and Right Relentlessly Censor Each Other* (New York: HarperCollins, 1992), 326; Kerouac, *On the Road*, 106; Johnson, *Minor Characters*, 231; Herb Caen, *Only in San Francisco* (New York: Doubleday, 1960), 251–52.

77. This network of clubs and musicians was connected by the Associated Booking Company (ABC) and its rival agency, MCA. Ironically, the circuit was largely dominated by one man: ABC owner Joe Glaser. Glaser, who started in the cabaret business in Chicago in the 1920s, managed Louis Armstrong for over three decades, while controlling the trumpeter's funds with infamous paternalism. Denounced by Barney Josephson as a racist misogynist with a criminal past, yet praised by Billie Holiday as a caring friend, it is difficult to disentangle the man from the myth. It is a small but telling detail that ABC itineraries sent to Dave Brubeck throughout the 1950s generally included the names of the venues in New York City and San Francisco, but other tour stops simply listed the city and the date. Chet Baker, *As Though I Had Wings: The Lost Memoir* (New York: St. Martin's Press, 1997), 64–65; Gillespie, *To Be or Not*, 296, 446; M. Gordon, *Live at the Village Vanguard*, 79–83; Holiday, *Lady Sings the Blues*, 34–41, 63–69, 104–16; Josephson, *Cafe Society*, 58–59; "Anita O'Day," in Gottlieb,

Reading Jazz, 191–92; Bert Block (ABC) to Dave Brubeck, August 27, 1954, box 1, folder 4, series 1.A, Brubeck Papers.

78. Paul Desmond to "Dad," "Monday" [ca. 1953], box 1, folder 4, Desmond Papers; Larry Bennett (ABC) to Dave Brubeck, January 26, 1956, box 1, folder 39, series 1.A, Brubeck Papers.

79. Ralph Gleason, "You Can't Play Here," This World, *San Francisco Chronicle*, September 21, 1958, 4; Ralph Gleason, "An Appeal from Dave Brubeck," February 18, 1960, 12–13, and "Perspectives," March 17, 1960, 43, both in *Downbeat*. See also various clippings, 1959–1960, series 1.E, Brubeck Papers, especially *New York Post*, February 24, 1959, and *Jet*, April 30, 1959, both unpaginated.

80. Von Eschen, *Satchmo*, 48; Stephen A. Crist, "Jazz as Democracy?: Dave Brubeck and Cold War Politics," *Journal of Musicology*, vol. 26, no. 2 (Spring 2009), 133–74.

81. B. J. Furgerson to Dave Brubeck, October 22, 1957, box 1, 1957: A–I, series 1.C, Brubeck Papers.

82. Howard Zinn, *SNCC: The New Abolitionists* (Boston: Beacon Press, 1964), 16; Gleason, "Appeal from Dave Brubeck"; Holiday, *Lady Sings the Blues*, 70–82; Jackie Kelso interview, UCLA; Poindexter, *Pony Express*, 87–88, 196–97. Poindexter's memoir described southern nightclubs in detail, and they were very similar to his experiences in the north. For black musicians, the difference came when they left the club, with meals and accommodations being hard to find.

83. Terea Hall Pitman, Everett P. Brandon, and Ellis H. Casson (NAACP) to Dave Brubeck, January 13, 1960, box 2, 1960: A–F, series 1.C, Brubeck Papers. See also Pamela Marsh Markmann, "Brubeck's Stand," letters to the editor, *San Francisco Chronicle*, January 19, 1960, 24.

84. George E. Pitts, "Give Brubeck Credit for a Slap at Bias," *Pittsburgh Courier*, January 13, 1960, unpaginated clipping in series 1.E, Brubeck Papers; Gleason, "Appeal from Dave Brubeck."

85. Zinn, *SNCC*, 17.

86. Ted Sirota, "Max Roach," November 17, 2011, Ted Sirota Music, www.tedsirota.com/music/max-roach; Ingrid Monson, *Freedom Sounds: Civil Rights Call Out to Jazz and Africa* (New York: Oxford University Press, 2007), 171–81. Monson offers a thorough examination of both the political and musical statements of *We Insist!*

87. Nat Hentoff, liner notes, *Charles Mingus Presents Charles Mingus*, Candid Records, LC 0585, 1997, CD, recorded in 1960.

88. Ibid.; Dave Hepburn, "Mingus Leaves United States, Will Live in Majorca," *New York Amsterdam News*, September 8, 1962, 18.

89. LeRoi Jones echoed this sentiment, declaring that cool jazz was a reaction to bebop separatism—and therefore represented the intellectualization of bop, as seen in Brubeck's popularity with college kids—but it was not a serious popular movement among black audiences (despite Miles Davis's own popularity). "Writings by CM," 199–202, box 45, folder 5, and 842–46, folder 10, Mingus Collection; Mingus, *Beneath the Underdog*, 188–89; Jones, *Blues People*, 204–14.

90. Charles Mingus to "Dear Max" [Max Gordon], undated [ca. 1965], box 54, folder 15, Mingus Collection; Mingus, *Beneath the Underdog*, 191. See also Timothy B. Tyson, *Radio Free Dixie: Robert F. Williams and the Roots of Black Power* (Chapel Hill: University of North Carolina Press, 1999).

91. Max Roach, quoted in Sirota, "Max Roach."

92. Farah Jasmine Griffin, *If You Can't Be Free, Be a Mystery: In Search of Billie Holiday* (New York: Free Press, 2001), 156–58; "Nina Simone," in Barnett, *I Got Thunder*, 146–47.

93. The explicit goal of Robin D. G. Kelley's biography of Thelonious Monk was to reveal the living human being behind the mysterious "high priest of bop." When I asked Lorraine Gordon, herself a politically active, progressive supporter of black rights—as well as a veteran of the jazz business and Monk's earliest press agent—how she felt about Kelley's praise for herself and her husband Max as strong supporters of the pianist, she responded with disapproval, complaining that Kelley's book had "demystified Monk." Author's interview with Lorraine Gordon, April 22, 2011, at the Village Vanguard, New York City.

94. Johnson, *Minor Characters*, 211.

95. Michael Magee, "Tribes of New York: Frank O'Hara, Amiri Baraka, and the Poetics of the Five Spot," *Contemporary Literature*, vol. 42, no. 4 (Winter 2001), 694–726; Baraka, *Autobiography of LeRoi Jones*, 234.

96. The Freedom Riders themselves had direct ties to the nightclub underground through one of their own, Bill Svanoe, who later formed the Rooftop Singers with Erik Darling, Pete Seeger's replacement in the Weavers. Svanoe's wife, Joan Darling, was also a member of a politically conscious satirical troupe, the Living Premise. Ingrid Monson, "Revisited!: The *Freedom Now Suite*," September 1, 2001, *JazzTimes*, http://jazztimes.com/articles/20130 -revisited-the-freedom-now-suite/; Stephen E. Kercher, *Revel with a Cause: Liberal Satire in Postwar America* (Chicago: University of Chicago Press, 2006), 263.

97. Art D'Lugoff oral history, 40, NYPL; "Reminiscences of Art D'Lugoff," 36–37; "Music In and Out of New York," *New York Times*, June 16, 1963, 98; Monson, *Freedom Sounds*, 158–59, 165; Kelley, *Thelonious Monk*, 293; Angelou, *Collected Autobiographies*, 702–3, 729, 735; Simone, *I Put a Spell*, 71, 101; press releases and photos, box 18, folder 6, and box 50, folder 20, and Ivan Black to Charles McHarry, press release, March 26, 1965, box 9, folder 12, all in Ivan Black Papers, JPB 06-20, Music Division, NYPL; Myers, "Interview: Art D'Lugoff"; Robert Healy, "Wallace Silent as Marchers Enter City," *Boston Globe*, March 25, 1965, 1. For a thorough and nuanced local study of the protests, see J. Mills Thornton III, *Dividing Lines: Municipal Politics and the Struggle for Civil Rights in Montgomery, Birmingham, and Selma* (Tuscaloosa: University of Alabama Press, 2002). Angelou also recalled *We Insist!* being smuggled into South Africa, as it was deemed a work of political subversion.

98. Ralph J. Gleason, "On and Off the Record," This World, June 18, 1961, 31, "Charles Is Riding the Crest of Several Waves Simultaneously," January 8, 1961, 15, and "Jazz Clubs Play for CORE Riders," June 27, 1961, 35, all in *San Francisco Chronicle*.

99. A. Philip Randolph credited Brubeck with raising "hundreds of thousands of dollars for the civil rights movement." Charmian Slade to Robert Bundy, September 24, 1963, folder 41, Bob Bundy to Dave Brubeck, September 26, 1963, folder 5, and A. Philip Randolph to Dave Brubeck, July 11, 1963, folder 9, all in box 6, Charles H. Boyle (Highlander Folk School) to Dave and Iola Brubeck, July 15, 1961, and Charles H. Boyle to Dave Brubeck, May 25, 1961, both in box 5, folder 10, C. Conrad Browne (Highlander Folk School) to Dave Brubeck, September 11, 1964, folder 12, and Iola Brubeck to Oscar Cohen, November 13, 1964, folder 38, both in box 8, all in series 1.A, Brubeck Papers; "Sit-In Benefit Bill Headed by Monk, Mingus," *Baltimore Afro-American*, February 2, 1963, 11; Ingrid Monson, "Monk Meets SNCC," in "New Perspectives on Thelonious Monk," *Black Music Research Journal*, vol. 19, no. 2 (Autumn 1999), 187–200.

100. Lorraine Hansberry and Robert Nemiroff to Dave Brubeck, March 6, 1963, and Theodore Bikel to Dave Brubeck, May 27, 1963, both in box 6, folder 9, series 1.A, Brubeck

Papers; "Reminiscences of Art D'Lugoff," 18; "Hearings Attacked at Two Rallies Here," *New York Times*, August 18, 1955, 14; "CORE Benefit at Five-Spot, Sun. Oct. 27," press release, 1963, box 13, folder 21, "SNCC," box 33, folders 14–18, and photos, box 50, folder 20, all in Black Papers.

101. Dave Brubeck to Phyllis Elkind, May 18, 1965, folder 34, and Dave Brubeck to Quin McLoughlin (CORE), August 11, 1965, folder 35, both in box 9, series 1.A, Brubeck Papers; Michael Levin, "Performer Dave Brubeck Speaks on Jazz Role," *Purdue (IN) Exponent*, October 15, 1968, unpaginated clipping, box 7, folder 17, series 1.D, Brubeck Papers.

102. Ed Sanders to Lawrence Ferlinghetti, January 9, 1964, September 19, 1961, May 15, 1962, and undated, box 11, folder 31, City Lights Books records, BANC MSS 72/107c, Bancroft Library, UC Berkeley; Paul Krassner, *Confessions of a Raving, Unconfined Nut: Misadventures in the Counter-Culture* (New York: Simon & Schuster, 1993), 35.

103. Sam Ridge, "Jazzville," vol. 1, no. 6 (January 6–13, 1965), 6, and vol. 1, no. 9 (February 3–9, 1965), 4, "Beatles Called a Red Menace," vol. 1, no. 12 (February 24–March 2, 1965), 4, Sam Ridge, "Jazzville," "Bradley Denies CORE Report," and "Homosexual Documentaries Set for Showing Soon," all in vol. 1, no. 5 (December 21–27, 1964), 4, and various articles and display ads in vol. 1, no. 11 (February 17–23, 1965) and vol. 1, no. 13 (March 3–9, 1965), all in (San Francisco) *Open City Press*, San Francisco History Center, SFPL.

Chapter 4. Beatniks and Blabbermouths, Bartok and Bar Talk

1. Ralph J. Gleason, "A Few Words in Defense of the Lowly Saloon," This World, *San Francisco Chronicle*, February 5, 1961, 25.

2. Brett Miller, "*Chelsea 8*: Political Poetry at Midcentury," in *Robert Duncan and Denise Levertov: The Poetry of Politics, the Politics of Poetry*, ed. Albert Gelpi and Robert J. Bertholf (Stanford, CA: Stanford University Press, 2006), 100–102.

3. "More Politics Than Poetry," *Washington Post and Times Herald*, October 12, 1954, 14; Margot Canaday, *The Straight State: Sexuality and Citizenship in Twentieth-Century America* (Princeton, NJ: Princeton University Press, 2009); Robin Blaser to Jack Spicer, October 23, 1950, Jack Spicer Papers, BANC MSS 2004/209, Bancroft Library, UC Berkeley; Lawrence Ferlinghetti to Kenneth Rexroth, "May 29" [ca. 1952], box 6, folder 13, Kenneth Rexroth Papers, collection 175, Department of Special Collections, Charles E. Young Research Library, UCLA; Nan Alamilla Boyd, *Wide Open Town: A History of Queer San Francisco to 1965* (Berkeley: University of California Press, 2003), 83.

4. Allen Brown, "Life and Love Among the Beatniks," This World, *San Francisco Chronicle*, June 22, 1958, 4.

5. Timothy Miller, *The Quest for Utopia in Twentieth-Century America, Volume I: 1900–1960* (Syracuse, NY: Syracuse University Press, 1998). Miller defines intentional communities by seven criteria: a common purpose separated from dominant society; self-denial in the group interest; geographic proximity; personal interaction; economic sharing; real existence; and a critical mass of at least five nonfamilial members (xx–xxii).

6. Knute Stiles interview, 69–70, May 30, 1982, conducted by Lewis Ellingham, at the East–West House, 733 Baker Street, San Francisco, box 4, folder 7, Lewis Ellingham's *Poet Be Like God* research materials, MSS 126, Special Collections and Archives, UC San Diego, courtesy of the Poetry Collection of the University Libraries, University at Buffalo, SUNY; Leo Krikorian interview in *The Beach*, directed by Mary Kerr (San Francisco: CA Palm, 1995), DVD; Jack Lind, *Leo's Place: An Oral History of the Beats in San Francisco's North Beach* (Søborg, Denmark: Det Danske Idéselskab, 1998), 23–24; Bill Morgan, *The Beat*

Generation in San Francisco: A Literary Tour (San Francisco: City Lights Books, 2003), 58–59.

7. US Bureau of the Census, "Supervisor's District no. 9, Enumeration District no. 10-93, Fowler (Fresno), CA," *Sixteenth Census of the United States: 1940*, 8-B, roll T627-00204, National Archives, Washington, DC; Jack Lind, "Paris, North Beach," *North Beach Magazine*, vol. 2, no. 3 (Fall 1986), 10–11, 35; Leo Krikorian interview in *The Beach*; Knute Stiles interview, Ellingham research materials; "List or Manifest of Aliens Employed on the Vessel as Members of Crew, SS *Marine Runner*, sailing from port of Nagoya, Japan, January 14, 1952, arriving at San Francisco, California, January 30, 1952," M1416:154, National Archives, Washington, DC

8. Leo Krikorian interview in *The Beach*; Lind, *Leo's Place*, 58, 24–27, 43, 31–34; Knute Stiles to Tram Combs, March 24, 1954, box 3, folder 3, Tram Combs Papers, Mandeville Special Collections Library, UC San Diego.

9. Knute Stiles to Tram Combs, March 24, 1954, Combs Papers; Knute Stiles interview, 1, Ellingham research materials.

10. Knute Stiles interview, 5–6, Ellingham research materials.

11. The Art Institute, originally called the California School of Fine Arts, was in the tradition of San Francisco's avant-gardism and had counted Diego Rivera among its faculty in the 1930s. Robert Duncan and Jack Spicer each had a radical background: Spicer's father had been in the IWW, and Duncan was a Trotskyist-anarchist veteran of the 1930s Left. Both critiqued the communists for their sexual prudishness, and Spicer was a strong proponent of the democratization of culture. Lewis Ellingham and Kevin Killian, *Poet Be Like God: Jack Spicer and the San Francisco Renaissance* (Hanover, NH: University Press of New England, 1998), 49–52; Robert Duncan interview, January 7, 1983, in San Francisco, box 5, folder 16, and Knute Stiles interview, 13, 19, both in Ellingham research materials.

12. Brown, "Life and Love"; Knute Stiles interview, 21–22, Ellingham research materials; Lind, *Leo's Place*, 18.

13. Knute Stiles interview, 22–23, 25, 36, Ellingham research materials.

14. The bartenders at the San Remo often wavered back and forth from protective of their patrons to hostile. While James Baldwin remembered these Italian Greenwich Villagers shielding him from a racist mob, Ronald Sukenick and Judith Malina each reported an incident in which co-owner and bartender John Santini brutally beat a customer unconscious, as well as other examples of tough bartenders. Judith Malina, *The Diaries of Judith Malina* (New York: Grove Press, 1984), 246; Ronald Sukenick, *Down and In: Life in the Underground* (New York: Beech Tree Books, 1987), 22–24.

15. In their capacity as public hosts, Stiles and Krikorian developed a division of labor that utilized their respective social skills. Stiles later recalled: "Krikorian and I agreed that I knew more people than he did so I would attend every night until we built up a clientele. And he would work during the day, do the clean-up and the buying; take care of the day crowd. . . . And actually after the habitués had gradually assembled I think Krikorian became . . . as popular as me in his way." Knute Stiles to Tram Combs, March 24, 1954, Combs Papers; Knute Stiles interview, 22–25, 36, Ellingham research materials; Lind, *Leo's Place*, 36; Dick Nolan, "Bulletin from Bohemia," *San Francisco Examiner*, April 22, 1958, unpaginated clipping, *Examiner* morgue, San Francisco History Center, SFPL.

16. Morgan, *Beat Generation in San Francisco*, 58–59; Ellingham and Killian, *Poet Be Like God*, 99; Ralph Gleason, "The Real Beatniks Flee Pasadena, North Beach," *Independent Star-News* (Los Angeles), April 4, 1960, 2–3.

17. Brown, "Life and Love"; Francis J. Rigney and L. Douglas Smith, *The Real Bohemia: A Sociological and Psychological Study of the "Beats"* (New York: Basic Books, 1961), 5; Leo Krikorian interview in *The Beach*.

18. Lind, *Leo's Place*, 38. Bohemians read local papers, as well as national magazines like *Time* and leftist-liberal journals, such as the *Nation* or *Partisan Review*. Television viewing was infrequent and largely limited to watching baseball games in bars. Radio, with stations such as New York City's WBAI and San Francisco's KPFA or KJAZ, was the most common form of electronic media. The more politically conscious subterraneans, like Allen Ginsberg, also read foreign journals and little magazines. See Allen Ginsberg to Louis Ginsberg, January 14, 1957, and Allen Ginsberg to "Dear Lou" [Louis Ginsberg], [undated], both in box 7, folder 15, and Allen Ginsberg to Louis Ginsberg, March 2, 1958, box 7, folder 16, all in Allen Ginsberg Papers, Rare Book and Manuscript Library, Columbia University Library; Allen Ginsberg, *The Letters of Allen Ginsberg*, ed. Bill Morgan (Philadelphia: Da Capo Press, 2008), 53, 97, 150, 212; Dennis McNally, *Desolate Angel: Jack Kerouac, the Beat Generation, and America* (Cambridge, MA: Da Capo Press, 1979), 221; Rigney and Smith, *Real Bohemia*, 5.

19. The routine garnered laughs with the punning suggestion that "we have nothing against homosexuals, nothing against homosexuals who write poetry, but we *do* have something against . . . poetry written by a small circle for a small circle." Clinton Robert Starr, "Bohemian Resonance: The Beat Generation and Urban Countercultures in the United States during the Late 1950s and Early 1960s," PhD diss., University of Texas at Austin (2005), 193, 227; Lind, *Leo's Place*, 38–39.

20. Brown, "Life and Love," 4–6; Russell FitzGerald diary, November 26, 1957, box 9, folder 1, Ellingham research materials.

21. Herb Caen, "Life in Lower Slobbovia," *San Francisco Chronicle*, February 11, 1958, unpaginated clipping, *Examiner* morgue, SFPL; "Blabbermouth Night at The Place," [ca. April 15, 1957], audio cassette recording, Intelirap Records, 2002. Poet Joanne Kyger and artist Nemi Frost carried on a correspondence through the late 1950s that exemplified this Freudian humor, reporting various shenanigans in North Beach, including an apparently symbolic dream in which Frost was thrown from The Place's balcony. See Nemi Frost to Joanne Kyger, undated [ca. 1958], box 7, folder 14, Joanne Kyger Papers, MSS 730, Mandeville Special Collections Library, UC San Diego.

22. Robert Duncan to Jack Spicer, August 26 and November 6, 1959, box 1, Robert Edward Duncan Papers, circa 1944–1966, BANC MSS 78/164c, Bancroft Library, UC Berkeley; Boyd, *Wide Open Town*, 16, 57–58; Morgan, *Beat Generation in San Francisco*, 34; quote from the "Certified Blabberlistener" award, featured in the Leo Krikorian interview in *The Beach*.

23. "Hunt Miss Smith in Holdup Plot," *San Francisco Examiner*, March 12, 1958. Tea Room owner Connie Smith signed over her beer and wine license following a series of legal troubles, including participation in a darkly comical botched robbery attempt.

24. Daniel Hurewitz, *Bohemian Los Angeles and the Making of Modern Politics* (Berkeley: University of California Press, 2007), 265–72.

25. Boyd, *Wide Open Town*, 124–25, 144–45.

26. Irving Rosenthal to Richard Edelstein, July 6, 1952, box 8, folder 1, Irving Rosenthal to Allen Ginsberg, October 19, 1963, and May 1, 1964, both in box 9, folders 7–8, all in Irving Rosenthal Papers, collection M1550, Department of Special Collections, Stanford University Libraries.

27. George Stanley interview, 1982, in San Francisco, box 7, folder 16, and Russell FitzGerald diary, May 20, 1958, both in Ellingham research materials; Ellingham and Killian, *Poet Be Like God*, 177–78.

28. Robert Duncan to Jack Spicer, undated [ca. 1947], box 1, Duncan Papers; George Stanley and Robert Duncan interviews, Ellingham research materials; Robert Duncan, "The Homosexual in Society," in *Selected Prose*, ed. Robert J. Bertholf (New York: New Directions, 1995), 48; John D'Emilio, *Making Trouble: Essays on Gay History, Politics, and the University* (New York: Routledge, 1992), 76–85. By the late 1950s, however, Duncan was less active in North Beach nightlife, having settled down with his partner, the painter Jess Collins, in Stinson Beach and only coming to San Francisco to attend Spicer's workshops.

29. Jack Spicer to "Dear Robin" [Robin Blaser], undated [ca. 1954], and Jack Spicer to "Dear Robin" [Robin Blaser], undated [ca. 1957], both in box 1, folder 7, Spicer Papers; Ellingham and Killian, *Poet Be Like God*, 46–49.

30. Henry Evans, *Bohemian San Francisco* (San Francisco: Porpoise Bookshop, 1953), 16, sent from Allen Joyce to Jack Spicer, box 2, folder 23, Spicer Papers.

31. Similarly, Joanne Kyger, who had many close gay friends, would later say of Jack Spicer that he might have been "cruel," but not "faggotty." Ellingham and Killian, *Poet Be Like God*, 151; Russell FitzGerald diary, November 24, 1958, and Ebbe Borregaard and Joanne Kyger interview, May 28, 1982, in Bolinas, California, both in box 5, folder 5, Ellingham research materials; Hurewitz, *Bohemian Los Angeles*, 73–74.

32. Starr, "Bohemian Resonance," 223; Jerry Kamstra, *Stand Naked and Cool Them: North Beach and the Bohemian Dream, 1950–1980* (n.p.: Peer-Amid Press, 1980), 91, self-published, photocopy in Special Collections, Bancroft Library, UC Berkeley; Gary Snyder to Allen Ginsberg, January 21, 1959, box 5, folder 27, Ginsberg Papers, Stanford.

33. Knute Stiles interview, 28–29, George Stanley interview, and Russell FitzGerald diary, October 20, 1957, all in Ellingham research materials; John D'Emilio, "The Homosexual Menace: The Politics of Sexuality in Cold War America," in *Making Trouble*. Nan Boyd does not even mention the Mr. Otis bar or Gino and Carlo's, an omission that further elides the connections between bohemia and queer culture.

34. Ellingham and Killian, *Poet Be Like God*, 116; Ebbe Borregaard and Joanne Kyger interview, Ellingham research materials.

35. Rigney and Smith, *Real Bohemia*, 92; Nemi Frost interview, 1982, at the East–West House, San Francisco, box 6, folder 9, Ellingham research materials.

36. Morgan, *Beat Generation in San Francisco*, 50; *Beat Narrative*, directed by Don Vigne (1960), film and "Amazing Footage Featuring Christopher Maclaine," directed by Don Vigne [ca. 1957–60], film, both in Berkeley Art Museum and Pacific Film Archive, Berkeley, California; Jerry Stoll and Evan S. Connell Jr., *I Am a Lover* (Oakland: Angel Island, 1961), unpaginated; Nemi Frost to Joanne Kyger, May 11, 1958, box 8, folder 7, Kyger Papers.

37. Herb Caen, "Onward & Upward," *San Francisco Examiner*, November 3, 1955, unpaginated clipping, *Examiner* morgue, SFPL; John Allen Ryan interview, 12–14, August 11, 1982, in San Francisco, conducted by Lewis Ellingham, box 4, folder 1, Ellingham research materials; "Night Life," *San Franciscan*, December 3, 1958, 5, Periodicals Collection, San Francisco History Center, SFPL; Boyd, *Wide Open Town*, 83.

38. John Allen Ryan to Allen Ginsberg, August 1, 1955, box 5, folder 15, Allen Ginsberg Papers, M0733, Department of Special Collections, Stanford University Libraries; John Allen Ryan to Jack Spicer, March 20, 1956, box 3, folder 27, Spicer Papers.

39. Joyce Johnson, *Minor Characters* (Boston: Houghton Mifflin, 1983), 156–57.

40. Jack Kerouac, quoted in Morgan, *Beat Generation in San Francisco*, 59; Ann Charters, *Kerouac: A Biography* (San Francisco: Straight Arrow Books, 1973), 283.

41. Johnson, *Minor Characters*, 156–58, 167.

42. George Stanley interview, Ellingham research materials; Ellingham and Killian, *Poet Be Like God*, 199.

43. Jerome Rothenberg and David Antin, "Interview with Kenneth Rexroth," April 1958, *Jacket*, http://jacketmagazine.com/23/rex-rothbg-antin-iv.html; Ellingham and Killian, *Poet Be Like God*, 101.

44. George Stanley interview and Jim Herndon interview, 1982, in San Francisco, box 6, folder 12, both in Ellingham research materials; Charters, *Kerouac*, 256–60, 344; Ellingham and Killian, *Poet Be Like God*, 107.

45. Ellingham and Killian, *Poet Be Like God*, 276–77; John D'Emilio, *Sexual Politics, Sexual Communities: The Making of a Homosexual Minority in the United States* (Chicago: University of Chicago Press, 2nd ed., 1998; first published 1983), 176–82; Marc Stein, *Rethinking the Gay and Lesbian Movement* (New York: Routledge, 2012), 54; John Patrick Diggins, *The Proud Decades: America in War and Peace, 1941–1960* (New York: W. W. Norton, 1988), 268–71; Todd Gitlin, *The Sixties: Years of Hope, Days of Rage* (New York: Bantam Books, 1987), 45–54; Howard Brick, *Age of Contradiction: American Thought and Culture in the 1960s* (Ithaca, NY: Cornell University Press, 1998), 69; Ned Polsky, *Hustlers, Beats, and Others* (New York: Anchor Books, paperback ed. 1969; first published 1967), 175. Ellingham and Killian, with their focus on the Spicer circle and its haunts, noted North Beach's influence on Allen Ginsberg. Yet even they set this in terms of poetic style, rather than the urban milieu as a whole.

46. For example, Allen Ginsberg gave fellow New York–San Francisco transplant Gerd Stern the manuscript of Neal Cassady's autobiography while Stern was an editor for Ace Books. Stern promptly misplaced it, leading Ginsberg to refer to him even years later as a goof. Allen Ginsberg to Lawrence Ferlinghetti, June 20, 1958, box 5, folder 2, City Lights Books records, BANC MSS 72/107c, Bancroft Library, UC Berkeley; Gerd Stern, "From Beat Scene Poet to Psychedelic Multimedia Artist in San Francisco and Beyond, 1948–1978," 11, 57, interview in 1996, conducted by Victoria Morris Byerly, Regional Oral History Office, Bancroft Library, UC Berkeley, 2001.

47. Arthur Rimbaud, "Bad Blood," from *A Season in Hell* (originally published in French 1891), in *Selected Poems and Letters*, ed. and transl. Jeremy Harding and John Sturrock (New York: Penguin Books, 2004), 145; Marcel Proust, *Remembrance of Things Past*, vol. 1, *Swann's Way: Within a Budding Grove*, transl. C. K. Moncrieff and Terence Kilmartin (New York: Random House, 1981; first published in English 1922), 694, 763; Louis-Ferdinand Céline, *Journey to the End of Night*, transl. John H. P. Marks (New York: New Directions Books, 1934; originally published in French 1932), 70, 203. For a thorough examination of Oswald Spengler's influence on the Beats' religio-philosophical New Vision, see John Lardas, *The Bop Apocalypse: The Religious Visions of Kerouac, Ginsberg, and Burroughs* (Urbana: University of Illinois Press, 2001).

48. John O'Connor, "The Beatnik Disease," *Vigilante*, vol. 3 (Summer 1960), 51, Periodicals Collection, SFPL; Jack Kerouac to Allen Ginsberg, December 22, 1954, box 11, folder 21, Ginsberg Papers, Columbia; Allen Ginsberg, *Journals: Early Fifties, Early Sixties*, ed. Gordon Ball (New York: Grove Press, 1977), 168.

49. Bill Morgan, *I Celebrate Myself: The Somewhat Private Life of Allen Ginsberg* (New York: Penguin Books, 2006), 177; Lind, *Leo's Place*, 49–50; Leo Krikorian interview in *The Beach*.

50. Wally Hedrick continued: "So we would go across town to The Place, and they would have their Blabbermouth Nights which were really Dada demonstrations. We didn't know it at the time, but it was just a rerun of Zurich, 1912–1914, where people could get up and say anything they want and then everybody'd pound on the tables and drink their beer and just generally raise hell." Michael McClure, "Poetry of the 6," in *Beat Down to Your Soul: What Was the Beat Generation?*, ed. Anne Charters (New York: Penguin Books, 2001), 370–77; Wally Hedrick interview, 12–18, June 10–24, 1974, Archives of American Art, Smithsonian Institution.

51. Allen Ginsberg to Kenneth Rexroth, undated [ca. October or November 1952], box 8, folder 1, Rexroth Papers.

52. Allen Ginsberg to Jack Kerouac, September 5, 1954, and Allen Ginsberg to Edith Ginsberg and Eugene Brooks, July 10, 1954, in Ginsberg, *Letters*, 101, 95; Allen Ginsberg, *Journals: Mid-Fifties, 1954–1958*, ed. Gordon Ball (New York: HarperCollins, 1995), 58–59, 116–17, 193–94; Morgan, *I Celebrate Myself*, 182–84.

53. Ellingham and Killian, *Poet Be Like God*, 55–59, 80, 99–103.

54. McClure, "Poetry of the 6," 370.

55. Jack Kerouac to Allen Ginsberg, undated [ca. March 1954], folder 20, "Don't sail with the NMU," undated [1951], folder 18, and Jack Kerouac to "Dear Allen" [Allen Ginsberg], undated [ca. May 1954], March 30, 1954, and July 30, 1954, folder 21, all in box 11, Ginsberg Papers, Columbia.

56. Jack Kerouac to Allen Ginsberg, August 23, 1954, and October 26, 1954, box 11, folder 21, Ginsberg Papers, Columbia. See also Bill Morgan, *The Typewriter Is Holy: The Complete, Uncensored History of the Beat Generation* (New York: Free Press, 2010), 52.

57. In his own way, Gregory Corso echoed this ideal, stating that his idol, Percy Shelly, was "revolutionary but he spilled no blood." Allen Ginsberg to Jack Kerouac, September 5, 1954, in Ginsberg, *Letters*, 107–8; Allen Ginsberg, Peter Orlovsky, Gregory Corso, and Jack Kerouac to "Dear Jim" [James Weschler], undated, box 9, folder 17, and Lawrence Ferlinghetti to Allen Ginsberg, March 16, 1961, box 5, folder 18, both in series 1, Ginsberg Papers, Columbia; Charters, *Kerouac*, 270, 275–77; Ed D'Angelo, "Anarchism and the Beats," in *The Philosophy of the Beats*, ed. Sharin N. Elkholy (Lexington: University Press of Kentucky, 2012), 227–42; Jack Kerouac to Allen Ginsberg, December 7, 1954, box 11, folder 21, Ginsberg Papers, Columbia.

58. Ginsberg, *Journals: Mid-Fifties*, 64–65, 115–17; Morgan, *Beat Generation in San Francisco*, 142–43, 25–26; Allen Ginsberg to Jack Kerouac, September 5, 1954, in Ginsberg, *Letters*, 101.

59. Ginsberg, *Journals: Mid-Fifties*, 5–7, 60–61; George H. White to Russell S. Munro, August 31, 1955, Alcoholic Beverage Control Board Appeals case files, F3718:291, subject files 1938–1970, series 5.1, California State Archives, Sacramento, California.

60. Lind, *Leo's Place*, 50; John Allen Ryan to "Dear Sikes" [Jack Spicer], undated [ca. September–October 1955], box 3, folder 27, Spicer Papers.

61. A previous tenant of the Montgomery Street apartment had been the activist poet Ruth Weiss. *Faust Foutu* (Faust Fucked) also starred Jack Spicer and Michael McClure. Ginsberg, *Journals: Mid-Fifties*, 80–89, 105, 115–25, 146–47, 179; Morgan, *I Celebrate Myself*, 197; McClure, "Poetry of the 6," 371–72.

62. Ginsberg, *Journals: Mid-Fifties*, 193–94.

63. Lind, *Leo's Place*, 53–55; John Allen Ryan to Jack Spicer, August 11, 1955, and January 15, 1956, both in box 3, folder 27, Spicer Papers; John Allen Ryan interview, 12, 109, Ellingham

research materials; Richard Cándida Smith, *Utopia and Dissent: Art, Poetry, and Politics in California* (Berkeley: University of California Press, 1995), 163, 486 n.26.

64. Allen Ginsberg to Kenneth Rexroth, undated [1952], Rexroth Papers; Allen Ginsberg, "Howl" and "Footnote to Howl," in *Collected Poems, 1947–1997* (New York: HarperCollins, 2006), 134–42, copyright © 1955 by Allen Ginsberg, reprinted by permission of HarperCollins Publishers.

65. The poem's influence is both measured and sustained in recent popular culture, ranging from a casual reference in the television show *Six Feet Under* to the eponymous film starring James Franco. On Ginsberg's guilt for acting callously toward Sheila Williams, see, for example, Morgan, *I Celebrate Myself*, 202. Williams went on to a tragic life of drug addiction and an early death while homeless.

66. Morgan, *I Celebrate Myself*, 128, 231.

67. Charters, *Kerouac*, 279, 401; Amiri Baraka [LeRoi Jones], *The Autobiography of LeRoi Jones* (Chicago: Lawrence Hill Books, 1984), 219–20.

68. Ellingham and Killian, *Poet Be Like God*, 35, 390 n.82. Spicer admired the essay, despite his disagreements with Paul Goodman when the latter had visited Berkeley and the Libertarian Circle in the 1940s.

69. Paul Goodman, "Advance-Guard Writing, 1900–1950," *Kenyon Review*, vol. 13, no. 3 (Summer 1951), 357–80. Goodman's essay, while suffering from clumsy prose, was prescient in its description of literary controversy, which applied to *Howl* six years later: "The audience reacted to the naturalistic offense with the specific sanction of censorship, on moral and political grounds. Yet this was obviously not a police-measure of defense, to protect the children, but a reaction of outraged sensibility; there had to be spectacular trials, to reaffirm the faith of the audience in itself. . . . Conscious of estrangement, serious writers, in their self-portraits and choice of protagonists, have more and more been describing marginal personalities— criminals, perverts, drunkards, underground people—or persons in extreme situations that make them 'existent' rather than universal. . . . The audience must respond to it by trying to annihilate the outcry, as if it had not been heard, or to prevent others from hearing it."

70. Jack Spicer to Robin Blaser, undated [ca. 1951], box 1, folder 7, Spicer Papers.

71. D'Emilio, *Sexual Politics*, 177.

72. Morgan, *I Celebrate Myself*, 242; Edward de Grazia, *Girls Lean Back Everywhere: The Law of Obscenity and the Assault on Genius* (New York: Random House, 1992), 333–37.

73. De Grazia, *Girls Lean Back Everywhere*, 333–37; Allen Ginsberg to Lawrence Ferlinghetti, June 10, 1957, box 5, folder 1, City Lights Books records, UC Berkeley. Ginsberg's pun refers to the 1930s communist ILWU leader, Harry Bridges.

74. For a critical account of how the idea of *communitas* developed in the 1960s, see Brick, *Age of Contradiction*, 98–123.

75. Lawrence Ferlinghetti to Allen Ginsberg, April 13, 1960, box 5, folder 17, Ginsberg Papers, Columbia; Morgan, *I Celebrate Myself*, 304; de Grazia, *Girls Lean Back Everywhere*, 338–39.

76. Paul O'Neil, "The Only Rebellion Around: But the Beats Bungle the Job in Arguing, Sulking and Bad Poetry," *Life*, November 30, 1959, 114–30; George B. Leonard Jr., "The San Francisco Bohemians: The Bored, the Bearded and the Beat," *Look*, August 19, 1958, 64–65; Rigney and Smith, *Real Bohemia*, 41, 69, 86, 93, 102, 107–12; Polsky, *Hustlers, Beats, and Others*, 154. Rigney and Smith were reluctant to openly declare a given percentage of bohemians to be mentally ill, so their figures are up for interpretation. By one calculation, 60% fit into categories suggesting an inability to fully function in society. Their own case studies, however,

undercut this view, with several individuals, particularly women, simply being nonconformists. More telling was that 22% were deemed the "most emotionally upset," with a little over half of those having been hospitalized for mental illness. Another 10% were in therapy, making 32% the highest possible number of documented cases—although only a few of those displayed socially dysfunctional behavior. The numbers in Polsky's study of the Village were even more obscure. He reported that "most beats are decidedly neurotic," but added that "their intelligence and native talents are likely to be superior when not average, and their neuroses usually do not incapacitate them."

77. Herbert Marcuse, *Eros and Civilization: A Philosophical Inquiry into Freud* (Boston: Beacon Press, 1966), 176–79.

78. Gitlin, *The Sixties*, 54.

79. Rigney and Smith, *Real Bohemia*, 176–83; Royce Brier, "Beatnik Problem Just Like Ours?," *San Francisco Chronicle*, April 6, 1959, 34.

80. Anne Dewey, "Poetic Authority and the Public Sphere of Politics in the Activist 1960s: The Duncan-Levertov Debate," in *Robert Duncan and Denise Levertov*, 112.

81. Cándida Smith, *Utopia and Dissent*, 169.

82. Lind, "Paris, North Beach," 35; Russell FitzGerald diary, November 27, 1958, Ellingham research materials; Lind, *Leo's Place*, 17–18.

83. Dan Wakefield, *New York in the Fifties* (New York: St. Martin's Griffin, 1992), 130–31; Malina, *Diaries*, 218–26, 299; Sukenick, *Down and In*, 19; Brenda Knight, *Women of the Beat Generation: The Writers, Artists and Muses at the Heart of a Revolution* (Berkeley, CA: Conari Press, 1996), 103.

84. Leo Krikorian interview in *The Beach*; Lind, *Leo's Place*, 13.

85. Joyce Johnson to Allen Ginsberg and Peter Orlovsky, October 28, 1957, box 1, folder 12, series 1, Peter Orlovsky Papers, Rare Book and Manuscript Library, Columbia University Library.

86. Jack Kerouac to "Dear Allen and Peter" [Allen Ginsberg and Peter Orlovsky], undated [ca. June 1956], box 12, folder 2, Ginsberg Papers, Columbia.

87. Ibid.; John Allen Ryan to Jack Spicer, "Friday" [1956], box 3, folder 27, Spicer Papers.

88. O'Neil, "Only Rebellion Around."

89. Joanne Kyger to Gary Snyder, March 23, 1959, box 7, folder 14, Kyger Papers.

90. George Murphy, "What's a Phony—and What's True?" *San Francisco Examiner*, September 26, 1957, 6, clipping, *Examiner* morgue, SFPL.

91. Fritz Bosworth, "Some Call It North Beach," *Today's San Franciscan*, vol. 2, no. 2 (May 1, 1959), 17–19, and Mark Green, "The Scene with Green: North Beach," *S.F. Territorial News*, vol. 4, no. 16 (May 1961), 2, both in Periodicals Collection, SFPL.

92. Polsky, *Hustlers, Beats, and Others*, 154. Maynard G. Krebs was a sympathetic character, however, acting as a usefully reticent foil to Dobie Gillis's overly ambitious schemes.

93. Mark Green to Sally Green, November 9, 1959, box 1, folder 2, General Correspondence: 1959–1976, Mark Green Papers, Archives of American Art, Smithsonian Institution.

94. John Wilcock, *The Village Square* (New York: Lyle Stuart, 1961), 14–15; Mark Stevens and Annalyn Swan, *De Kooning: An American Master* (New York: Alfred A. Knopf, 2004), 362.

95. Characteristically, Kenneth Rexroth later took credit for suggesting this tactic, asserting: "People on the West Coast work. . . . And I said [to Ginsberg], 'Ship out. Do you realize that when they go into the Bering Sea, you are in hot water? . . . That means double pay.'" Jack Kerouac to Allen Ginsberg, "Don't sail with the NMU," undated [1951], box 11, folder 18, Ginsberg Papers, Columbia; Charles Modecke interview in *The Beach*; "Kenneth Rexroth (1969),"

interview, in *San Francisco Beat: Talking with the Poets*, ed. David Meltzer (San Francisco: City Lights Books, 2001), 232.

96. Although utopian, Goodman's most famous work on urban planning, *Communitas* (1947), proposed several concrete plans. One revolved around a dual subsistence/market economy, in which mandatory public service for seven years provided the option of either a lifetime minimum income or education for use in the free market. This neo-functionalist scheme aimed at both decentralization and the efficiency of what he referred to as "life as a whole." Kingsley Widmer, *Paul Goodman* (Boston: Twayne, 1980), 42–49.

97. Wilcock, *Village Square*, 16.

98. Hettie Jones, "How I Became Hettie Jones," in *The Greenwich Village Reader: Fiction, Poetry, and Reminiscences, 1872–2002*, ed. June Skinner Sawyers (New York: Cooper Square Press, 2001), 588.

99. While both the marriage and John Gruen's tenure were short lived, Grove Press went on to be a crucial force, disseminating cutting-edge writing through the 1990s. Barney Rosset himself was long a part of socially conscious Left networks. He embraced leftist politics as a youth in Chicago and, after World War II, made a film on civil rights called *Strange Victory. Obscene: A Portrait of Barney Rosset and Grove Press*, directed by Neil Ortenberg and Daniel O'Connor (New York: Double O Film Productions, 2007), DVD; John Gruen, *The Party's Over Now: Reminiscences of the Fifties—New York's Artists, Writers, and their Friends* (New York: Viking Press, 1972), 41–49.

100. Sukenick, *Down and In*, 34–37.

101. Dan Wakefield interview, February 7, 1993, box 1, folder 94, Maurice Isserman research files for *The Other American: The Life of Michael Harrington*, TAM.239, Tamiment Library / Robert F. Wagner Labor Archives, Elmer Holmes Bobst Library, New York University.

102. Kerouac, quoted in *Greenwich Village Reader*, 418–19; Sukenick, *Down and In*, 35, 75; author's interview with Todd Gitlin, October 14, 2009, in New York City; "The Prevalence of Paul Goodman," *New York Times*, April 3, 1966, SM-36; John Gruen, *The New Bohemia: The Combine Generation* (New York: Shorecrest, 1966), 86, 126; Students for a Democratic Society, *Port Huron Statement* (New York: Students for a Democratic Society, 2nd printing, 1964; first published 1962), 5–7.

103. Rigney and Smith, *Real Bohemia*, 21–23; Polsky, *Hustlers, Beats, and Others*, 149, 145–54, 171–75; data for 1960 from Bureau of Labor Statistics, "Changes in Men's and Women's Labor Force Participation Rates," TED: The Economics Daily, https://www.bls.gov/opub/ted /2007/jan/wk2/art03.htm. Rates of work for bohemian men and women were around 65%, with 70% of that employment in blue-collar jobs and 30% in white-collar ones. Both Rigby and Smith's and Polsky's studies suffered from small sample sizes and assumptions about race, class, and gender that skewed their interpretations by making white, middle-class men their standard, although Rigney and Smith were better in this regard. See also Cándida Smith, *Utopia and Dissent*, 265, 330–31.

104. Alice Denham, *Sleeping with Bad Boys: A Juicy Tell-All of Literary New York in the Fifties and Sixties* (n.p.: Book Republic Press, 2006), 57–60, 113–32, 177–79; Elsa Gidlow, *Elsa, I Come with My Songs: The Autobiography of Elsa Gidlow* (San Francisco: Booklegger Press, 1986), 255–56; Johnson, *Minor Characters*, 106–10, 136–37, 236–37; Albert Goldman, *Ladies and Gentlemen—Lenny Bruce!!* (New York: Random House, 1971), 58–70, 286; Suze Rotolo, *A Freewheelin' Time: A Memoir of Greenwich Village in the Sixties* (New York: Broadway Books, 2008), 280–81; Robert Gottlieb, ed., *Reading Jazz: A Gathering of Autobiography, Reportage,*

and Criticism from 1919 to Now (New York: Pantheon Books, 1996), 185–99; Rigney and Smith, *Real Bohemia*, 82–97.

105. Joanne Kyger to Gary Snyder, June 9, 1959, box 7, folder 15, Kyger Papers; Denham, *Sleeping with Bad Boys*, 179.

106. Russell FitzGerald diary, October 1, 1957, Ellingham research materials; Lind, *Leo's Place*, 79–80; Christopher Lowen Agee, *The Streets of San Francisco: Policing and the Creation of a Cosmopolitan Liberal Politics, 1950–1972* (Chicago: University of Chicago Press, 2014), 48–49.

107. Jack Kerouac to Allen Ginsberg, September 8, 1945, box 11, folder 14, Ginsberg Papers, Columbia.

108. Although more research is needed, Lisa Lindquist Dorr gives the frequency of such incidents, noting that in oral histories of women who experienced unwanted pregnancies, 7% were the result of date rape. She further cites sociological studies indicating that over 50% of women in the 1950s experienced "offensive episodes at some level of erotic intimacy" while on dates. Lisa Lindquist Dorr, "The Perils of the Back Seat: Date Rape, Race and Gender in 1950s America," *Gender and History*, vol. 20, no.1 (April 2008), 27–47.

109. Maya Angelou, *The Collected Autobiographies of Maya Angelou* (New York: Modern Library, 2004), 713.

110. Joanne J. Meyerowitz, "Introduction" and Wini Breines, "The 'Other' Fifties: Beats and Bad Girls," in *Not June Cleaver: Women and Gender in Postwar America, 1945–1960*, ed. Joanne J. Meyerowitz (Philadelphia: Temple University Press, 1994), 11, 3; Cándida Smith, *Utopia and Dissent*, 257–64.

111. Joanne Kyger to Gary Snyder, March 27 [1959], folder 14, June 26, 1959, folder 15, and August 17, 1959, folder 16, all in box 7, Kyger Papers.

112. Gary Snyder to Joanne Kyger, June 10, 1959, folder 15, "March about the 19th" [1959] and April 1, 1959, folder 14, and July 14, 1959, folder 16, all in box 7, Kyger Papers.

113. California law prohibited women bartenders, unless they owned the establishment—a discrepancy that garnered nary a peep from bohemians.

114. Polsky, *Beats, Hustlers, and Others*, 144–49. Polsky's epigraph to his Beat chapter acknowledges this adolescent formative aspect, but he fails to do so in the body of the text.

115. Ebbe Borregaard and Joanne Kyger interview, Ellingham research materials; Lind, "Paris, North Beach," 11; Ellingham and Killian, *Poet Be Like God*, 32–33; Jack Spicer, *My Vocabulary Did This to Me: The Collected Poetry of Jack Spicer*, ed. Peter Gizzi and Kevin Killian (Middletown, CT: Wesleyan University Press, 2008), xv; Lind, *Leo's Place*, 28.

116. Wilcock, *Village Square*, 16; Baraka, *Autobiography of LeRoi Jones*, 454; Michael Harrington, "The Death of Bohemia," in *Greenwich Village Reader*, 458–66; Michael Harrington, "A San Remo Type: The Vanishing Village," in *The Village Voice Anthology (1956–1980): Twenty-Five Years of Writing from the* Village Voice, ed. Geoffrey Stokes (New York: William Morrow, 1982), 151.

117. Although the League for Industrial Democracy was the institution through which Students for a Democratic Society first congealed, Harrington was quick to denounce them, mistakenly pegging them as too soft on communism. Tellingly, Harrington's biographer suggests that "had Michael and Tom Hayden sat around a table in the back room of the White Horse in June 1962 to hash out these issues, they might have found that they agreed more often than they disagreed. . . . But the meeting hall at Port Huron was not the back room of the White Horse. The setting aroused instincts in Michael more akin to those he used to feel in the dusty YSL [Young Socialist League] loft where he sharpened his rhetorical skills in the

1950s." Maurice Isserman, *The Other American: The Life of Michael Harrington* (New York: Public Affairs, 2000), 236–37.

118. Russell FitzGerald diary, September 7, 1957, and March 26, 1958, Ellingham research materials.

119. Mary Perot Nichols interview, March 16, 1995, 2, folder 65, Eileen Fantino Diaz interview, 2, 8, March 16, 1995, folder 15, Dan Wakefield interview, 1, February 7, 1993, folder 94, Jane Warwick interview, 4, January 6, 1999, folder 96, George Rawick telephone interview, August 17, 1984, folder 71, and Bogdan Denitch interview, December 21, 1990, folder 14, all in box 1, Isserman research files; Isserman, *The Other American*, 158–59; Dan Wakefield, "Land of the Free," *Nation*, vol. 181, no. 14 (October 1, 1955), 284–85.

120. Gary Snyder, "Notes on the Beat Generation," in *Beat Down*, 519–20; Polsky, *Hustlers, Beats, and Others*, 155.

121. J. R. Goddard, "The Wonderful World of the White Horse," *Village Voice*, June 22, 1961, in *Village Voice Anthology*, 93–94; "B. F." [unidentified] to Joanne Kyger, May 9, 1958, box 18, folder 26, Kyger Papers.

122. Jack Kerouac, *On the Road* (New York: Viking Press, 1957), 123–24. This concern was similar to C. Wright Mills's reaction in *The New Men of Power* to the solidification of union power by the AFL-CIO after World War II, which took place in tense cooperation with the federal government, followed soon thereafter by the Treaty of Detroit in 1950.

123. Ingrid Monson, "Monk Meets SNCC," in "New Perspectives on Thelonious Monk," special issue, *Black Music Research Journal*, vol. 19, no. 2 (Autumn 1999), 187–200; "Black Out Over," October 7, 1949, unpaginated clipping, *San Francisco Examiner*, *Examiner* morgue, SFPL; Agee, *Streets of San Francisco*, 84–85; "Gangster Issue Revived Over AFL Election," *Chicago Daily Tribune*, March 21, 1950, A-7; Matthew Josephson, *Union House, Union Bar: The History of the Hotel and Restaurant Employees and Bartenders International Union, AFL-CIO* (New York: Random House, 1965), 211–14.

124. "Statement to the Court, 1963," box 20, folder 8, Alvah Bessie Papers, Wisconsin Historical Society, Madison.

125. Fielding Dawson, *An Emotional Memoir of Franz Klein* (New York: Pantheon Books, 1967), 52–56, 94.

Chapter 5. Rise of the "Sickniks"

1. Ralph Gleason, liner notes for *The Sick Humor of Lenny Bruce*, Fantasy Records 7001, 1958. LP.

2. The most notable of these is Stephen E. Kercher, *Revel with a Cause: Liberal Satire in Postwar America* (Chicago: University of Chicago Press, 2006). See also Jesse Bier, *The Rise and Fall of American Humor* (New York: Holt, Rinehart & Winston, 1968); Joseph Boskin, *Rebellious Laughter: People's Humor in American Culture* (Syracuse, NY: Syracuse University Press, 1997).

3. Howard Brick, *Age of Contradiction: American Thought and Culture in the 1960s* (Ithaca, NY: Cornell University Press, 1998), 59. See also Todd Gitlin, *The Sixties: Years of Hope, Days of Rage* (New York: Bantam Books, 1987); Paul Krassner, *Confessions of a Raving, Unconfined Nut: Misadventures in the Counter-Culture* (New York: Simon & Schuster, 1993); Gerald Nachman, *Seriously Funny: The Rebel Comedians of the 1950s and 1960s* (New York: Pantheon Books, 2003); Theodore Roszak, *The Making of a Counter Culture: Reflections on the Technocratic Society and Its Youthful Opposition* (Garden City, NY: Anchor Books, 1969); Stephen Whitfield, *The Culture of the Cold War* (Baltimore: Johns Hopkins University Press, 1991).

4. The one quasi-exception was Dustin Hoffman's Oscar-nominated portrayal of Bruce—some eight years after the comedian's death—in the 1974 film *Lenny*, directed by Bob Fosse.

5. See Miriam Hansen, *Babel and Babylon: Spectatorship in American Silent Film* (Cambridge, MA: Harvard University Press, 1991); Walter Benjamin, "The Work of Art in the Age of Mechanical Reproduction," in *Illuminations*, ed. Hannah Arendt, transl. Harry Zohn (New York: Schocken Books, 1968).

6. Robert Shelton, "Ancient Art of Poking Fun—on LP," *New York Times*, March 22, 1959, X-22; Sherri Cavan, *Liquor License: An Ethnography of Bar Behavior* (Chicago: Aldine, 1966), 167–70; Jon E. Rocklein, *The Psychology of Humor: A Reference Guide and Annotated Bibliography* (Westport, CT: Greenwood Press, 2002), 17–18, 185; Margaret Stutley, *Shamanism: An Introduction* (London: Routledge, 2003), 1–21; "Mort Sahl Double-Header," *Pasadena (CA) Independent*, February 3, 1959, 12; Murray Schumach, "Storm Is Brewed in Pool at Metro," *New York Times*, May 12, 1959, 38; Norman Mailer, "The White Negro," in *Advertisements for Myself* (New York: Berkeley Medallion Books, 1959), 327.

7. "Mort Sahl Up and Down the Organization," *Chicago Metropolitan News*, February 24, 1973, 17; Mort Sahl, *Heartland* (New York: Harcourt Brace Jovanovich, 1976), 150; Nachman, *Seriously Funny*, 54–55; Herbert Mitgang, "Anyway, Onward with Mort Sahl," *New York Times*, February 8, 1959, SM-32.

8. Babior divorced Sahl in 1958, charging that he had been loud and abusive toward her in public. Sahl, *Heartland*, 6–11; "Mort Sahl Up and Down"; Kercher, *Revel with a Cause*, 203–4; Albert Goldman, *Ladies and Gentlemen—Lenny Bruce!!* (New York: Random House, 1971), 192; "Night-Club Comic Mort Sahl Divorced," *San Francisco Chronicle*, March 28, 1958, 14.

9. Sahl, *Heartland*, 10–11.

10. "Mort Sahl: The Loyal Opposition," directed by Robert Weide, American Masters Series, PBS, aired September 18, 1989, Paley Center Archives, New York City; "Last Laughs 2004: Comedian Mort Sahl," interview conducted by Terry Gross, *Fresh Air*, WHYY, December 30, 2004; Nachman, *Seriously Funny*, 56.

11. Ralph J. Gleason, "Beatnik Poets Move Out, the Tourists Move In: North Beach Haunts Are 'Going Commercial,'" *San Francisco Chronicle*, August 30, 1960, 1, 6; Goldman, *Ladies and Gentlemen*, 192.

12. Sahl, *Heartland*, 12–13, 5; John D. Weaver, "San Francisco: hungry i," *Holiday*, vol. 29 (April 1961), 125–38.

13. Untitled article, September 6, 1950, "3d. St. Bar Operator Loses License in Vice Case Echo," November 16, 1951, Ralph J. Gleason, "Banducci Closes One 'i' and Opens Another," October 20, 1969, and "Bay City Beat," November 5, 1970, all unpaginated *San Francisco Examiner* clippings, *Examiner* morgue, San Francisco History Center, SFPL.

14. Banducci later insisted the name meant "hungry id." Gerald Nachman, "A Funny Thing Happened to the hungry i," *Oakland Tribune*, January 11, 1970, 3-EN; Dick Boyd, *Broadway North Beach, The Golden Years: A Saloonkeeper's Tales* (San Francisco: Cape Foundations, 2006), 37–39; Mort Sahl and Enrico Banducci interview, in "Enrico Banducci's hungry i: San Francisco's Legendary Nightclub," hungry i exhibition video loop, 1997, San Francisco Performing Arts Library & Museum; Nan Alamilla Boyd, *Wide Open Town: A History of Queer San Francisco to 1965* (Berkeley: University of California Press, 2003), 22.

15. John Allen Ryan interview, 12–21, August 11, 1982, in San Francisco, conducted by Lewis Ellingham, box 4, folder 1, Lewis Ellingham's *Poet Be Like God* research materials, MSS 126, Special Collections and Archives, UC San Diego, courtesy of the Poetry Collection of

the University Libraries, University at Buffalo, SUNY; Don Steele, "Going Places," *Oakland Tribune*, June 12, 1954, D-11; *The Pizza Pusher*, hungry i exhibition video loop. *The Pizza Pusher*, which was written by Jack Goodwin, also starred the artist Sargent Johnson.

16. Michael Denning, *The Cultural Front: The Laboring of American Culture in the Twentieth Century* (London: Verso, 1997), 349–60; "A Record Success Story," *Wisconsin State Journal* (Madison), August 30, 1977, I-17.

17. Alvah Bessie to Enrico Banducci, January 3, 1964, box 20, folder 8, and Alvah Bessie-Lenny Bruce Correspondence: 1959–1960, box 2, folder 12, Alvah Bessie Papers, Theater Division, Wisconsin Historical Society, Madison.

18. James Gavin, *Intimate Nights: The Golden Age of New York Cabaret* (New York: Grove Weidenfeld, 1991), 120, 148–50; "In One Ear," August 17, 1964, and "For the Old hungry i," September 10, 1968, both unpaginated *San Francisco Examiner* clippings, *Examiner* morgue, SFPL. The Kingston Trio purchased and ran the club for a few years in the mid-1960s.

19. "Enrico Banducci: 1922–2007," *Chicago Tribune*, October 16, 2007, 6; Howard Taubman, "Special to the *New York Times*," *New York Times*, May 13, 1961, 11; Weaver, "San Francisco: hungry i."

20. Mort Sahl, *Live at Sunset*, Fantasy Records 7005, 1958, LP, Recorded Sound Reference Center, Library of Congress; Sahl, *Heartland*, 21; Walter Kerr, "The Fast-Talking Man in a Sweater Has Started Something," This World, *San Francisco Chronicle*, April 13, 1958, 21; Gross, "Last Laughs."

21. Nachman, "A Funny Thing Happened"; Sahl, *Heartland*, 21; Weaver, "San Francisco: hungry i"; Mort Sahl and Enrico Banducci interview, hungry i exhibition video loop.

22. Dan Steele, "Going Places," June 12, 1954, D-11, August 18, 1954, D-35, and September 1, 1954, 32, all in *Oakland Tribune*; Sahl, *Heartland*, 16–17.

23. Nachman, "A Funny Thing Happened."

24. "Mort Sahl: The Loyal Opposition."

25. Mort Sahl and Enrico Banducci interview, hungry i exhibition video loop.

26. "Interview: Enrico Banducci," *San Francisco Focus*, March 1987, unpaginated clipping, Enrico Banducci biography file, San Francisco History Center, SFPL. Banducci reported that jazz singer Ella Fitzgerald, visiting the club to see folk artist Josh White, was so impressed by the no-drink policy that she included it in her contract at other venues.

27. Weaver, "San Francisco: hungry i."

28. Sahl, *Heartland*, 34–38.

29. Paul Krassner, *Impolite Interviews* (New York: Seven Stories Press, 1999), 162.

30. Mort Sahl and Enrico Banducci interview, hungry i exhibition video loop.

31. Howard Taubman, "Spawning Ground of the Offbeat," *New York Times*, May 13, 1961, 11; Sahl, *Heartland*, 20.

32. Wood Soanes, "This Seems to Prove No Business Like Show Biz," *Oakland Tribune*, March 25, 1954, 52-E.

33. Taubman, "Spawning Ground"; Nachman, *Seriously Funny*, 58; Kercher, *Revel with a Cause*, 204.

34. John Patrick Diggins, *The Proud Decades: America in War and Peace, 1941–1960* (New York: W. W. Norton, 1988), 99; Lizabeth Cohen, *A Consumer's Republic: The Politics of Mass Consumption in Postwar America* (New York: Vintage Books, 2003), 166–73, 138–41; Margot Canaday, *The Straight State: Sexuality and Citizenship in Twentieth-Century America* (Princeton, NJ: Princeton University Press, 2009).

35. Dan Steele, "Going Places," *Oakland Tribune*, June 12, 1954, D-11; Sahl, *Heartland*, 16–18; Paul Desmond to "Duke," undated, Paul Desmond Papers, MSS 309, Holt-Atherton Special Collections, University of the Pacific, Stockton, California.

36. "Review Spotlight on Albums," *Billboard*, October 27, 1958, 28; Wally George, "Court of Records," *Los Angeles Times*, January 4, 1959, J-34; Nachman, *Seriously Funny*, 57–63; Sahl, *Live at Sunset*; Lewis Funke, "Sahl Views Political Campaign in 2 Performances at Town Hall," *New York Times*, October 24, 1960, 24.

37. Sahl, *Heartland*, 25; Jules Feiffer, *Backing into Forward* (New York: Doubleday, 2010), 230–31; Carrie Pitzulo, *Bachelors and Bunnies: The Sexual Politics of Playboy* (Chicago: University of Chicago Press, 2011). Pitzulo challenges the simple notion that *Playboy*'s sexual politics were only in objectifying women, citing the magazine's liberatory impact on the sexual revolution, as well as its intermittent support of feminism.

38. "Verve August Sales Surge," August 8, 1960, 8, "Mort Sahl," March 6, 1961, 2, 52, "Comedy Album Sales Brighten," November 20, 1961, 13, 18–19, and "Funny Men Score on Sales Chart in Houston Area," January 23, 1961, 3, 28, all in *Billboard*; Thomas Weyr, *Reaching for Paradise: The Playboy Vision of America* (New York: Times Books, 1978), 88; Russell Miller, *Bunny: The Real Story of Playboy* (London: Michael Joseph, 1984), 75; Nachman, *Seriously Funny*, 84; *Playboy's Penthouse* television series, 1959–61, episode list, IMBd, www.imdb .com/title/tt0052503/episodes/.

39. Elizabeth Fraterrigo, *Playboy and the Making of the Good Life in Modern America* (Oxford: Oxford University Press, 2009), 69.

40. Feiffer, *Backing into Forward*, 230–31.

41. Walter Winchell, "Broadway and Elsewhere," *Pharos-Tribune* (Logansport, IN), November 26, 1954, unpaginated; Lloyd Johnson, "Star Time," January 8, 1955, 4, and January 15, 1955, 4, both in *San Francisco News*; Lloyd Johnson, "Star Time," *San Francisco Call-Bulletin*, January 22, 1955, 4.

42. Sahl, *Heartland*, 40–44, 53–54; Tad Hershorn, *Norman Granz: The Man Who Used Jazz for Justice* (Berkeley: University of California Press, 2011), 3–8, 256–57. Sahl's introduction to the Chicago nightclub scene illustrates how jazz social networks plugged him into the national club circuit. Desmond was the first to encourage Sahl to venture outside San Francisco, introducing him to Newport Jazz Festival organizer and Boston club owner George Wein, which led to shows in Chicago after the owner of the jazz venue Mister Kelly's caught Sahl's act. In the Windy City, Sahl made key connections with both Hugh Hefner and Norman Granz, the owner of Verve Records, who was known in jazz circles as a left-leaning champion of civil rights and was therefore a perfect match to help bring Sahl into wider popularity. In addition to anchoring Sahl's recording career, Granz was briefly the comic's manager—although the mercurial Sahl quickly backed out of their arrangement, as he had done with others several times previously. Verve provided another slender thread tying Sahl to the literary underground, as the label also released spoken-word albums by Dorothy Parker, Jack Kerouac, and Alice B. Toklas.

43. Sahl, *Heartland*, 54.

44. Dan Wakefield, *New York in the Fifties* (New York: St. Martin's Press, 1992), 164, 313; Ronald Sukenick, *Down and In: Life in the Underground* (New York: Beech Tree Books, 1987), 32; Charles Kaiser, *The Gay Metropolis: 1940–1996* (Boston: Houghton Mifflin, 1997), 135–36.

45. Lawrence Ferlinghetti, *A Coney Island of the Mind* (New York: New Directions, 1958), 60; Richard Cándida Smith, *Utopia and Dissent: Art, Poetry, and Politics in California* (Berkeley: University of California Press, 1995), 63–66.

46. Krassner, *Impolite Interviews*, 156, 163, 178; Sahl, *Heartland*, 31.

47. Mort Sahl, *At the hungry i*, Verve Records MG V-15012, 1960, LP; Krassner, *Impolite Interviews*, 156; "Mort Sahl: The Loyal Opposition."

48. Mort Sahl, "Satire Is Shorthand," December 7, 1958, SM-26, and John Canaday, "Mort Sahl Links Up String of Asides," June 19, 1964, 34, both in *New York Times*; Sahl, *Heartland*, 37.

49. Kerr, "Fast-Talking Man."

50. "Theatre: 'Next President,'" *New York Times*, April 10, 1958, 34; "Nightclubs: The Sickniks," *Time*, July 13, 1959, 44–45; Nachman, *Seriously Funny*, 56; "Observer: Kremlin Esthetics," *New York Times*, May 2, 1965, E-10; Russell Baker, "Convention Show Moves Outdoors," *New York Times*, July 16, 1960, 6.

51. Sahl, *Live at the hungry i*; Cavan, *Liquor License*, 160–63.

52. Murray Schumach, "Mort Sahl Knows No Party," *New York Times*, June 2, 1960, 27; John Pagones, "Listening Is Key to Sahl's Success," *Washington Post*, December 2, 1960, B-10; Canaday, "Mort Sahl Links Up"; Arthur Gelb, "Cabaret Menu: Roast Politician," *New York Times*, June 4, 1962, 32.

53. "What's So Funny?," *Bell and Howell Close-Up!* television series, ABC, 1962, Paley Center Archives, New York City.

54. Comedy albums, particularly of the risqué blue, or sophisticated, type, were frequently called party albums and were listened to during social gatherings. *Playboy* magazine referred to hi-fi systems and party records as part of the culture of bachelor-pad sophistication that it promoted. "Comedy Album Sales Brighten," *Billboard*, November 20, 1961, 19; Kercher, *Revel with a Cause*, 238; Sahl, *Heartland*, 18–19.

55. "Ellington, Mort Sahl Feud over Top Billing, So Duke Takes a Walk," *Chicago Defender*, July 12, 1960, 21; "Duke Quits Date in Feud with Night Club Comedian," *Baltimore Afro-American*, July 16, 1960, 15.

56. "An Impolite Interview with Mort Sahl," *Realist*, no. 43 (September 1963), 24–25.

57. Ibid., 26.

58. Ronald K. L. Collins and David M. Skover, *The Trials of Lenny Bruce: The Fall and Rise of an American Icon* (Naperville, IL: Sourcebooks, 2002), 11–75, 345.

59. Kercher, *Revel with a Cause*, 397–440; Goldman, *Lenny Bruce*, 204–7, 345, 456–79.

60. *People v. Bruce* trial transcript, 291, San Francisco City and County Court, March 5–8, 1962, San Francisco History Center, SFPL.

61. Henry Miller to Richard "Lord" Buckley, February 15, 1955, box 7, folder 3, Henry Miller Papers, collection 110, Department of Special Collections, Charles E. Young Research Library, UCLA.

62. Sigmund Freud, *Totem and Taboo: Some Points of Agreement between the Mental Lives of Savages and Neurotics*, transl. James Strachey (New York: W. W. Norton, 1952; originally published in German 1913), 14; *Obscene: A Portrait of Barney Rosset and Grove Press*, directed by Neil Ortenberg and Daniel O'Connor (New York: Double O Film Productions, 2007), DVD; "Interview: Enrico Banducci," Banducci biography file. Even conventional comedy occasionally tackled taboos in mild form. Freud noted that one of the strictest social taboos forbids close male relationships with mothers-in-law, the root of one of Western culture's most time-worn gags.

63. The inability of Bruce's humor to translate onto the page is essentially part of his role as a modern shaman. Like the music and chants that accompany tribal myths, Bruce's routines had a flow and a cadence that were intrinsic to their appeal. See Claude Levi-Strauss,

Mythologiques, vol. 1, *The Raw and the Cooked: Introduction to a Science of Mythology*, transl. John Weightman and Doreen Weightman (New York: Harper Torchbooks, 1969; originally published in French 1964), 28.

64. Goldman, *Lenny Bruce*, 73–98, 109–12, 471; Kercher, *Revel with a Cause*, 397–98.

65. Russ Wilson, "S.F. Turns Back on New Network Show," *Oakland Tribune*, April 20, 1958, B-19; Lenny Bruce, *How to Talk Dirty and Influence People* (New York: Fireside, first Fireside ed., 1992; first published by Playboy Enterprises 1965), 16–22, 50.

66. George Laine, "Everybody's in Calypso Act," *Independent Star News* (Los Angeles), June 6–7, 1957, 11-Z1–Z2, 9-Z3; Norwood "Pony" Poindexter, *The Pony Express: Memoirs of a Jazz Musician* (Frankfurt, Germany: JAS, 1985), 189–90; Jack Lind, "When Jazz Was King," *North Beach Magazine*, vol. 1, no. 2 (Fall 1985), 6–11, 34–37.

67. Bill Morgan, *The Beat Generation in San Francisco: A Literary Tour* (San Francisco: City Lights Books, 2003), 82–83; Lenny Bruce to Lawrence Ferlinghetti, January 23 and 24, 1963, both in box 2, folder 10, City Lights Books records, BANC MSS 72/107c, Bancroft Library, UC Berkeley; Goldman, *Lenny Bruce*, 345, 205–7, 256.

68. J. D. Salinger was among the literati who went to the Blue Angel. Colby, *Bitter End*, 29; Lenny Bruce, *Lenny Bruce—American*, Fantasy Records F 7011, 1959, LP; Sukenick, *Down and In*, 83; Max Gordon, *Live at the Village Vanguard* (New York: St. Martin's Press, 1980), 75–77; witness testimony notes, box 3, folder 1, Ephraim London Papers, MS 6260282, Rare Book and Manuscript Library, Columbia University; Kercher, *Revel with a Cause*, 422.

69. Lenny Bruce, *The Sick Humor of Lenny Bruce*, Fantasy Records 7001, 1958, LP.

70. Lenny Bruce to Alvah Bessie, March 23, 1960, box 2, folder 12, Bessie Papers; Bruce, *How to Talk Dirty*, 17.

71. "David Amram Remembers," in *Empty Phantoms: Interviews and Encounters with Jack Kerouac*, ed. Paul Maher (New York: Thunder's Mouth Press, 2005), 421–23; Philip Whalen journal, 21, June 17, 1964, San Francisco, box 1, folder 7, April 21, 1964–February 24, 1966, BANC MSS 2000/93, Philip Whalen Papers, Bancroft Library, UC Berkeley.

72. Helen Weaver to Reinhold Niebuhr, July 30, 1964, box 3, folder 1, London Papers; Kercher, *Revel with a Cause*, 419. Niebuhr later admitted that he was unfamiliar with Bruce's material and that signing Ginsberg's petition was a mistake, but he also never spoke out against the comic.

73. *Lenny Bruce: Swear to Tell the Truth*, directed by Robert Weide, Whayaduck Productions, HBO documentary, 1998.

74. Bruce's transgressive language backfired badly when he faced Justice Thurgood Marshall during his obscenity trial appeal. Attempting to perform a routine that illustrated the hypocrisy of white liberals with a scene featuring a white defendant before an all-black jury, Bruce concluded, "They gave me twenty years for raising my voice—those niggers." With this, Marshall's "head jerked up immediately," leaving a fumbling Bruce unable to explain the joke. Collins and Skiver, *Trials of Lenny Bruce*, 304; Bayard Rustin to Lenny Bruce, April 19, 1960, box 2, folder 12, Bessie Papers. See also Randall Kennedy, *Nigger: The Strange Career of a Troublesome Word* (New York: Vintage Books, 2002).

75. By all accounts, Bruce's relationship with Eric Miller was close, perhaps even sexual. But according to Albert Goldman, Dick Gregory once asked Bruce to participate in a civil rights rally, to which Bruce responded: "No, man, I'd just bring a lotta heat on you! Besides, the marchers are sloppy: [blind singer] Al Hibbler walks right into people!" "Enrico Banducci Interview," Banducci biography file; Kercher, *Revel with a Cause*, 404; Goldman, *Ladies and Gentlemen*, 504–7.

76. Nat Hentoff, "The Humorist as Grand Inquisitor," *Liberation* (May 1963), 27–29; Lenny Bruce, *The Carnegie Hall Concert*, CDP 7243 8 34020 2 1 (Hollywood, CA: World Pacific, 1995), CD.

77. Lenny Bruce to Alvah Bessie, September 12, 1960, and June 15, 1959, and Alvah Bessie to Lenny Bruce, November 5, 1960, all in box 2, folder 12, Bessie Papers.

78. Kenneth Tynan, "Introduction," in Lenny Bruce, *How to Talk Dirty*, xiii; Cándida Smith, *Utopia and Dissent*, 274.

79. Arthur Gelb, "Comic Gives Shocks with Moral," *New York Times*, December 8, 1960, 44; Hentoff, "Humorist as Grand Inquisitor"; Collins and Skover, *Trials of Lenny Bruce*, 144–45.

80. Hentoff, "Humorist as Grand Inquisitor"; Bruce trial transcript, 289–90, SFPL; Abigail Hastings and Grace Goodman, "Howard Moody, 91, Activist Pastor Who Led Judson Church," September 20, 2012, *Villager*, http://thevillager.com/2012/09/20/howard-moody-91-activist-pastor-who-led-judson-church/. Hastings and Goodman note that "most would be surprised to learn that the first occasion of the word 'fuck' to appear in the pages of the *Voice* was Moody's article."

81. For an overview of both cases, see Collins and Skover, *Trials of Lenny Bruce*, 11–75. See also Christopher Lowen Agee, *The Streets of San Francisco: Policing and the Creation of a Cosmopolitan Liberal Politics, 1950–1972* (Chicago: University of Chicago Press, 2014), 110–43.

82. Goldman, *Lenny Bruce*, 345, 205–7, 256; Lenny Bruce to Lawrence Ferlinghetti, January 23 and 24, 1963, both in box 2, folder 10, City Lights Books records.

83. Orrin Keepnews, *The View from Within: Jazz Writings, 1948–1987* (New York: Oxford University Press, 1988), 150; Ernest van den Haag, "Kerouac Was Here," *Social Problems*, vol. 6, no. 1 (Summer 1958), 21–28.

84. Transcribed in Collins and Skover, *Trials of Lenny Bruce*, 48.

85. Knute Stiles interview, 14, 17, May 30, 1982, conducted by Lewis Ellingham, at the East–West House, 733 Baker Street, San Francisco, box 4, folder 7, and John Allen Ryan interview, 117, both in Ellingham research materials; Agee, *Streets of San Francisco*, chapters 2–3.

86. Collins and Skover, *Trials of Lenny Bruce*, 50–51.

87. *Lenny Bruce: Swear to Tell the Truth*; Edward de Grazia, *Girls Lean Back Everywhere: The Law of Obscenity and the Assault on Genius* (New York: Random House, 1992), 461–79.

88. Bruce trial transcript, 14, 304–5, SFPL.

89. Ibid., 193, 202, 234, 324, 78–79, as well as 48–49, 73–80, 235–64. Ralph J. Gleason, "An Unorthodox Pulpit for Lenny Bruce," *San Francisco Chronicle*, October 10, 1961, 35; Michael Harris, "Lenny Bombs in Court Scene," *San Francisco Chronicle*, November 18, 1961, 3.

90. Bruce trial transcript, 199, 308, SFPL.

91. Ibid., 44–49.

92. Ibid., 29–31, 44–45, 87–88.

93. Ibid., 201–2.

94. James Joyce, *Ulysses* (New York: Vintage International, 1990; originally published in Paris 1922), 742; Bruce trial transcript, 306, SFPL.

95. Bruce trial transcript, 210–15, 196, SFPL.

96. Ibid., 50–51. This gendered concern was echoed in Bruce's New York trial, as sociologist Herbert Gans affirmed that such language was "used with groups of women together" and "in mixed company" among the subjects of his suburban studies. Collins and Skover, *Trials of Lenny Bruce*, 254.

97. Bruce trial transcript 73–79, 180, 195, 109–14.

98. John P. Shanley, "TV Review," *New York Times*, May 13, 1959, 75; Gelb, "Comic Gives Shocks"; Jonathan Miller, "The Sick White Negro," *Partisan Review*, vol. 30 (Spring 1963), 149–55. As Albert Goldman notes, quoting Eldridge Cleaver, beatniks were often considered "a clutch of middle-class white kids adopting the life-style of 'niggers.'" Goldman, *Lenny Bruce*, 189.

99. Lawrence Laurent, "Time and the Pioneers of Humor March On," *Washington Post and Times Herald*, July 10, 1959, D-5; "A Look at the Legal Obscenity Laws in the Soviet Union, in France," December 1963, 2, and "The Forgotten People—the Community," November 1963, 4, both in *Operation Yorkville* (New York City) newsletter, box 2, folder 1, London Papers; de Grazia, *Girls Lean Back Everywhere*, 434. Bruce saw his prosecutions as an organized conspiracy, and went as far as filing a complaint with the FBI office in San Francisco. Unsurprisingly, the bureau did not take him seriously. A newspaper clipping sent to J. Edgar Hoover by a concerned citizen was telling in this regard, as was Hoover's thankful reply. The journalist, supportive of Bruce, had stated in the article that the comic had little chance for justice "in a place whose standards of morality were set by Frank Hogan and Cardinal Spellman and J. Edgar Hoover." "Subject: Lennie Bruce," FBI Records: The Vault, https://vault.fbi.gov/Lenny%20Bruce/.

100. Collins and Skover, *Trials of Lenny Bruce*, 72–77, 251–55; Marin Garbus to Art D'Lugoff, July 13, 1964, box 3, folder 1, London Papers; Free Speech Movement records, carton 2, folder 48, CU-309, Bancroft Library, UC Berkeley. Collins and Skover report that Kilgallen's testimony moved Bruce to tears, with him finding more validation in her middle-American viewpoint than in the *Village Voice* or the ACLU.

101. Arthur E. Bondy to Mayor Robert Wagner, April 4, 1964, box 3, folder 1, London Papers; George P. Selaiden, attorney at law, to Lenny Bruce, May 4, 1960, Bessie Papers; Goldman, *Lenny Bruce*, 363; Krassner, *Confessions*, 73. As Krassner later asserted, on at least one occasion, prosecutor Richard Kuh played Bruce's records in his apartment to impress a date.

102. Collins and Skover, *Trials of Lenny Bruce*, 272–73; Richard H. Kuh, *Foolish Figleaves?: Pornography In and Out of Court* (New York: Macmillan, 1967), 175–211; *People v. Bruce*, trial transcript, June 17, 1964, part 2-C, 4, Criminal Court of New York, County of New York, in London Papers.

103. Andrew Ross, *No Respect: Intellectuals & Popular Culture* (New York: Routledge, 1989), 82–90.

104. In a rare glimpse of the bohemian mutual-aid economy at work in the nightclub culture, in 1958 Peter Orlovsky wrote to Allen Ginsberg, stating that he would go hear Kerouac read at a Village club "if I can get in free but so many of Jack's friends want to get in free so don't know if I can do it." Peter Orlovsky to Allen Ginsberg, March 20, 1958, box 4, folder 41, Allen Ginsberg Papers, M0733, Department of Special Collections, Stanford University Libraries.

105. Lenny Bruce to Alvah Bessie, March 23, 1960, box 2, folder 12, Bessie Papers. This makes Bruce a prime example what theorist Antonio Gramsci terms an organic intellectual.

106. In a letter to his lawyer, Ephraim London, concerning public outrage at his conviction in New York, Bruce wrote: "Don't you know who will reap the hostility? The poor policeman, the foot soldier. The newspaper[s] . . . bring forth the statement from the liberals, 'Gestapo police, how 'bout that, the Goddamn police.' It's not the Goddamn police, but it's 'God damn you,' for denying the trial court something they can judge. Did it ever occur to you that the expert witnesses couldn't relate to the court? The words they used were too

esoteric." Goldman, *Lenny Bruce*, 452; Ross, *No Respect*, 92; de Grazia, *Girls Lean Back Everywhere*, 450; Jack Lind, *Leo's Place: An Oral History of the Beats in San Francisco's North Beach* (Søborg, Denmark: Det Danske Idéselskab, 1998), 90; Kercher, *Revel with a Cause*, 410–12.

107. Bruce, *Carnegie Hall Concert*; Lenny Bruce, *Lenny Bruce—American*, Fantasy Records F 7011, 1959, LP; Collins and Skover, *Trials of Lenny Bruce*, 4, 18; Kercher, *Revel with a Cause*, 408–11.

108. Jeffrey Shandler, *Adventures in Yiddishland: Postvernacular Language and Culture* (Berkeley: University of California Press, 2006), 4, 16–23, 155–76; Kercher, *Revel with a Cause*, 408, 439; James D. Bloom, *Gravity Fails: The Comic Jewish Shaping of Modern America* (Westport, CT: Praeger, 2003); Sahl, *Live at the hungry i*.

109. Goldman, *Lenny Bruce*, 282–83; "Comic Lenny Bruce Douses Pearl Bailey with Acid," *Baltimore Afro-American*, July 9, 1960, 15.

110. Arthur Knight, "Movies and the Racial Divide," in *American Cinema of the 1950s: Themes and Variation*, ed. Murray Pomerance (New Brunswick, NJ: Rutgers University Press, 2005), 222–43; Thomas Doherty, *Cold War, Cool Medium: Television, McCarthyism, and American Culture* (New York: Columbia University Press, 2003), 70–79. Doherty is correct to point out that perpetual reruns of domestic sitcoms like *Leave It to Beaver* have whitened collective memory. Variety shows that featured black performers were live and not recorded, making them impossible to syndicate and adding to the image of a lilywhite 1950s. Yet he overstates the significance of such performances, as they rarely featured material that challenged the cultural status quo, with edgy comics such as Moms Mabley and Redd Foxx banned from the airwaves. See also Andrew J. Falk, *Upstaging the Cold War: American Dissent and Cultural Diplomacy, 1940–1960* (Amherst: University of Massachusetts Press, 2010), 175–77.

111. "Negroes in Cambridge Protest Wallace Talk," *Los Angeles Times*, May 11, 1964, 4; "Soldier Shot, Others Hurt in Maryland: Guardsmen Put Down Racial Demonstration," *Chicago Tribune*, May 26, 1964, 12; Douglas D. Connah Jr., "Gregory Cancels Show, Bids Whites Close Theaters Too," May 28, 1964, 50, and "Plan to Ease Cambridge Tension Set," June 1, 1964, 36, both in *Baltimore Sun*.

112. See Joseph Boskin, *Sambo: The Rise and Demise of an American Jester* (New York: Oxford University Press, 1986); Mel Watkins, *On the Real Side: Laughing, Lying, and Signifying—the Underground Tradition of African American Humor that Transformed American Culture, from Slavery to Richard Pryor* (New York: Simon & Schuster, 1994).

113. Paul Krassner, "Dick Gregory," *Playboy* (August 1964), 39–48.

114. Janet Coleman, *The Compass* (New York: Alfred A. Knopf, 1990); Giovana P. Del Negro, "The Bad Girls of Jewish Comedy: Gender, Class, Assimilation, and Whiteness in Postwar America," in *Jews and Humor*, ed. Leonard J. Greenspoon (West Lafayette, IN: Purdue University Press, 2011); Nachman, *Seriously Funny*. There is a similarity between Nichols and May and the style of Joanne Kyger and George Stanley's *Carola* letters, read at Robert Duncan's last class at the San Francisco Public Library.

115. Dick Gregory, with Robert Lipsyte, *Nigger: An Autobiography* (New York: Pocket Books, 1964), 1–65, 105–7, 127–37; "Club Apex Offers Hit Acts, Fine Music, Food," *Chicago Daily Defender*, March 10, 1959, 18; Kercher, *Revel with a Cause*, 286–87.

116. Gregory, *Nigger*, 142–44.

117. Maureen Cavanaugh and Megan Burke, "Comedian Activist Dick Gregory Is Still Speaking His Truth," KPBS, aired February 22, 2011, KPBS News, www.kpbs.org/news/2011

/feb/22/; Eugene Brooks to Allen Ginsberg, November 19, 1962, box 1, folder 13, series 1, Allen Ginsberg Papers, Rare Book and Manuscript Library, Columbia University Library; Fraterrigo, *Playboy*, 65–73, 141–48; Hugh M. Hefner, *The Playboy Philosophy* (Chicago: HMH, 1963), 10–17, 27–35; Weyr, *Reaching for Paradise*, 24–77.

118. Watkins, *On the Real Side*, 503.

119. Dick Gregory, *In Living Black and White*, Colpix Records CP 417, 1961, LP, reissued by Collector's Choice Music, 2008, CD; Kercher, *Revel with a Cause*, 291; Watkins, *On the Real Side*, 92, 498.

120. Ted Watson, "Comedians 'Warm' behind Dick Gregory's Success," *Pittsburgh Courier*, March 4, 1961, A-23; Arthur Gelb, "Comic Withers Prejudice Clichés," *New York Times*, March 20, 1961, 34; Kercher, *Revel with a Cause*, 290–91; Watkins, *On the Real Side*, 498.

121. Dick Gregory, *East & West*, Colpix Records CP 420, 1961, LP; reissued by Collector's Choice Music, 2008, CD.

122. Ibid.

123. Ibid.

124. Gregory, *Nigger*, 181.

125. Press releases, November 27, 1964, and undated, both in box 18, folder 6, Ivan Black Papers, JPB 06-20, Music Division, NYPL.

126. Gregory, *Nigger*, 191; Krassner, "Dick Gregory." For an example of this financial challenge at ground level, see "Cabaret in Queens Drops Dick Gregory," *New York Times*, April 18, 1963, 38; Dick Gregory and James R. McGraw, *Up from Nigger* (New York: Stein & Day, 1976), 87–89, 150–51; Larry Wilde, "Dick Gregory," in *The Great Comedians* (Secaucus, NJ: Citadel Press, 1968), 256–64.

127. John A. Williams, "Dick Gregory: Desegregated Comic," *Swank* (August 1961), in *Flashbacks: A Twenty-Year Diary of Article Writing* (Garden City, NY: Anchor Press/Doubleday, 1973), 231–39.

128. Kercher, *Revel with a Cause*, 442, 287; Watkins, *On the Real Side*, 496.

129. Gregory, *Nigger*, 105, 132–35; Kercher, *Revel with a Cause*, 291–92.

130. Watkins, *On the Real Side*, 502; Gregory, *Nigger*, 201–9.

131. Dick Gregory and Sheila P. Moses, *Callus on My Soul: A Memoir* (New York: Dafina, 2003), 110–11; "Federal Bureau of Investigation, NW 32621: FBI Chicago Field Office File 157–347, Richard Claxton Gregory, 100-40346," vol. 1, serials 1–149, National Archives, College Park, Maryland.

132. J/B, "Lenny Bruce Obit Was Just a Bit Premature," *Open City Press*, February 17, 1965, 1–2, little magazine collection, San Francisco History Center, SFPL.

Chapter 6. The New Cabaret

1. Paul Colby, with Martin Fitzpatrick, *The Bitter End: Hanging Out at America's Nightclub* (New York: Cooper Square Press, 2002).

2. Michael Harrington, *Fragments of the Century* (New York: Saturday Review Press/E. P. Dutton, 1973), 50; Bob Dylan, "Outlined Epitaphs," *The Times They Are A-Changin'*, Columbia Records CK 8905, 1964, LP.

3. Dan Wakefield, "Night Clubs," *Nation*, January 4, 1958, 19–20.

4. Joyce Johnson, *Minor Characters* (Boston: Houghton Mifflin, 1983), 221. Johnson also suggests that a level of self-sabotage was at work, with Kerouac *predicting* that the readings would be a failure. Legends about his drunkenness at the Village Vanguard abound, including that he threw up into the piano during one performance.

5. Jack Kerouac to Kenneth Rexroth, January 14, 1958, box 11, folder 18, Kenneth Rexroth Papers, collection 175, Department of Special Collections, Charles E. Young Research Library, UCLA.

6. Ronald Sukenick, *Down and In: Life in the Underground* (New York: Beech Tree Books, 1987), 38.

7. In 1954, Malcolm Cowley had already praised the works of Ralph Ellison and Nelson Algren for their postwar return to social conflict. Foreshadowing his attraction to Kerouac, Cowley wrote of Algren, "Instead of leaving us with a feeling of defeat, he celebrates the unconquered personality and humor in the lowest of men: hustlers, junkies, stoolies, dips, stewbums, 'the Republic's crummiest lushes.'" Gilbert Millstein, "O Tempora O Vanguard," *New York Times*, June 16, 1957, SM-7; Malcolm Cowley, "Personalism: A New School of Fiction," *New Republic*, October 18, 1954, 16–18. For a discussion of Cowley's views, see Lawrence Lipton to Kenneth Rexroth, August 21, 1954, box 14, folder 7, Kenneth Rexroth Papers, collection 175, Department of Special Collections, Charles E. Young Research Library, UCLA.

8. Sukenick, *Down and In*, 38–39.

9. Wally Hedrick interview, 16–17, June 10–24, 1974, Archives of American Art, Smithsonian Institution.

10. David Meltzer, "Poetry and Jazz," in *Beat Down to Your Soul: What Was the Beat Generation?*, ed. Anne Charters (New York: Penguin Books, 2001), 399–403.

11. Ibid.

12. Max Gordon, *Live at the Village Vanguard* (New York: St. Martin's Press, 1980), 42; Lawrence Ferlinghetti, "Note on Poetry in San Francisco," *Chicago Review* (Spring 1958), quoted in *Beat Down*, 168; Francis J. Rigney and L. Douglas Smith, *The Real Bohemia: A Sociological and Psychological Study of the "Beats"* (New York: Basic Books, 1961), 178.

13. Kenneth Rexroth, "San Francisco's Mature Bohemians," in *On Bohemia: The Code of the Self-Exiled*, ed. Cesar Grana and Marigay Grana (New Brunswick, NJ: Transaction, 1990), 212–18; Kenneth Rexroth, "Some Thoughts on Jazz as Music, as Revolt, as Mystique," in *Bird in the Bush* (New York: New Directions, 1959), 19–41; Philip Whalen to Allen Ginsberg, October 12, 1959, box 5, folder 49, Allen Ginsberg Papers, M0733, Department of Special Collections, Stanford University Libraries.

14. Allen Ginsberg to Kenneth Rexroth, October 21, 1959, and September 29, 1959, box 8, folder 1, and Jack Kerouac to Kenneth Rexroth, January 14, 1958, box 11, folder 18, all in Rexroth Papers. Ginsberg suggested that, as evidence, Rexroth listen to Fantasy Records' recent recording of a Beat reading and the audience's interaction.

15. "The Cool, Cool Bards," *Time*, December 2, 1957, 71; Sascha Feinstein, *Jazz Poetry: From the 1920s to the Present* (Westport, CT: Greenwood Press, 1997), 61–88.

16. Jazz poetry was not limited to San Francisco or New York City. In 1958, *Chicago Review* editors Irving Rosenthal and Paul Carroll contacted Ginsberg and Kerouac about a poetry reading at the Gate of Horn to benefit the magazine, which was fighting censorship by its publisher, the University of Chicago. Rosenthal noted that the club's owner, Albert Grossman, "sponsors folk singers mainly, I think Jazz too," adding excitedly that Grossman "is also the *manager* of Odetta." This tentative connection became solidified in the early 1960s, when Grossman began to manage Bob Dylan—a fan of Allen Ginsberg, with whom Dylan sometimes collaborated. Grossman was well known as a tough and streetwise manager. (Dylan later recalled that Grossman often carried a gun.) Yet other scenesters, such as Suze Rotolo, also remembered him as attentive to his artists and dedicated to racial justice. For a fascinat-

ing view of Grossman in action, see *Bob Dylan: Don't Look Back*, directed by D. A. Pennebaker (New York: Pennebaker Hgadus Films, 1967), DVD. Irving Rosenthal to Allen Ginsberg and Jack Kerouac, "Dec. 123456789, oy," 1958, box 5, folder 12, Ginsberg Papers, Stanford; Bob Dylan, *Chronicles: Volume One* (New York: Simon & Schuster, 2004), 97; Suze Rotolo, *A Freewheelin' Time: A Memoir of Greenwich Village in the Sixties* (New York: Broadway Books, 2008), 138–39; Linda Hamalian, *A Life of Kenneth Rexroth* (New York: W. W. Norton, 1991), 278–83; "Daddy-O," Talk of the Town, *New Yorker*, May 3, 1958, 29–30; Les Matthews, "Oust Coleman from School Board Post: Baker Czar?" *Chicago Daily Defender*, February 11, 1958, A-9; John S. Wilson, "Jazz and Poetry Share Program: Charles Mingus Quintet and Kenneth Patchen Attempt Accompanied Readings," *New York Times*, March 17, 1959, 42.

17. Rexroth, "Some Thoughts on Jazz," 39–40; Rexroth, "San Francisco's Mature Bohemians," 217.

18. *The Beat Generation: An American Dream*, directed by Janet Forman (New York: WinStar, 1987), VHS; Amiri Baraka [LeRoi Jones], *The Autobiography of LeRoi Jones* (Chicago: Lawrence Hill Books, 1984), 427; J. Michael Lennon, *Norman Mailer: A Double Life* (New York: Simon & Schuster, 2013), 240.

19. Rigney and Smith, *Real Bohemia*, 67–69; Tom Clark, "A Hipster Poet's Nocturnal Muse," undated and unpaginated clipping, Bob Kaufman file, Biography Collection, San Francisco History Center, SFPL; A. D. Winans, "Bob Kaufman," *American Poetry Review*, vol. 29, no. 3 (May/June 2000), 19–20. In Rigney and Smith's book, Kaufman is identified under the pseudonym "Ed." See also James Smethurst, "'Remembering When Indians Were Red': Bob Kaufman, the Popular Front, and the Black Arts Movement," in "Jazz Poetics," special issue, *Callaloo*, vol. 25, no. 1 (Winter 2002), 146–64.

20. US Bureau of the Census, "Enumeration District 84, New Orleans Ward 5, Orleans, Louisiana," *Fourteenth Census of the United States, 1920*, 7-B, roll T625-62, Records of the Bureau of the Census, Record Group 29, National Archives, Washington, DC; Maria Damon, *The Dark End of the Street: Margins in American Vanguard Poetry* (Minneapolis: University of Minnesota Press, 1993), 32–34. Louisiana records list Joseph E. Kaufman and Lillian Rose Vignes' marriage date as January 5, 1914.

21. Lillian Vignes was from a prominent family, light-skinned and classified as "mulatto" in the 1910 and 1920 censuses (and probably able to pass as white), as was Kaufman's father, Joseph. Joseph's racial ambiguities are further implied by his family name and by his eye color, listed as grey on his 1917 draft card, supporting Bob's claim of German Jewish ancestry. Tellingly, as racial lines hardened with Jim Crow policies, by 1930 the Kaufmans were simply labeled "Negro." Lillian's ability to pass as white is supported by the fact that two of her sisters, Leontine Vignes and Cora Vignes Wilson, did precisely that. In the 1920 and 1930 censuses, they were listed as "white," along with Cora's husband Robert Wilson, who had also been "mulatto" in 1910. Moreover, the 1920 census shows Lillian's race marked originally as "octoroon," which was crossed out and replaced with "mulatto," suggesting that she, too, might have been able to pass, had she not married the more visibly African American Joseph. By 1940, Lillian was widowed and heading the family, with support from sons Joseph and George and daughter Marion, who did library research for the NYA. Bob himself began working by age seventeen, shipping out in June 1942—not as a merchant marine but as a messman—on various merchant vessels and US Army transport ships. US Selective Service System, "Registration State: Louisiana, Registration County: Orleans, Draft Board 4," *World War I Selective Service System Draft Registration Cards, 1917–1918*, roll 1684917; US Bureau of the Census, "Enumeration District 0057, Census Place: New Orleans Ward 4,

Orleans, Louisiana," *Thirteenth Census of the United States, 1910*, 6-A, roll T624-520; US Bureau of the Census. "Enumeration District 104, Census Place: New Orleans, Orleans, Louisiana," *Fifteenth Census of the United States, 1930*, 24-A, roll 804; US Bureau of the Census, "Enumeration District 36-183, Census Place: New Orleans, Orleans, Louisiana," *Sixteenth Census of the United States, 1940*, 5-B, roll T627-1424; "Crew Lists of Vessels Arriving at New Orleans, Louisiana, 1910–1945," microfilm T939, roll 285, and "List or Manifest of Aliens Employed on the Vessel as Members of Crew, *S.S. Harold L. Winslow*, arriving New York, NY, June 21, 1944," *Passenger Lists of Vessels Arriving at New York, New York, 1820–1897*, microfilm publication M237, roll 6836, Records of the US Customs Service, record group 36, all in National Archives, Washington, DC. See also Damon, *Dark End of the Street*, 33, 248 n.2; David Henderson, "Introduction," in Bob Kaufman, *Cranial Guitar* (Minneapolis: Coffee Table Press, 1996). For a full examination of New Orleans's racial categories and the history of Storyville, see Emily Epstein Landau, *Spectacular Wickedness: Sex, Race, and Memory in Storyville, New Orleans* (Baton Rouge: Louisiana State University Press, 2013), 48–76.

22. While Cecil Taylor has talked extensively about the influence of Robert Duncan, LeRoi Jones, and Jack Kerouac on his work, apparently Kaufman took the cake. The pianist declared that an all-night talk session with Kaufman, after meeting the latter at the Five Spot, left him completely transformed. Jack Lind, "The Lives of Bob Kaufman," *North Beach Magazine*, vol. 2, no. 1 (Spring 1986), 28–32, 42–44, in Periodicals Collection, San Francisco History Center, SFPL; Christopher Funkhouser, "Being Matter Ignited: An Interview with Cecil Taylor," *Hambone* no. 12 (1995), 17–39; Eileen Kohl Kaufman interview, circa 1959–1996, Bob and Eileen Kaufman Papers, BANC MSS 2007/159, Bancroft Library, UC Berkeley. Various accounts place Bob Kaufman's arrival in San Francisco as early as 1953 or as late as 1957. The documentary record shows he married Eileen in 1958, making even the later date plausible. He visited San Francisco as a port of call in the 1940s, probably making contact with the scene several times before staying there.

23. Richard "Specs" Simmons is another example of the North Beach nocturnal tradition. He met his wife at Vesuvio, and his bar has since carried on the Rebel Café tradition, with its Spanish Civil War posters, living room feel, and declarations of "No sexism or racism allowed" and "There's no juke box or TV here. It's really about people sharing stories and their lives." One story relates that when Kerouac biographer Dennis McNally first arrived in the Bay Area, he went to Specs, telling Simmons, "I just moved to San Francisco," to which the bar owner replied, "Welcome home." Lind, "Lives of Bob Kaufman"; Scott Lettieri, "Peering in at Specs," *North Beach News* (Summer 2004), unpaginated clipping, Specs file, Biography Collection, SFPL.

24. Leo Krikorian recalled that "customers did things like that because they wanted to be out of the ordinary" and that Bob Kaufman would "break my front window every three or four months." The Coexistence Bagel Shop resignedly took a pragmatic approach and "divided the window into smaller panes, so when they broke, it was only a matter of spending ten dollars at a time." Michelle Marin Boleyn, "'Black American Rimbaud': Legendary Beat Poet Bob Kaufman Dies," *San Francisco Chronicle*, 7, undated clipping, Bob Kaufman file, SFPL; Lewis Ellingham and Kevin Killian, *Poet Be Like God: Jack Spicer and the San Francisco Renaissance* (Hanover, NH: University Press of New England, 1998), 131–38, 164; Eileen Kaufman, "From Who Wouldn't Walk with Tigers?," in *Women of the Beat Generation: The Writers, Artists and Muses at the Heart of a Revolution*, ed. Brenda Knight (Berkeley, CA: Conari Press, 1996), 113; Lind, "Lives of Bob Kaufman," 29, 43–45; Lind, *Leo's Place*, 66–68.

25. Russell FitzGerald diary, November 7, 1957, box 9, folder 1, Lewis Ellingham's *Poet Be Like God* research materials, MSS 126, Special Collections and Archives, UC San Diego, courtesy of the Poetry Collection of the University Libraries, University at Buffalo, SUNY; Lind, "Lives of Bob Kaufman," 29; Lind, *Leo's Place*, 66.

26. Quoted in Rigney and Smith, *Real Bohemia*, 119–20.

27. Tony Seymour, "Don't Forget Bob Kaufman," *San Francisco Sunday Examiner and Chronicle*, April 25, 1976, unpaginated clipping, Bob Kaufman file, SFPL; Lind, "Lives of Bob Kaufman," 30, 32, 42; E. Kaufman, "From *Who Wouldn't Walk*," 107.

28. Bob Kaufman, "Abomunist Manifesto" in *Beat Down*, 262–72; John O'Connor, "The Beatnik Disease," *Vigilante*, vol. 3 (Summer 1960), 14, Periodicals Collection, SFPL.

29. Rigney and Smith, *Real Bohemia*, 170–75; Arthur Hoppe, "Beatniks Go After Cop— in Verse," August 14, 1959, 1, 4, "Lawman Rips Poems Off Wall," August 14, 1959, 1, 4, and "Beatnik Cop Wins, Is Moved," August 31, 1960, 4, all in *San Francisco Chronicle*; US Bureau of the Census, "Supervisor's District no. 5, Enumeration District no. 38-243, Census Place: San Francisco, CA," *Sixteenth Census*, 15-A, <roll T627-00307, National Archives, Washington, DC. See also Christopher Lowen Agee, *The Streets of San Francisco: Policing and the Creation of a Cosmopolitan Liberal Politics, 1950–1972* (Chicago: University of Chicago Press, 2014). The episode also showed the conflicts over definitions of or claims on community. Bigarani came from a local San Francisco family: his father was a watchman, and his aunt—like Kaufman's sister—worked for the NYA. His stance was like that of many ethnic whites who resented the influx of blacks amid war mobility in the 1940s, despite the objective similarity of their working-class, New Deal backgrounds. Bigarani was later charged with corruption, stemming from unrelated incidents.

30. Rotolo, *Freewheelin' Time*, 112–15. Rotolo considered Dave Van Ronk's politics, which she described as part of the anti-CP Trotskyite Left, to be an influence on both Dylan and herself.

31. Tram Combs's correspondence and literary ties to *Liberation* illustrate these networks. Although he rarely published in the magazine, he identified himself as the sole subscriber in the US Virgin Islands and stayed in contact with editors Bayard Rustin and David McReynolds, also of the War Resisters League. In addition, Combs maintained ties with radical bohemians, such as Gerd Stern and Philip Lamantia, through correspondence and during visits to New York City. See various correspondence, box 2, folder 10, and box 3, folder 2, Tram Combs Papers, Mandeville Special Collections Library, UC San Diego.

32. Maurice Isserman, *The Other American: The Life of Michael Harrington* (New York: Public Affairs, 2000), 219; Harrington, *Fragments of the Century*, 47–48; Michael Harrington interview, November 19, 1982, folder 35, Dan Wakefield interview, 14, February 7, 1993, folder 94, and George Rawick telephone interview, August 17, 1984, folder 71, all in box 1, Maurice Isserman research files for *The Other American: The Life of Michael Harrington*, TAM.239, Taminent Library / Robert F. Wagner Labor Archives, Elmer Holmes Bobst Library, New York University. If Ginsberg was in the YSL, he certainly remained on the fringes. It was reportedly a YSL event with Max Shachtman, however, that was the source for the line in "Howl" asking "Who threw potato salad at CCNY lectures on Dadaism?" George Rawick recalled that Lawrence Ferlinghetti also had ties to the Shachtmanites.

33. Isserman, *The Other American*, 108, 199, 219, 227–29, 270–74; Harrington, *Fragments of the Century*, 50.

34. Jane Warwick interview, 2, 6, 11–12, January 6, 1999, box 1, folder 96, Isserman research files.

35. Jane Jacobs, *The Death and Life of Great American Cities* (New York: Random House, 1961), 29, 36, 40–41, 244–45; Anthony Flint, *Wrestling with Moses: How Jane Jacobs Took On New York's Master Builder and Transformed the American City* (New York: Random House, 2009), 104–8, 132, 155, 176. Flint also reports that Bob Dylan wrote a protest song (left unnamed) against the Lomex Crosstown Freeway over Lower Manhattan, another small link between the Rebel Café and politics. Jacobs did note that too great a concentration of entertainment businesses could also have deleterious effects, as seen in the Third Street bar scene, where large numbers of tourists caused disruptions.

36. Ned Polsky, *Hustlers, Beats, and Others* (New York: Anchor Books, paperback ed. 1969; first published 1967), 150; Harrington, *Fragments of the Century*, 50.

37. Larry Rivers and Arnold Weinstein, *What Did I Do?: The Unauthorized Autobiography* (New York: HarperCollins, 1992), 201; Lawrence Lipton to Kenneth Rexroth, April 23, 1956, box 14, folder 7, Rexroth Papers. See also Johnson, *Minor Characters*, 26–30.

38. Bob Dylan, *Chronicles: Volume One* (New York: Simon & Schuster, 2004), 9–17, 47, 55, 73, 83, 235, 258–62.

39. Rotolo, *Freewheelin' Time*, 14–15, 43–49, 250, 364–65.

40. *Hart's Guide to New York City* (New York: Hart, 1964), 875; Lorraine Gordon, as told to Barry Singer, *Alive at the Village Vanguard: My Life In and Out of Jazz Time* (Milwaukee: Hal Leonard, 2006), 106–9.

41. Sherri Cavan, *Liquor License: An Ethnography of Bar Behavior* (Chicago: Aldine, 1966), 161–70.

42. Gilbert Millstein, "Lament for New York's Night Life," *New York Times*, May 22, 1955, 233; Arthur Gelb, "Barbs Salute the Blue Angel, 20," *New York Times*, April 16, 1963, 31.

43. This discourse also surrounded Chicago nightclubs, such as the Gate of Horn and the Blue Note, which featured performers like Josh White and Dave Brubeck. Nat Hentoff, however, scoffed at Blue Angel crowds as being falsely sophisticated and concerned only with their sense of dress and style, in contrast to the Village Vanguard's crowds of socially conscious young liberals. Lawrence E. Davies, "Audiences Vary, Satirists Find," *New York Times*, August 31, 1963, 9; Knight Rambler, "Bright Lights: Kay Thompson Wins Fans," *San Francisco News*, May 22, 1954, 4; Margaret Cairns, "Local Groundlings," letter to the editor, *San Francisco Chronicle*, March 9, 1962, 32; Will Leonard, "On the Town," September 10, 1961, E-5, and September 25, 1955, E-10, both in *Chicago Daily Tribune*; Nat Hentoff, *Free Speech for Me—but Not for Thee: How the American Left and Right Relentlessly Censor Each Other* (New York: HarperCollins, 1992), 328.

44. Gene DeForrest, "About Town," *San Francisco Call-Bulletin*, July 17, 1954, 8; J. L. Pimsleur, "The Canoon, the Oud and a Belly Dancer," *San Francisco Chronicle*, October 15, 1961, 4; Herb Caen, *Only in San Francisco* (New York: Doubleday, 1960), 211–12.

45. Elaine Tyler May, *Homeward Bound: American Families in the Cold War Era* (New York: Basic Books, 1988); Wini Breines, *Young, White, and Miserable: Growing Up Female in the Fifties* (Boston: Beacon Press, 1992), 6–22, 127–66; Cavan, *Liquor License*, 166. Breines convincingly argues that black culture's influence was often missed by academics, such as by David Riesman. Yet its racial objectification was another example in which the myth of African American male hypersexuality combined with what Farah Jasmine Griffin calls the "white supremacist aesthetic of beauty" to negate black womanhood. Farah Jasmine Griffin, *If You Can't Be Free, Be a Mystery: In Search of Billie Holiday* (New York: Free Press, 2001), 178–79.

46. L. Gordon, *Alive at the Village Vanguard*, 112; author's interview with Charles and Marlene Inman, June 19, 2011, in Sutter Creek, California; Maxwell T. Cohen, *The Police Card Discord* (Metuchen: Scarecrow Press and Institute of Jazz Studies, Rutgers–The State University of New Jersey, 1993), 19–20; Paul Chevigny, *Gigs: Jazz and the Cabaret Laws in New York City* (New York: Routledge, 2nd ed., 2005; first published 1991), 59; Mark Caldwell, *New York Night: The Mystique and Its History* (New York: Scribner, 2005), 310. Economic and social control issues also guided nightclub regimens. Performances were often held twice nightly, in an effort to bring in enough income to pay performers, which necessitated assigned seating. Additionally, New York's municipal government maintained more oversight on nightclubs with entertainment than on bars. Thus nightclubs could regularly count on police raids to spot performers who skirted the city's cabaret card requirement and owners who hid their earnings to avoid the cabaret tax. As a result, it's unsurprising that nightclub owners maintained careful vigilance over the behavior of their audiences, always aware of law enforcement's prying eyes.

47. M. Gordon, *Live at the Village Vanguard*, 75; author's interview with Lorraine Gordon, April 22, 2011, New York City; "The Reminiscences of Art D'Lugoff," 11, interviews on September 20 and November 6, 1996, conducted by Christiane Bird, Oral History Research Office, Columbia University, 1999. Lorraine Gordon, noting the Vanguard's liberal policies, told a story, with a certain amount of affection, about meeting two beautiful transvestites in the women's room.

48. Johnson, *Minor Characters*, 187–88.

49. Fritz Bosworth, "Some Call It North Beach," *Today's San Franciscan*, vol. 2, no. 2 (May 1, 1959), 17–19, Periodicals Collection, San Francisco History Center, SFPL; John Wilcock, *The Village Square* (New York: Lyle Stuart, 1961), 154–55.

50. Such alliances were also fraught with divisions. Gay bohemians like Jack Spicer and Allen Ginsberg displayed their fair share of misogyny, and Denise Levertov once asserted that while she had "individual homosexual friends," she nonetheless found "homosexual males & lesbians uncongenial in groups, when they reinforce each other's sexism toward heterosexuals." Ellingham and Killian, *Poet Be Like God*, 117, 125–26, 138, 392 n.23.

51. Ann Bannon, *I Am a Woman* (Greenwich, CT: Fawcett, 1959), 5–9, 27, 30–42, 64–72, 80–90, 193–94, 222–24.

52. Susan Sontag, "Notes on Camp," in *Against Interpretation and Other Essays* (New York: Farrar, Straus & Giroux, 1966), 283; Nan Alamilla Boyd, *Wide Open Town: A History of Queer San Francisco to 1965* (Berkeley: University of California Press, 2003), 57–62, 210–12, 242.

53. "Self-Taught Painter Shows at De Young,"1, and "Peggy Tolk Watkins Paints for Kids & Adults," 7, undated clippings, Harriet Sohmers Zwerling, "Peggy," and photograph of Richmond, California, mural, dated 1945, listing Peggy Tolk as "instructor," all courtesy of Ragland Tolk Watkins (also archived in the San Francisco Historical Society); author's interview with Ragland Tolk Watkins, December 4, 2012, New York City; US Bureau of the Census, "Supervisor's District no. 10, Enumeration District no. 24–634, Census Place: New York, NY," *Sixteenth Census*, 3-B, roll T627-02562, National Archives, Washington, DC; "Tin Angel's Peggy Tolk-Watkins Dies," *San Francisco Chronicle*, June 26, 1973, and "Tin Angel Operator Dead at 51," *San Francisco Examiner*, June 26, 1973, unpaginated clippings, Peggy Tolk-Watkins file, *Examiner* morgue, San Francisco History Center, SFPL.

54. Rafael Marin, "Marin Musings," June 2, 1949, 1, and September 29, 1949, 1, and "Deyala Missed Fun of His Celebration at Sausalito Regatta," September 26, 1949, 1–3, all in *Independent Journal* (San Rafael, CA).

55. "Foster, Watson, and Norman Art Exhibits," November 3, 1950, 20, and "Tin Angel Sold: Glad Hand to Take Its Place," July 6, 1951, 18, both in *Independent Journal* (San Rafael, CA); Ralph J. Gleason, "Days of Peggy and Helen," This World, *San Francisco Chronicle*, July 8, 1973, 33; "Tin Angel," 33-A, unidentified and undated clipping, courtesy of Ragland Tolk Watkins; author's interview with Ragland Tolk Watkins.

56. Harriet Sohmers Zwerling, "Peggy," courtesy of Ragland Tolk Watkins. See also Harriet Sohmers Zwerling, *Abroad: An Expatriate's Diaries* (New York: Spuyten Duyvil, 2014).

57. Gleason, "Days"; Dick Nolan, "Stuff & Nonsense," December 4, 1958, and April 7, 1960, both unpaginated, *San Francisco Examiner* clippings, Peggy Tolk-Watkins file, *Examiner* morgue, SFPL; Peggy Tolk-Watkins to Bill and Joan Roth, undated [ca. 1960], courtesy of Ragland Tolk Watkins (also archived in the San Francisco Historical Society).

58. Gleason, "Days"; B. C., "And Then There Was San Francisco," *Metronome* (November 1955), 23.

59. Gleason, "Days"; "Tin Angel Is Peggy's—Sale Off," *San Francisco Chronicle*, November 6, 1956, unpaginated clipping, Peggy Tolk-Watkins file, *Examiner* morgue, SFPL.

60. "The Cool, Cool Bards," *Time*, December 2, 1957, 71; Brio Burgess, *Wail!: An American Journey; A Novel in Autobiographical Vignette Form* (Tempe, AZ: Jacob's Ladder Books, 2002), 47–49, 26–34; John Allen Ryan to Jack Spicer, March 20, 1956, box 3, folder 27, Jack Spicer Papers, BANC MSS 2004/209, Bancroft Library, UC Berkeley; "Agreement Contract: *Peggy Tolk-Watkins and Irmine Droeger v. Tin Angel, Inc.* (Max Weiss, et al.), Dismissal of Superior Court of California Case #473967," July 30, 1961, courtesy of Ragland Tolk Watkins. Droeger enlisted in 1944, and her occupation was written down as a reporter and editor. World War II Army Enlistment Records, record group 64, National Archives, College Park, Maryland; Suzette, "Pot Pourri of Romantic News, Travel and Fashion Shows," *Oakland Tribune*, February 28, 1961, 17.

61. Herb Caen, "La Triviata," December 1, 1955, and untitled articles, October 17, 1955, and December 7, 1955, all unpaginated *San Francisco Examiner* clippings, Fallen Angel file, *Examiner* morgue, SFPL.

62. Sally Stanford was clearly a model or mentor for Peggy Tolk-Watkins, as Stanford was a fiercely independent woman who owned a restaurant in Sausalito, the Valhalla, after closing her brothel on Pine Street. Born Mabel Busby, Stanford collected noms de plume, including Marcia Spagnoli and Claire Gold. Stanford was also politically active, often speaking out on issues in Sausalito and making an impressive, through unsuccessful, run for city council in 1962. Author's interview with Ragland Tolk Watkins; "Peggy Tolk-Watkins," undated and unpaginated article, courtesy of Ragland Tolk Watkins; Curt Gentry, *The Madams of San Francisco: An Irreverent History of the City by the Golden Gate* (Garden City, NY: Doubleday, 1964), 163–66, 275–78, 310–11.

63. Boyd, *Wide Open Town*, 83–88; John D'Emilio and Estelle B. Freedman, *Intimate Matters: A History of Sexuality in America* (Chicago: University of Chicago Press, 2nd. ed., 1997; first published 1988), 256–64.

64. "Peggy Tolk-Watkins," courtesy of Ragland Tolk Watkins; author's interview with Ragland Tolk Watkins.

65. Ralph J. Gleason, "The Kid Is Down 'On the Levee' Blowing Good," *San Francisco Chronicle*, September 14, 1958, 25; Herb Caen, "Business as Usual," This World, September 25, 1956, "Sausalito's Free Spirits Swing into Action," May 27, 1959, and "It Was a Fist, Not a Glass," June 2, 1959, all unpaginated *San Francisco Chronicle* clippings, Peggy Tolk-Watkins file, *Examiner* morgue, SFPL.

66. Burgess, *Wail!*, 47, 89–90.

67. Susan Sontag, *Reborn: Journals and Notebooks, 1947–1964*, ed. David Rieff (New York: Farrar, Strauss & Giroux, 2008), 23–25.

68. "Notebook #21," May 7, 1949–May 31, 1949, box 123, folder 5, Susan Sontag Papers, collection 612, Department of Special Collections, Charles E. Young Research Library, UCLA.

69. Sontag, *Reborn*, 24–27.

70. "Notebook #21," Sontag Papers; Sontag, *Reborn*, 25–26. "Peggy Tolk-Watkins" is written in the margin of the original notebook but omitted from *Reborn*.

71. Sontag, *Reborn*, 27.

72. Ibid., 27–29, 34.

73. Ibid., 31–36; "Notebook #21," entries for May 28, 1949, March 23, 1950, April 3, 1950, and April 22, 1950, Sontag Papers; Zwerling, *Abroad*, 264–94.

74. Sontag, *Reborn*, 44, 70, 160–83, 198–208; "Notebook #22," June 1, 1949–September 16, 1949, folder 6, "Notebook #24," December 28, 1949–[undated], folder 8, and "Notebook, 1956–1957," folder 10, all in box 123, "Notebook, 1957–60," folder 5, "Notebook, 1960," folder 6, and "Notebook, 1963–5," folder 11, all in box 124, Sontag Papers.

75. Sontag, *Reborn*, 95, 173, 220, 159, 244. See also Alice Kaplan, *Dreaming in French: The Paris Years of Jacqueline Bouvier Kennedy, Susan Sontag, and Angela Davis* (Chicago: University of Chicago Press, 2013).

76. Sontag, *Against Interpretation*, 274, 277, 7, 10, 13–14, 288; "Notebook, 1957," undated entry, box 124, folder 1, Sontag Papers.

77. Sontag, *Against Interpretation*, 277, 14. For a brief but cogent queer feminist view on Sontag's public role, see Yoshie Furuhashi, "Sexing Susan Sontag," May–June 2005, Solidarity, www.solidarity-us.org/site/node/287/.

78. Greil Marcus, *Lipstick Traces: A Secret History of the Twentieth Century* (Cambridge, MA: Harvard University Press, 1989), 284.

79. Edward Downes, "'Poeme' by Varese Has United States Premiere," November 10, 1958, 36, and "Rebel from Way Back," November 16, 1958, X-11, both in *New York Times*; Cohen, *Police Card Discord*, 56; Dan Wakefield, *New York in the Fifties* (New York: St. Martin's Griffin, 1992), 313; Philip Benjamin, "'Villager' Accuser Will Help Police," April 13, 1961, 36, and "City Is Criticized on Cafe Licensing," May 10, 1961, 32, both in *New York Times*.

80. Sidney E. Zion, "Lindsay Placates Coffeehouse Set," *New York Times*, May 3, 1966, 49; Sukenick, *Down and In*, 100–101; Norman Mailer, "Lindsay and the City," *Village Voice*, October 28, 1965, in *Village Voice Anthology*, 113. See also *Greenwich Village News*, September 2 and 8, 1960, for more general accounts of local insistence on neighborhood preservation.

81. Murray Schumach, "'Villagers' Are Facing Summer's Din with Quiet Despair," *New York Times*, April 24, 1967, 35.

82. John Allen Ryan to Jack Spicer, March 20, 1956, box 3, folder 27, Spicer Papers; "Only Dignity Injured in Bagel Shop 'Bombing,'" *San Francisco Chronicle*, July 15, 1958, "Bagel Interlude: Bomb Jolts Beatniks," July 21, 1958, and "Beatnik 'Bomb' Called Harmless," July 22, 1958, all unpaginated *San Francisco Examiner* clippings, Coexistence Bagel Shop file, *Examiner* morgue, SFPL.

83. *Beat Narrative*, directed by Dion Vigne (1960), film, and *Amazing Footage Featuring Christopher Maclaine*, directed by Dion Vigne [ca. 1957–1960], film, Berkeley Art Museum and Pacific Film Archive, Berkeley, California; Jerry Stoll and Evan S. Connell Jr., *I Am a Lover* (Oakland, CA: Angel Island, 1961), unpaginated; Rigney and Smith, *Real Bohemia*, 159–61; untitled, May 13, 1958, and "Ahern Denies 'Going After' Bagel Shop," July 8, 1959, both

unpaginated *San Francisco Chronicle* clippings, Coexistence Bagel Shop file, *Examiner* morgue, SFPL.

84. "This Is a Tale of 'Beatniks'," and "S.F. Police Arrest Negro Publisher-Physician," both in *Los Angeles Tribune*, August 7, 1959, 6; "Bearded Agents Lead Dope Raid on S.F. Beatniks," *San Francisco Chronicle*, January 23, 1960, 1, 4.

85. Robert LaVigne to Allen Ginsberg, June 22, 1958, box 4, folder 5, and John Allen Ryan to Allen Ginsberg, February 15, 1957, box 5, folder 15, both in Ginsberg Papers, Stanford; Jack Lind, *Leo's Place: An Oral History of the Beats in San Francisco's North Beach* (Søborg, Denmark: Det Danske Idéselskab, 1998), 92.

86. "Welcome to My Pad? Like Union (Square, Man): 100 Beatniks Visit the Real World," *San Francisco Chronicle*, August 12, 1958, 1, 5; Rigney and Smith, *Real Bohemia*, 161.

87. "Big Beatnik Rally to Protest Raids," *San Francisco Chronicle*, January 31, 1960, 1, 5; Lee Stothers, "Protests Doomed to Failure," *S.F. Territorial News and Hickory Stick Almanac*, vol. 3, ed. 1 (July 1960), 1–2.

88. While bohemians had occasional conflicts with minority populations, geographer Brian Godfrey argues, subcultures nonetheless offered internal order and stability that simultaneously embraced multiculturalism and civility. Clinton Robert Starr, "Bohemian Resonance: The Beat Generation and Urban Countercultures in the United States during the Late 1950s and Early 1960s," PhD diss., University of Texas at Austin, 2005, 300–303, 311–25; Rigney and Smith, *Real Bohemia*, 163–65; "Red Probers Booed by Crowd When They Appear on Balcony," May 15, 1960, "60 in Riot Leave Fate to Judge: Waive Trial, Civil Actions," May 28, 1960, and Jerry Kamstra, "The Grim Plight," December 7, 1969, all in *San Francisco Examiner*, and Maitland Zane, "Ex-Smuggler . . . Jailed," *San Francisco Chronicle*, July 12, 1974, all unpaginated clippings in Jerry Kamstra file, *Examiner* morgue, SFPL; Brian J. Godfrey, *Neighborhoods in Transition: The Making of San Francisco's Ethnic and Nonconformist Communities* (Berkeley: University of California Press, 1988), 15–17, 208.

89. Donovan McClure, "Police Visit Black Hawk, Play It Cool," *San Francisco Chronicle*, January 26, 1961, 1, 4.

90. Ralph J. Gleason, "Cops Are Confused about the Black Hawk," January 26, 1961, 27, "Rhyme Your Squawk about the Black Hawk," January 31, 1961, 27, letters to the editor, January 31, 1961, 26, and "Christopher Swings at Black Hawk," February 13, 1961, 36, all in *San Francisco Chronicle*.

91. "Black Hawk Owners Ask Trial," February 1, 1961, 34, Tom Mathews, "Blackhawk Massacres the Mayor," February 22, 1961, 1, 8, "Mayor Blasts State over Blackhawk," February 23, 1961, 1, 7, and "Mayor Taps Foot as Judge Clears Blackhawk," February 24, 1961, 3, all in *San Francisco Chronicle*.

92. "Cops Again Raid Black Hawk, Oust Teen-Agers," January 27, 1961, 1, 5, letters to the editor, February 2, 1961, 26, and Ralph J. Gleason, "A Few Lonely Words in Defense of the Lowly Saloon," This World, February 5, 1961, 25, all in *San Francisco Chronicle*.

93. Letters to the editor, *San Francisco Chronicle*, January 27, 1961, 24.

94. "Big Beatnik Rally to Protest Raids," *San Francisco Chronicle*, January 31, 1960, 5; Harrington, *Fragments of the Century*, 42.

95. Lennon, *Norman Mailer*, 271–79.

96. Through the 1940s and early 1950s, Gallup polls consistently showed that between 70% and 80% of Americans supported restricting the rights of communists to jobs and civil liberties. Although Joseph McCarthy's methods eventually grew unpopular, even as late as Janu-

ary 1954, he still found support among a plurality of those polled, with 40% registering approval and 35%, disapproval.

97. Lewis Allan [Abel Meeropol], composer of "Strange Fruit," adopted the two Rosenberg boys, one of whom, Robert Meeropol, went on to be an activist in the 1960s New Left.

Conclusion. Playboys and Partisans

1. "Speaker to Student Union 3-5-65 Noon Rally," container 2, folder 4, carton 2, folders 4–53, and carton 3, folders 6 and 31, all in Free Speech Movement Papers, Bancroft Library, UC Berkeley.

2. Lawrence Ferlinghetti to Allen Ginsberg, December 9, 1954, box 5, folder 3, series 1, Allen Ginsberg Papers, Rare Book and Manuscript Library, Columbia University; Dorothy Bowman, "Battle of the Beatniks," *Daily Tribune* (Great Bend, KS), December 10, 1964, 2; David Smothers, "Noisy New Left Draws Young Radicals," (Phoenix) *Arizona Republic*, July 28, 1965, 12.

3. Robert Cohen and Reginald E. Zelnik, eds., *The Free Speech Movement: Reflections on Berkeley in the 1960s* (Berkeley: University of California Press, 2002), 222–23.

4. Michael Kazin, *American Dreamers: How the Left Changed a Nation* (New York: Alfred A. Knopf, 2011), 212–16, 251.

5. Tram Combs to Mattachine Society, February 25, 1966, carton 1, folder 31, 1956–1973, Tram Combs Papers, BANC MSS 79/48, Bancroft Library, UC Berkeley.

6. Leo Krikorian interview in *The Beach*, directed by Mary Kerr (San Francisco: CA Palm, 1995), DVD; Russ Wilson, "Ross Show Recalls Band Era," *Oakland Tribune*, January 9, 1972, 5-EN; "Coffee Gallery," *San Francisco Chronicle*, February 5, 1971, unpaginated clipping, Coffee Gallery envelope, *Examiner* morgue, San Francisco History Center, SFPL.

7. Peter Coyote, *Sleeping Where I Fall: A Chronicle* (Washington, DC: Counterpoint, 1998), 8–15; Gary Snyder to Philip Whalen, October 11, 1966, box 7, Philip Whalen Papers, Rare Book and Manuscript Library, Columbia University.

8. "State Opens Hearing on Topless Waitresses," *Independent* (Pasadena, CA), September 28, 1965, 15; Claire Leeds, "Playboy Club's Preview Party with a Heart," *San Francisco Examiner*, November 7, 1965, 14; Elizabeth Fraterrigo, *Playboy and the Making of the Good Life in Modern America* (Oxford: Oxford University Press, 2009), 128–32; Thomas Weyr, *Reaching for Paradise: The Playboy Vision of America* (New York: Times Books, 1978), 153–54; "Bunny Girls Are Covered by Union Suit: U.S. Ponders Inquiry on Playboy Clubs' Hiring," *Baltimore Sun*, March 14, 1964, 3. See also clippings in Playboy Club envelope, *Examiner* morgue, SFPL.

9. Wallace Turner, "'Topless' Is Tops in San Francisco," March 5, 1966, 15, and "Denver Clubs Go Topless," January 14, 1968, 70, both in *New York Times*; Margo St. James, "Foreword," and Dick Boyd, "Margo St. James" chapter in *Broadway North Beach: The Golden Years; A Saloon Keeper's Tales* (San Francisco: Cape Foundation, 2006), xi–xii, 49–56; Weyr, *Reaching for Paradise*, 225–47.

10. "1,000 Women Appeal to NATO," *Cedar Rapids (IA) Gazette*, May 13, 1964, 13-B; Fulton Lewis Jr., "Commies Identified among the Vietniks," *Brownsville (TX) Herald*, December 3, 1965, 4; Amy Swerdlow, *Women Strike for Peace: Traditional Motherhood and Radical Politics in the 1960s* (Chicago: University of Chicago Press, 1993), 132, 194–95, 214–15; Mary Hershberger, *Traveling to Vietnam: American Peace Activists and the War* (Syracuse, NY: Syracuse University Press, 1998).

11. Max Gordon, *Live at the Village Vanguard* (New York: St. Martin's Press, 1980), 123–29; Gerald Nachman, "A Funny Thing Happened to the hungry i," *Oakland Tribune*, January 11,

1970, 3-EN; "Racial Debate Displaces Jazz Program," *New York Times*, February 10, 1965; Ingrid Monson, *Freedom Sounds: Civil Rights Call Out to Jazz and Africa* (New York: Oxford University Press, 2007), 251–76.

12. *Rag Baby*, vol. 1, no. 2 (October 1965) and *Soulbook*, vol. 1, no. 2 (Spring 1965), carton 2, folders 42 and 48, Free Speech Movement Papers.

13. Abbie Hoffman was fully aware that the Chicago Eight judge, Julius Hoffman, had tried Lenny Bruce on obscenity charges four years previously. The YIP leader did his best to channel Bruce in the courtroom, satirizing the judge at every turn. Hoffman's initial arrest was for public indecency, after he attended a protest with the work "Fuck" written on his forehead. See various press releases and clippings, box 18, folder 6, Ivan Black Papers, JPB 06-20, Music Division, NYPL; Dick Gregory and James R. McGraw, *Up from Nigger* (New York: Stein & Day, 1976), 43–44, 87–89, 148–60; Todd Gitlin, *The Sixties: Years of Hope, Days of Rage* (New York: Bantam Books, 1987), 235; Jon Wiener, ed. *Conspiracy in the Streets: The Extraordinary Trial of the Chicago Eight* (New York: New Press, 2006), 13, 148–50, 188–91; Stephen E. Kercher, *Revel with a Cause: Liberal Satire in Postwar America* (Chicago: University of Chicago Press, 2006), 443.

14. Mailer had also held a book release party for *An American Dream* at the Village Vanguard in 1965. Maurice Isserman, *The Other American: The Life of Michael Harrington* (New York: Public Affairs, 2000), 285; Joe Flaherty, *Managing Mailer* (New York: Coward-McCann, 1969), 107–9, 129; Russell Baker, "Observer: Cheers for Politerates," *New York Times*, May 6, 1969, 46; J. Michael Lennon, *Norman Mailer: A Double Life* (New York: Simon & Schuster, 2013), 348.

15. John S. Wilson, "Max Loew Transports Schmaltz to Diners near Central Park," November 17, 1965, 52, Richard F. Shepard, "New Year's Eve Merrymakers, Flu Permitting, Will Fill Clubs," December 30, 1968, 26, and Freed Ferretti, "Copa Is Back as a Disco," October 15, 1976, 53, all in *New York Times*.

16. "Opening Tonight: 'Discotheque,'" February 17, 1964, 1, Charles Mohr, "World of Affluent Youth Favors 'In' Dancing at City Hideaways," March 30, 1964, 31, Philip H. Dougherty, "Now the Latest Craze Is 1-2-3, All Fall Down," February 11, 1965, 28, Marylin Bender, "Fashion Had Its Go-Go Fling during 1965, and Now for . . . ," December 31, 1965, 24, all in *New York Times*; Mark Caldwell, *New York Night: The Mystique and Its History* (New York: Scribner, 2005), 314; *New York in the '50s*, directed by Betsy Blankenbaker (New York: First Run Features, 2001), DVD.

17. John Gruen, *The New Bohemia: The Combine Generation* (New York: Shorecrest, 1966), 8, 16; Grace Glueck, "A Little Be-In Goes a Long Way," May 15, 1966, D-20, Louis Calta, "Brooklyn Loses Two Nightclubs," October 6, 1966, 55, and Ellis Rabb, "Unfashionable?," letter to the editor, October 13, 1968, D-8, all in *New York Times*.

18. Allen Ginsberg to Louis Ginsberg, various letters, 1965, box 7, folder 19, Allen Ginsberg Papers, and Philip Whalen to Robert LaVigne, September 29, 1964, box 1, folder 29, Robert LaVigne Papers, both in Rare Books and Manuscripts Library, Columbia University. See also Amiri Baraka [LeRoi Jones], *Black Music* (New York: William Morrow, 1967), 180, 206–7.

19. For instance, Dashiell Hammett's book, *The Maltese Falcon* (1929), opens with a description of Sam Spade as a "blond satan" whose face displayed a "v-motif," with "his chin a jutting v under the more flexible v of his mouth." Thomas Pynchon, *V.: A Novel* (Toronto: Bantam Books, 1963), 208–32, 276–77, 428; Steven Weisenburger, *Fables of Subversion: Satire and the American Novel, 1930–1980* (Athens: University of Georgia Press, 1995).

20. Both films starred George Peppard as a struggling young writer.

21. David Hinckley, "Art D'Lugoff Dies at 85: Longtime Owner of the Village Gate, His Conscience Shaped Counterculture," *(New York) Daily News*, November 5, 2009, www .nydailynews.com/entertainment/music-arts/art-lugoff-dies-85-longtime-owner-village-gate -conscience-shaped-counterculture-article-1.416926/.

22. Kenneth Rexroth, *The Alternative Society: Essays from the Other World* (New York: Herder & Herder, 1970), 45; "Kenneth Rexroth (1969)," in *San Francisco Beat: Talking with the Poets*, ed. David Meltzer (San Francisco: City Lights Books, 2001), 255, 239.

23. Ibid., 252, 259.

24. Herbert Marcuse, *Eros and Civilization: A Philosophical Inquiry into Freud* (Boston: Beacon Press, 1966), 207; Alice Echols, *Daring to Be Bad: Radical Feminism in America, 1967–1975* (Minneapolis: University of Minnesota Press, 1989), 6, 83–91, 142–43, 244–45.

25. John D'Emilio, *Sexual Politics, Sexual Communities: The Making of a Homosexual Minority in the United States, 1940–1970* (Chicago: University of Chicago Press, 1983), 231–33; Nan Alamilla Boyd, *Wide Open Town: A History of Queer San Francisco to 1965* (Berkeley: University of California Press, 2003), 9–10; Marc Stein, *Rethinking the Gay and Lesbian Movement* (New York: Routledge, 2012), 79–81; Thomas Heise, *Urban Underworlds: A Geography of Twentieth-Century American Literature and Culture* (New Brunswick, NJ: Rutgers University Press, 2011), 167–96.

26. For example, Lawrence Lipton, in his glossary of Beat terms, defined a "spade cat" as "Negro. The holy barbarians, white and negro, are so far beyond 'racial tolerance' and desegregation that they no longer have to be polite about it with one another." Lawrence Lipton, *The Holy Barbarians* (New York: Julian Messner, 1959), 317.

27. Gary R. Edgerton, Michael T. Marsden, and Jack Nachbar, eds., *In the Eye of the Beholder: Critical Perspectives in Popular Film and Television* (Bowling Green, OH: Bowling Green State University Popular Press, 1995), 28. In perhaps the Rebel Café's most literal—and simultaneously most absurd—1970s film permutation, the Rebel Alliance's resistance to the Empire in George Lucas's 1977 *Star Wars* was successfully solidified when Han Solo first met Luke Skywalker in a galactic cabaret.

28. The movie included *Saturday Night Live*'s Bill Murray in his first Hollywood role (uncredited), playing a bohemian recently returned from Mexico.

Index

abortion, risks of, 147
absurdity, ethos of, 9, 16–17
Adams, Ansel, 117
African Americans: and cabaret culture, 37–47; and the Communist Party, 6; discrimination faced by, 1–2, 79, 105–12; and the GI Bill, 161–62; Mort Sahl's antipathy toward, 166–67; and social change, 6–7. *See also* bebop jazz; black culture; civil rights movement; jazz clubs; jazz culture; racial equality
Allan, Lewis, 38
Allen, Steve, 155, 168
Allen, Woody, 90, 155, 186
Altman, Robert, 234
American Civil Liberties Union (ACLU), 139
Amram, David, 82, 83, 138, 174
anarchist-libertarian networks, 66–67
Angelou, Maya, 77, 104, 107, 111, 148
Ann's 440, 114, 122, 170, 178, 180
Ansen, Alan, 133
anti-Semitism: as issue in jazz clubs, 103
Anxious Asp, 122, 125, 127, 144
Apex, the, 186
Aquatic Park, 125
Arbuckle, Arlene, 127
Armstrong, Louis, 89
art/artists: and the Rebel Café, 2, 4, 19, 25, 27, 29–31, 33, 52, 53, 54, 59, 80, 118, 144, 211; as social criticism, 8–9, 17, 29–31, 33, 36, 39; women as 74–75
Artman, Charles E., 227, 228
atomic age: social and political response to, 9–10, 45, 80, 105, 122, 129
Auden, W. H., 70
Auerbach, Art, 87, 177
authenticity: and African American identity, 184; as countercultural value, 2, 8, 14, 35, 168, 202; and elitism, 77; and gender roles, 148–49; and live comedy, 155; and performativity, 238; and the Rebel Café, 194, 197, 235

Babior, Susan, 157
Baez, Joan, 193
Bailey, Pearl, 184
Baker, Chet, 105, 109
Baker, Josephine, 22; as advocate for racial equality, 78–79
Baldwin, James, 14–15, 57, 59, 74, 75, 78, 78, 90, 146, 168, 237; *Another Country*, 91
Banducci, Enrico, 157–58, 159–60, 161, 188–89, 230
Bannon, Ann, 210
Baraka, Amiri (Leroi Jones), 43, 82, 88, 90, 108, 110, 137, 150, 228, 230–31, 236; *Blues People*, 145; on jazz clubs and political struggle, 94–95; on poetry and activism, 200
Barnes, Djuna, 23; *Nightwood*, 19, 211, 217
bartenders: role of in bohemian cafés, 118, 120
Barth, Belle, 186
Basin Street East, 95
Battle of the Beatniks, 195, 221–22, 224, 226
Battle of the Black Hawk, 195, 222–23, 224
Bay of Pigs invasion, 225
Beatles, the, 232–33; *Sgt. Pepper's Lonely Hearts Club Band*, 233
Beats, the, 10, 50, 57, 58, 60, 63–66, 69, 72–73; and Lenny Bruce, 168–74; and consumerist society, 114–15; frugal lifestyle of, 144–45; as literary influence, 129–31, 138–40; and mainstream sensibilities, 228; popular appeal of, 208; publicity surrounding, 140–44; and queer culture, 123–29. *See also* Ginsberg, Allen; "Howl"; Kerouac, Jack
Beauvoir, Simone de, 63–64, 147, 218
bebop jazz, 38, 42–45, 49, 82, 100, 155, 197
Beck, Julian, 142
Behan, Brendan, 31
Belafonte, Harry, 104, 111, 171, 184, 237
Bendich, Al, 139, 177, 179, 181, 204
Benjamin, Walter, 17
Berlin: cabarets in, 17–18
Berman, Wallace, 176
Bessie, Alvah, 153, 158, 175

- wants to link old cult + all   p. 89
         (ruins)   (nightclubs)
      compare to Dionysian

- what about art clubs?? overly romanticized
                                    Kapow universities

- doesn't use model - but infotainment
      a good working lens

- ~~makes~~ jams cultural theories together

- what's next Kansas City ??

- Jasper Johns, John Cage

- Boldness's formalism - p. 35

- Lacanian political - p. 66

- mysticism of anarchism - p. 68.

- Rebel Cafe? egalitarian ideal - 68

- clubs - p. 94
                  p. 104
- Belgrade - more sophisticated readies

pp. 110-11 - good connection.

p. 112 - transition - World